of God

ALIVE-O

3

The glory of God is people fully alive.

Saint Irenaeus

A re-presentation of *Show Us The Father*

Written by Maura Hyland,

Eleanor Gormally and Clare Maloney

VERITAS

Published 1998 by
Veritas Publications
7-8 Lower Abbey Street
Dublin 1

ISBN 1 85390 430 9

Veritas would like to thank:
The teachers, pupils, parents and Primary
Diocesan Advisers in Religious Education in the
Dioceses of Ardagh & Clonmacnois, Armagh,
Dromore, Dublin, Elphin, Ferns, Limerick and
Ossory for their assistance in the piloting of this
programme;
the Chairperson of the Joint Board Fund,
Education and Library Boards, Northern Ireland,
for sponsoring a residential workshop of
Catholic maintained school teachers at
Burrendale, Newcastle, and the teachers who
participated;
Mary Immaculate College of Education,
Limerick, who made it possible for Eleanor
Gormally to participate in the writing of this
programme.

Resource Team: Hilary Musgrave
                          Anne Hession
                          Piaras Jackson
                          Andy McNally

Theological Advisers: Dermot Lane DD
                          Úna O'Neill DD

Series Coordinator: Finola Mc Laughlin
Editor: Elaine Campion

Art Director: Bill Bolger
Music Director: Patricia Hegarty
Illustrator: Jeanette Dunne
Worksheet Illustrations: Mary Cawley
Typesetting: Colette Dower
Music Setting: Top Type Music Bureau

Origination by Accuplate Ltd, Dublin
Printed in Ireland by Betaprint Ltd, Dublin

Contents

*Welcome to **Alive-O 3**.*

*While most of the children who are beginning First Class/Primary Three this year have been using **Alive-O** for two years now, this may well be your first encounter with it. Leaving aside a programme with which you have become very familiar is not easy. However, most teachers of Infant Classes have found the effort worthwhile and are happy with the positive impact **Alive-O** is having on both children and parents.*

*So what has changed? The first change you will notice is probably in the format of the lessons. After the introduction for the teacher you will find the aims for the week outlined under the headings: **What am I trying to do?** and **Why?** We have also included a short reflection for the teacher. You may find that you don't always have time to read this at the beginning of the week. However, at some stage during the week you might read through it. The hope is that it would help you to tune into the main focus of the lesson.*

Each lesson is divided into five parts, one for each day of the week, with each day's work ending with a prayer. As usual, each week's resources will contain at least one story, a song, a poem, a worksheet, some artwork and other activities. Within this you can choose the materials which are most suited to your own class situation. In fact, the programme has been constructed with a view to the many variations which exist in the make up of the different classes where the programme will be used. Depending on the ability of the pupils in your class, you may find that there is too much to be covered and that you need to omit, let's say, the poem or the artwork, or that the 'chatting' could be shortened. You are free to do this, to make choices, regarding the best possible way to use the resources in your class.

*You will notice quite a difference in the approach to prayer in **Alive-O**. As has always been the case in the **Children of God** series, we seek not only to teach the children prayers but to teach them to pray. **Alive-O** tries to help the children, particularly through these prayertimes, to experience God's love and care for them. Each day contains a place for prayer. Already the children have been introduced to quiet meditative prayer since they were in Junior Infants/Primary One. Teachers have found that the children respond very easily to this, and in **Alive-O 3** we seek to build on their ability to enter into times of quiet, meditative prayer. In doing so we deepen their capacity to experience prayertimes as times when they are aware of themselves being in God's presence and being loved and cared for by God.*

*You will find some new characters and new stories in **Alive-O 3** and you may be disappointed that some old favourites are missing. We say goodbye to Zacchaeus for the moment. Through the story of **The Lost Sheep** the children explore the never-ending love of God for them, even at times when they are 'lost'. Teachers who piloted this part of the programme and who worked with the story of **The Lost Sheep** found that the children entered into it with enthusiasm and enjoyed the activities that accompany it.*

There are also a number of opportunities during the year to invite the parents and the local priest or other parish personnel to join in prayer with the children. Whether or not this is possible will depend on the circumstances in your own situation. However, teachers of Infant Classes, who have had the opportunity to invite the parents to take part in such prayer celebrations, have found them to be very good experiences for everyone involved. At the appropriate times in the text you will find some indications as to how these might be organised, but you will, of course, need to adapt them to your own local circumstances.

As you are aware, it is no longer possible to presume that children come to school from a context where faith is taken for granted. Some children will not have heard of God or of Jesus or may not have been inside a church until they come to school. While the school cannot replace what is missing from such children's experience, it can nevertheless provide for some children the first context wherein they are introduced to God. It is also, for some children, the first place where they feel loved and valued as the unique individuals which they are. Indeed, the work teachers in Catholic schools do is immeasurable in terms of their contribution to the faith formation of the children in their classrooms – a work which, as it becomes more and more difficult, is increasingly more and more significant.

We wish you a good year.

The Glory of God is people fully alive.
(St Irenaeus)

Alive-O 3 is the third programme in the re-presentation of the *Children of God* catechetical series. The title *Alive-O* reflects one of the overriding aims of religious education, namely, to enable people to become fully alive to the presence of God in themselves, in others, in the Church and in the world around them.

Home, school and parish in partnership are responsible for the religious education of children. The primary educators of the child are the significant adults in the home – the parents/guardians. They are the ones who are responsible for the nurture and care of the child. They are the ones who, at Baptism, in presenting their child before the Christian community, agreed to raise their child as a member of that community. Without the support of the home, the school can achieve very little. The support and co-operation of the parents/guardians are indispensable at every stage of the children's religious and moral education.

In the changing cultural climate, teachers need to be aware of and sensitive to the individual contexts from which the children in their class emerge. We can no longer assume or take for granted the faith patterns of the past. It is important, however, that each child, regardless of home circumstances, be valued and respected as unique and special to God.

Together with the home and school, the parish has a role to play in the religious education of children. It is in the parish that the children, together with the Christian community, gather to take part in the liturgical rituals of the Church. The sacramental initiation of the children is a significant aspect in the life of the parish. Six- and seven-year-olds have a limited experience of parish. However, through the school, they can come to know their local priest/parish sister/parish representative. Several times during the year opportunities are provided for the priest, parish sister or parish representative to join with the children in prayer and celebration. These Prayer Services take place either in the local church or in the classroom.

Alive-O 3 seeks to be a resource for teachers. It can also offer resources to parents/guardians and those who work at parish level. It encourages their active participation in the faith development of the children.

Some Characteristics of Six- and Seven-Year-Olds

The catechesis of children is necessarily linked with their life situation and conditions.
(*General Directory for Catechesis*, 178)

*A*live-O 3 takes into account the children's age, needs and capacity to learn. As religious educators it is important to be aware of some of the characteristics of the six- and seven-year-old.

- Six- and seven-year-olds are continuously discovering more about themselves and about their world. Everything is new and exciting. Because they are open and spontaneous and, as yet, unfettered by the conventions of adulthood, they can be easily motivated to celebrate and give thanks.

- Six- and seven-year-olds have a desire to be with others, to be part of whatever is happening. They have a desire to belong. It is appropriate then to help them to begin to reflect on the challenge of trying to live with others in a way that is creative and life-giving. We lead them to an awareness of the reality that their actions and attitudes impact on the lives of those around them.

- Six- and seven-year-olds emerging from their egocentric world are beginning to take on another perspective and to see things from other people's points of view. We can help to develop this capacity in them by encouraging them to relate to others with respect and to become aware of the needs of those around them.

- Six- and seven-year-olds have a natural capacity for awe and wonder. They are fascinated by the world of nature. They take nothing for granted. They have a sense of mystery. This programme takes every opportunity to provide the children with the experience of exploring and reflecting on the wonder and mystery in the natural world around them.

- Six- and seven-year-olds learn through their senses. Maria Montessori sums it up thus: 'I hear and I forget, I see and I remember, I do and I understand'. Their attention is best maintained when they are actively involved in whatever they are learning.

- Six- and seven-year-olds continue to imitate adult behaviour. Children are always learning from the adults around them, from the things they do and say and from the way in which they relate to others.

- Six- and seven-year-olds need to feel loved and accepted. They learn best in an atmosphere where they feel affirmed and appreciated for the unique individuals that they are. In this secure context they are best able to learn how to relate appropriately to the world around them and to others. It is through their experience of the love and care of others that they will ultimately understand the love and care of God and learn how to relate to God.

- Six- and seven-year-olds are very limited in their understanding of abstract religious concepts. Researchers in Faith Development, Fonald Goldman and James Fowler, remind us of the literal and concrete nature of children's thought at this age. Throughout the programme we try as much as possible to present material to the children in a language that is in line with their age and comprehension. In situations where children are being introduced to abstract theological concepts, it is important to be aware of the children's stage of faith development and to acknowledge that a fuller and more meaningful understanding of the rich truths of our Christian heritage will come later.

Aim of Religious Education

Faith is a personal act – the free response of the human person to the initiative of God who reveals himself. But faith is not an isolated act. No one can believe alone, just as no one can live alone. You have not given yourself faith as you have not given yourself life. The believer has received faith from others and should hand it on to others. Our love for Jesus and for our neighbour impels us to speak to others about our faith. Each believer is thus a link in the great chain of believers. I cannot believe without being carried by the faith of others, and by my faith I help support others in the faith.

(*Catechism of the Catholic Church,* 166)

The aim of religious education is to foster and deepen the children's faith. People of faith perceive themselves and their world in a special way. Faith is active. As people of faith we are aware of God as a presence in our lives. We see things in relation to God. This awareness calls for a response. Our lives become a response to a compassionate and loving God. Faith is our response to God's self-communication to us through revelation. God's initiative is a gift, an invitation. The response we make is our choice, our decision. It is a response that no one can make on behalf of another, neither can it be forced from anyone. What is possible, however, is the creation of a context wherein people have the opportunity to become aware of God's invitation, to hear God's word and to explore how best they can respond in their own lives.

The presence of God in our lives is revealed in a unique way through the person and teaching of Jesus Christ. Those involved in the religious education of children today are offered the same challenge which Jesus offered his followers:

> An argument arose among them as to which one of them was the greatest. But Jesus, aware of their inner thoughts, took a little child and put it by his side, and said to them, 'Whoever welcomes this child in my name welcomes me, and whoever welcomes me welcomes the one who sent me; for the least among all of you is the greatest' (Luke 9:46-48).

The apostles judged who was the greatest according to a particular narrow set of values. Jesus, however, pointed out a different way of viewing the situation, which caused the apostles to review their previously held judgements. He continually challenged the people who were with him to new perspectives. He viewed life from a particular viewpoint – God's viewpoint.

Faith as a Response to Revelation

Revelation is God's self-communication to us.

Sources of Christian Revelation

Faith is our personal response to this communicating presence. As religious educators we need to ask ourselves:

- Where do we experience God's self-communication today?
- Where can we hear God's word?
- Where are the signs of God's presence among us; of God's love for us; of God's work for our salvation?

These guiding questions help us as adults to develop our own faith and as religious educators to nurture the faith of children. The explicit signs of God's presence and action in our lives are scripture, the teachings of the Church (tradition), the liturgy and the lives of believers.

Scripture
From the beginning God revealed himself to those who lived in Old Testament times, thus establishing a relationship of intimacy and familiarity with the people. 'I will be their God, and they shall be my people' (2 Cor 6:16).

Before the coming of Jesus, God spoke to the people through the events of history and through the prophets. The fullness of God's revelation comes through Jesus, 'the word made flesh' who 'dwelt amongst us'. In his person, in his teaching, in his way of relating to others and to the natural world, Jesus shows us most clearly who God is, what God is saying to us, and what God asks of us in response.

> The Word of God, incarnate in Jesus of Nazareth, Son of the Blessed Virgin Mary, is the Word of the Father who speaks to the world through his Spirit... He is 'the Way' that leads to the innermost mystery of God.
> (*General Directory for Catechesis*, 99)

Tradition
The Church, in every age, reflects on the message of Christ and applies it to a modern and often complex world. Aided by the Holy Spirit, the Church expounds its teachings in its creeds, its dogmas and its doctrinal statements. The name given to this collection of Church teachings is Tradition.

> Sacred Tradition and Sacred Scripture, then, are bound closely together, and communicate one with the other. For both of them, flowing out from the same divine well-spring, come together in some fashion to form one thing, and move towards the same goal. (*Dei verbum*, 9)

> Each of them makes present and fruitful in the Church the mystery of Christ, who promised to remain with his own 'always, to the close of the age'. (*Catechism of the Catholic Church*, 80)

Liturgy and Sacraments
The Risen Christ is present in the Mass and in the sacraments. Through him, God continues to speak to us and to offer us salvation.

The Lives of Believers
Down through the ages there have always been people who, in remarkable ways, have tried to make Christ present in their world. Some of them have been written into history and are well known. Others have lived quiet lives and will never be known except to a few. In their work, in their lives, in their prayer, they show us who God is and what God is asking of us.

Other Sources of Revelation

Human experience and the natural world are also signs of Christian revelation. They speak to us of a Creator God, a God who is not far away, a God who is among us, who loves and cares for us.

The Natural World
> The heavens proclaim your glory, O God,
> and the firmament shows forth the work of your hands.
> Day unto day takes up the story

and night unto night makes known
the message.
No speech, no word, no voice is heard
yet their span extends through all the
earth,
their words to the utmost bounds of
the world. (Psalm 19: 1-5)

When we look at the natural world around us
we see many things which are signs of God's
action, power and wisdom. The cycle of the
seasons, the grandeur of nature and the
mystery of new life all speak of the power and
mystery of God. The plan whereby day follows
night, spring follows winter and new life
follows death and decay, shows the
providence, love and care of God for all
creation.

Human Experience

It is the task of catechesis to make
people aware of their most basic
experiences, to help them to judge in
the light of the Gospel the questions
and needs that spring from them, as
well as to educate them in a new way
of life.
(*General Directory for Catechesis*, 152)

Human beings are created in the image and
likeness of God. More than anything else we
have the capacity to show the world who God
is and what God is like.

Our experience of being alive, of using our
creative talents, of growth, success and
achievement, of sadness, failure and sickness,
can all tell us something about God and about
God's plan for us. The love, care, concern, co-
operation, trust, honesty, truthfulness and
respect which we experience in our human
relationships all speak to us of God's
relationship with us.

Through our experience of human
relationships and of the natural world we can
be helped to come to know God, not only as
someone who is far removed from our human
experience, whose power and greatness is
beyond our human understanding, but as
someone who is close by, who lives among us,
who is intimately concerned for our well-
being, growth and development, who loves
and cares for us unconditionally.

As we try to enable the children to grow as
people of faith, we hope that they will become
as articulate in this area as in any other area of
the curriculum. We hope that eventually they
will be able to give an account of the faith that
is in them, to say what they believe and why.
This familiarity with the content of faith will be
achieved gradually as the children move from
class to class, and as their ability to understand
difficult language and concepts increases. Faith,
however, is not only something to be
understood, it is also something to be lived.
The kind of 'knowing' that we seek is not only
one which leads to clarity of thought and
articulation, but one which profoundly
influences the whole of an individual's
approach to life. We seek to lead the children to
become the kind of people who see the world
around them and all that is happening in it
through the eyes of faith, and whose
interpretations of what is happening and
responses to it are all influenced by their faith.

In order for this to become a possibility we
help the children to become the kind of
people who are aware. Aware not just of what
is happening in their experience, but also of
the significance of what is happening in terms
of their relationship with those around them,
with the natural world, and with God.

Thus there are many signs of God's presence
and love, and in the course of the primary
catechetical programme, the children will be
introduced progressively to these different
signs.

Religious Education must lead children to
respond to God here and now with faith, love
and gratitude. Therefore, we must communicate
the Christian message to them in a manner
appropriate to their age, stage of faith
development and life experience.

The Theme of Journey

This is what Yahweh asks of you: only
this, to act justly, to love tenderly and
to walk humbly with your God.
(Micah 6:8)

The image of journey is very powerful. It can
speak to us in a variety of ways about the shape
of our lives, our quest for wholeness and well-
being, our spiritual growth, our search for God.

'Walking humbly with your God' is a core theme in both the Old and New Testaments. Many great biblical events are framed within a journey experience – the movement of the Israelites from Egypt; the Passover meal; the wanderings in the wilderness; Mary and Joseph journeying to Bethlehem; Jesus' journey to Jerusalem as a boy; the Way of the Cross; the women going to the tomb.

Throughout the course of his life, Jesus was one who constantly and consistently walked with others – often the outcast and the marginalised. He was there to share his stories, his food and his vision for the Kingdom of God with those who had ears to hear. He spoke of a God of love and compassion, a God who searches us out, a God who is with us always, a God who never forgets us.

Many of these same biblical journeys were punctuated with rests and breaks. In the Old Testament we hear of how Elijah, resting on his journey to Horeb, was fed by an angel, then 'strengthened by that food… walked forty days and forty nights to the mountain of God, Horeb' (1 Kings 19). Jesus too broke his journeys to take a drink of water at the well; to share meals with his friends; to pray to his Father.

The theme of journey connects into the content of this year's programme in many instances. While six- and seven-year-olds have a limited experience of life, and the full significance of the journey theme is beyond their comprehension, they can, nonetheless, begin to tap into the richness of this archetypal theme. In the programme we help them to do this by enabling them to reflect on what it is like:

- to begin a new year;
- to leave behind the 'old' class and move into a 'new' class;
- to take part in the rhythm of the school day;
- to get in touch with the movement and rhythm of their body;
- to feel time moving on;
- to watch the changing seasons;
- to learn to belong with others as they go through the year;
- to celebrate the completion of their year's journeying together as a class;
- to experience, as with the cycles in the natural world, how, as one journey is ended, a new journey beckons them forth.

We introduce them to:

- the journey of Jesus to Jerusalem with Mary and Joseph for the celebration of Passover;
- the journey in time towards the first Christmas;
- our journey through the season of Advent as we encounter the different moments of preparation for Christmas;
- the journeying of the Chosen People through the desert;
- the searching of the shepherd as he looked for the lost sheep;
- the journey of Jesus to Calvary;
- a celebration of the children's journey through the year.

We explore the experience of journey in the light of the Christian message. The children's experience of journey becomes revelatory for them when an adult believer accompanies them and sheds the light of God's word on their experience of journeying. We hope to create in the children an openness and awareness of the presence of God in their lives. We hope that they will come to see in their everyday lives, in their relationships with others, in the changing seasons, a hint of the love and care of God for all living things.

The gift of life has come from God – the gift of time and place, rhythm and movement all come from God. God wants us to 'have life and have it to the full' (Jn 10:10). Jesus shows us best how to live for God and for others and sends the Holy Spirit to help us. As the Christian community gathers together, to tell the story and to break the bread, the Risen Jesus is with us as we journey together in faith.

The image of journey can help us to come to a deeper sense of the significance of the different stages and seasons in our lives. Our life is a journey through time. This year is a particular time on the life journey of each child, which brings with it unique opportunities for growth. It is a gift of time to be taken hold of and explored, which is what *Alive-O 3* seeks to enable them to do, right now, in the hope that they will continue to live life to the full as they grow through time into their adult years.

The most important signs of God for six- and seven-year-olds are the faith, prayer and lives of the Christian adults they live with and admire, at home, at school and in the parish.

The children are, however, also introduced to other privileged signs of God's revelation in a manner suited to their age and development:

- simple Old Testament and New Testament biblical tests;
- the liturgical feasts;
- reconciliation and Eucharist;
- doctrine in the form of hymns, prayers, verses and simple statements.

Throughout the year, framed in the image of journey, we explore with the children their experience of themselves, others and the world around them. We help them to discover there signs of God's presence and love.

Use of the Bible

The Bible is a source of inspiration for Christians. It is a significant resource book at all levels. However, at this stage, it is important that the teacher present the Bible and the biblical message in a manner appropriate to the age and development of the children.

The Word of God

> Now since in the Bible God has spoken through human agents to humans, if the interpretation of Holy Scripture is to understand what God has wished to communicate he [or she] must carefully investigate what meaning the biblical writer had in mind; that will also be what God chose to manifest through their words. (*Dei verbum*)

The writers of the Old and New Testaments used stories, songs, letters, statements and poems to convey to the people the messages they wished them to understand about themselves, about themselves in relation to others and the natural world, and about themselves in relation to God. They succeeded in doing this by filling their writings with images and experiences which were familiar to those for whom the message was intended. They were writing for adults. If they were trying to communicate the same message in today's world they would use different experiences and images which would mirror the reality of life in today's world.

In our religious education programme for six- and seven-year-olds today, we seek to lead the children to a sense of God's creative, loving presence in them and in the world. To do this we use stories and images which are true to their experience.

The Bible is the Word of God. It has something to say about every human situation. It has something to say about every activity and experience explored in the programme. Therefore, each theme and each lesson is accompanied by an appropriate biblical text and a short reflection, which provide background information for the teacher. This will help the teacher to approach the experience of the child from a biblical and Christian standpoint.

The biblical texts and reflections preceding each lesson are, of course, meant only for the teacher. They should not be taught to the children.

New Testament

The New Testament presents the life and teaching of Jesus. The children are too young to be introduced to the text of the New Testament. Therefore, New Testament stories and events are often paraphrased or expanded in order to make them more intelligible to the children. In the New Testament, we find Jesus trying to open the eyes of his disciples to the signs of God's presence, goodness and care for all creatures in the ordinary things around them. He often did this through the use of parables.

The children are introduced for the first time to two parables: The Parable of The Lost Sheep and

The Parable of the Sower. Parables are complex stories. Their language is metaphorical and the images that are used are deeply symbolic. In telling the parables, Jesus challenged people to question their preconceived ideas about themselves, others and the world, and to reconsider their values and attitudes. First Class/Primary Three children are not ready to understand the more abstract implications of the parables. So we introduce them to the richness of the stories by presenting them in a manner appropriate to their age and development – remembering that children are always ready to enter enthusiastically into story-telling of every form. Some New Testament stories connected with significant events in the life of Jesus and with significant images of Jesus have also been included.

Old Testament

The entire programme is profoundly biblical, in the sense that it presents God as a living God who is present and active in our daily lives. Through the programme we help the children to relate their discovery of themselves, of other people and of the world, to God who is the creator of all things, the source of all life, who loves and cares for each of them and is always with them. While in many instances the language used and the stories told in the exploration of the child's experience are not from the Bible, the approach is biblical.

The Israelites had a keen awareness of the gracious presence of God in all the activities and experiences of human life. They saw signs of God's majesty, splendour, love, wisdom and providence in everything around them: the human person, the seasons of the year, birds, flowers, trees, rain. This awareness permeates the Old Testament, especially the Psalms. In this sense, the themes explored in the programme are biblical themes.

The hymns and prayers in which the children express their love and gratitude for God's goodness, and their wonder and awe at the beauty of God's creation, are also biblically inspired. They are, in fact, the Psalms in the language of children. Old Testament stories are chosen at this stage for inclusion in the programme when they can be retold in a way which is faithful to the meaning and content of the passage in scripture, while at the same time enhancing a particular theme which is being explored in the programme.

Reverence for the Bible

We encourage the children to be aware of the importance of the Bible for Christians.

This year we introduce the children to the formal reading of the Bible as the Word of God. We do this by involving the children in a Bible Procession Ritual. For this, the children are asked to form a simple procession – one child carrying the Bible, another carrying the unlit candle (children could carry other items like flowers, incense stick, grains of incense, cloth, etc.) – and process to a table where the Bible and candle are placed with reverence.

Taking a Gospel story with which the children are already familiar, a short Bible reading follows. Because of the reading ability of most six- and seven-year-olds, it would not be feasible to read the full text of the story from the Bible. A pre-selected phrase, written on a flashcard, is placed between the covers of the Bible. A child is appointed reader and is asked to read this short sentence from the Bible. Through this ritual the children are taught various responses to the Scripture readings from the Liturgy of the Word, and are helped to see the link between the biblical stories they hear in class and the Liturgy of the Word at Mass.

It is hoped that this ritual will create in the children a sense of respect for the Word of God in the Bible and ultimately help them to be able to participate in and understand more fully the Liturgy of the Word in the Eucharist.

At every stage and in every lesson of *Alive-O 3* we have a threefold concern:

Focus: to help the children to focus on their experience of living in the world with others (experiential).

Explore/Reflect: to provide opportunities for the children to develop an awareness of the presence and action of God in their lives (doctrinal).

Response: to help them to respond to God's love in the liturgical celebration and in their everyday lives (moral and sacramental).

Doctrine

In presenting doctrine, it is important to stress the central truths of faith in order to achieve a proper perspective. Catechesis on all levels must take account of the most important truths of faith:

- the mystery of God the Father, the Son, the Holy Spirit;
- the mystery of Christ the incarnate Word;
- the mystery of the Holy Spirit;
- the mystery of the Church, in which the Virgin Mary holds a prominent place.

These central truths of faith are highlighted in this year's programme. However, they are presented in a manner suited to the age and faith development of six- and seven-year-olds.

The Trinity

Through Baptism, the children are already sons and daughters of God, sisters and brothers of Jesus Christ and temples of the Holy Spirit. Religious education in the home, in the school and in the parish liturgical celebrations, help the children to enter into a conscious and personal relationship with each person of the Trinity.

God is presented as the one:
- who, as Creator, gives life to us and to all living things and whose beauty is reflected in the world around us;
- who loves us as a loving father and who cares for us like a loving mother;
- who has given us a mind to learn and a body to grow;
- who has given us the gift of others with whom we belong and who help us to grow and to learn and to live lives that are full and happy;
- who calls us to find places and spaces to communicate with him;
- who brought the Israelites from slavery to freedom;
- who was with the Israelites as they journeyed through the desert;
- who is with us at all times, particularly in times of emptiness and struggle – in our wilderness times;
- who has sent Jesus to show us how much he loves us and to teach us how to love others;
- who raised Jesus to new life;
- who searches for us and for all who are lost;
- who is always waiting to forgive us;
- who wants us to be happy with him in heaven;
- who deserves our praise and thanks.

Jesus, Son of God, is presented as the one:
- who was born in Bethlehem and whose presence among us we celebrate at Christmas;
- who grew up like other Jewish boys in Nazareth;
- who shows us what God is like;
- who tells us about God's love for each one of us;
- who is a true friend, especially to children;
- who journeyed through life sharing his time and his love with those with whom he lived;
- who shared himself with others in story, in food and in love;

- who recognised hidden goodness in the hearts of those who were outcast in the society of his time;
- who taught us about God in his stories and in his actions;
- who is the Word of God made flesh;
- who withdrew into the desert to spend time in prayer with the Father;
- who teaches us how to pray;
- who invites us to share his closeness with God when he tells us to address God as 'Abba';
- who shows us the love and forgiveness of God;
- who, like the Good Shepherd, searches for us when we stray;
- who saw the goodness in the people he lived with, and who forgives us when we don't live up to that goodness;
- who died on the cross for us;
- who was raised from the dead by God the Father and continues to be with us;
- who sent his Spirit to the apostles on Pentecost Sunday;
- who is with us today
  in Baptism,
  in the Sacrament of Reconciliation,
  in the Eucharist,
  in the Holy Spirit.

The Holy Spirit is presented as the one:
- who inspired the life and prayer of Jesus;
- who led Jesus into the wilderness to pray;
- who was sent by Jesus to the apostles on Pentecost Sunday;
- who helps us to live and love like Jesus;
- who is with us in Baptism and when we renew our baptismal vows;
- who together with God the Father and the Son deserves our praise.

The Church
Through Baptism, the children are already members of the Church. Their first real contact with the Church should occur in the family, among those with whom they live, where they become aware of the Christian life expressed in family relationships, family prayer, celebration of feasts, church-going and care for others. However, for some children the Catholic school may well be their first real contact with the Church community. While the school can never replace what may be missing at home, it can, nevertheless, provide for some children their first experience of a context where an effort is made to model life and shared living on Christian values.

In this year's programme we deepen the children's awareness of belonging with others at home, at school, in the neighbourhood and with the Christian community called Church as it gathers together in the liturgical celebrations. This community

- believes in Christ's resurrection;
- is inspired by the Holy Spirit;
- tries to live in accordance with Jesus' teaching;
- gathers together every week to praise and thank God with the Risen Jesus;
- celebrates the forgiveness of God in the Sacrament of Reconciliation;
- celebrates the birth, death and resurrection of Jesus;
- looks forward to eternal happiness with God.

Mary
Children may have seen pictures and statues/icons of Mary in their Junior Infants/Primary One or Senior Infants/Primary Two pupil books, in their classroom/school, perhaps in the home or church. They have heard her name in prayers such as the *Hail Mary*. In this year's programme Mary is presented as the one:

- who responded to God's will to become the Mother of Jesus;
- who is the Mother of God's son, Jesus, and our Mother too;
- who loved God deeply;
- who lived, cared for and nurtured Jesus as he grew up in Nazareth;
- who was at the foot of the cross when Jesus died;
- who is honoured in the Rosary;
- who deserves our love and devotion;
- who loves us and protects us.

Grace
The terms grace, sanctifying grace (state of grace) and actual grace (the grace given for each particular act) are not used in the children's text. This does not mean that the reality underlying these concepts is ignored. We cannot ignore the intimate communion of life which we as Christians share with God.

'Now we have received not the spirit of the world, but the Spirit that is from God, so that we may understand the Gifts bestowed on us by God' (1 Cor 1:12). The Spirit of God then is within us, enabling us and prompting us to become, like Christ, children of God. 'For all who are led by the Spirit of God are children of God (Rm 9:14). We approach this truth from different angles:

- we are God's friends; we are God's children;
- we share in the risen life of Jesus Christ;
- we are sisters and brothers of Jesus Christ;
- the Holy Spirit dwells in us;
- the Holy Spirit helps us to live like Jesus.

Heaven and Hell

As Christians, we believe that we are called to eternal happiness with God. Children sometimes ask questions about heaven and hell. We cannot give complete answers but we should take account of the following considerations:

- St Paul tells us that we already share in the life of the risen glorified Jesus: 'God made us alive together with Christ ... and raised us up with him and seated us with him in the heavenly places' (Eph 2:4-6).

- This life will one day lead to a fullness of life and joy which we cannot imagine but to which we all aspire. This new life is a union with Christ (1 Cor 13:12; Phil 1:21-25).

- It is through the resurrection of Christ that the possibility of this new life with him and with others has been achieved: 'God will wipe away all tears from their eyes; there will be no more death and no more mourning or sadness' (Apocalypse 21:3-4).

- Heaven is not static, as children sometimes imagine. It is a fuller life than we can imagine: 'What no eye has seen nor ear heard, nor the human heart conceived, all that God has prepared for those who love him' (1 Cor 2:9).

- The word 'heaven' suggests a place to which we go after death. However, we should not think of heaven as a place but rather as a state of happiness with God. This state of happiness consists of living with God and with others forever in a relationship of knowledge and love.

- The word 'hell' can cause difficulties, especially with children who have been exposed to frightening images of hell or have been threatened with hell. We do not at this stage introduce the children to the word 'hell' or the spiritual reality underlying this word: namely, those who refuse to love God and to love others cannot live with God. They will remain separated from God. Neither do we introduce the term 'mortal sin' at this stage.

In speaking to children, it is better to confine ourselves to positive statements which express the realities underlying the terms 'heaven', 'hell', 'mortal sin': for example, all those who love God and others will be happy with God for ever.

Some children have heard of the 'devil' and ask questions about who the 'devil' is. Sometimes they are frightened of the power of the devil. Sometimes they can be overly influenced by what they see on television and in films. In dealing with the children's questions in this matter it is essential to frame all answers in the context of the Christian's belief in eternal happiness with a loving God:

- that God has constant love for us;
- that God has also given us free will and each one of us has the power to direct our lives towards God and to act according to conscience, to seek truth;
- that we have the power to turn away from God, to make ourselves blind to the light of conscience, and deaf to the call of God and of others;
- that God will never fail to love us no matter what we do;
- that it is God, not the devil, who is the supreme power;
- that when we try to be good, God is with us.

Mission Awareness

By definition, all Christians are missionary. We hope that the children will gradually be led to understand themselves as belonging to a missionary Church. Jesus asked his followers to follow his example in showing care and concern for all people. We are challenged to help all people to know the good news that God sent Jesus to show them how much God loves and cares for them.

In the early years, this spirit has to be caught rather than taught. There may be times during the year when our television screens and newspapers carry pictures of people who are suffering because of natural disasters or unjust government policies. These provide appropriate opportunities to help children to come to an awareness that there are people who do not enjoy the same quality of life as they do. As they give thanks to God for the gifts they have been given, we encourage them to be aware of those who are less well off and to realise gradually that they can and ought to help when possible.

Liturgical and Sacramental Initiation

Catechesis prepares the Christian to live in community and to participate actively in the life and mission of the Church. The Second Vatican Council indicates the necessity for pastors to form genuine Christian communities and for catechumens '[to] learn to co-operate actively in building up the Church and its work of evangelisation'. (*General Directory for Catechesis*, 86)

Parents, priests and teachers play a significant role in the liturgical and sacramental initiation of children. The experience of parish liturgy and the practice of parents and of the Christian community are vital elements for the sacramental initiation of children. Without these, little can be achieved at school.

Without faith, we cannot participate meaningfully in the liturgical and sacramental life of the Church. However, liturgy and sacraments enrich and deepen faith. Initiation into the liturgical and sacramental life of the Church is therefore an integral part of religious education.

Sacramental catechesis must be adapted to the children's age and stage of development. We should not attempt to say everything during these first years. The children will be introduced gradually and progressively to all aspects of the sacraments in the course of the primary programme.

In the course of the year we endeavour to explore with the children the human values and attitudes which are central to an understanding of and meaningful participation in these sacraments:

- a sense of their own goodness;
- a sense of belonging with others;
- a sense of celebration;
- a recognition of wrongdoing;
- a respect for self and others;
- a capacity to forgive and to be forgiven.

In the First Class/Primary Three programme we formally introduce the children to two sacraments: the Eucharist and the Sacrament of Reconciliation. We deal also with the main events in the liturgical year: Feast of All Saints/Souls, Advent, Christmas, Lent, Easter, Holy Week. Catechesis on the sacraments is not confined to those lessons that deal specifically with these themes, but is integrated throughout the entire programme. In the presentation of each sacrament we must acknowledge the limitations in the experience, understanding and faith development of six- and seven-year-olds.

The Sacraments of Penance and Eucharist are presented as the actions of Christ. They make his salvation visible, accessible and efficacious for us today. It is Christ who offers us the forgiveness of God in the Sacrament of Reconciliation. It is Christ who is present in the Eucharist, speaking to us in the Scriptures, leading us in our praise, thanksgiving and worship to God, giving himself to us as the Bread of Life and sending us out to show his love in our world.

Eucharist

Catechesis on the Eucharist is not confined to the specific lessons on the Eucharist. Throughout the year, we try to develop in the children attitudes which will help them to participate consciously in the celebration:

- an ability to work with symbol and to take part in ritual;
- a sense of coming together with others;
- listening to the Word of God;
- a sense of gratitude and thanksgiving;
- a sense of the meaning of celebration;
- reflecting on the life, death and resurrection of Jesus Christ;
- a desire to be a follower of Jesus.

The *Directory on Children's Masses* highlights the importance of cultivating such attitudes in children as a preparation for understanding and participation in the Eucharist. It writes:

> All those who are concerned with education should work and plan together to ensure that the children, besides having some idea of God and the supernatural, should also, in proportion to their years and degree of maturity as persons, have experience of those human values which are involved in eucharistic celebration: for example, acting together as a community; exchanging greetings; the capacity to listen; to forgive and to ask forgiveness; the expression of gratitude; the experience of symbolic actions, conviviality and festive celebration. (9)

Term Three of *Alive-O 3* focuses on four fundamental aspects of the Eucharist, each of which are central to the life of Jesus: shared story, shared meal, shared memory and shared living. During the year some children will be celebrating their First Communion.

Shared Story
Throughout the year the children have heard many stories which were told by Jesus. It is these stories which hold together and inspire the Christian community today to continue to live as his followers. When we come together to celebrate the Eucharist the Risen Jesus is present in the words of Scripture which are read at the Liturgy of the Word.

Shared Meal
A shared meal is a sign of friendship, trust, hospitality, unity and love. For Jesus, meals were one medium through which he made himself present and available to people.

On the night before he died, Jesus shared his Last Supper. At the Last Supper, he took bread, blessed and broke it. He took wine, blessed and shared it. In this action he wove together his life of love and service and his approaching death. What Jesus did at the Last Supper, he told his disciples to do in memory of him. When we come together to celebrate the Eucharist, we remember the Last Supper. The Risen Jesus is present in the consecrated bread and wine which we share in the Eucharist.

Shared Memory
As followers of Jesus we need to remember the things he did and said so that we can keep alive the connectedness between the original events which shaped the Christian community and our present-day experiences of being part of that community. When we come together as a community to celebrate the Eucharist, we recall the life, death and resurrection of Jesus. Through him, with him and in him we offer ourselves to God. We remember and make present in a special way the actions of Jesus at the Last Supper and on the cross. The Risen Jesus is with us as we remember.

Shared Living
Shared living is characterised by a spirit wherein people share their stories, their memories and their food.

In the Eucharist, as followers of Jesus, we remember the way he asked us to share our lives and our love. We celebrate the way in which we have been doing this in his memory. The Risen Jesus is with us as we gather in our families and communities and as we renew and live out our desire to live as Jesus asked us to. During the year some children will be celebrating their First Communion.

Sacrament of Penance

In First Class/Primary Three we put the children in touch with their own individual goodness, with the collective goodness of childhood, and with the goodness that is at the heart of human nature. Made in the image and likeness of God, we reflect something of the goodness of God. Jesus is the one who above all embodied the full potential of that human goodness and who revealed what the goodness of God is like. It is in this context that we situate the Sacrament of Reconciliation for the children.

In this unit the children are led on a particular journey through which they come to recognise their essential goodness and rejoice in it, become aware of their failures, and are led to say sorry for the times when their behaviour has been destructive or has caused pain or hurt. In other words, the children are becoming aware of the steps necessary for reconciliation to take place. This process of reconciliation is set in the context of the secure knowledge of the never-ending love of God for each one of them, in spite of any failure on their part. During the year some children will be celebrating the Sacrament of Reconciliation for the first time.

Sacrament of Baptism

In this programme, while not dealing specifically with the Sacrament of Baptism, we hope to lay a firm foundation for a future understanding of Baptism as the sacrament through which we share in the new life of the Risen Jesus and which marks our belonging to the Church.

In First Class/Primary Three we explore the children's sense of belonging with others in the class. We seek to engage them in a process of reflection on their experiences of sharing their life with others in the classroom so as to heighten their awareness of the identity which shapes any group of people who hold a common sense of belonging. In an effort to concretise this reality, the children, at the beginning of the year, will be invited to take part in a Celebration of Enrolment. For some, this ceremony will mark their initiation into a new class. For others, it will mark the beginning of their preparation for First Communion and their first celebration of the Sacrament of Reconciliation. In this ceremony the children, along with their parents/guardians, will be asked to renew their baptismal vows.

Throughout the year, the children are led to a deep awareness of God's love for each one of them, that they are indeed God's children, that they share in the life of the Risen Jesus whose spirit is always with them as they try to live as Jesus lived.

Moral Education

Through Baptism we share in the life and love of God. Christian living is an expression of this life. Our aim, in the moral education of children, is to help them to grow into mature Christians.

Developing a Christian conscience, and learning to live as a Christian, are lifelong tasks. Knowledge is not sufficient for moral development. Emotional and psychological immaturity are as much obstacles to moral growth as is a lack of knowledge. Therefore, to teach rules and commandments is not sufficient. We must also foster the children's personal and emotional development. The following are important considerations in the moral development of six- and seven-year-olds:

- First Class/Primary Three children are beginning to emerge from their egocentric world where everything is judged in terms of themselves and their own needs. They must be helped and encouraged in this development as they become increasingly aware that others also have needs and that they must learn to be sensitive to and respond to those needs.

- Children's moral sense first develops in response to the rules, precepts and expectations of adults. They accept, unquestioningly, the rules, standards and attitudes of the adults whom they love and admire, especially their parents and teachers. Six- and seven-year-olds essentially are motivated to do what is right, in order to gain approval from the adults around them.

- Parents contribute most to children's moral growth and development of conscience. They provide the love, security, discipline and correction which children need to develop self-acceptance, self-criticism and self-control. They provide an example of Christian living and an experience of the Christian values of love, respect, tolerance, generosity, forgiveness and self-sacrifice. The school also has an important role to play in the moral education of children, supporting and deepening the work of parents. Sometimes, of course, it must supply what the parents have neglected, or correct wrong attitudes already formed.

- The atmosphere of the school is very important for personal and moral growth. An atmosphere of love, respect for others, sympathy and forgiveness contributes to the six- and seven-year-old's self-confidence and self-acceptance, and develops their capacity to relate to others and to God.

- In the classroom and at play, six- and seven-year-olds are helped to develop the moral qualities of self-discipline, perseverance, determination, patience, fair play and consideration of others. The teacher serves as a model and an example. The children are influenced by her or his attitudes towards individuals and reactions to situations. Like the parent, the teacher seeks to develop in the children a habit of self-discipline, a sense of responsibility and concern for others.

- Six- and seven-year-olds need the security of order and discipline in the classroom. Obedience to rules and observance of certain standards of behaviour help them to develop self-control and to realise that there are limits to their freedom. The teacher must be prepared to correct and challenge the children, if necessary. However, God should never be used to threaten the children or to coax them to do what is required of them.

- To help children to develop into free, mature Christian adults, we should allow them a certain amount of freedom to make choices, even at this early stage. This will help them to develop self-confidence, to discover the consequences of their choices, and to realise that they are responsible for their own actions. This year the children are being offered a unique opportunity to take collective responsibility to create their own classroom atmosphere by formulating, in partnership with the teacher, their own Class Code.

- Stories that are told to six- and seven-year-olds at this stage can contribute to their personal and moral growth. Good stories often highlight the distinction between good and evil, right and wrong, the triumph of good over evil, and, indirectly, convey many moral values. Children can recognise in such stories, situations and conflicts which parallel their own experience. In this way they learn to come to terms with fear, anger, frustration, disappointment and death.

- Moral development is a slow and gradual process and must be viewed in the context of the children's overall psychological, emotional and intellectual development.

- The egocentricity of children makes it difficult for them to respond altruistically to others. In this year's programme we seek to put the children in touch with their own individual goodness, which is at the heart of human nature, and with the collective goodness of childhood which was recognised by Jesus when he said: 'Unless you become like little children...'.

We help them to reflect in a critical way upon some aspects of their behaviour when they don't live up to the goodness that is potentially theirs.

- Children of six and seven are limited in their capacity to choose freely. Sin should only be linked with conscious and deliberate choices. Children will always be influenced by their family context and background. We should be aware of and sensitive to the variety of situations out of which children emerge, recognising the importance of not expecting more than some children may be capable of giving.

Moral Development Theories

The works of Jean Piaget, Lawrence Kohlberg and Carol Gilligan are important considerations for anyone involved in moral education. While differing from each other in many ways, all three theorists acknowledge that moral development is a very gradual process and that environment and perspective of self in relation to others are significant influencing factors in the motivation of an individual's behaviour. Children of six and seven years of age, in particular, need to be encouraged to continue to emerge from their self-centred perspective, to acknowledge the perspective of those around them and to move towards more co-operative, mutual interaction with others.

Moral Education Related to God

In this programme, we are helping the children to become more aware of themselves and of the people and things around them. This is important for their personal development and moral growth. They are being helped to know themselves, to accept themselves, to appreciate their human abilities and to have more confidence in themselves. This develops their capacity to relate to the world, to others and to God.

In alerting them to the beauty and usefulness of the natural things around them, we are helping the children to develop positive attitudes towards the world and a responsible attitude towards creation. We help them to see these things as gifts from God. They are signs of God's love and care for creation. The children will then recognise that their attitude to these things is relevant to their relationship with God.

Lessons which explore the children's relationships with other people are also important for their moral formation. Children of six and seven years of age must be helped to realise that others have rights and needs which must be respected. We help them to discover the values of co-operation, sharing and respect for others and their property. Through living, working and playing with others, they will gradually come to discover the unhappy consequences of their selfish behaviour and the value of helping others and sharing with them.

During this year the children come to know, love and admire Jesus. They are old enough now to appreciate him as a model, as someone who tells us that if we are to find life, we must love God with all our hearts, and our neighbour as ourselves (Lk 10:27-28).

Through Baptism we share in the life of the Risen Jesus. We are called to live as Jesus lived. The Holy Spirit helps us to become more like Jesus and to love as he loved. Jesus gives himself to us in the Eucharist as the Bread of Life so that we may grow in love. When we are sorry for having failed to love, we celebrate God's forgiveness in the Sacrament of Reconciliation. We begin to live like Jesus once more.

We do not mention the commandments of God at this stage. However, the values underlying the commandments are stressed throughout the programme: respect and love for God, respect for others, respect for life, truth, honesty and property.

We take Jesus' commandment of love as our starting point – the commandment that calls us to love God through our love and compassionate care of others. We help children to identify ways in which they fulfil this commandment in their own lives.

Here again, the children gradually become aware that respect and love for others is not separate from their relationship with God, or their response to God, especially if they see that their parents and teachers live these values as part of their own response to God.

Prayer

'Prayer is the raising of one's mind and heart to God or the requesting of good things from God.' But when we pray do we speak from the height of our pride and will, or 'out of the depths' of a humble and contrite heart? Only when we humbly acknowledge that 'we do not know how to pray as we ought' are we ready to receive freely the gift of prayer. (*Catechism of the Catholic Church*, 2559)

Religious education seeks to help children to hear about God and to begin to explore questions about who God is and what God is like. However, more importantly, we are also seeking to help the children to know God, to relate to God as someone who is interested in them, who cares about them, who knows them by name, who has counted the hairs on their heads. We want them to know God as someone who gave them the gift of life, who is interested in their well-being and who sustains the gift of life in them. While both of these aims are obviously interrelated, working with the first does not necessarily achieve the second. If we want to sustain a relationship with anyone, we must spend time with that person. We must try to find the way in which we can best communicate with one another. Likewise, with God, if we want to help children to relate to God, we need to help them to become aware that God is present in their lives. We also need to help them to communicate with God: to be able to talk to God in prayer and to be able to listen to God speaking to them in the silence of their own hearts.

Therefore, in any religious education programme, prayer should be given a central place. The children's faith in God is fostered through prayer and they can learn to express this faith in prayer. Teaching children to pray is not the same as teaching definitions of prayer, nor is it as simple as teaching prayer formulas – though this is also important and is accommodated in the programme. Teaching prayer begins by making an effort to foster certain attitudes in the children.

An Awareness of God's Presence

Children are intuitive by nature and learn a lot from the atmosphere in which they live. Therefore, an atmosphere which is conducive to the recognition of and responds to God's presence in the ordinary events of every day is one in which children's own sense of God's presence is alerted and encouraged. A child's faith is fostered in school and the ability to pray is developed not only in the activity which is timetabled for religious education but in the opportunity which is provided to engage in relationships with other children, with the adults in the school and with the environment, which are shaped by a sense of God's presence in other people and in the natural world.

Atmosphere of Prayer

A child's natural sense of awe and wonder can flourish in a classroom where there are objects from the natural world, e.g. water, clay, sand, rocks, shells; living things, e.g. plants, flowers, seeds; seasonal signs, e.g. branches, leaves, corn, rushes; where there are seasonal pictures showing details of the countryside as we move through the year; where there is an abundance of colour and shape. A classroom where there is a sense of openness and listening between pupils themselves and between pupils and teacher is a place where children learn to respect others and come to have a sense of their personal dignity and self-worth. This will enhance their potential to build healthy relationships in the future, not only with other people but also with God.

Music, songs and hymns can help stimulate the children's sense of awe; the songs and hymns in their programme provide them with a language in which to express this. Religious images – good quality pictures and statues; pictures of nature scenes; liturgical symbols: a lighted candle, incense, sprinkling of Holy Water – can evoke attitudes of prayer or provide a focus for a time of prayer in the classroom. The way in which any of these are used should vary from prayertime to prayertime. However, the classroom could also contain a 'prayer corner', where some of the objects described above would be available for the children to hold or to touch; these could be varied frequently.

Witness

Watching Jesus pray awoke in the disciples the desire to pray. Children learn most of what they know by copying the adults around them. Likewise, with prayer, one of the best ways of teaching children to pray is to provide them with the opportunity to hear adults pray and to join in when they can. There was a time when practically every child would have this opportunity at home and would have had a sense of prayer instilled before ever coming to school. For some children that is still the case. For others, the first adult they will hear pray is the teacher in the classroom. An important part of the child's education in prayer is the opportunity to listen to a Christian adult express his or her faith in prayer and to recognise that this is a meaningful activity for the adult concerned. The prayertimes provide opportunities for the teacher to express her/his faith with the children as she/he feels appropriate for them.

Different Expressions of Prayer

> The Lord leads all persons by paths and in ways pleasing to him.... However, Christian tradition has retained three major expressions of prayer: vocal, meditative and contemplative.
> (*Catechism of the Catholic Church*, 2699)

There are many different expressions of prayer which are true to the Christian tradition of prayer. It is important to provide children with the opportunity to experience different expressions of prayer. Often when people say 'I can't pray', what has in fact happened is that they are not aware of or have not tried the type of prayer which might best suit their individual needs and personality type. Just as

we will choose different ways in which to communicate with others, so it is with prayer.

Vocal Prayer
Vocal prayer is usually the first type of prayer we encounter. When we pray vocally we put words on our experiences of God in our lives. We need to express in words what we feel and believe. This is part of our human condition. Through vocal prayer we can both express and understand better our relationship with God. Vocal prayer takes many forms, all of which can be introduced to children at a very young age.

Meditative Prayer
> Meditation engages thought, imagination, emotion and desire.
> (*Catechism of the Catholic Church*, 2708)

As this quotation from The *Catechism of the Catholic Church* states, meditation involves the whole person. Children can be introduced in a simple way to meditation at a very early age. A methodology for doing this will accompany suggestions for meditative prayer as they occur in the text. A meditative prayer might, for example, lead children to imagine themselves in a space where they can talk to God about whatever they wish. At a later stage they would be led to imagine themselves in a Gospel story. The children are encouraged to take on the role of one of the characters in the story. As such, they can meet with Jesus. They can tell him in their imagination what they are thinking or feeling. They can imagine his response. Children have very little difficulty with this type of prayer since they have little difficulty entering the world of the imagination. All they need are suggestions and guidance.

Contemplative Prayer
> What is contemplative prayer? St Teresa answers: 'Contemplative prayer in my opinion is nothing else than a close sharing between friends; it means taking time frequently to be alone with him who we know loves us'.
> (*Catechism of the Catholic Church*, 2709)

Usually when we communicate with people we do so through words, gestures or images. At certain times, though, we can communicate without using these tools. When we know someone very well and feel particularly close to that person, we can communicate silently at a very deep level, even through something as simple as a glance. So it is with God. Though we usually use words, gestures or images when we communicate with God, we can also communicate silently from deep within our hearts. One prerequisite for this type of prayer is the ability to achieve a level of quiet and stillness from within. To help the children to begin to achieve a level of stillness and to move beyond images, we introduce the children to praying the mantra. A short phrase like 'Jesus is Lord' is repeated quietly and gently until the mind and heart become still and the children rest in deep silence with God. It is possible to begin to help children to do this from a very early age, while recognising that, like any form of prayer, it takes time to practise and to learn.

Forms of Prayer

Prayer of Petition

When we think of prayer, a prayer of petition is the one which comes to mind most easily. Those of us who rarely pray probably do so in times of need or crisis. This is also the kind of prayer which probably comes most naturally and easily to children. While we would not want to confine their thinking about prayer to 'asking God for', it may be that this is the place where prayer begins to make sense to some children. It is only if we use no other form of prayer that there is something lacking in prayer of petition. It is, however, important from the beginning to direct children's prayers of petition away from the magical understanding of God as the Great Santa Claus in the sky – 'Please, God, can I have a new bike for my birthday?'

Prayer of Thanksgiving

Children are equally open to prayer of thanksgiving. It is, however, important that their 'Thank you, God, for...' is linked to a concrete experience in their lives. Prayer of thanksgiving then comes most appropriately at the end of a period of time spent raising the children's awareness in some particular area, e.g. after spending a week exploring the season of autumn, it makes sense that the children might pray 'Thank you, God, for the colours of autumn'.

Prayer of Praise

Prayer of praise is the prayer which praises God simply because God is God. As children are gradually led to some simple understanding of the wonder and glory of God, it makes sense to introduce them to prayer of praise.

Prayer of Sorrow and Repentance

Prayer of sorrow and repentance should probably begin all our prayers. As soon as children begin to recognise that they do wrong, we can introduce them to prayer of sorrow and repentance – prayer of asking God's forgiveness for the wrong that we do.

Prayer of Intercession

We have all asked people to 'say a prayer for me'. Even to know that someone is praying for us is a help. Prayer of intercession characterised the prayer of Jesus, who often prayed on behalf of his followers. From the very beginning, children can be encouraged to pray for others' needs – a parent who is sick, a grandparent whom they haven't seen for a while, etc.

Prayer in the Classroom

It is important to develop in the children from the beginning a sense that they can 'talk to God' at any time and in any place and that God is always listening to and interested in what they have to say. We would encourage them, therefore, to pray at certain times during the day – morning, evening, meal times. To this end, it is important from an early stage to provide space within the day's work in the classroom when the child can pray personally. This can be either vocal spontaneous prayer or silent prayer.

Education in common prayer will help the children to come to an awareness of themselves as participating members of the Church community. Education in prayer includes the learning of prayer formulas, which are the formal prayer language of the Church and education in the liturgy. These take place gradually over the course of the children's years in the primary school in line with their developing understanding and vocabulary. In the normal ongoing course of the religion class, common prayer can take place in different contexts:

- *Occasional prayer arising out of everyday events*
  In every class special moments will occur which provide occasions for prayer: a new baby brother or sister; death of a family member; good news of a new job for someone's parent; an accident, etc. These can be prayers of petition, of thanksgiving, of praise, etc., as the occasion demands.

- *Prayer in the context of the religion lesson*
  In every religion class the children will be helped to explore some aspect of their experience in order to discover its significance, the questions posed by it, etc. They will also be helped to relate their own story to the Christian story. The hope is that they will grow in their understanding of their own experiences and of the implications of the Christian story for their lives. We hope that they will also become more aware of the way in which God speaks to them in their concrete, everyday experiences. Awareness is fostered through expression. They will be given many opportunities to express their understanding of what they are doing: in art, in drama, in story, etc. They should also have the opportunity to express this in the language of prayer. In every lesson there will be opportunities for the children to pray. Their prayer experiences will be as varied as possible – some in the context of a day's religious education work, some as a response to an entire lesson.

- *Celebrations*
  Sometimes these moments of prayer will be more solemn. They will be more formal and will seek to introduce the children to the liturgy by using symbols, gestures, movements, etc. They may be linked to a series of lessons which have been completed or they may be linked to an occasion: the Feast of All Saints, Advent, Lent, the end of the school year, etc. Sometimes a number of classes might take part in these together. On one occasion during each term of the First Class/Primary Three programme, it is hoped the parents or other family members will be invited to join with the children in a Prayer Service. A celebration of this nature might also be led by the local priest or parish sister.

- *The language of prayer*
  Children should be encouraged from the beginning to express their prayers spontaneously, that is, in whatever language comes most easily to them. This will foster in them a sense that God is always interested in and listening to their concerns. It is the attitude of the heart which counts, not the accuracy of the words. Once they understand what is happening, children generally have no difficulty with this. However, because the children are not yet able to express their thoughts accurately, the wording of these prayers may not be of a very high standard. It is important always to remember that it is the sincerity which counts, while at the same time encouraging the children to go beyond what they are at present capable of. For instance, if the spontaneous prayers around a class are echoing 'please, God, make my granny better', 'please, God, help my daddy to get a new job', etc., a gentle nudge which would suggest, 'does anybody want to thank God for something?', might be all that's needed to introduce a new dimension. Spontaneous prayers can be prayers of petition, of love, of thanks, of praise, of sorrow, etc.

Traditional prayer formulas form the common prayer language of the Church. They are the prayers which constitute the prayer language of the adults with whom the children live and of the community with whom they pray in the local church. So, while excessive dependence on traditional prayer formulas can lead to routine in prayer, they can also be a genuine expression of faith and it is important that children learn them. This is done gradually as they move through the primary school: new prayers are introduced as their capacity for understanding and use of language grows.

Spontaneous prayer and traditional prayer formulas should not be seen as being in opposition to one another. It should never be an either/or situation. One can be enriched by the other and the children's faith can be helped to grow and develop by using both.

Using the Programme in the Classroom

Stories

Listening to and telling stories is an important part of the process of every lesson in this programme. Children love stories. They will listen to the same story hundreds of times. Adults are compulsive story-tellers. As we grapple with the great moments of life and death, with good, with evil, with the mystery which touches our lives, story-telling is always important. Story-telling, however, is not always valued as a serious activity and is often seen as belonging to the world of entertainment, of children, of the frivolous.

The ability to think in abstractions has always been highly valued in western education. We are heirs to Greek philosophy. We are encouraged to seek out 'good', 'beauty', 'truth'. For a child, however, it is impossible to think in abstraction. A child can only come to some understanding of 'goodness', 'truth' or 'beauty' by experiencing the actions of a good person, by being told what is true, by seeing beautiful things.

Stories have the capacity to explore abstractions in terms of images and interpersonal experiences. They provide a stage peopled by characters exemplifying the great forces that have shaped humanity and where we can see love, hatred, greed, generosity, compassion and jealousy in action. A good story is a mirror which shows us the heights and the depths of human experience, and in doing so gives us the opportunity to view our own experience at a safe distance.

The stories in the programme are closely linked to the children's experience. A story can be an experience for both the teacher and the children, if it is told in an open atmosphere of participation, where the children are encouraged to identify with its characters and the happenings. Stories help children make sense of their experience. Children are never outside the immediacy of a well-told story and teachers will readily agree that story-telling time is one of the 'magical' moments in the classroom. A story is outside calendar time and so the listener and the teller can come back into it again and again.

Through story-telling, children can be helped to come to terms with and understand their own experience. They can learn to value the significance of the things that happen to them. If we allow the stories we tell to evoke the children's own stories, we can help them to articulate their experiences and to begin to put a shape on their world.

In the Christian tradition, story-telling is not an innovation. Jesus told stories which challenged the people of his day to look again at their experiences. Through his stories he challenged them to re-evaluate these in the light of the values of God's Kingdom, which he explored in concrete terms in his stories.

Poetry

Poetry plays a central role in *Alive-O 3* because of its capacity to express and to hold in creative tension varying elements of the human struggle to become fully alive.

The struggle to become fully alive is one which unfolds through experience and is expressed through language. In a particular way, experience and language are what poetry works with too. Without the language which poetry puts on human experience, that experience can be hollow and empty. It can amount to no more than what T. S. Eliot describes in 'The Family Reunion' when a young man says to his relations:

> You are all people
> To whom nothing has happened, at most a continual impact
> Of external events.

Poetry works with experience in a way that transforms life from being a mere series of events which happen to us, into something we experience. All poetry does this by working with image. The success of the best poetry – (reflecting the original working with image, i.e. the creation of humankind in God's image) – lies in the exactitude of its images. The role of poetry in a programme which aims to celebrate the liveliness and 'life-fullness' of young children, therefore becomes obvious. At least one poem is included in each lesson so that the children have an opportunity, metaphorically, to poke and prod words and images with their fingers, toes and tongues. In the saying of these poems the child is holding a kind of aural mirror up to her or his ear. In it, as in a looking glass, the child can 'hear' his or herself reflected in sound, cadence and rhythm. The child may also catch a glimpse over her or his shoulder of the 'sound' of the language of the present-day community and the communities which preceded it. The child may begin to develop an aural dimension to her or his developing imagination. And because of the context, content and nature of the imagery in many of the poems, the child may develop a keenly religious imagination. These are the opportunities which it is the duty of any religion programme aimed at enhancing fullness-of-life, to offer. However, it is important to realise that the extent to which these opportunities can be taken up by the child depends on the level of enjoyment she or he finds in the saying, and in the considering, of these poems.

Enjoyment of poetry is the kind of phenomenon of which Seamus Heaney says: it is its own reward. It is hoped that repeated recitation or incantation of some of the poems in the programme will be an *experience* for children's tongues, minds, voices and ears of:

> ...all those anglings, aimings, feints and squints...
> ...all those
>
> Hunkerings, tensings, pressures of the thumb,
> Test-outs and pullbacks and re-envisagings...
> as they begin to tackle life to the full.
> (*Seeing Things*, Seamus Heaney)

Art

While engaged in the task of awakening in the children a consciousness of the wondrous, we must consider the importance of the gift for imagery. More than any formal, abstract means of communication, such as language or writing, the image is the immediate personal language of the senses. In a world where many things are transitory, it alone remains as a meaningful record of an event, a sensation, an experience, an emotion. The ever-changing world of the child needs art as a means of expression. It makes possible the externalisation of what might otherwise remain a confused mass of uninterpreted, unrelated stimuli. Art allows the many stimuli – aural, sensory and emotional – to find unity in expression.

The border constantly shifts between reality and fantasy, the secular and the sacred, in a world where children explore all that impinges on them with a burning honesty. Children can explore this world in line, in symbol, in colour, with a degree of freedom and concentration otherwise found only in the works of great artists.

In their paintings and drawings, children are allowed to express their reactions and fears, without fear of correction or contradiction. It is one discipline which allows for acceptance of the children for what they are, rather than for what they might be or might know.

When the children express themselves in picture form, they learn to look at and assess their own vision. They are continually adjusting their understanding of the world as part of an ongoing process.

In drawing a picture, a necessary cross-over point is reached from sound into silence and from a public world into a private one. It serves the need for contemplation and provides a necessary transfer point from the objective to the subjective, and from the group to the individual. In leading children into the world of art, we are giving them the right of access to a development which aids and makes plain and meaningful their confrontation with the exciting and demanding process of coming to maturity.

Music

Music and song speak to the heart in a way that often transcends the spoken word. Music uplifts the spirit and renews the soul. Each lesson in the programme contains at least one song. Each of these is recorded and available on the audio tapes and CDs which accompany the programme. The songs are related to the theme and content of the lessons for which they are intended. The songs vary from being bright, lively and action-oriented to being quiet and prayerful. They can be listened to each day during the week and the children will know all or part of them by the time the lesson has been completed. The songs seek to explore in words and music the spirit of each lesson. They are one way through which the children can be helped to reflect on and remember what they have learned. Towards the end of the week they can be incorporated into the Prayer Service.

Chatting About...

Each lesson contains a number of 'chatting' opportunities, about the story, sometimes about the poem/art, about some aspect of experience which is relevant to the lesson, etc. The aim of these is to engage the children in dialogue/conversation with the teacher and with each other about the content of the lesson. The learning process is helped by giving the children the opportunity to put words on what they are learning or experiencing. In so doing they make their own of something new or different.

Different children from different classes will have varying abilities for doing this exercise.

The exercise as it is laid out in the text simply provides an example of what might be done. It is not in any way envisaged that every question be asked. Neither is it meant to be a question and answer exercise in which each child is expected to know the correct answer to each question. As the title suggests, it simply seeks to get the children 'chatting' and so thinking about what they are learning. The chatting can be changed and adapted as best suits the individual class.

Memorisation

The importance of memorisation should not be overlooked. It is good to encourage children to know something 'by heart'. To know 'by heart' in the truest sense means that what is learnt resonates with the child and is internalised by her/him. Throughout the year the children are provided with countless opportunities to 'learn by heart' – songs, hymns, poems, Mass responses, traditional prayers and informal prayers, which sum up and express the core content of a given lesson.

To further develop the children's capacity for memorisation, *Alive-O 3* introduces:
- *Remember and Say:* simple theological statements presented in verse format;
- *Now We Know:* simple doctrinal questions and answers which summarise core content in language that is accessible to six- and seven-year-olds.

Did You Know?

Sometimes it is necessary to present information directly to the children. Such material is highlighted under the heading *Did You Know?* It is envisaged that the teacher would chat to the children about the content as it is being presented to them.

Sacramental Classes
To facilitate teachers of sacramental classes, material specifically orientated to children who will be celebrating the sacraments of Reconciliation and Eucharist is presented in a closed box.

Process Followed in the Lessons

The duties of catechesis correspond to education of the different dimensions of faith, for catechesis is integral Christian formation, 'open to all the factors of Christian life'. In virtue of its own internal dynamic, the faith demands to be known, celebrated, lived and translated into prayer.
(*General Directory for Catechesis,* 84)

The following is the process used in each lesson in the infant programme.

Focus

We begin each lesson by focusing on particular significant experiences which are part of the life of a child of their age. Children's experience is limited, as is their understanding and vocabulary. It is not easy for an adult to enter into the world of the child and to explore with the child his or her experience, not from the adult's but from the child's point of view. The programme in its choice of experiences seeks to provide the teacher with the resources to do this. It may be 'returning to school', 'the changing seasons', 'the thrill of being alive', 'watching, waiting, wondering'. We begin by offering the children a number of activities which focus on the particular experience that is being explored in a particular lesson. It may be a game, or a story, or an art activity. Sometimes, even those things which seem to be most obvious escape us. We can have eyes that fail to see or ears that fail to hear. We seek to enable the children to become the kind of people who have eyes which see and ears which hear, people who are capable of a level of awareness which seeks not only to answer the question 'what is this?', but also the question 'what does this mean for me?, for me in relation to others?, for me in relation to God?'.

We take for granted much of what happens in our daily lives. Only in rare moments do we stop and think and ask questions about the significance of the ordinary events of our lives. In this religious education programme we seek to provide the opportunity for the children to do that: to stop and think; to ask questions; to explore; to wonder.

Explore/Reflect

At this point in the lesson we offer the children the possibility of dwelling on the experience which is being explored, so that they may become more aware of what is happening. They may engage in activities such as listening to a story, drawing pictures, acting out a scene, making something. We hope, for example, that they will become more aware of the feelings associated with being part of a class and be helped to cope with these feelings; or that they will be more alert to the beauty of the world in autumn and experience something of the wonder and mystery of the natural world; or that they will have a greater consciousness of the gift of life in their own bodies and feel the excitement of being alive; or that they will be more aware of the creativity of which they are capable and see this as a gift. We explore the Christian story as it bears light on their experience.

We seek to provide opportunities for the children to become reflective people who will take time to stop and think, so that they will have the capacity to become aware of the presence and action of God in their lives and in the world around them. 'Indeed he is not far from each one of us. For "In him we live and move and have our being" ' (Acts 17:28).

Sometimes important information needs to be given to the children, and because of the nature of this information it cannot be readily elicited from them. In this situation the programme presents such content under the heading 'Did You Know?'. It is hoped that the teacher, having presented the information, would then reflect on it with the children.

Response

An important stage in the learning process is that moment when a person is able to say 'this is what I learned', 'this is how that affects me', 'this is what that means for me in my own life'. For six- and seven-year-old children this expression must take many and varied forms. They can say it in words, draw it in pictures, act it out in a play, sing it in a song. One of the ways through which they will always be encouraged to express what they have learnt in a particular lesson is through prayer. Where appropriate, in line with the capacity of a child of this age, they are also encouraged to respond in an action which shows that there are implications in what they have learnt for the way in which they live their lives. So, for instance, it may be that they have spent some time thinking about those at home who love them. A response might be, that they would make a card saying 'thank you' to those people. It may be that having spent some time thinking about the wonder of the natural world, they take time to pick up litter in the school playground.

Lesson Structure for Each Week

Each lesson is divided into five parts, one for each day. This is intended to help teachers in their efforts to structure a week's work in the classroom. **However, should this prove too rigid in any situation, the teacher can feel free to disregard the way in which the lesson is divided and to choose from the material as she or he sees fit.**

Being Sensitive

In *Alive-O 3* we help the children to discover signs of God in their experience of self, others and the world. We can help the children to find more immediate signs of God's splendour, love and care in their experiences of pleasant and beautiful things: joy, happiness and love at home and at school; beautiful things in the world. Therefore, the programme assumes that most children have some experience of love and happiness at home and that they have opportunities to observe and enjoy the beautiful things in the world around them.

Religion is about life. Children learn from their experience, so it is vital that every child finds his/her real experience reflected in the programme.

While most children have some experience of love and happiness, it is important to be aware that this may not be true for all children, all of the time. Some children may have a physical or mental handicap. Some children may have experienced the loss of a parent or a brother or sister. Some children may not live in the typical family unit. They may live with one parent or with a grandparent. All children experience times of hardship, fear, sadness, loneliness, disappointment, loss and sickness. These experiences are not explicitly explored in the programme. However, they cannot be ignored and must be acknowledged by everyone involved in the religious education of children, and, as Christians, must be interpreted in the light of our faith.

The following points should be borne in mind in the interpretation of unpleasant experiences.

Throughout the programme we endeavour to help children to realise that:

- God's goodness is unfailing. God is loving and compassionate. God is always with us. God is with us when we are lonely, neglected and sad. God never ceases to love us but constantly calls us to grow and to change, to become fully human, fully alive.

- We should never associate evil with God. In this year's programme the children come to know Jesus as one who loved and cared for everybody. Jesus shows us what

God our Father and our Creator is really like – loving, caring and compassionate. Therefore, when something unpleasant happens to children, they should not be given the impression that God is punishing them for bad behaviour. This would give the children a distorted image of God.

- It is not God's will that anyone be deprived, suffer hardship or have a disability. No matter what disabilities we may have, we are still cherished by God. We are all unique in God's eyes. God wants us all to lead as full a life as possible. We should help the children to come to terms with the limitations and disabilities they may have. We should stress that disabilities can be overcome and that many people with disabilities succeed in living full and enriching lives. In fact, for some people, difficult experiences in life may encourage them to lead a fuller and more meaningful life than they would otherwise have.

- God wants us to grow up and to come to terms with the realities of life. We cannot grow up and mature unless we learn to face up to and cope with the difficulties and hardships we meet in life. We should not, therefore, lead the children to expect God to deliver them immediately from hardships and disappointments. We should rather help them to develop confidence in God's goodness and wisdom, and in God's help in facing up to and overcoming the difficulties and trials of life. In this programme they will be introduced to the example of Jesus, his patience during suffering, his confidence in God's presence and goodness, and his determination to do his Father's will, in spite of pain and suffering.

- Children can be helped to discover immediate signs of God's love and care in beautiful and happy experiences. In unpleasant and unhappy experiences, they can find God's love, care, goodness, justice, wisdom and forgiveness mediated through a sympathetic and fair-minded adult. Therefore, it is important that the children should feel loved and wanted. They should always have the security of knowing that they can rely on the love, sympathy and forgiveness of a parent/guardian, a teacher or some other significant adult. The teacher should, in the context of the classroom and where it is appropriate, offer the children the care and attendion of a loving adult.

The Teacher's Kit

The teacher's kit, of which this book is a part, comprises several elements.

Teacher's Book

This text is a resource, primarily for teachers but also for those such as priests or other parish personnel who visit classrooms regularly. It provides teachers with background material in the areas of theology, scripture, catechetical methodology and personal reflection.

For each week there is a lesson, which contains resources in the following areas: story, song, prayer, art, poetry, activities and classroom conversation. An indication is given in the overview for the week and in the text as to what might be covered on any given day.

Every classroom is different, in terms of teacher's preferences, children's ability, social and cultural context, number of children in the class, number of classes in the room, etc. The teacher's text is designed to offer teachers a choice, and while all the material in the teacher's text may not be covered in any one classroom in any year, it is offered so that teachers will have a useful resource which provides them with an option to pick and choose.

Pupil Book

The pupil book is colourful and child-centred and designed to capture the child's imagination and attention. It contains full-page, full-colour illustrations of the stories in the teacher's book. The pupil book offers the children a visual representation of most of the stories in the teacher's book. It also provides an invaluable link with the home. It is not, however, an English Reader! It can be read to the children by the teacher in school or by the parent/guardian in the home. Sometimes, depending on the child's ability, it can be read by the child herself/himself. It offers a useful starting point for further conversation about the stories, thereby furthering the pupil's ability with language and with observation.

It is a book which the children will enjoy and have fun using. The book also contains notes for parents, the formal prayers the children are learning, and some simple prayers written in a language which children can easily understand. This will enable parents to engage in conversation and prayer with their children in a way that is related to what the children are learning at school.

Worksheets and Workbook

The kit also contains a set of photocopiable worksheets, one for each lesson in the teacher's text. These worksheets are also available in the form of a workbook. The teacher can, therefore, choose which format is best suited to his or her own situation, taking into account the advantages and disadvantages of each.

One of the principal functions of this resource is to provide a further link between the school and the home. Once again, each worksheet, or workbook page, contains notes for the parents. The worksheets can be given freely to the children to take home without the concern that they may not be returned safely. While the worksheets demand extra work and time spent photocopying on the teacher's part, they are re-usable and offer a greater flexibility in that the teacher can choose which ones to use. On the other hand, the workbook offers the greater possibility of building up, over the year, a record of the child's work. You may, or may not, consider this necessary, since the child will have benefited from the worksheet simply by using it. It is not recommended that the workbook is seen as an alternative to the pupil text, since these do not fulfil the same function for the child.

Posters

A set of twelve posters is available to be used at the teacher's discretion as an optional extra. These are A1 size reproductions of some of the pictures in the pupil text. They have the potential to provide a focal point for classroom discussion or for prayer.

Video

The video is sixty minutes long and contains five units which are linked to the themes and content covered in the programme.

Tapes/CDs

The music is recorded both on cassette and on CD, which contain at least one song for each lesson.

Guided by the **What am I trying to do?** and **Why?**, teachers can use the **Overview of the Week** as a guide in the selection of the material they feel appropriate to their situation, especially if they are teaching in a multi-context class. Choosing from the diverse resources and suggestions, they can use the variety of approaches over time.

A Note on Cultural Background

It is important for teachers to talk to children in ways appropriate to the children's own experience and culture. This presents a challenge to the authors of printed materials, who must take account of the wide variety in their readers' situations. There will be differences in relationships (not all children have two parents), race, social class, religion, sex, proper names, idiom, urban or rural environment.

This programme is written in Ireland and can be adapted where the cultural background is different. We hope that teachers will adapt the language to match their own children's understanding: 'Mammy' may become 'Mum', 'Seán' could be replaced by 'Ian' or 'John', the doctor may be a man or a woman, and the countryside may become the local park.

The Role of the Teacher

The teacher is one of the most significant people in the life of any school-child. While the teacher cannot and should not be expected to take on the role of the parent or make up for what can sometimes be missing from the parent/child relationship, many people will look back on their relationship with a particular teacher as being one of the most formative influences in their lives.

A teacher can create in the classroom an open, respectful, caring, trust-filled atmosphere where children can feel valued and have a sense that their uniqueness and potential are recognised. In such an atmosphere they can be helped to form and develop as people who will have a respect for themselves, for others, for the world in which they live and for God. For many children the school may be the first place where they will feel cared for and valued. While no school can make up for what is missing at home, whatever a teacher can do to give such children a sense of being lovable and loved is significant.

In the religious education class, a teacher who respects each child and each child's experience, who tries to take where the children are at as a starting-point, can do much to help the children to grow as people of faith. A teacher can help the children to know that they are individually known and loved by God and that God, who has given us the gift of life, is caring for and sustaining that life. She or he can help the children to become aware of the fact that God is always listening to them and that they can talk to God about their good and their bad experiences. Helping the children to take part in the Prayer Service at the end of each lesson will lead them to become comfortable with a number of different ways of praying. By encouraging them to be aware of the needs of the others in the class, to share and to be truthful, to care for the environment both inside and outside of the classroom, the teacher can help the children to become people who will have a sense of their inter-dependence on one another, on the physical world, and on God. By reminding them to acknowledge, respond to and give thanks for the love and care they receive from those with whom they live at home, they are being encouraged to see their own potential for being loving, caring people.

More important than any of this is the example children see in the way in which the teacher responds to each member of the class and the effort made by her or him to create an atmosphere of respect and care among the children for one another.

Relationships and Sexuality Education

The *Alive-O* programmes seek to help the children to grow and develop into healthy mature adults, capable of realising their full potential as human beings created in the image and likeness of God. One aspect of that growth is the development of the children's ability to relate to others and to have a positive understanding of their own sexuality.

In *Alive-O* this is not seen as a separate element of the programme but is integrated throughout. The table below shows where *Alive-O 3* explicitly deals with the topics given in the guidelines for relationships and sexuality education as outlined in the Department of Education's document.

This material is only relevant to schools in the Republic of Ireland.

Myself

I am Unique

SELF-ESTEEM

- **Acquire a growing sense of self-esteem**

Term 2, Lesson 2: Entire Lesson
Term 2, Lesson 3: Entire Lesson

- **Develop an appreciation of personal strengths, abilities and personal characteristics**

Term 2, Lesson 2: Entire Lesson
Term 2, Lesson 3: Prayertime (Day 1, 2 & 5), Art (Day 3)
Term 2, Lesson 8: Ritual (Day 5)

DEVELOPING AND
EXPRESSING SELF-CONFIDENCE

- **View him/herself as special and unique**

Term 1, Lesson 5: Song, Activity (Day 2), Prayertime (Day 5)
Term 2, Lesson 2: Entire Lesson
Term 2, Lesson 3: Entire Lesson

- **Express personal opinions and preferences, listen to and acknowledge those of others, and comment upon them**

Chatting throughout the programme

- **Cope with a variety of new situations**

Term 1, Lesson 1: Entire Lesson
Term 1, Lesson 5: Entire Lesson

- **Appreciate and make use of quiet time**

Term 2, Lesson 1: Entire Lesson
Term 2, Lesson 4: Chatting (Day 1 & 2), Prayertime (Day 1 & 2),
Prayertime throughout the programme

My Body

- **Name and identify external parts of the male and female body and their associated functions**

Term 1, Lesson 3: Song, Prayertime (Day 2 & 3), Game (Day 3), Art (Day 4)
Term 2, Lesson 6: Prayertime (Day 4)

- **Appreciate the need to care for the body in order to keep it strong and healthy**

Term 1, Lesson 7: Prayertime (Day 4)
Term 3, Lesson 3: Prayertimes
Term 3, Lesson 5: Chatting (Day 1 & 3), Activity (Day 1), Prayertime (Day 1)

As I grow, I change

- **Understand that physical growth has taken place since birth**

Term 1, Lesson 4: Prayertime (Day 2), All of Day 3

- **Compare and contrast the development of social and intellectual skills and other abilities from infancy onwards**

Term 1, Lesson 4: Day 3, Poem, Chatting, Activity, Prayertime

- **Recognise that growing up brings increased responsibility for oneself and others**

Term 1, Lesson 1: Story, Chatting (Day 1)
Term 1, Lesson 3: Story, Chatting (Day 2)
Term 1, Lesson 5: Day 1 and Day 2

New Life

- **Appreciate and celebrate the wonder of new life**

Term 1, Lesson 13: Chatting (Day 1)
Term 1, Lesson 15: Chatting (Day 1)
Term 3, Lesson 1: Chatting (Day 3)

- Become familiar with the cycles of some common plants and animals

Term 1, Lesson 1: Story, Chatting (Day 2)
Term 1, Lesson 3: Story, Chatting (Day 2)
Term 1, Lesson 4: Story (Day 2)

- Appreciate what is necessary in order to provide and care for new-born babies in both the animal and human world

Term 3, Lesson 1: Story (Day 2), Chatting (Day 3)

Keeping Safe

- Recognise dangerous situations and how to seek help

Term 1, Lesson 8: Song, Art (Day 1), Chattings throughout the Lesson, Prayertime (Day 1, 2 & 3)
Term 1, Lesson 11: Chatting (Day 1)
Term 1, Lesson 14: Chatting (Day 1)
Term 2, Lesson 5: Prayertime (Day 3)
Term 3, Lesson 1: Chatting (Day 5)

- Identify people who make him/her feel unsafe

Term 2, Lesson 5: Art (Day 5)

- Develop appropriate observational skills to promote personal safety

Term 1, Lesson 8: Chatting (Day 1, 3, 4 & 5), Art (Day 1), Prayertime (Day 1 & 3)

Feelings and Emotions

- Identify and name positive and negative feelings which can be experienced

Term 1, Lesson 2: Chatting (Day 4), Prayertime (Day 4)
Term 2, Lesson 1: Chatting (Day 1), Prayertime (Day 1, 2 & 4)
Term 2, Lesson 2: Chatting, Stories
Term 2, Lesson 5: Prayertime (Day 4 & 5)
Term 2, Lesson 6: Entire Lesson
Term 2, Lesson 7: Entire Lesson
Chatting throughout the programme

- Differentiate between physical and emotional hurt

Term 2, Lesson 6: Entire Lesson
Term 2, Lesson 7: Entire Lesson

- Realise the various ways that feelings can be expressed and choose which is most appropriate and socially acceptable

Term 2, Lesson 6: Story, Chatting, Prayertime
Term 2, Lesson 7: Story, Chatting, Prayertime, Poem (Day 2 & 4)
Chatting throughout the programme

Making Decisions

- **Recognise the choices that are made every day**

Term 1, Lesson 1: Chatting throughout Lesson
Term 1, Lesson 2: Chatting throughout Lesson
Term 1, Lesson 5: Chatting (Day 1 & 2)

- **Discuss factors which may influence personal decisions and choices**

Term 1, Lesson 5: Chatting, Activities
Term 2, Lesson 6: Entire Lesson
Term 2, Lesson 7: Entire Lesson

- **Identify risky behaviour and the consequences of same**

Term 2, Lesson 6: Stories, Chatting
Term 2, Lesson 7: Stories, Chatting

- **Begin to realise that he/she will be given more opportunities to make choices as the trust of others is earned**

Term 1, Lesson 5: Entire Lesson

Myself and Others

Myself and my family

- **Explore and discuss how the family functions as a unit**

Term 1, Lesson 13: Chatting, Activity (Day 5)
Term 3, Lesson 3: Chatting (Day 3 & 4)

- **Understand and accept that all families are not the same**

Term 1, Lesson 11: Story (Day 2), Chatting

- Identify the ways in which members of a family can help one another

Term 2, Lesson 5: Prayertime (Day 2 & 5)
Term 2, Lesson 6: Stories and Chatting throughout entire Lesson
Term 2, Lesson 7: Stories and Chatting throughout entire Lesson
Term 3, Lesson 1: Chatting (Day 3)
Term 3, Lesson 3: Chatting (Day 2, 3 & 4)

Myself and my friends

- Identify, explore and discuss qualities and skills associated with friendship

Term 1, Lesson 1: Entire Lesson
Term 2, Lesson 2: Story, Chatting, Activity, Prayertime (Day 2)
Term 2, Lesson 6: Entire Lesson
Term 2, Lesson 7: Entire Lesson
Term 3, Lesson 8: Song

- Identify, explore and discuss the different ways one can lose a friend, and begin to develop the necessary skills to cope with such a loss

Term 2, Lesson 6: Entire Lesson
Term 2, Lesson 7: Entire Lesson

- Acknowledge that friends often circulate in groups, which can be healthy/unhealthy

Term 1, Lesson 5: Chatting (Day 2)

Other people

- Begin to appreciate how people depend on each other in the family, school and the wider community

Term 1, Lesson 3: Prayertime (Day 4)
Term 1, Lesson 5: Activity (Day 1 & 2), Chatting (Day 2), Prayertime (Day 3)
Term 1, Lesson 10: Poem (Day 2)
Term 1, Lesson 12: Chatting (Day 1), Activity (Day 1)
Term 1, Lesson 13: Art (Day 3)
Term 1, Lesson 14: Prayertime (Day 1 & 3)
Term 1, Lesson 15: Prayertime (Day 5)
Term 2, Lesson 3: Story (Day 1)
Term 2, Lesson 4: Chatting, Activity (Day 5)
Term 3, Lesson 8: Entire Lesson

- Begin to develop sensitivity and empathy towards others, including those who may be different

Term 1, Lesson 10: Prayertime (Day 1)
Term 1, Lesson 11: Story (Day 2), Chatting (Day 2)
Term 1, Lesson 13: Art (Day 3)
Term 1, Lesson 14: Prayertime (Day 5)
Term 2, Lesson 1: Art, Prayertime (Day 5)
Term 3, Lesson 8: Activies throughout Lesson, Prayertime (Day 5)

Relating to others

COMMUNICATING

- Listen to others and hear what is being said

Term 1, Lesson 9: Song, Ritual (Day 1), Game (Day 2), Poem (Day 3)
Term 1, Lesson 10: Activity (Day 4)
Term 1, Lesson 12: Activity (Day 1), Chatting (Day 1), Prayertime (Day 1)
Term 3, Lesson 4: Game (Day 3)
Term 3, Lesson 6: Activity (Day 2)
Chatting throughout entire programme

- Talk about and reflect on a range of everyday experiences, feelings and emotions

Chatting and Prayertime throughout entire programme

- Use language, gestures and other appropriate behaviours to perform social functions

Term 1, Lesson 1: Chatting (Day 1), Prayertime (Day 2)
Term 1, Lesson 7: Prayertime (Day 5)
Term 1, Lesson 13: Art (Day 3), Prayertime (Day 3)
Term 1, Lesson 15: Prayertime (Day 5)

- Express and/or record experiences, opinions, feelings and emotions in a variety of ways

Chatting, Art and Activities throughout the entire programme

SHARING AND CO-OPERATING

- **Learn to share and co-operate with others**

Term 1, Lesson 1: Chatting, Activity, Prayertime (Day 4)
Term 1, Lesson 2: Story, Chatting (Day 2)
Term 1, Lesson 5: Entire Lesson
Term 1, Lesson 10: Prayertime (Day 2 & 4), Story (Day 1)
Term 1, Lesson 13: Art (Day 3)
Term 1, Lesson 15: Activity, Prayertime (Day 5)
Term 2, Lesson 9: Ritual (Day 2)
Term 3, Lesson 2: Activity (Day 1)
Term 3, Lesson 3: Story, Activity (Day 1), Prayertime (Day 5), Chatting throughout Lesson
Term 3, Lesson 8: Entire Lesson

RESOLVING CONFLICTS

- **Explore and practise, through discussion, role-play and other techniques, how to handle conflict without being aggressive**

Term 2, Lesson 6: Stories, Chatting
Term 2, Lesson 7: Stories, Poems, Chatting
Term 2, Lesson 8: Entire Lesson

Education for Love

The *Education for Love* programme is designed for and used by the primary schools in Northern Ireland. There are a variety of reasons as to why the programme was initiated in 1990.

The Church both universally and here in Ireland has stressed, especially in recent years, the importance of sexuality education within the moral and spiritual framework, thus building up and forming a healthy respect for the gift of sexuality and personal relationships.

The Vatican Council has always emphasised the need for a 'positive and prudent' approach to sexuality education, and the essential need for the involvement of parents and other intrinsically linked supports, as in school or parish. The Irish Bishops in their 1985 Pastoral Letter *Love is for Life* stressed that:

> Sexuality must not be isolated from its emotional, moral, spiritual and religious dimensions.

The Church has also become increasingly aware of the profound changes in the social fabric and society in general. There is now improved health in the population in general and thus a corresponding physical maturing at an earlier age; such maturing is no longer so clear cut. Moreover, there is the ever-present media, which in its presentation of the issues involving family life have made them more explicit. As a consequence, children are exposed to considerable information, which presupposes that children should be introduced to the whole understanding of human sexuality, specifically within a Catholic framework.

One other reason for the introduction of such a programme is to complement existing programmes which centre solely upon children protecting themselves against abuse. Accordingly, this sexuality programme focuses upon the inherent goodness and sacredness of the divine gift of sexuality.

Finally, the Department of Education, giving the viewpoint of another interested party in 1987, issued a circular stating:

> The department considers that sex education should be an important element in the curriculum of all schools. It should be taught in a sensitive manner which is in harmony with the ethos of the school or college and in conformity with the moral and religious principles held by parents and school management authorities. Teaching should take place, therefore, within a caring moral context, stressing the importance of stable personal relationships, parental responsibilities and family life.

> Each school should have a written policy on sex education which sets out the aims of the programme and describes the topics to be included, their sequencing and depth of treatment and teaching methods and materials to be employed. The policy should be endorsed by the school's Board of Governors and communicated to parents. All teachers, whether or not they are centrally involved in teaching the programme, should be aware of its details and their implications.

While it is absolutely important to focus upon the reasons for such a programme, it is equally important to state who the programme involves as central to the question of educating for love.

> The first task of the Catholic school in its programme of *Education for Love* must be to ensure the involvement of parents. The school should recognise, as do the bishops, that the first responsibility to educate for love lies with *parents*. In this regard, it is suggested that the school also has responsibilities. Schools should aim:

> • to provide support for all parents in *their* role as educators for love;

- to involve parents in drawing up both the school policy and the school programme in *Education for Love*;

- to provide opportunities for all parents to understand the work of the school in *Education for Love*.

Providing Support for Parents
The school should reassure parents that no-one is better qualified in this regard than they are and that the work of the school is to build on the foundations which have been laid by parents. No school programme can substitute for the role of parents in educating for love. Parents must be helped to see how vital is their role and how irreplaceable is their qualification in this regard; the message must be that God 'qualified' them by giving them children.

It has to be recognised, of course, that many parents are inhibited by the prospect of sex education. One of the reasons for this may be the perception that sex education is about the giving of biological information and parents can be shy about this, feeling perhaps that they lack the necessary vocabulary or are ill at ease in using the vocabulary. But the main way in which the home is the first school of love is through example – the example of caring parents, the example of the sharing family, the example of forgiveness and reconciliation. The school must emphasise to parents, therefore, that the principal way in which they educate for love is through daily life in a loving, caring, sharing and forgiving home.

The sad reality in our society, however, is that many families are broken by death or by separation, by bitterness or domestic violence, by alcoholism or gross selfishness. Many of our children grow up in a single-parent family. Some parents who are coping in these circumstances may feel that they cannot give the example of family love. They must be reassured by the school that, however difficult their situation is, they are still helping their children to grow in love. For example, the mother who drinks too much and is painfully aware of her family's suffering can talk to her children about how difficult family life has been for them and implore them to be responsible in their attitude to alcohol. And the father whose attitude has been that child-rearing is solely a woman's role, can compensate to some extent by admitting his mistake and by urging his children, especially his sons, to see their role as fathers as more important than any of their other roles in life.

Involving Parents in Planning
It would be a matter for the school to determine how this should be achieved; consultation with the parents' representative(s) on the Board of Governors might be a starting point.

Providing Information for Parents
Parents should be introduced to the aims and process of the school programme at each Key Stage; they have the right to be fully informed about the content and terminology of the classroom strategies which are planned for their children.

There are many facets of the school curriculum which are already pointing towards the whole area of sexuality education and impinge upon this area. As well as the teacher, the school and the parish, parents are vital in this programme. The school curriculum involves Health Education, Science, Pastoral Care and Guidance, and so these aspects form a model that marries well with the *Education for Love* programme. Accordingly, the *Education for Love* programme is essentially about formation, initiation and information, all carefully balanced and rooted firmly in the context of Catholic values.

Aims of Education for Love

Primary One

- to help each pupil to see that he/she is a member of a family;

- to introduce pupils to the preparations for the birth of a new baby, including Mary's preparations for the birth of Jesus;

- to emphasise to the pupils that our bodies and our families are gifts from God and that we should thank God for these gifts.

Primary Two

- to reinforce the idea of family membership through introducing pupils to the extended family network;

- to help pupils to see how they have grown from conception to five years of age;

- to encourage pupils to use the proper names for the different parts of their body, including their external sexual organs;

- to introduce pupils to the stages of growth of Jesus from conception to boyhood;

- to remind pupils that family love and human life are gifts from God and that we should thank God for these gifts.

Primary Three

- to reinforce the idea that God our Father gives the gift of life;

- to emphasise the fact that people marry because they love each other, and through their love new life begins;

- to focus on the Holy Family as an example of family life that we should try to imitate by sharing love.

The resources for the programme consist of the workbooks for each year from Primary One to Primary Seven. These workbooks will continue to be used as the *Education for Love* programme is woven into the new re-presentation.

The ITV 'What Next?' Video

In this short video there is a clear presentation of:

- stages of growth;

- changes in girls/boys as they grow;

- conception and birth of a baby.

The approach is through a nine-year-old boy and his eleven-year-old sister explaining to a robot the differences between humans and robots. The explanation happens during a dream sequence and the emphasis is on how human life begins and the care which babies need.

While some felt that the dream sequence was a gimmick, this video was generally welcomed as simple, thoughtful and clearly presented. It was the most popular of the videos. *The 'What Next?' video has, therefore, been unreservedly recommended for use with the Primary Seven programme (see Pupil Workbook).*

This programme, *Education for Love*, respects the place of the parental role, which has centre stage, and facilitates the development of skills for imparting and unfolding the gift of sexuality from God within the Catholic context and with the invaluable assistance of school and parish. Accordingly, the children grow in maturity in so many comprehensive ways, recognising sexuality as a real gift from God.

Alive-O 1 – Education for Love Workbooks

Alive-O 2 – Education for Love Workbooks

FRIENDSHIP
Term 1

Lesson 2	Together Again	7 and 8
Lesson 4	Getting Along Together	7 and 8
		(on p. 7 it should now read: Ask your child to sing for you, 'I am Special, So Are You')

Alive-O 3 ~ Education for Love Workbooks

MARRIAGE AND BABIES
Term 1

Lesson 14	The Moment They'd All Been Waiting For	1, 2 and 3

GROWTH AND CHANGE
Term 1

Lesson 4	Time Moves On	4

FAMILIES (THE HOLY FAMILY)
Term 1

Lesson 7	Introducing Jesus	5, 6 and 7

Term 3

Lesson 1	Mary Our Mother	5, 6 and 7

RELATIONSHIPS
Term 2

Lesson 5	The Lost Sheep	8 and 9
Lesson 6	Losing My Way	8 and 9
Lesson 7	Still Losing My Way	8 and 9
Lesson 8	Blessing Ritual/ Celebrating God's Forgiveness	8 and 9

Written by St Mary's Training College and Fr Martin O'Hagan for the Diocesan Advisers

A Quick Guide Through The Programme

Lesson Title	Song	Story	Poem	Prayertime
Term 1				
We Begin Together	Alive-O/Time and Time and Time Again/Together Again	Peas and Beans	Belonging	Prayertime
Anytime	Look at the Clock	Tick and Tock	Out-time, In-time	Prayertime
Inside Time	My Body Clock	Back in Granny's Garden	Off to Africa	Prayertime
Time Moves On	Old Man Time/Round and Round	Old Daddio	Goodness How You've Grown/It Takes Time!	Prayertime
We Belong Together	Christ is my Light/Together Again		Where I Belong	Enrolment Ceremony with parents and guardians in the classroom/church
We Remember Together	Remember Them/Columba	Columba	All Saints, All Souls	Prayertime
In Jesus' Time	The Passover Song	The Passover	Jesus Growing Up	Prayertime
Jesus – Journey Man	We Go on a Journey	Shortening the Road/Jesus goes to Jerusalem	Many Ways to Travel	Bible Procession Ritual
Jesus – Story-teller	Once Upon a Time	A Story Remembered/The Parable of the Sower	Wait Till I Tell You	Prayer Service with parents and guardians/Bible Procession Ritual
Jesus – Sharer of Bread	The Bread Song	The Magic Loaf/Micah's Story	Farmer	Bible Procession Ritual
Jesus – Diviner	Water Litany	Tojo's Garden/The Woman at the Well	Granny's Finger/Water	Bible Procession Ritual
Jesus – Teacher	Amen	Jesus Prays	When I Want To Pray	Bible Procession Ritual
One Moment	Mary	One Moment	Mary's Song/A Few Little Moments	Prayertime
Watching, Waiting, Wondering	Following a Star	Watching, Waiting, Wondering	Could it Be?/The Christmas Star	Prayertime
The Moment They'd All Been Waiting For	This is the Moment/Away in a Manger/Carol of the Journey	The Moment They'd All Been Waiting For	A Few Little Moments/The Crib Community	Prayertime

Lesson Title	Song	Story	Poem	Prayertime
Term 2 *A Different Time*	*Christ Be Beside Me*	*The People in the Wilderness*	*It'll be O-K*	*Prayertime*
My Goodness	*Beings/ We Thank You, God, We Do*	*Being Friends/ Being Eager*		*Prayertime*
We Are The Greatest	*We are the Greatest*	*We are the Greatest*	*Great!*	*Prayer Service with parents and guardians*
Lent – Turning Time	*Wilderness*			*Rituals: Lent/ Ash Wednesday*
The Good Shepherd	*The Lost Sheep*	*The Good Shepherd/The Lost Sheep's Story*		*Prayertime*
Losing My Way	*I'm Sorry*	*Being Destructive/ Being Violent*	*One Day*	*Prayertime*
Time To Change	*I'm Sorry God*	*The Lost Temper/ Being Selfish/ Being Jealous*	*Huff/Sulk*	*Prayertime*
I Was Lost, I Am Found	*The King of Love*	*We are the Greatest/The Good Shepherd*		*Sacrament of Penance Rites 1 & 2 with parents and guardians/ Celebration of God's blessing in the classroom*
Time For Joy	*Alleluia*	*The Last Supper/ An Easter Surprise*	*Jesus Stumbles*	*Rituals: The Last Supper/ Stations of the Cross/An Easter Surprise*

Lesson Title	Song	Story	Poem	Prayertime
Term 3				
Mary's Joy	*Mary, Our Mother*	*One Moment/ Two Cousins/The Moment They'd All Been Waiting For/ Anna and Simeon/ Jesus Goes to Jerusalem*		*Prayertime*
A Time To Share Stories	*Once Upon a Time/ Happy in the Presence*	*The Market-Place/ The Parable of The Sower/The Good Shepherd*	*Let the Children Come*	*Bible Procession Ritual*
A Time To Share Meals	*Eat this Bread/ Céad Míle Fáilte Romhat*	*Names in the Pot/ The Last Supper*	*Sharing Meals*	*Shared Meals Celebration with parents and guardians*
A Time To Share Memories	*I Remember*	*Jenny and the Computer/A Special Meal*	*Remember*	*Prayertime*
A Time To Share Life	*Do this in Memory of Jesus*	*Jesus Visits Three Special Friends*	*Shared Living*	*Prayertime*
Holy Spirit Help Us	*Come Holy Spirit*	*The Story of Pentecost*	*Help us Holy Spirit*	*Prayertime*
Treasures From Long Ago	*Round and Round/ Christ Be Beside Me*	*The Children of Lir*		*Prayertime*
Time To Go – Alive-O!	*Alive-O*			*Celebratory Ritual*

Prayers for the Year

The Sign of the Cross
In the name of the Father, and of the Son, and
of the Holy Spirit. Amen.

Our Father
Our Father who art in heaven
Hallowed be thy name.
Thy kingdom come,
Thy will be done
On earth as it is in heaven.
Give us this day our daily bread
And forgive us our trespasses
As we forgive those who trespass against us.
And lead us not into temptation.
But deliver us from evil. Amen.

Hail Mary
Hail Mary, full of grace,
The Lord is with thee.
Blessed art thou among women
And blessed is the fruit of thy womb, Jesus.
Holy Mary, mother of God,
Pray for us sinners,
Now, and at the hour of our death. Amen.

Glory be to the Father
Glory be to the Father,
And to the Son,
And to the Holy Spirit.
As it was in the beginning,
Is now and ever shall be,
World without end. Amen.

Morning Prayer
Father in heaven, you love me,
You're with me night and day.
I want to love you always
In all I do and say.
I'll try to please you, Father.
Bless me through the day. Amen.

Night Prayer
God, our Father, I come to say
Thank you for your love today.
Thank you for my family,
And all the friends you give to me.
Guard me in the dark of night,
And in the morning send your light. Amen.

Grace before Meals
Bless us, O God, as we sit together.
Bless the food we eat today.
Bless the hands that made the food.
Bless us, O God. Amen.

Grace after Meals
Thank you, God, for the food we have eaten.
Thank you, God, for all our friends.
Thank you, God, for everything.
Thank you, God. Amen.

Prayer to Jesus
Christ be with me.
Christ be beside me.
Christ be before me.
Christ be behind me.
Christ at my right hand.
Christ at my left hand.
Christ be with me everywhere I go.
Christ be my friend, for ever and ever. Amen.

*Confiteor
I confess to almighty God,
And to you, my brothers and sisters,
That I have sinned through my own fault,
In my thoughts and in my words,
In what I have done,
And in what I have failed to do;
And I ask blessed Mary, ever virgin,
All the angels and saints
And you, my brothers and sisters
To pray for me to the Lord our God. Amen.

*Act of Sorrow
O my God, I thank you for loving me.
I am sorry for all my sins, for not loving
others and not loving you.
Help me to live like Jesus and not sin again. Amen.

*Prayer for Forgiveness
O my God, help me to remember the times
when I didn't live as Jesus asked me to.
Help me to be sorry and to try again. Amen.

*Prayer after Forgiveness
O my God, thank you for forgiving me.
Help me to love others.
Help me to live as Jesus asked me to. Amen.

Prayer to the Trinity
Praise to the Father.
Praise to the Son.
Praise to the Spirit.
The Three in One. Amen.

Prayers to Mary
Mary, mother of Jesus,
I want to live and love like you.
I want to love the Father,
I want to love like Jesus. Amen.

Mother of Jesus, blessed are you.
Mother of Jesus, my mother too.
Help me to live like Jesus
And help me to live like you. Amen.

Prayers to the Holy Spirit
Holy Spirit, I want to do what is right.
Help me.
Holy Spirit, I want to live like Jesus.
Guide me.
Holy Spirit, I want to pray like Jesus.
Teach me. Amen.

Spirit of God in the heavens.
Spirit of God in the seas.
Spirit of God in the mountain-tops.
Spirit of God in me.
Spirit of God in the sunlight.
Spirit of God in the air.
Spirit of God all around me.
Spirit of God everywhere.
Holy Spirit, Spirit of God, help me. Amen.

Journey Prayer
Arise with me in the morning,
Travel with me through each day,
Welcome me on my arrival.
God, be with me all the way. Amen.

Mass Responses
'The Lord be with you.'
'And also with you.'
'A reading from the Holy Gospel according
to_____.'
'Glory to you, O Lord.'
'The Gospel of the Lord.'
'Praise to you, Lord Jesus Christ.'

'Let us proclaim the mystery of faith.'
'Christ has died, Christ is risen, Christ will
come again.'

'The Body of Christ.'
Amen.

Lord have mercy.
Lord have mercy.
Christ have mercy.
Christ have mercy.
Lord have mercy.
Lord have mercy.

Glory to God in the highest
and peace to his people on earth.

Holy, holy, holy Lord,
God of power and might.
Heaven and earth are full of your glory.
Hosanna in the highest.
Blessed is he who comes in the name of the
Lord.
Hosanna in the highest.

Lamb of God, you take away the sins of the
world, have mercy on us.
Lamb of God, you take away the sins of the
world, have mercy on us.
Lamb of God, you take away the sins of the
world, grant us peace.

Prayer before Communion
Lord Jesus, come to me.
Lord Jesus, give me your love.
Lord Jesus, come to me and give me yourself.

Lord Jesus, friend of children, come to me.
Lord Jesus, you are my Lord and my God.
Praise to you, Lord Jesus Christ.

Prayer after Communion
Lord Jesus, I love and adore you.
You're a special friend to me.
Welcome, Lord Jesus, O welcome.
Thank you for coming to me.

Thank you, Lord Jesus, O thank you
For giving yourself to me.
Make me strong to show your love
Wherever I may be.

Be near me, Lord Jesus, I ask you to stay
Close by me forever and love me, I pray.
Bless all of us children in your loving care
And bring us to heaven to live with you there.

I'm ready now, Lord Jesus.
To show how much I care.
I'm ready now to give your love
At home and everywhere. Amen.

*These prayers are particularly relevant to those children
preparing for First Communion and First Penance.*

Lesson 1: We Begin Together

... there will be one flock, one shepherd.
(John 10:16)

As a new school year begins, the children are once again moving into a new class and experiencing all the feelings which go with that: strangeness, anxiety, anticipation, etc. They are moving out of a situation with which they were familiar, and where they felt comfortable with themselves and with the others in Senior Infants/Primary Two. They had come to belong there.

This year we focus on the children's experience of changing from class to class in such a way as to provide them with the opportunity to explore what it feels like to belong and what it feels like when we do not belong. In doing this we are leading the children towards an awareness of the human need to belong.

We also seek to help the children to realise that arriving at a sense of belonging is a gradual process. During the year they will be learning what it means to belong in this new situation and will gradually become better able to understand the significance of belonging with others and the challenge it holds for the way in which they live together. The last lesson in the programme will celebrate the way in which they have learned to live out a sense of belonging during the year. They will then be ready to move on – a process that is mirrored again and again in the cycles of the natural world and in the pattern of human life. This is the backdrop against which we begin to help the children to realise what it means to belong to the Church, leading towards an understanding of what it means to take part in the Eucharist as one who belongs to the community of the Church, the followers of Jesus.

FOR THE TEACHER:

A thought before beginning

Pathways

Lord, today brings
>Paths to discover
>Possibilities to choose
>People to encounter
>Peace to possess
>Promises to fulfil
>Perplexities to ponder
>Power to strengthen
>Pointers to guide
>Pardon to accept
>Praises to sing
and a Presence to proclaim.
>*David Adam*

What am I trying to do?

To set a context for the children to appreciate and develop among themselves a sense of belonging as a class.

Why?

So that a context may be built within which they can understand the concept of belonging to the Christian community called Church.

Note: Throughout the programme the relevant songs can be found at the end of each lesson.

Overview of the Week

Song: *Alive-O/Time and Time and Time Again/Together Again*			Continue song Recall story Repeat poem	
Chatting about the new class	Continue song Story: *Peas and Beans*		Chatting about a class code	
Activity: *Can you guess what I'm looking forward to?*	Chatting about the story	Continue song Poem: *Belonging* Art: *Class Tree*	Activity: *Our Class Code*	Chatting about the picture
Prayertime	Prayertime	Prayertime	Worksheet Prayertime	Prayertime

Day One

Song

Alive-O

Time and Time and Time Again

Together Again

Chatting

...about the new class

What class are we in now? In what way will being in this class be different from being in Infants/Primary One/Two? How do you think you will like being in First Class/Primary Three? Does anyone think they would be happier to go back to their old class? Why? Why not?

(If there are any new children in the class)
Most of us here know each other. How has that happened? We have a new person/people in the class, perhaps we should introduce ourselves. Perhaps the new children would like to tell us a bit about their old school. When someone is new to a class, everything may feel a little strange. Let's think about what might feel strange. Perhaps *(name the new child/children)* can be a special help to us here.

If we all think back to when we started school, we will probably remember how everything seemed strange. Can you remember the day you started school? Let's talk about it. It takes time to settle into a new class but, gradually, we come to feel we belong there. Can you remember how long it took before you began to feel that you belonged in your new class?

Even though all/most of us know each other and have been together for some years now, we might not have been in First Class/Primary Three before. Being in First Class/ Primary Three is a little bit strange to us now. We have different work to do. Let's talk about how our work will be different. *(Where applicable: We are in a different classroom now. Let's look around and see what is strange and new about it.)* We have grown and we are older and bigger than we were this time last year. Let's talk about how different it feels to be in a class that is bigger and older. Let's look ahead and see if there is anything particular in this year, in First Class/Primary Three, that we look forward to. Hopefully when we have spent some weeks and months together in our new class we will feel that we belong in it.

ACTIVITY

Can you guess what I'm looking forward to?

Ask the children to form pairs and to chat together about what it is they are looking forward to this year.
Ask them to choose one thing that they are looking forward to and to think of a way to mime it.
Invite the children to act out their mime for the class while the others try to guess what it is.

PRAYERTIME

Sign of the Cross.

Teacher *(as the candle is lit)*
God is the light, the light of our lives.
God is the light, the light of each day.

As we begin this year in a new class, as we look forward to our year together, let us ask God's blessing as we pray:

All
God bless us and keep us each day.

Teacher
We look forward to being together in our new class.

All
God bless us and keep us, we pray.

Teacher
We look forward to learning new things together.

All
God bless us and keep us, we pray.

Teacher
We look forward to making new friends.

All
God bless us and keep us, we pray.

Teacher
Close your eyes and think of what it is you are most looking forward to.
With your inside voice that no one else can hear, tell God about it. *(Pause)*
Now ask God to look after you during this year in First Class/Primary Three. *(Pause)*

We pray:

All
Our Father…

Sign of the Cross.

Note: *In art on Day Three you will be making a class tree. For this you will need a bare branch (with lots of side branches) secured in a pot of sand or compost.*

Day Two

Continue song: *Alive-O/Time and Time and Time Again/Together Again*

STORY

Peas and Beans

The Peas and Beans in the seedling-tray were very excited. They had lived and grown together for a long time. They knew each other well. They felt as though they really belonged together in their tray. But now it was time for them to move on in their lives.

'I wonder what it will be like to move out into the big wide garden world,' said a rather nervous little Pea.

'I don't think I want to leave my seed-tray,' said a nervous little Bean. 'What will we do out in the garden when the nights are cold and dark and we have no warm tray to keep us safe? Have you thought about that?'

But there wasn't time to think about it now. For just at that moment the gardener came and lifted the tray of seedlings and carried them out into the fresh air and the bright light. The gardener set them down beside the vegetable plot. Then he took a hoe and a rake and began to prepare a spot for each of them.

'Just look at that lovely clay,' said some excited Peas. 'We can't wait to get our roots into it.'

A large Crow squawked overhead. Several little Beans jumped with fright. 'What's that?' they asked, and their little leaves began to quiver.

'Never mind, it's only an old Crow,' said a wise old Carrot from the far side of the vegetable plot.

Next thing the gardener lifted the seedlings one by one and planted them in the ground. The gardener dug a little hole and placed each one in gently. Then he packed the soil in around their roots and finally gave each one a long drink of water.

'Oooh, delicious!' said the Peas as the cool water soaked into their roots and made it easy for them to stretch and wiggle deep into the earth.

'The soil is very different to our seed-tray,' said the nervous little Bean, 'and everything is so big. Look at the size of the sky, and the hedges, and look at all these other vegetables, they are so much bigger than we are. I think I'd like to go back inside to my seed-tray.'

'Don't worry,' said a friendly Cabbage from the far side of the plot. 'I felt just like you when I came out here first, but you will soon get used to it.'

'Indeed you will,' said all the Lettuces. 'There is so much more to see and do out here. Life in the garden is so interesting. Every morning the birds sing their dawn chorus to awaken us, some days the bees and the butterflies come to visit, and have you ever seen a sky full of stars, or the moon playing hide-and-seek with the clouds?'

'No,' said the little Peas and Beans together. 'Tell us more! Tell us more!' they shouted.

'Aha!' said a tall Onion, as the older vegetables in the far side of the plot smiled knowingly at one another, 'I could tell you, but it will be much better for you to wait and to see for yourselves.'

'We can't wait! We can't wait!' they shouted together, but the older vegetables simply turned their leaves to the sun and got on with the business of growing.

Left to themselves, the little Peas and Beans explored every inch of their new world together. They soaked up the warmth of the sun and the softness of the rain on their leaves. They danced in the wind and listened to the stories and songs that little birds told them. They got to know the hardness of the stones and the wiggliness of worms in their part of the vegetable plot.

But most importantly of all, underneath the ground they spread out their roots, like long spindly fingers, stretching until they touched each other as if they all held hands. They intertwined their roots so that they now felt they belonged together in a closer way than ever before.

'You know what,' whispered the nervous little Bean to the Butterfly resting on her leaves, 'I wouldn't go back to my seed-tray now even if I could. This is where I belong, in my garden with all of my friends.'

CHATTING

...about the story

Do the Peas and Beans in the story remind you of anything? At the beginning of the story the Peas and Beans are ready to move out into the big wide garden world. Has anything like that ever happened in your life/in the life of the class? The Peas and the Beans have different kinds of feelings about going into the garden: some are excited and some are nervous. How did you feel when you were going into First Class/Primary Three? There were some older vegetables in the garden. Why do you think the older vegetables would not tell the Peas and Beans what life in the garden would be like? Do you think they were right to do that? If you could ask some of the older pupils in school what it will be like to be in their class, what do you think they would say? Are there any other questions you would like to ask them? Perhaps we could ask some older pupils to come and chat to us about life outside Infants/Primary One/Two. Do you think that would be a good idea or do you think we should take the advice of the older vegetables and wait until we find out for ourselves?

As they grew, the Peas and Beans learned all about life in the garden. Can you remember some of the things they learned? As they grew together, their roots intertwined closely. How did this make them feel? Can you see a change in the nervous little Bean by the end of the story? How do you think this change came about?

PRAYERTIME

Sign of the Cross.

Teacher (*as the candle is lit*)
God is the light, the light of our lives.
God is the light, the light of each day.

God, you are with us right now. Be with us all year long.

All
God, be with us on our way.

Teacher
As we leave behind our old class.

All
God, be with us on our way.

Teacher
As we start First Class/Primary Three.

All
God, be with us on our way.

Teacher
As we discover new things about ourselves.

All
God, be with us on our way.

Teacher
As we discover new things about others.

All
God, be with us on our way.

Teacher
Let's turn to the person on our right, shake their hand and welcome each other to this class.
Let's turn to the person on our left, shake their hand and wish each other well for the year. Together we pray:

Teacher (*with children repeating*)
It's good to be back in school, God,
thank you for this class of ours.
Thank you for a new exciting school year.

Sign of the Cross.

Day Three

Continue song: *Alive-O/Time and Time and Time Again/Together Again*

POEM

Belonging

All of the leaves
That hang on a tree
Belong together
Indefinitely.

When the sun shines bright
They bask in its glow,
They hang in together
When cold winds blow.

They shelter together
When rains pitter-patter,
Bid each other 'Goodbye'
In autumn – and scatter.

All of the leaves
That hang on a tree
Belong together
Indefinitely.

God bless all the leaves
Together on the tree.
God bless all my classmates.
God bless me.

ART

Class Tree

Show the children the bare branch. Explain to them that they are going to make a class tree by hanging their names like leaves from its branches.

For each child you will need:
- a piece of paper/card
- a piece of wool
- scissors

To make the leaves:
Distribute the paper (you may like to use coloured paper). Ask the children to draw a large leaf on the page and to cut it out. Ask them to write their name on the leaf, to decorate the leaf and then to make a little hole at the top of the leaf with a pencil. Thread some wool through the hole and tie it to make a loop. The leaves can then be hung on the tree by the loop.

Alternatively, you might draw a large tree on cartridge paper. Ask the children to paint the tree. Ask them to draw a leaf, write their name on it, then decorate and cut it out. The leaves that the children make could then be pasted onto the tree (or put on with Velcro).

The placing of the leaves on the tree will take place during the prayertime.

PRAYERTIME

Note: In preparation for the prayertime, place the tree in a prominent position where every child can reach it with ease. Ask the children to place their leaf on the desk in front of them.

Sign of the Cross.

Teacher *(as the candle is lit)*
God is the light, the light of our lives.
God is the light, the light of each day.

As a sign that we all belong to this class, let's place our names on our class tree.
We ask God to bless us. We pray:

All
God bless us and keep us, we pray.

Invite each child to come forward and to put his/her name on the tree (or stick their leaf on the 'paper' tree). As each child comes forward the class say:

All
God bless us and keep us, we pray.

Teacher
We ask God to bless all who belong to this school.
Bless _____ (name of school).

God bless all the leaves
Together on the tree.
God bless all my classmates.
God bless me.

All
Our Father…

Sign of the Cross.

Day Four

Continue song: *Alive-O/Time and Time and Time Again/Together Again*

Recall story: *Peas and Beans*

Repeat poem: *Belonging*

CHATTING

...about a class code/'way of being together'

Note: *This chatting offers an opportunity for the children along with the teacher to draw up a short, simple statement/statements describing their vision of how they can live together as a class. This code (or whatever you wish to call it) will hopefully reflect something of what the children will later come across in Jesus' teaching on 'The Kingdom of God'.*

The emphasis in drawing up this 'code' is more on the principles underlying how we behave, rather than on rules saying 'you must not do this' or 'you must not do that'.

We are a class together. We spend time together every weekday. We share a classroom and all of the things in the classroom. We eat together and we work together and we play together. We share our 'being together'. How would you like to be treated in this class? How do you think we could help to ensure that everyone in our class is happy here? What kind of place would you like your classroom to be? *Brainstorm for words like fair, happy, peaceful, etc. Finally, if it hasn't already come up in the conversation ...* what about the word 'love'? How do people know that we love them? People know we love them because they can see it and feel it in the way we treat them. You know you are loved because you see it and feel it in the way you are treated by the people who love you. Do you think *everyone* in our class, not only those who are our best friends, should be loved? Why? Do you think God loves everyone in the class? Why? If

everyone in our class is to be loved, how then do we need to treat each other?

Let's try to draw up a statement or statements for our class, reminding us of how we should live together.

ACTIVITY

Our Class Code

Depending on what has come up in the discussion with your class, formulate a statement or series of statements. Display on a large chart under the heading 'Our Class Code'.

WORKSHEET

If you wish to use the worksheet or workbook page which accompanies this lesson, this is an appropriate time to do so.

PRAYERTIME

Sign of the Cross.

Teacher *(as the candle is lit)*
God is the light, the light of our lives.
God is the light, the light of each day.

We pray that our class code will help us to belong together in love and in friendship.

All
Help us, God, to live according to our class code.

Teacher
By loving others.

All
Help us, God, to live according to our class code.

Teacher
By _____. *(use the words/phrases that have come up in the 'chatting')*

All
Help us, God, to live according to our class code.

Teacher
By _____.

All
Help us, God, to live according to our class code.

Teacher
By _____.

All
Help us, God, to live according to our class code.

Teacher
We know that sometimes it won't be easy.
We know that God will be with us as we try.

All
Glory be to the Father...

Sign of the Cross.

Day Five

CHATTING

...about the picture on page 1

Can you name all the different plants in the picture? If you could be in the picture, who or what would you like to be? Which little Bean do you think is the nervous one? Have you ever been nervous about something? What do you think Bertie the Crow is looking at? Do you think the Carrots are all friends? Why? Can you think of names for the different Beans and Peas? The old tree looks happy. Do you think he likes being in the garden? Does he remind you of anyone? How old do you

think he is? He must have seen lots of vegetables and plants come and go. Has your teacher seen lots of classes of girls and boys come and go?

PRAYERTIME

Sign of the Cross.

Song: *Alive-O/Time and Time and Time Again/Together Again*

Teacher *(as the candle is lit)*
God is the light, the light of our lives.
God is the light, the light of each day.

Close your eyes.
Place your feet on the floor.
Place your hands gently on your lap.
Listen to your breath as it brings oxygen to every part of your body.

You are sitting in your new classroom with all the others in the class.
Picture all the different faces.
Think about how you feel right now.
Maybe you feel different, more grown-up.
Maybe you feel excited, maybe you feel a little worried.
Maybe you feel glad to be in a new class.
With your inside voice say thank you to God for this class.
Thank God for all the people who belong in your class this year.
Ask God to be with you and everyone in the class in a special way this year.

Open your eyes.

Look around at all the faces of the children in your new class.

Stretch.

Poem: *Belonging*

Now let's hold hands *(if possible, ask the children to form a big circle)*. Together we say:

All
Our Father...

Sign of the Cross.

8

Alive-O!

Words: Clare Maloney
Music: Fran Hegarty

Chorus:

Be - ing, be - long - ing, to - geth - er as friends, yeah,

yeah! A - live - O!

Be - ing, be - long - ing, be - gin - ning to end, yeah,

yeah! A - live - O! To-geth-er as friends.

1. Say Be! Say We! Say You! Say Me!
   Say Yes, Yes, YES! Because we are ALIVE-O!
   Say Sow! Say Grow! Ready, Steady, say GO!
   Say Hey! Praise God! Because we are ALIVE-O!

2. Say Do! Say Don't! Say Will! Say Won't!
   Be all you can be, because we are ALIVE-O!
   Say Try! Say True! Say Good through and through!
   Say Hey! Praise God! Because we are ALIVE-O!

Together Again

Frances O'Connell

Chorus:

To - geth - er a - gain,__ to - geth - er a - gain.__ We're
back! To - geth - er a - gain.__ With
each new day__ we shout 'Hur- ray!'__ It's
good to be to- geth- er a - gain.__ 1. We're
start - ing on__ a new ad - ven - ture to -
geth- er ev - 'ry step of the way,_____ so
much to learn,__ so much to say,__ and
God is with us as__ we pray._____

2. There's me and you, there's teacher too,
   We work together all the day through,
   With songs to sing and games to play,
   And God is with us as we pray.

10

Time and Time and Time Again

John O'Keeffe

Time and time and time a - gain praise—— God, praise—— God.

Lesson 2: Anytime

From the time it came to be I have been there.
(Isaiah 48:16)

That which is, already has been;
that which is to be, already is;
and God seeks out what has gone by.
(Ecclesiastes 3:15)

In Celtic spirituality the rhythmic movement of time is often symbolised as an all-embracing, inclusive circle. This unbroken circle of time is reflected in the months of the year, in the changing seasons, in each and every day. In each liturgical year we move through the rhythm of the Christian times and seasons, stopping to name and to celebrate each one as it comes and goes. The seasonal moods and changes which we see in the natural world around us are a reflection of the moods and changes within ourselves. 'For everything there is a season and a time for every matter under heaven' *(Eccl 3:1)*. In Junior Infants/Primary One and Senior Infants/Primary Two we offered the children an opportunity to recognise the 'seasons of the heart' and to realise that the changes in the world around us mirror the changes which take place in the life-cycle of each one of us and in the moods and feelings which we experience at the heart of human life. In this lesson we move between the inner rhythm of the 'seasons of the heart' and the outer rhythm of time which structures human activity.

We focus on the school day, which for the child has its own familiar patterns and sequences. We explore how each school day brings its own rhythm. The children's time in school is punctuated by all kinds of 'times': morning-time, break-time, play-time, prayertime, lunchtime, home-time. Each time signals something different within the unity of the day, and each day these times are repeated. Repetition brings with it a rhythm and a familiarity leading to a deeper awareness and understanding. In fact, the rhythm of life in the classroom fluctuates between the introduction of the new and the repetition of the familiar.

FOR THE TEACHER:

A thought before beginning

Days

O God of the morning, Christ of the hills,
O Spirit who all the firmament fills,
O Trinity blest who all goodness wills,
Keep us all our days.
Philip Larkin

What am I trying to do?

To offer the children an opportunity to explore their experience of the rhythm of time in the context of their school day.

Why?

So that the children may
- appreciate the significance of the rhythm of each new day;
- begin to learn to value each moment of their lives;
- come to see time as a gift from God;
- lay the foundation for an understanding of the concept of the timelessness of God.

12

Overview of the Week

Song: *Look at the Clock*	Continue song	Continue song	Continue song, art	
Chatting about school break-times	Story: *Tick and Tock*	Chatting about different times during the school day	Recall story	
Activity: *What's the time Crocodile?*	Chatting about the story	Art: *My Special School-Time Clock*	Poem: *Out-time, In-time*	Activity: *What's my special school-time?*
Prayertime	Worksheet	Prayertime	Chatting about 'a good time' and 'a bad time'	Chatting about the picture
	Prayertime		Prayertime	Prayertime

Day One

SONG

Look at the Clock

CHATTING

...about school break-times

Last year you went home at___, this year your school day is longer. What time will you go home at this year? Which do you like best – the longer day or the shorter day? Why? What time does school begin in the morning? What time do we have our first break? How long does it last? How do we know when it is time to take the morning break (use whatever terminology exists in your school for this break, e.g. 'Little Lunch' etc.) How do we know when it is over? At what time do we have our lunch? How long does lunchtime last? What time is it over? How do we know when it is time to begin and end our breaks? (If your school has a 2 o'clock break, you might chat similarly about it.) Why do you think we have break-times during the school day? What do you think it would be like if we had no breaks at all?

ACTIVITY

What's the time Crocodile?

How to play:

* One player is the Crocodile. She/he walks at random around the room followed by the rest of the children.
* The other players ask continually, 'What's the time Crocodile?', to which the Crocodile responds 'eight o'clock', 'half past three', etc.
* When the Crocodile finally tires of their taunts and calls 'Dinner-time', he/she proceeds to turn around and chase the others, who must reach the safety of a wall without being caught.
* The first person to be caught becomes the new Crocodile.

PRAYERTIME

Sign of the Cross.

Teacher (*as the candle is lit*)
God is the light, the light of our lives.
God is the light, the light of each day.

All time belongs to God. All time is God's time. Let's thank God for all the time we have had to do things this morning. Let us pray to God:

13

Teacher *(with children repeating)*
Time and time and time again.
Praise God, praise God.

Teacher
For time to say hello to all our friends.

All
Time and time and time again.
Praise God, praise God.

Teacher
For time to learn *(sums/poems/songs, etc.)*

All
Time and time and time again.
Praise God, praise God.

Teacher
For break-time to run and play.

All
Time and time and time again.
Praise God, praise God.

Teacher
For time to chat and tell stories.

All
Time and time and time again.
Praise God, praise God.

Teacher
Now close your eyes and think of the time you
liked best this morning. It might be the time
you were writing or reading, it might be the
time you were listening to the teacher, it
might be the time you chatted with your
friend.

Pause

Tell God about this time and why you liked it.

Teacher
For all God's time let us pray:

All
Glory be to the Father…

Sign of the Cross.

Continue song: *Look at the Clock*

STORY

Tick and Tock

Once upon a time there were two little friends.
One was called Tick and the other was called
Tock. Although Tick and Tock were as different
as day and night, they had one thing in
common: neither Tick nor Tock had any idea
of time. Time meant nothing to them.

Their days were topsy-turvy. Tick would go to
bed first thing every morning and get up first
thing every night. Tock would have her dinner
at breakfast-time and her lunch at supper-
time. And when they met each other they
would say 'Isn't it a lovely month' instead of
'Isn't it a lovely day'.

Although both their lives were topsy-turvy,
Tick thought that Tock was having the time of
her life. She arranged to go on holidays once a
week instead of once a year. When Tick was
running out of time to get things done, Tock
seemed to have all the time in the world. But,
then, Tock would think nothing of sending a
Christmas card when it should have been a
birthday card and she would eat chocolate
eggs in November if it suited her.

To Tock, Tick was a nuisance, he would think
nothing of asking her to 'Wait an hour!' when
he should only have asked her to 'Wait a
minute'. And if Tock arranged to meet him, he
would be either too early or too late but he
would never be right on time. Tock wouldn't
have minded whether he was late or early if
only he would tell her first. In the end they
kept missing each other because they had no
set time to meet.

Tick would say 'It's time we met', but Tock
would reply 'Time enough'. And they would

try to set a time but it never worked. Time meant nothing to either of them.

Very soon Tick's and Tock's lives were in chaos. There was neither top nor bottom, neither head nor tail, beginning nor end to their days. There was only a muddle in the middle. 'This cannot continue,' said Tock to Tick, when he woke her up in the middle of the night to go out to play. 'It's about time we did something about Time.'

'You are right, Tock,' said Tick, 'It's time to call a halt to the way we are living, but what can we do?'

One day Tick was out walking and Tock was out walking too. Neither of them was watching where they were going when, suddenly, quite by accident, they just happened to bump into each other.

'Tick!' exclaimed one.

'Tock!' exclaimed the other.

'Tick Tock, Tick Tock, Tick Tock,' they both said together.

And at that very second a wonderful thing happened. Everything fell exactly into place for Tick and Tock. They found each other! They found a rhythm! They found time! Once they managed to meet each other, Tick and Tock could not bear to be separated again. From that day to this Tick and Tock have stayed together. You never hear of Tick without Tock, or Tock without Tick. All day every day, and right around the clock, they accompany each other – Tick and Tock; Tock and Tick.

CHATTING

...about the story

It might be fun to live with Tick and Tock. Can you think of some things that would be fun about living with them? On the other hand it might be annoying to live with Tick and Tock. Can you think of some things that would not be such fun about living with them? What do you think it would be like for Tick and Tock to live with you? How do you think they would manage being at school on time, getting the bus on time, etc. Have you ever been late for something? When? What happened? Have you ever had to wait for someone who was late? What was that like? Do you think it's important that everyone knows that school starts at a certain time? Why? What do you think would happen if everyone could just come at whatever time they wished?

Everything fell into place for Tick and Tock when they got their Tick-Tock rhythm going. Why do you think that was?

WORKSHEET

If you wish to use the worksheet or workbook page which accompanies this lesson, this is an appropriate time to do so.

PRAYERTIME

Sign of the Cross.

Teacher *(as the candle is lit)*
God is the light, the light of our lives.
God is the light, the light of each day.

We pray:

Teacher *(with children repeating)*
God, our Creator,
We thank you for giving us your time;
time to run,
time to walk,
time to start,
time to stop,
time to drink,
time to eat,
time to wake,

time to sleep,
time to laugh,
time to cry,
time for hello,
time for goodbye,
time to work,
time to play,
time to watch,
time to pray.
Thank you, God,
for your time every day.
Amen.

Sign of the Cross.

Day Three

Continue song: *Look at the Clock*

CHATTING

...about different times during the school day

We have lots of different times during the day. Can you name them? Which of these times (Maths, English, etc.) do we have every day? Are there any times that we only have once a week (e.g. PE)? Are there times during the day when you find you run out of time? What happens then? Are there times when you feel that the time is very long, when time goes very slowly, perhaps you have finished your work more quickly than you expected to? What do you do then? How does time feel when you are waiting? Tell us about one time when you had to wait and time went very slowly. Tell us about a time when you were really enjoying yourself and suddenly it was time to stop, or it was time to go home. How did that feel?

ART

My Special School-Time Clock

For 'My Special School-Time Clock' each child will need:

*   A paper plate
*   Markers/crayons/colouring pencils
*   Scissors

Tell the children that they are going to make a special clock.
Instead of showing the time of the day this clock will show 'school-time'. For example, it could show Morning-time or Break-time or Afternoon-time or Home-time. Ask the children to think of their favourite time in the school day.

Chat to the children a little about these times.

Using crayons/markers/colouring pencils, the children could draw their favourite time on their paper plate.

Display the clocks on the wall with a title such as 'Our Special School-Time Clock'. You may like to display the 'clocks' in sequence, reflecting the rhythm of the school day.

Alternatively, you could ask the children to divide their paper plate into four quarters and to draw their favourite morning-time, break-time, afternoon-time and home-time.

PRAYERTIME

Note: *As this prayertime encourages the children to thank God for the time spent during the school day, you might like to keep this prayertime for the end of the school day, just before the children go home.*

Sign of the Cross.

Teacher *(as the candle is lit)*
God is the light, the light of our lives.
God is the light, the light of each day.

Every time we laugh, God is with us. Every time we cry, God is with us. Every time we sing and talk, God is with us. God is with us all the time. God has been with us all day. Let's think about the times that God has been with us today.

Close your eyes.
Place your hands gently on your lap.
Place your feet on the floor.
Listen to your heart beat.
Feel the air as it goes in and out of your lungs bringing life and oxygen to every part of your body.

God, who created you, breathes the breath of life through your body every day. God loves you very much. You are special to God. God takes care of you. God has been with you all day today. Talk to God about your day. Tell God about the best parts of the day. Maybe it was play-time. Maybe it was PE-time. Maybe it's home-time. With your special inside voice you can tell God about any time you wish. God listens to us all the time. *Pause.*

Now, open your eyes.
Look around the classroom.
This is where you have spent all your time today. Think of all the activities you did in the classroom today. As our school day comes to an end let's thank God for this place where we have spent our time today. Thank you, God, for our classroom.

Thank you, God, for the time we have spent in our classroom today.
We know that you are with us all day.
We know that all time belongs to you.
We pray:

All
Each day's a very busy place,
Each time has something to do,
Milk time, play time, home time, bedtime,
Night-time and prayertime too.
So help me, God, to clear a space
In the middle of all I do,
To say a word, or think a thought,
And offer a little prayer to you.

Sign of the Cross.

Day Four

Continue song: *Look at the Clock*

Recall story: *Tick and Tock*

Continue art: *My Special School-Time Clock (if not already completed)*

POEM

Note: Movements are suggested by the verse. Begin by standing in a circle, moving out etc. as the verse suggests. At the beginning of the second verse the children come back and join hands to form a circle.

Out-time, In-time

Out-time, out-time,
run around and shout time,
shake it all about time,
out-time, out-time.

In-time, in-time,
it's time to begin time,
stop the noisy din time,
in-time, in-time.
Brian Moses

CHATTING

...**about 'a good time' and 'a bad time'**

Sometimes we talk about 'a good time'. What does that mean? Do you have a good time in school? Have you had times when you felt really excited at school? Have there been times when you felt sad at school? Did you ever have a bad time in school? What about 'good times and bad times'? Have you had both? Do you think everyone has both good times and bad times? Which would you like to last longest – the exciting times or the sad times? Why? Can you help someone at school to have a good time? Do you sometimes cause someone at school to have a bad time?

PRAYERTIME

Sign of the Cross.

Teacher *(as the candle is lit)*
God is the light, the light of our lives.
God is the light, the light of each day.

Let us ask God to be with us during our good times and our bad times. Let us pray to God.

Teacher
For the times when you find it hard to listen. The Lord be with you.

All
And also with you.

Teacher
For the times when you feel excited and happy. The Lord be with you.

All
And also with you.

Teacher
For the times when you feel sad and lonely. The Lord be with you.

All
And also with you.

Teacher
For the times when you feel angry and lose your temper. The Lord be with you.

All
And also with you.

Teacher
For the times when you laugh and have fun. The Lord be with you.

All
And also with you.

Teacher
God loves us like a mother loves her child at all times.

God cares for us like a father cares for his child all the time.
God loves each one of us in a special way.
God loves you and is with you all the time.

We ask God to be with us all day long. Let us pray:

All
Each day's a very busy place,
Each time has something to do,
Milk time, play time, home time, bedtime,
Night-time and prayertime too.
So help me, God, to clear a space
In the middle of all I do,
To say a word, or think a thought,
And offer a little prayer to you.

Sign of the Cross.

Day Five

ACTIVITY

What's my special school-time?

- A child comes forward and becomes the 'School-Time Reader'.
- Ask the child to look at the 'Special School-Time Clocks' which are displayed on the wall and to visually choose a particular time.
- He/she then asks the class: 'What's my special school-time?'
- The class can ask three questions, to which the 'School-Time Reader' can answer only 'Yes' or 'No'.
- When the right time is guessed, the child points to the time on the 'Special School-Time Clock'.
- The child who guesses the right 'time' gets to be the next 'School-Time Reader'.
- You may like to chat to the children about the various times that are chosen as the game is played.

CHATTING

...about the picture on page 2

Can you find Tick? Can you find Tock? Can you see what happened when they joined together? Imagine one of your hands is Tick and the other is Tock, *before* they joined together. What kinds of things are they doing 'on their own'? Now join them together. What can they do now? Tick and Tock are words that go together – they have a rhythm. Can you think of any other words that go together, for example, yoo-hoo, sing-song, etc?

PRAYERTIME

Sign of the Cross.

Song: *Look at the Clock*

Teacher *(as the candle is lit)*
Our clock reminds us that all time belongs to God.
Let's pick a time and say 'thanks' to God.

All
Time for work
And time for play,
We thank you, God,
For the time in each day.

Teacher
Who would like to pick a special school-time?

Invite a child to choose a time and to name the time for the class:

Child
My special school-time is_____ .

Teacher
Let us pray to God.

All
Time for work
And time for play,
We thank you, God,
For the time in each day.

Invite a child to choose another time.

Child
My special school time is _____.

Teacher
Let us pray to God.

All
Time for work
And time for play,
We thank you, God,
For the time in each day.

Note: *Several children may be invited to name a special time.*

All
God, our Creator,
We thank you for giving us your time;
time to run,
time to walk,
time to start,
time to stop,
time to drink,
time to eat,
time to wake,
time to sleep,
time to laugh,
time to cry,
time for hello,
time for goodbye,
time to work,
time to play,
time to watch,
time to pray.
Thank you, God,
for your time every day.
Amen.

Sign of the Cross.

Look at the Clock

Words: Ger Walsh
Music: Daniel Walsh

1. Look at the clock, the clock on the wall.

Look at the clock, the big clock on the wall. It's

time for school, it's half past eight, and the

clock's tick-ing out 'Don't be late!'

Chorus:

Tick, tock, tick, tock,

tick, tock, tic - ke - ty tock,

tick, tock, tick, tock,

tic - ke - ty, tic - ke - ty tock!

2. In the school yard we'll meet our friends
   And plan for the day we hope never ends.
   We'll play hide-and-seek all through break-time
   Till the clock in the school starts to chime.

3. Look at the clock, the clock on the wall,
   We've finished school and in no time at all
   It's time to go home and we say 'Bye, bye!'
   'See you tomorrow!' we cry.

Lesson 3: Inside Time

I will cause breath to enter you,
and you shall live...
and you shall know that I am the Lord.
(Ezekiel 37:5)

There are many ways of looking at time. We all have the experience of being regulated by external time, by world-time. A certain clock-time calls forth a certain response or activity. To stay in tune with the given routine of the day we can often feel compelled to move along in a manner that is dictated by something outside of, rather than inside of, ourselves.

There exists a more subtle, often unexplored, unacknowledged experience of time, inner-time. This is the time that moves inside each of us as human beings; it moves on a physical, emotional and spiritual level. There is the inside time of the constant movement of the heart and lungs, which measures and sustains life. There is the movement of the breath in the lungs, inhaling and exhaling, bringing oxygen to every part of the body. This silent rhythm sustains life. There is a sense in which the body knows its own time, time for eating, time for sleeping, etc. The wise tune into the rhythm of their own physical and spiritual well-being. Even when it is forced upon us we often ignore the salient signals and hints. When we are in alignment with the rhythm of our bodies, emotions and wills, we are in touch with our own 'time'.

Deep within us we can be in touch and in tune with God in whose presence we 'live and move and have our being', and who lives within each one of us at the deepest core of our inner world. When we are in contact with God we are fully alive, fully living.

FOR THE TEACHER:

Something Told the Wild Geese

Something told the wild geese
It was time to go.
Though the fields lay golden
Something whispered – 'Snow'.
Leaves were green and stirring,
Berries, lustre-glossed,
But beneath warm feathers
Something cautioned – 'Frost'.

All the sagging orchards
Steamed with amber spice,
But each wild beast stiffened
At remembered ice.
Something told the wild geese
It was time to fly –
Summer sun was on their wings,
Winter in their cry.
Rachel Field

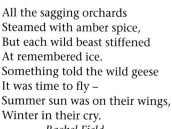

What am I trying to do?

To build on the children's awareness of the inner rhythms of life as experienced in their own bodies and in the world of nature.

Why?

So that they can become more aware of God dwelling in each of us, and begin to acknowledge and celebrate the hidden action of God at the heart of all life.

Overview of the Week

		Continue song		
	Continue song	Recall story		
	Repeat poem	Chatting about	Continue song	Worksheet
Song: *My Body Clock*	Story: *Back in*	heartbeats	Art: *Make a Heart*	Chatting about the
Poem: *Off to Africa*	*Granny's Garden*	Activity: *Take a*	*Badge* or *Make a*	picture
Chatting about the	Chatting about the	*Breather* or *Have a*	*Heart Card*	Prayertime
poem and the song	story	*Heart*	Prayertime	Now We Know
Prayertime	Prayertime	Prayertime		

Day One

Song

My Body Clock

Poem

Off to Africa

On the wire they gather
in a nearly-ready row,

They won't shiver in the winter
when the cold winds blow.

I wonder: which wee swallow
has the job of shouting GO!
Sam McBratney

Chatting

...about the poem and the song

How did the swallows know when it was time for them to fly to Africa? What would have told them to get ready? What do you think it would be like to be the swallow who shouted 'Go!'? Have you ever shouted 'Go'? Tell us about a time when you said 'Go'. The swallows knew deep inside themselves that it was time to fly away. Do you think we know things deep inside ourselves? What kind of things might we know? Would we get any hints from our song *My Body Clock*? Let's listen to our song again.

Can you think of something that your body might tell you? How about right now? Do you think it's good to have a body clock? Do you think it is good to listen to your body clock? Why? Why not?

Prayertime

Sign of the Cross.

Teacher (*as the candle is lit*)
Praise to the Father.
Praise to the Son.
Praise to the Spirit.
The Three in One.

Let us praise God who gives all living things the gift of inside-time.
You tell the swallows when to fly away.

All
Praise to the Father.
Praise to the Son.
Praise to the Spirit.
The Three in One.

Teacher
You tell the leaves when to fall from the tree.

All
Praise to the Father.
Praise to the Son.
Praise to the Spirit.
The Three in One.

Teacher
You tell the seeds when to grow.

All
Praise to the Father.
Praise to the Son.
Praise to the Spirit.
The Three in One.

Teacher
You tell the flowers when to bloom.

All
Praise to the Father.
Praise to the Son.
Praise to the Spirit.
The Three in One.

Teacher
You tell our bodies when to sleep and when to wake up.

All
Praise to the Father.
Praise to the Son.
Praise to the Spirit.
The Three in One.

(Encourage the children to name other times.)

Teacher
We pray together:

All
Praise to the Father.
Praise to the Son.
Praise to the Spirit.
The Three in One. Amen.

Sign of the Cross.

Day Two

Continue song: *My Body Clock*

Repeat poem: *Off to Africa*

STORY

Back In Granny's Garden

Robert looked at the big red apple hanging from the top branch of Granny's apple tree. He stood on tiptoes and stretched his hand up towards it. He could not reach it. 'Ready… Steady… GO!' he shouted to the apple. But of course the apple did not fall. 'When will the apple fall from the tree?' Robert asked Granny. 'When the apple is ripe it will fall,' Granny answered with a smile. 'Squawk,' said Bertie the crow.

The next day Robert went out into the garden. He looked up at the big red apple hanging from the top branch. 'The apple is still there,' he said to Granny. Then he jumped as high as he could and grabbed hold of one of the bottom branches of the tree. He shook it hard. The whole tree quivered, as though Robert's hardest shake was only a tickle making its leaves giggle. The apple did not fall. 'When will the apple fall?' Robert asked Granny. 'When the apple is ripe it will fall,' Granny said and smiled. 'Squawk,' said Bertie the crow.

The next day Robert went out into the garden. The wind was blowing in strong gusts, whirling and swirling leaves here, there and everywhere. Robert looked up at the big red apple on top of the tree. It was swinging and swaying to and fro. Robert stood underneath the tree with his hand outstretched. 'Ready… Steady… GO!' he called to the apple, above the noise of the wind, but of course the apple did not fall. Robert watched and waited, but it was no good. Soon the wind died down, the garden grew calm, and the big red apple clung stubbornly to the topmost branch of the tree.

'When will the apple fall?' Robert asked Granny. 'When the apple is ripe it will fall,' Granny said and smiled.

The next day Robert went out into the garden. He looked at the big red apple hanging from the top branch of the tree. 'The apple is still there,' he said to Granny. Just then along came Bertie the crow. He perched on a twig just beside Robert's apple. He cast a beady eye, first on Robert and then on the apple. He hopped closer to the apple. Suddenly a terrible screeching and squawking filled the sky above Granny's garden as all the other crows descended on the tree. Bertie rose flapping and chattering from his perch. The crows and Bertie scolded and argued over the big red apple. Just then it started to lash rain. The birds turned tail and flew off to the hedges for shelter. Robert and Granny ran inside. Relieved, the big red apple clung to its branch.

The next day Robert went out into the garden. He looked at the big red apple hanging from the topmost branch of the tree.

'I don't think that apple will ever fall,' said Robert, and as he and Granny cycled out the gate he turned to look back at the apple. 'Squawk,' said Bertie the crow.

At that moment a smiling, shining, autumn sun stole silently out from behind the cloud. It filled Granny's whole garden with warm sunlight. The big red apple felt its rays. They reached into the core of the apple. Deep in the heart of the big red apple, inside each of its pips, it knew that it was the right moment to fall from its branch. Bit by bit the apple's stem lost its grip on the branch of Granny's apple tree. Ready… steady… go! The big red apple let go and fell silently and happily to the ground.

'Granny! Granny…,' shouted Robert. Granny did not hear him. But who do you think did? 'Squawk! Squawk! Squawk!' he said.

CHATTING

…about the story

Tell us about a garden you have been in. What was in the garden? How many trees were in the garden? Do you know anyone who looks after a garden? Have you ever helped to look after a garden? What kind of work needs to be done in a garden? Do you think different kinds of work need to be done at different times of the year – like cutting the grass for example? Let's talk about the different times of the year in the garden. Do you know the name for a special kind of garden in which fruit trees grow? Have you ever picked an apple from a tree?

What do you think Granny meant when she said 'When the apple is ripe it will fall'. Sometimes we feel like Robert, we are impatient for things to happen, we want them to happen straight away, right this minute. Tell us about a time when you felt like that.

Tell us about a time when you said 'Ready, steady, go' to somebody. Has anyone ever said 'Ready, steady, go' to you? – perhaps you were playing a game, or going to jump into the pool, or perhaps it was something different. Have you ever said 'Ready, steady, go' to yourself, then at the last minute changed your mind and you didn't 'go'? Sometimes it can happen that there is something we want to do and we try to make ourselves do it but we can't, because we're not ready just yet. Tell us about a time when that happened to you? How do you know when you are really ready? How do you know when the time is right for you?

How do you know when it's time to go to sleep? How do you know when it's time to have a drink? Did your body ever help you to know that it was the right time for something? When?

Do you think the apple was happy to let go of its branch? Do you think it might have felt any sadness at all, having to let go? Have you ever had to let something go? Perhaps you had to let go of someone's hand; perhaps you had to say goodbye; perhaps you had to give away something that belonged to you. How did you feel then? How do you feel now?

PRAYERTIME

Sign of the Cross.

Teacher *(as the candle is lit)*
Praise to the Father.
Praise to the Son.
Praise to the Spirit.
The Three in One.

As we breathe in and out we know that oxygen is bringing life to every part of our bodies. As we breathe in and out we know that the breath of God fills us. Our body is a gift from God.

Let us thank God for the gift of our bodies. Let us pray:

All
Thank you, God, for the gift of my body.

Teacher
When my tummy rumbles maybe I need to eat all of my breakfast.

All
Thank you, God, for the gift of my body.

Teacher
When my eyes get itchy maybe I need to go to bed.

All
Thank you, God, for the gift of my body.

Teacher
When my throat goes dry maybe I need to be quiet for a while.

All
Thank you, God, for the gift of my body.

Teacher
When my head hurts maybe I need to turn off the TV.

All
Thank you, God, for the gift of my body.

Teacher
When my tummy aches maybe I need less sweets.

All
Thank you, God, for the gift of my body.

Teacher
When I sweat maybe I need to stop and take a rest.

All
Thank you, God, for the gift of my body.

Teacher
When I shiver maybe I need to come in out of the cold.

All
Thank you, God, for the gift of my body.

Teacher
Close your eyes. How are you now? Are you feeling happy or sad? Are you feeling hungry or thirsty? Talk to your body. Ask it how it is right now.

God cares for us a lot. God cares about our bodies. Tell God about the way you feel at the moment. Talk to God with your inside voice that nobody can hear.

Now open your eyes. Stretch.

All *(repeating after teacher)*
Praise to the Father.
Praise to the Son.
Praise to the Spirit.
The Three in One. Amen.

Sign of the Cross.

Continue song: *My Body Clock*

Recall story: *Back in Granny's Garden*

CHATTING

...about heartbeats

Do you know where your heart is? Do you know what your heartbeat does? It sends your blood flowing all through your body. Do you know how many times a minute your heart beats? It beats between 70 and 80 times a minute. Can you feel your heartbeat? Can you listen to your friend's heartbeat? Your heart is a little bit like a clock that keeps ticking away inside you all through your life. It ticks away through the whole year – spring, summer, autumn and winter. It ticks away through the day when you are wide awake and through the night when you are fast asleep. Let's listen again to our own heartbeat.

ACTIVITY

Take a Breather *or* Have a Heart

Note: This game offers the children an opportunity to reflect on the changes taking place in their bodies as they move from a time of activity to a time of quiet and peace.

- Play any active warm-up exercise with which the children are familiar, e.g. Traffic Lights, Follow the Leader, O'Grady Says, etc.

- After a few minutes shout 'Take a Breather' or 'Have a Heart', and everyone must find a space to lie down.

- Ask the children to close their eyes and then instruct them as follows:
  Put your hands on your ribs: feel them go in and out with your breath.
  Put your hands around your mouth and nose: feel your warm breath in your hands.
  Listen to your breath as it gets slower and slower.
  Put your hands on your chest: feel your heartbeat.
  Listen to your heartbeat as it gets slower and slower.

- With your inside voice that no one else can hear, talk to your body.
  How is it?
  Is it feeling tired or rested?
  Is it feeling happy or sad?
  Is it feeling relaxed?
  Is it feeling ready to go again?

When the children say 'Yes' the activities can be repeated.

Finish the exercise with a big stretch.

PRAYERTIME

Sign of the Cross.

Teacher *(as the candle is lit)*
Deep inside us our hearts are beating, beating, beating.
All day long our hearts are beating.
All night long our hearts are beating.

Sometimes we forget that we have a little clock ticking away inside us all the time.
Let's give God thanks and praise for our heart today as we say:

Each beat of my heart praises you, O God.

Become quiet and still.
Put your hand on your chest and feel your heart beating.
Let us give God thanks and praise as we say.

All
Each beat of my heart praises you, O God.

Teacher
Put your hand on the side of your head.

With your fingers feel the pulse of your heart as it beats.
Let us give God thanks and praise as we say:

All
Each beat of my heart praises you, O God.

Teacher
God gives us life. Our heartbeat tells us that we are alive.
It is good to be alive. It is good to hear our heart beat.
Thank you heart for beating every day.
Thank you, God, for my heartbeat.

Sign of the Cross.

Day Four

Continue song: *My Body Clock*

ART

Make a heart badge

For each child you will need:
- Coloured paper/card
- Scissors
- A safety-pin
- Adhesive tape

Distribute the paper/card.
Ask the children to draw a heart and to cut out the heart shape.
Decorate the heart.
Stick the safety-pin on the back of the heart to make a badge.

or

Make a heart card

You will need:
- A sheet of paper for each child
- Markers/crayons, etc.

Distribute the paper.
Ask the children to fold the page in two.

On the outside of the card draw a big heart.
Write a verse on the inside, e.g.:

Alive-O! Together as friends.
Praise God! Because we are Alive-O!

Decorate the card on the inside.
You might add a caption to the card, e.g. 'Each beat of my heart praises you, O God'.

PRAYERTIME

Sign of the Cross.

Teacher (*as the candle is lit*)
Time and time and time again.
Praise God, praise God.

All time is God's time and God is with us at all times. Let us use God's times well.

Let us pray: Help us, God, to know the right time.

Help us, God, to know when to say 'I am sorry'.

All
Help us, God, to know the right time.

Teacher
Help us, God, to know when to ask 'can I help' at home.

All
Help us, God, to know the right time.

Teacher
Help us, God, to know when to talk and when to listen.

All
Help us, God, to know the right time.

Teacher
Help us, God, to know when to say 'yes' and when to say 'no'.

All
Help us, God, to know the right time.

Teacher
Help us, God, to know when to say 'you're my friend'.

All
Help us, God, to know the right time.

Teacher
For all God's time we give thanks and praise.

All
Time and time and time again.
Praise God, praise God.

Sign of the Cross.

Note: Ask the children to bring in a stone for tomorrow's prayertime. If you feel this suggestion is not appropriate for your class, instead of a stone use a piece of Plasticine.

Day Five

WORKSHEET

If you wish to use the worksheet or workbook page which accompanies this lesson, this is an appropriate time to do so.

CHATTING

...about the picture on page 3

The apple is falling. Do you think Bertie or Robert will catch it before it hits the ground? Why? Do you have a granny? Does she ride a bike? Can you ride a bike? What might the sunflowers be thinking as they look at what is happening? Have you ever waited and waited for something to happen – and then almost missed it?

PRAYERTIME

Note: In preparation for the prayertime ask the children to place the stone or Plasticine on the desk in front of them.

Sign of the Cross.

All
Sing: *My Body Clock*

Teacher *(as the candle is lit)*
We light the candle.
We remember that God is with us.

Take your stone (Plasticine) in your hand.
Cup your hands together and hold the stone (Plasticine).
Close your eyes so that you can feel the stone (Plasticine).

Feel it very carefully.
Is it smooth? Is it rough?
Your stone (Plasticine) is very still. It isn't moving. It is still because it doesn't have a heartbeat. It doesn't have life. Feel how cold and still it is. The stone (Plasticine) has no life. Gently, put the stone (Plasticine) down on the desk.

Now place your hands on your ribs. Feel them move as your breath flows in and out of your body.

Feel the breath coming in. *Pause.*
Now feel the breath going out.
Repeat the sequence again.

Our breath flows through our bodies.
Our breath keeps us alive.
Our breath gives us life.

On your next breath as you breathe in, feel your body filling up with God's love. *Pause.*
As you breathe out, feel the love of God going out to everyone in the room.
Repeat the sequence again.

Let us thank God for the breath of life.

Thank you, God, for the breath of life that flows through all living things.

Thank you, God, for the heartbeat that brings
life to every part of our body.

Open your eyes.
Stretch.
Relax.

All
Sing: *Alive-O chorus*

Sign of the Cross.

Q. Who gives us the gift of life?

A. God Our Father gives us the gift of life.

My Body Clock

Words: Clare Maloney
Music: Fran Hegarty

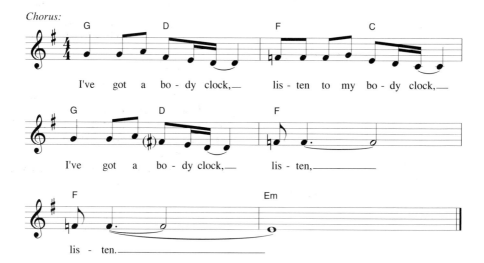

1. My body has a timer though it isn't like a clock.
   It doesn't show the hour and it doesn't say tick-tock.
   It doesn't hang upon the wall or sit upon a shelf
   But my body has a timer way down deep inside myself.

2. It tells me when I'm hungry, that it's time for me to eat.
   It keeps time to the music and it makes me tap my feet.
   It tells me when I'm feeling sad, it's time to have a cry.
   It makes my chin start quivering and tears come to my eye.

3. And when I'm feeling tired but I don't want it to show
   My body starts to yawn and yawn so Mum is sure to know.
   'It's time for you to go to bed', says Mum but I say, 'No!'
   Then my body gives another yawn and off to bed I go.

4. As verse 1.

Lesson 4: Time Moves On

For everything there is a season,
and a time for every matter under heaven.
(Ecclesiastes 3:1)

Time is constantly moving and changing.
There is the cyclical movement of the
seasons and the chronological, linear
movement of life from birth to death. These
are signs of the tangible creative plan of God
at the heart of all life. With this movement
comes growth and development and also
death. It is, perhaps, this echo of mortality in
every changing moment that sometimes
causes us to want to hold on to the present
rather than embrace the future. Within the
overall content of the programme we will
endeavour to lead the children to an
awareness of the insight which we find in
Ecclesiastes 3:1 'For everything there is a
time...'.

What am I trying to do?

To help the children to become aware of the call
to 'move on' as experienced in the world of
nature and in human life.

Why?

So that they will be better able to understand the
need to continually take hold of the 'not yet' and
to be able to negotiate it with confidence in
God's continuing presence with them.

FOR THE TEACHER:

A Blessing

May the light of your soul guide
you.
May the light of your soul bless
the work you do with the secret
love and warmth of your heart.
May you see in what you do the beauty of
your own soul.
May the sacredness of your work bring
healing, light and renewal to those who work
with you and to those who see and receive
your work.
May your work never weary you.
May it release within you the wellsprings of
refreshment, inspiration, and excitement.
May you never become lost in the bland
absences.
May the day never burden.
May dawn find you awake and alert,
approaching your new day with dreams,
possibilities and promises.
May evening find you gracious and fulfiled.
May you go into the night blessed, sheltered
and protected.
May your soul calm, console and renew you.
    John O'Donohue

Overview of the Week

		Continue song		
		Recall story		
Song: *Old Man Time/*		Poem: *It Takes Time!*	Continue song	
Round and Round		or *Goodness How*	Recall poem: *It Takes*	
Chatting about	Continue song	*You've Grown*	*Time!* or *Goodness*	
seasonal time	Story: *Old Daddio*	Chatting about	*How You've Grown*	Worksheet
Activity: *Me in the*	Chatting about the	changes in human	Art: *Make an Egg-*	Chatting about the
Changing Seasons	story	life	*timer*	picture
Prayertime	Prayertime	Prayertime	Prayertime	Prayertime

Day One

SONG

Old Man Time

Round and Round

CHATTING

...about seasonal time

What time of the year is it now? What happens at this time of the year? How does the world of nature tell us that it is autumn time? What do you like about this time of the year? Name the other times of the year? What's special about summertime? About wintertime? About springtime? Which time do you like best? Why? How do the seasons change? Tell us about some of the changes you see each year. Do we wear the same sort of clothes in every season? What would we wear in summer that is different from what we wear in winter? Do we eat different kinds of food in each season? Tell us about some of the foods you might eat in autumn/in winter. If you were to think of a colour for each season, what colour might you choose for summer? For spring? For winter? For autumn?

ACTIVITY

Me in the Changing Seasons

Ask the children to divide a page into quarters. Each section represents one of the four seasons. Ask the children to draw themselves wearing the typical clothes for each season.

PRAYERTIME

Sign of the Cross.

Teacher (*as the candle is lit*)
God is our light.
Our light for all time.

Seasons change all the time. Summer moves along for autumn to come. Autumn moves on for winter. Winter changes into spring and spring turns into summer.

We ask God who holds all time to bless the seasons of the year. We pray:

The seasons come and the seasons go,
They each move on for us to grow,
So thank you, God, you love us so.

For summer and its sunshine.

All
The seasons come and the seasons go,
They each move on for us to grow,
So thank you, God, you love us so.

Teacher
For autumn and its golden colours.

All
The seasons come and the seasons go,
They each move on for us to grow,
So thank you, God, you love us so.

Teacher
For winter and its frosty skies.

All

The seasons come and the seasons go,
They each move on for us to grow,
So thank you, God, you love us so.

Teacher

For spring and its bright green shoots.

All

The seasons come and the seasons go,
They each move on for us to grow,
So thank you, God, you love us so.

Teacher

Let's make an autumn wish.
At birthday-times we wish each other 'Happy Birthday'.
At morning-time we wish each other 'Good Morning'.
At night-time we wish each other 'Good Night'.
It's autumntime now. Let us wish each other a 'Happy Autumn'.

Children turn to each other, shake hands and wish each other a happy autumn.

Teacher

Let us give glory and thanks to God for the seasons.

All

Glory be to the Father...

Sign of the Cross.

Day Two

Continue song: *Old Man Time/Round and Round*

Note: *In the following story the children meet again familiar characters from the Junior Infants/Primary One and Senior Infants/Primary Two stories.*

STORY

Old Daddio

Once upon a time there was an old man whose proper name was Mr E. Ternity, but everyone called him Old Daddio. He had a long white beard and he wore an old sack tied in the middle with a rope. He looked for all the world like an egg-timer with arms and legs. In the middle of his baldy old head, two green twinkly eyes sparkled as brightly as the day they were born. Old Daddio was always on the move. He walked from here to there to everywhere. He never stood still, not for one minute. Everywhere he went he carried an old brown suitcase. When anyone asked him what was in it, he would smile.

'Time,' he would say, '...all the time in the world.'

One day he walked down the road, around the corner and straight into the middle of a moment of mid-summer madness. Summertime had come, it had stayed, and now it refused to go. It stood still. It had stopped its clock. Bertie the Crow sat on his perch. He refused to peck and gobble his luscious strawberry. Instead he looked at it, he tried to lick it, he admired it. The farm animals and the zoo animals who had swopped places and gone on holiday refused to come home. The sun refused to stop shining, the flowers refused to let go of their blooms, and the days refused to shorten their stride. This threw all the other seasons into a fluster. They stood jammed in a huge pile-up behind King Combine, who was revving with rage because the corn refused to turn golden for the autumn harvest. Peter and Paul and all the other swallows were lined up on the wires but there was no cold to give them a nip and send them off. Dinny and Dolly were very cross because people kept asking them when Auntie Jemima was coming for the End-Of-Summer Sale.

'How can we have a sale when summertime refuses to end?' they snapped back.

And these were just the autumn dwellers. Behind them Fiona's snowman wanted to know when he could get re-built and her snowdrops were all confused about whether or not to start putting down their roots. Hoggy was fed up with all the sleepy animals asking him, 'Can we get into Jamie's bed yet?'

'No!' he answered crossly. 'How can you hibernate when there's no wintertime to hibernate through?'

And over the shoulders of winter's inhabitants, Mrs Spring and all her crew were in a tizzy. Griselda was particularly cross. 'No wonder I cannot wake up,' she said, 'when I cannot even get to bed on time!'

'Do something Old Daddio!' the seasons cried. 'Do something!'

Old Daddio spoke gently to the summer sun. 'What is the matter Sun?' he asked. 'Don't you think it's time for you to move on?'

'Summertime is a happy time,' said the sun. 'I don't like it when summertime is over. I am afraid that it will never come back again. Imagine what it would be like if there was never another summer.'

But the other seasons grew more impatient. 'Move over summer, it is time for autumn now,' they cried, 'and then it'll be wintertime and then springtime.'

'All in good time, all in good time,' said Old Daddio, gently. He lifted his old suitcase above his head.

Then he opened the brown suitcase and shook it. All the time in the world flew up, up, into the air. The seasons watched in amazement. Bertie gobbled his strawberry, the days grew shorter, the cold nipped the swallows and they set off, and by the time all that had happened autumn was well underway. The other seasons lined up, ready to follow, each in their turn. 'Take your time and remember,' said Old Daddio, 'there's always time; all the time in the world.' And he walked on.

CHATTING

...about the story

Do you know anyone who reminds you of Old Daddio? Have you ever seen an egg-timer? Why do you think it is called an egg-timer? Do you like boiled eggs? How long do you like your egg boiled for? Why do you think Old Daddio never stood still? Do you know anyone like that?

Can you remember any of the people mentioned in the story? Old Daddio walked right into the middle of a moment of madness and mayhem. Can you remember what was happening? What did you think about what the summertime characters were doing? Have you ever been enjoying something and not wanted it to end? Tell us about it. Have you ever not enjoyed something and wished it would be over right away? Tell us about that.

PRAYERTIME

Sign of the Cross.

Teacher *(as the candle is lit)*
God is our light.
Our light for all time.

Let us take this time and give thanks to God, the creator of all time.
God, our Creator, you created the earth.

All
Blessed are you, Lord, God of all creation.

Teacher
You planned the changing seasons.

All
Blessed are you, Lord, God of all creation.

Teacher

You are with us as we grow and change.

All

Blessed are you, Lord, God of all creation.

Teacher

God loves and cares for us always.
We ask God to bless us as we grow and change
with each passing day.

All

Our Father…

Sign of the Cross.

Day Three

Continue song: *Old Man Time/Round and Round*

Recall story: *Old Daddio*

 POEM

It Takes Time!

I can grow hair
    grow nails
    grow teeth.
I can grow bigger
    grow older
    grow tall.
I can grow better
    grow wiser
    grow stronger.
But there's one 'grow' I cannot
    at all.
From all the 'grows' that
    I can do,
If I could take
    my pick
I wouldn't choose any of these
    at all.
I'd simply choose to
    grow quick!

'Cos after all the time
    I've spent
Growing in body
    and mind
I've learned one thing
    about growing,
I've learned that – growing
    TAKES TIME!

or

Goodness How You've Grown

Whenever Granny Cronin comes, she pats me
on the head,
Smothers me with kisses 'till I wish that I were
dead.
Says 'Goodness gracious me child, how the
time has flown,
Since last I came to see you, you have grown
and grown and grown!'

Whenever Uncle Harry comes he slaps me on
the back,
Swings me round and throws me up, then
dumps me like a sack.
Says 'Goodness gracious me child, how the
time has flown,
Since last I came to see you, you have grown
and grown and grown!'

Whenever Auntie Mary comes she ruffles up
my hair,
Gazes at me lovingly, then hugs me like a bear.
Says 'Goodness gracious me child, how the
time has flown,
Since last I came to see you, you have grown
and grown and grown!'

Whenever Grandad Murphy comes he shakes
me by the hand,
Slips me 50p and says 'Hello, you're looking
grand.
It's very nice to see you, you haven't changed
a jot.'
O Grandad you're a smasher and I like you
such a lot!

CHATTING

...about changes in human life

Can you remember when you were a baby? What's it like to be a baby? What's good about being a baby? What do you think is not so good about being a baby? Did anyone ever tell you what your first words were? Or when you took your first step? Or when your first tooth appeared? What was it like when you were three and you still weren't at school? What did you do all day? Who can remember their first day in school? What was it like? How did you feel? What's it like to be in First Class/Primary Three now?

Have you changed over the years? What is different? Who would like to show us a picture of themselves when they were younger? Maybe we'll play a game and I'll show you a photo of someone in the class and you can tell me if you know who it is! *(You might like to play this game a few times, each time chatting about the changes in the person.)*

PRAYERTIME

Sign of the Cross.

Teacher *(as the candle is lit)*
Time and time and time again.
Praise God, praise God.

Let us thank God for all the changes that have happened to us since we were babies.
Today let's thank God that we are growing all the time. We pray:

All
Time and time and time again.
Praise God, praise God.

Teacher
For the day we were born.

All
Time and time and time again.
Praise God, praise God.

Teacher
For our first steps.

All
Time and time and time again.
Praise God, praise God.

Teacher
For our first words.

All
Time and time and time again.
Praise God, praise God.

Teacher
For our first day at school.

All
Time and time and time again.
Praise God, praise God.

Teacher
For our first day in this class.

All
Time and time and time again.
Praise God, praise God.

Teacher
For all the growing that we have done so far.

All
Time and time and time again.
Praise God, praise God.

Teacher
It is good that time moves on.
It is good that we grow and get bigger.
It is good that we change as we grow.
We ask God to bless us and to be with us as we grow in the days and weeks and years ahead.

All
Our Father...

Sign of the Cross.

Note: For the art on Day Four you will be making an egg-timer. You will need two plastic bottles (with their caps), a knitting needle, and a cupful of rice. You might like to bring in an actual egg-timer to show to the children. Alternatively, you could ask the children to bring in a selection of egg-timers.

Continue song: *Old Man Time/Round and Round*

Recall poem: *It Takes Time!* or *Goodness How You've Grown*

ART

Make An Egg-Timer

Note: This artwork is done by the teacher. Many children may never have seen an egg-timer. However, it is a useful instrument in helping the children to understand the concept of time moving on. It visualises in a concrete and measurable way for the children the passing of time. If the children have brought some egg-timers into school, show them to the class.

You will need:
- Two plastic bottles with caps
- Knitting needle
- Cup of rice

With the knitting needle make a hole in the end of the bottle-caps, large enough for a grain of rice to pass through. Then pour the cupful of rice into one bottle. Place the bottles together, cap to cap, and secure with adhesive tape around both caps. Watch as the rice goes from one bottle to the other. Explain to the children how egg-timers are used to measure the time it takes to boil an egg. They can watch it and see how time moves on!

PRAYERTIME

Note: If possible, gather the children around the egg-timer.

Sign of the Cross.

Teacher *(as the candle is lit)*
Today we are going to thank God for time, time that is always moving. To help us to thank God for time, we are going to get a little help from an egg-timer. Egg-timers let us know when our egg is cooked. Egg-timers help us to measure time. They show us that time never stands still. As we watch our timer we will remember that all time belongs to God.

As we turn the timer we remember that God is always with us.
This time is God's time. So let us be quiet for a moment.

Look at the timer.
Look at the shape of the timer.
Look at the grains in the timer.
Look at the grains as they fall gently.

Time is moving on. As you watch the little grains, feel the time moving slowly. This is God's time. God is with us as the grains fall. God is with us as time moves.

All
Glory be to the Father…

Sign of the Cross.

Note: For prayertime on Day Five you will need a birthday candle.

Day Five

WORKSHEET

If you wish to use the worksheet or workbook page which accompanies this lesson, this is an appropriate time to do so.

CHATTING

...about the picture on pages 4 and 5

Look at all the little pictures. Can you find the characters who are mentioned in the story *Old Daddio*? Can you remember who the others are? Have you ever seen anyone like Old Daddio? Can you name all the time-things which flew out of the suitcase? Which of these things would you find in your home? Which would you find outside? Which is your favourite?

PRAYERTIME

Note: Instead of the normal candle used for prayertime you might like to light a birthday candle – it will burn more quickly and will concretise the passing of time for the children.

Sign of the Cross.

Song: *Old Man Time/Round and Round*

Teacher (*as the candle is lit*)
Our burning candle is a symbol of time passing.
As we watch our candle we can see time passing.

All
God, our Creator,
We thank you for giving us your time;
time to run,
time to walk,
time to start,
time to stop,
time to drink,
time to eat,
time to wake,
time to sleep,
time to laugh,
time to cry,
time for hello,
time for goodbye,
time to work,
time to play,
time to watch,
time to pray.
Thank you, God,
for you time every day.
Amen.

Sign of the Cross.

Round and Round

Fran Hegarty

1. Sum - mer fades to au - tumn gold,
leaves fall to___ the ground.
Days are get - ting short - er as the
sea - sons turn a - round.
Au - tumn days get cold - er, soon the
win - ter winds___ will blow.
In be - tween comes Hal - low - e'en___ when the
chan - ges start to show.

Oh like the night time al - ways turns to day, the tides they come and go but the o - cean's here to stay. The sea - sons change and yet it all re - mains the same go - ing round and round.

2. Winter snows melt away and buds are on the trees,
Days are getting longer as the buds turn into leaves,
Spring is here and sunshine soon will drive away the rain,
When the summer's over, it will all go round again.

Coda:

Round and round yet still the same,
Round and round yet still the same.

40

Old Man Time

Finbar O'Connor

1. Old Man Time walks a - long the road and the road goes e - ver___ on. Though we know that his steps are slow, when we look for him he's___ gone. And he will not stay, he will not de - lay as his wea - ry way he___ wends. Old Man Time walks a - long the road and his jour - ney ne - ver___ ends.

2. Old Man Time walks along the road
   On his long and weary way.
   Though we try, as he passes by,
   We can never make him stay.
   No he will not stay, he will not delay
   As his weary way he wends.
   Old Man Time walks along the road
   And his journey never ends.

Lesson 5: We Belong Together

Live as children of light.
(Ephesians 5:8)

In this lesson we reaffirm the children's experience of belonging with others. We focus in particular on their experience of belonging to their new class. We seek to deepen their understanding of what it means to be part of a group by engaging them in a series of activities to reinforce their identity as a class. In so doing we are exploring with them the identity which shapes any group of people who hold a common sense of belonging.

We began this year by providing the children with an opportunity to reflect on what it was like to move into First Class/Primary Three. Through the year we seek to help them to develop their awareness that belonging to any group is a gradual process. Hopefully by the end of the year they will have learnt something of the significance of belonging with others. In this lesson we invite the children and their parents/guardians to participate in a Celebration of Enrolment. For children of classes where First Communion and First Penance are not being celebrated this Celebration of Enrolment marks the present stage in their emerging identity as members of their class.

Some children in First Class/Primary Three, however, are preparing to celebrate First Communion/First Penance this year. For these children the content of this lesson will provide a background to help them begin to understand what it means to belong to the community of the Church. The Celebration of Enrolment marks a stage in the process of their initiation into membership of the Church.

Parents help children to participate as fully as possible in life. As children, we were baptised into the Christian community in the presence of our families. It is the children's families who help them to enter more fully into the life of the Church. Offering an invitation to parents/guardians/godparents to take part with their children in this Celebration of Enrolment may help these adults to understand their role in relation to their children as they begin their preparation for First Communion/First Penance. It is envisaged that the Celebration of Enrolment would take place in the local parish. Grounded in the philosophy of the home-parish-school partnership, we help to prepare the children for their celebration of First Communion/First Penance.

For the Teacher:

A thought before beginning

The first steps any of us make
are faltering and slow.
It takes time to learn to walk,
and our first words are unclear,
just mumbled sounds.
It takes time to learn to talk.

Within each of us
the kingdom of God grows.
Its qualities are
compassion and courage,
forgiveness and faith,
hope and harmony,
peace, joy and love.

As we need patience with learning
in our first words and first steps –
for these are skills learned gradually –
we need similar patience
as God's life grows within us.
Donal Neary SJ

What am I trying to do?

To further explore and celebrate the children's experience of belonging in First Class/Primary Three.

For those children who will celebrate First Communion and First Penance.
To begin to heighten their awareness of belonging to the local Church community. Through the Ceremony of Enrolment we provide an opportunity for parents/guardians to recognise their role in relation to their children's preparation for these sacraments.

Why?

So that they will be more aware of themselves as belonging to First Class/Primary Three and understand better the sense of identity that goes with the experience of belonging.

For those who will celebrate First Communion and First Penance:
So that parents/guardians/godparents and children will have a sense of this time as one of preparation for the parish's celebration of First Communion/First Penance.

Overview of the Week

Song: *Christ is my Light/Together Again* Chatting about the class Activity: *Class Crest or Badge* Worksheet Prayertime	Continue songs Poem: *Where I Belong* Chatting about belonging to a group Activity: *Enrolment Book* Prayertime	Continue songs Chatting about preparing for a celebration Activity: *Making Banners* Prayertime	Continue activities Prepare for the Enrolment Ceremony Prayertime	Enrolment Ceremony in the Classroom *or* Enrolment Ceremony in the Church Now We Know

Day One

Note: This lesson prepares the children for an Enrolment Ceremony. For children of classes where First Penance and First Communion are not being celebrated the ceremony may take place in the classroom on Day Five. For children preparing for First Communion/First Penance the ceremony could take place in the local church. Ask these children to being their baptismal candle in to class during the week.

It is important to give the children the opportunity to participate fully in this preparation so that they have a sense that the ceremony belongs to them. Over the week, therefore, the children will be involved in a range of activities which will culminate in the Celebration of Enrolment.

It is not necessary to do all the activities. From the variety of activities offered, choose what is appropriate to your class and situation.

SONG

Christ is my Light

Together Again

CHATTING

...about the class

What is the name of our school? Do you know why it is called by that name? Does our class have a name? If you could choose a name, what name might you call this class? Is there anything special about our class? Now that you have been in it for a few weeks, what do you like about being in this class? How would you describe our class? Let's look for words that describe what our class is like.

What sort of class would we like to be? What about our Class Code – does that tell us anything? Does anyone know what a crest is? A crest tells us through pictures and symbols what a group is like. Do you have a school crest? Let's look at it. *(If you have one, talk with the children about the crest – what's on it, what it says, etc.)* Do you know your family crest? Sometimes when you belong to a group/club/team you get a badge. The badge tells you something about the group/club/team. Does anyone here have a badge like that? Do you know anyone who has a badge like that? Could anyone describe a badge for the class? Would the badge/crest have words or pictures on it? Why do you think it would have pictures? What sort of words would it have? These words are often called mottos.

Let's see if we could make a badge/crest for our class. How do you think we might do that? Does any one special thing come into your mind when you think about our class? Tell us about it. What sort of pictures could we put on our badge/crest? Our pictures would want to tell others what our class is like. Close your eyes and think about this for a minute.

ACTIVITY

Note: In preparation for this activity, draw a very large crest/badge outline on a sheet of chart paper and cut it out.

Ask the children to decide what pictures will go on their Class Crest/Badge. These pictures will tell others what their class is like. Give each child a small piece of white card on which to draw a

picture of something they like about their class or something they like doing as a class. Cut out the picture.

When all the pictures for the Class Crest/Badge are drawn and cut out, discuss what the caption/motto might be. Write the caption/motto on the Class Crest/Badge.

WORKSHEET

If you wish to use the worksheet or workbook page which accompanies this lesson, this is an appropriate time to do so. The worksheet or Enrolment Certificate will be used during the Celebration of Enrolment which takes place in the Church.

PRAYERTIME

Note: In preparation for the prayertime, place the Class Crest/Badge in a prominent position.

Sign of the Cross.

Teacher *(as the candle is lit)*
Christ is my light.
Help us to live as children of the light.

Place your picture for the Class Crest/Badge on the desk in front of you.
Close your eyes and think of what this picture is saying about our class.

All
Help us to live as children of the light.

Invite each child to come forward and stick their picture on the crest/badge. If time allows, each child could make a statement about his or her picture, e.g. 'Our class is a fun class', 'Our class is a hard-working class'. After each child places his/her picture, the class responds:

All

Help us to live as children of the light.

Teacher

Let us look at all the pictures that make up our Class Crest/Badge.

Let's read our Class Motto together.

Let us stand, hold hands, as we sing (or listen to the tape): *Christ is my Light.*

All

Sing: *Christ is my Light*

Sign of the Cross.

Day Two

Continue song: *Christ is my Light/Together Again*

POEM

Where I Belong

No, No,
I didn't want to go,
My heart was beating very fast,
My feet were very slow.
Why should I leave my comfy bed?
There's something very wrong.
Why should I leave to go to school?
I simply won't belong.

Yes, Yes,
I simply must confess,
I love to meet my friends each day,
I love the games we always play.
I'm glad I came to school to learn
To read or sing a song.
Why do I leave to go to school?
'Cos that's where I belong!

Christy Kenneally

CHATTING

...about belonging to/enrolling in a group

Let's make a list of all the people we belong with – at home, at school, in the neighbourhood. How do we come to belong to a group? How do you come to belong to a family? How did you come to belong to this school? Does anyone belong to a club/team? How did you come to belong to that club/team? What did you have to do? Did you have to sign-up? Did someone ever put your name down or give your name to someone so that you could join a group? What does it mean to enrol in a group? Tell us about a time you enrolled for something. When you enrol for something it means that you begin to belong to something. Have you ever enrolled for anything? What did you have to do? Who was there? What happened? Did you have to say anything special? Did you have to dress in any special way?

ACTIVITY

Enrolment Book

This activity involves the gathering of each child's photograph into a class Enrolment Book.

For each child you will need:
- An individual photograph
- An A4 sheet of paper, preferably coloured
- Adhesive
- Scissors

Ask the children to stick their photograph in the centre of the A4 sheet of paper. Discuss with the children the different designs that can be seen on picture frames. Ask them to design a crest-like frame for their photo. Alternatively, ask the children to frame their photo with pictures of the people to whom they belong. Gather all the photos together as one book.

Discuss the cover of the Enrolment Book. Discuss a possible title, e.g. 'We Belong Together'.
If there is a class photo, put it at the end of the Enrolment Book. Discuss with the children where the Enrolment Book may be placed in the classroom.

You might like to create the Enrolment Book during the Enrolment Ceremony on Day Five. If you decide to do this, you may need to ask the children to punch holes at the side of their picture so that each sheet may slot with ease into a binder/folder, thus making the Enrolment Book.

PRAYERTIME

Sign of the Cross.

Teacher *(as the candle is lit)*
Christ is my light.
Help us to live as children of the light.

Christ be with me.

All
Christ is my light.

Teacher
Christ be beside me.

All
Christ is my light.

Teacher
Christ be before me.

All
Christ is my light.

Teacher
Christ be behind me.

All
Christ is my light.

Teacher
Christ on my right hand.
Christ on my left hand.

All
Christ is my light.

Teacher
Christ be with me everywhere I go.
Christ be my friend for ever and ever.

All
Christ is my light.

Sign of the Cross.

Continue song: *Christ is my Light/Together Again*

CHATTING

...about preparing for a celebration

Have you ever helped to prepare for a birthday party or any sort of party? What did you do? Did you ever make your own decorations? Did you send out invitations? How did you do that? How did you feel as you were getting ready for the party? How did you decide whom to invite? Did you enjoy preparing? What was the easiest part? What was the most difficult part?

ACTIVITY

Making Banners

Write out one or a selection of the following captions on chart paper:
    Let's Celebrate!
    We Belong Together.
    First Class/Primary Three Have Fun Together.
    First Class/Primary Three Learn Together.
    It's Good To Be In Our Class!
    It's Good To Be In First Class/Primary Three!

Divide the children into four/five groups.
Give each group a separate caption.
Ask the children to colour in the letters and to
draw pictures of themselves around the
caption.

PRAYERTIME

Sign of the Cross.

Teacher *(as the candle is lit)*
God bless all the people who will help us to
work and to grow together as a class during
the coming year.
We are gathered in your name. We know you
are with us.

All
We are gathered in your name.

Teacher
For our class friends.

All
We are gathered in your name.

Teacher
For our principal _____ *(name)* and our vice-
principal _____ *(name)*.

All
We are gathered in your name.

Teacher
For all the teachers in the school.

All
We are gathered in your name.

Teacher
For all who look after us in school.

All
We are gathered in your name.

Teacher
We thank you, God, for everyone in our
school.
Let's hold hands as we say:

All
Our Father...

Sign of the Cross.

Continue activity: *Banners (if not already
completed)*

Prepare for the Enrolment Ceremony

PRAYERTIME

Sign of the Cross.

Teacher *(as the candle is lit)*
As we light our candle we know that God is
with us.
God loves each one of us.
God loves us when we are by ourselves.
God loves us when we are with others.
God loves us when we are together in our
class.

Close your eyes.
Still your hands.
Place your feet on the floor.
Listen to your heart beat.

Go into your inside world where it is dark and
warm and quiet and peaceful. Feel your breath
as it moves in and out of your body.

(Pause)

Think of all the people who belong to this
class.
Send your love and friendship out to each
person.

(Pause)

God loves each one of us in this class. Each
one of us is special to God. With your inside
voice that no one else can hear, tell God about
our class. Tell God about how you feel now
that you belong to this class.

Open your eyes.
Stretch.
Let us hold hands as we say:

All
Glory be to the Father...

Sign of the Cross.

Enrolment Ceremony – In the Classroom

Preparing the Room: Involve the children in the preparation of the room. Arrange the banners, the Class Crest/Badge, the Enrolment Book for the celebration. Alternatively you might like to create the Enrolment Book during the actual ceremony. To do this you will need a folder of some kind, e.g. a ring-binder, so that each child can come forward and place their sheet in the folder.

Place the table with the lighted candle in a central position. If possible, gather everyone in a circle around the table.

Sign of the Cross.

All
Sing: *Together Again*

Teacher
Today we celebrate the fact that we are now in a new class and have begun a new year.
We thank God for all the people we belong with.
We belong with our families at home.
We belong with our class at school.
We belong with the followers of Jesus.
Today we celebrate our belonging to this class, this year.
We pray:

All
Blessed be God.

Teacher *(calling out each child's name in the order in which they appear in the Enrolment Book)*
_____ *(name)*, what class do you belong to?

Child *(stands and answers)*
I belong to First Class/Primary Three.

If time allows you might like to ask each child to come forward and sign the Enrolment Book. Or if you are creating the Enrolment Book during the ceremony, invite each child to come forward and to place her/his sheet in the book.

All
Blessed be God.

Teacher *(on raising the Enrolment Book)*
God, we know that you are always with us.
We know that you will be with us each day of the new year.
Bless our class as we belong together.
Let's stand, hold hands and sing:

All
Sing: *Christ is my Light*

Sign of the Cross.

Enrolment Ceremony – In the Church (for children celebrating First Communion/First Penance)

Note: *If appropriate, you might suggest integrating the following celebration into the Vigil Mass or one of the Sunday Masses. While this ceremony is primarily directed at those children who will be celebrating their First Communion this year, some people may also like to enrol those children who will not be celebrating First Holy Communion, thus extending their period of preparation.*

The lighted Paschal Candle should be placed in the sanctuary area before the ceremony begins.

All
Sing: *Christ is my Light*

Entrance Procession: Children form a procession, each carrying their baptismal candle (unlit). One child carries the Enrolment Book while another child carries the Class Crest/Badge. When the children reach the top of the church they bow, then return to join their parents or accompanying adults in their seats. The two children carrying the Enrolment Book and the Class Crest/Badge go to the front of the altar where the priest receives their gifts. Children bow, then return to join the parents or guardians, who will have their baptismal candles.

The priest welcomes the children, their parents/guardians, and the teachers.

Welcome
Priest
God our Father, we know that you love us as a mother loves her child. We know that you care for us as a father cares for his child. Today we come together to ask you to bless

the children of First Class/Primary Three, as they prepare for their First Penance and First Communion.

Liturgy of the Word
Children, as a class, recite poem Where I Belong.

Priest
The Lord be with you.

All
And also with you.

Priest
A reading from the Holy Gospel according to Mark.

More and more people came to see Jesus. Everyone wanted to speak to him face to face. They wanted to tell him all their worries and troubles. They wanted to tell him about the good things that were happening to them. They waited for hours to get near him. It took a long time to get close to Jesus because Jesus listened carefully to each person's story. Then he gave each one his blessing. The crowds got bigger and bigger. The line of waiting people grew longer and longer. 'How strong he is,' thought the apostles. 'He can stand for hours meeting people and listening to them. Does he ever get tired?'

As the sun was beginning to set, a group of grown-ups and their children came over the hill towards Jesus. 'We have come to see Jesus,' they said, 'We want him to bless our children.' But the apostles said, 'No, it is too late. It's impossible. Jesus is tired. You must go home. He can't see you.'

The people pleaded with the apostles, 'But we want Jesus to bless our children. We have come a long way.'

Still the apostles said no. 'It's getting dark,' they said, 'Jesus has been here talking to people and blessing them all day long. There is no time for anyone else. Go home and come back another day.'

Just then, Jesus saw what was happening. 'Let the children come to me. Don't stop them,' he said. 'God loves children in a very special way.' So the children were brought to Jesus and Jesus talked to them and listened to them. He took the younger ones in his arms. He laid his hands on them and he blessed them. They knew that he loved them and they felt very happy. That evening they thanked God for Jesus.

Homily

Rite of Renewal of Baptismal Commitment
Priest
We invite the parents/guardians to come forward and light their children's baptismal candle.

Parents/guardians return to their seats and together with the child they hold the baptismal candle.

Priest
As these children prepare to celebrate their First Penance and First Communion we remember the day you first brought them to the church. We remember the promises you made for them that day. Now you promise to continue to love and support them as they prepare for First Penance and First Holy Communion.

I invite the adults to stand up.

Do you believe in God the Father?

All
We do.

Priest
Do you believe in Jesus Christ?

All
We do.

Priest
Do you believe in the Holy Spirit?

All
We do.

Priest
Do you promise to love and support these children as they prepare to celebrate First Penance and First Holy Communion?

All
We do.

Priest
As you do, may the love of God the Father support you; may the light of Jesus Christ, the Son of God, guide you; may the Holy Spirit strengthen you.

All
Amen.

Priest

I now invite the children to stand and to help hold their baptismal candle.

As you look forward to your First Penance and First Communion, do you promise to work with your teachers and all the people who love you at home, to learn about Jesus and his love for God the Father and for all of us?

All

We do.

Priest

May God the Father, Son and Holy Spirit bless you and may you know God's love in your hearts and learn to share it with others.

All

Amen.

Rite of Enrolment
Priest

Parents/guardians, as the name of your child is called, come forward and present her/him as a candidate for First Penance and First Communion.

We welcome _____ *(name of child)* as he/she enrols for First Penance and First Communion. We ask you to support him/her during the coming year.

Child receives Enrolment Certificate and returns to her/his seat with her/his parents/guardians.

Round of applause.

Prayers of the Faithful
Priest

The Lord be with you.

All

And also with you.

Priest

For all the children of the parish who are preparing for First Penance and First Communion. We pray to God.

All

Lord, hear our prayer.

Child

For everyone in our class. We pray to God.

All

Lord, hear our prayer.

Child

For all the people who love us at home as they help us to prepare. We pray to God.

All

Lord, hear our prayer.

Child

For the teachers in our school. We pray to God.

All

Lord, hear our prayer.

Priest

For the people in our community. We pray to God.

All

Lord, hear our prayer.

Invite a parent/guardian to read the reflection for parents at the end of this lesson.

Blessing
Priest

May God bless us and keep us.

All

Amen.

Priest

May we know the presence of God, the Father, Son and Holy Spirit in our hearts, in our lives, in our school and in our community at this special time in the life of our parish.

All

Amen.

Sing: *Christ is our Light*

NOW WE KNOW

Q. Who gives us the gift of life with others?

A. God Our Father gives us the gift of life with others.

Christ is my Light

Capo 3: Play D.

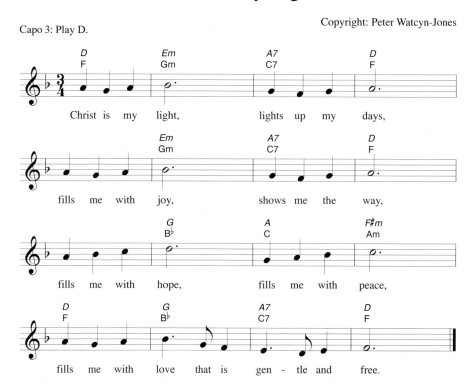

Christ is my light, lights up my days,

fills me with joy, shows me the way,

fills me with hope, fills me with peace,

fills me with love that is gen - tle and free.

52

Together Again

Frances O'Connell

Chorus:

To - geth - er a - gain,___ to - geth - er a - gain.___ We're

back! To - geth - er a - gain.___ With

each new day___ we shout 'Hur - ray!'___ It's

good to be to - geth - er a - gain.___ 1. We're

start - ing on___ a new ad - ven - ture to -

geth - er ev - 'ry step of the way,_____ so

much to learn,___ so much to say,___ and

God is with us as___ we pray.___

2. There's me and you, there's teacher too,
We work together all the day through,
With songs to sing and games to play,
And God is with us as we pray.

Reflection for Parents

Our Children

O Lord our God,
We have loved them in our longing,
Long before they flourished in the womb
Or stretched out into the world at birth.
We have held them in our arms
And cuddled them against all cold and care
As Mary and Joseph did for Jesus.

We have blessed them with a name
That someone in our family bore,
Or blessed them with a name
That no one of our tribe has ever held before,
As the Baptist's parents did for John.

We have nourished them at our table
And bring them now to yours,
To break the bread we break in memory
Of your Son, and in memory
Of those now gone before.

We pray,
That they may do for theirs
As we have done for them.
Amen.
Christy Kenneally

Lesson 6: We Remember Together

But I have said these things to you so that ...
you may remember.
(John 16:4)

Remember now, O Lord...
How I have walked before you in faithfulness
with a whole heart.
(Isaiah 38:3)

November is a dark month when days shorten and nights close in. We arise in the dark, we return home in the dark. We have moved towards the winter solstice, a time of transition between autumn and winter, a journeying between two worlds. At this time nature forces us to slow down. Bad weather draws us indoors. This mirrors another kind of drawing-in, a drawing into ourselves, a remembering.

Traditionally, November is the month when we remember our dead. It is a time to recall past events and people who shared our lives. We remember those who have gone before us marked with the sign of faith. We remember so that we can understand our own lives and our inevitable death.

As we approach the Feasts of All Saints and All Souls we help the children to talk about people they have known, or people they have been told about, who have died but whose memories have been kept alive. In this lesson we tell the children the story of Saint Columba, sometimes known as Saint Colmcille, and his Sean-Chapall Bán (his old white horse). They learn how this great saint approached his impending death with dignity and hope. We invite the children to journey with Columba as he prepares to say goodbye to this world. At the end of the story, instead of the usual chatting about the story, we ask the children to remain in silence so that they can savour for themselves the richness of the narrative.

FOR THE TEACHER:

A thought before beginning

A Blessing for Death

I pray that you will have the blessing of being consoled and sure about your own death.
May you know in your soul that there is no need to be afraid.
When your time comes, may you be given every blessing and shelter that you need.
May there be a beautiful welcome for you in the home that you are going to.
You are not going somewhere strange. You are going back to the home that you never left.
May you have a wonderful urgency to live your life to the full.
May you live compassionately and creatively and transfigure everything that is negative within you and about you.
When you come to die may it be after a long life.
May you be peaceful and happy and in the presence of those who really care for you.
May your going be sheltered and your welcome assured.
May your soul smile in the embrace of your anam cara.
J. O'Donohue

What am I trying to do?

To help the children to reflect on their own experience of remembering and to provide them with an opportunity during the month of November to remember those who have died.

Why?

So that the children may begin to be aware of the importance of remembering those who have died and be able to link this month with the liturgical year, the Feast of All Souls and the Feast of All Saints.

Overview of the Week

		Continue song		
		Poem: *All Saints, All Souls*		
Song: *Columba/ Remember Them*				
Chatting about remembering		Chatting about those who have died	Continue song, art	
	Continue song		Recall story	
Activity: *Guess who is Missing*	Story: *Columba*	Art: *Making a Story Cross*	Chatting about the picture	Worksheet
Prayertime	Prayertime	Prayertime	Prayertime	Prayertime

Day One

Song

Columba

Remember Them

Chatting

...about remembering

Let us see what we can remember about the last few weeks since school began. Does anyone remember the first day at school this year? What happened? What was the weather like then? Can you remember how you felt beginning school again? Can you remember anything else that happened in September? Is it easy to remember? Why/why not? How far back can you remember? Can you remember when you were a very small child? Tell us about something you remember from when you were small. What would happen if we could never remember?

Activity

Guess Who is Missing

How to play:
- Invite the children to sit in a semi-circle.
- One person is 'on' and leaves the room or goes aside and closes his/her eyes.
- A second player is pointed out and asked to 'hide' so that she/he is completely out of sight.
- The remaining players all change seats.
- The person who is 'on' is recalled and asked to say who is the 'missing' person.
- You may want to allocate a certain time-frame within which the 'missing person' is to be found.

PRAYERTIME

Sign of the Cross.

Teacher *(as the candle is lit)*
God the light of yesterday.
God the light of today.
God the light of tomorrow.

Sometimes in our hearts or in our special inside world we keep pictures of all the different things that have happened in the past. It's like having a photo album or a video of the things that have happened. Sometimes we can pick out one of these 'pictures' and we can remember where we were and what we were doing. Sometimes we remember a happy time. Sometimes we remember a sad time. We know that God has been with us at all times. Let us remember sometimes that are past and give glory to God in the highest.

Close your eyes…
Still your body…

Let us remember:
Summer holidays when the days were long and bright.
Let us pray:

All
Glory to God in the highest.

Teacher
Let us remember:
The day when we packed our bags for school to begin again.
Let us pray:

All
Glory to God in the highest.

Teacher
Let us remember:
The past weeks we have spent together in this classroom.

All
Glory to God in the highest.

Teacher
God the light of yesterday.
God the light of today.
God the light of tomorrow.

All
Glory be to the Father…

Sign of the Cross.

Day Two

Continue song: *Columba/Remember Them*

STORY

Columba

Most stories begin with beginnings,
    This story begins with the end,
Of an old man's life on an island
    And a horse's goodbye to his friend.

One Saturday morning Columba
    Woke up in bed and just knew
That this, the last day of the week,
    Was going to be his last day too.

He jumped out of bed, determined,
    It being the day that was in it,
To continue his life as he had always done,
    Living, to the very last minute.

Resting his head in his hands he prayed,
    *[1]'Buíochas le Dia go deo!
Molaimid thú, móraimid thú
    Thall 's abhus 's anseo.'*

Patting the pillow, 'Goodbye Bed,' he said,
    In you I have known rest 'n peace,
No matter how dark or dreary the night
    You cradled me, *[2]'rís 's arís.*

Goodbye Window,' he said, opening it wide,
    'You brought fresh air and light to my life.
You helped me breathe; you helped me see
    Through troubles and struggles and strife.

Goodbye Room,' he said, as he closed the door,
    'You gave me space – just to *be*
On my own, with you, when I needed –
    Just the two of us; you Room, and me.'

57

Neither Bed, Window nor Room
 Moved or uttered a word,
But the old saint knew, as old saints do,
 That each one had listened and heard.

It was May, the first month of summer,
 Columba's last of the year.
His friends were at work in the western fields,
 They stopped as the old man drew near.

'I have this notion,' Columba said,
 'Don't ask me how, what or why,
But I know in my heart, I feel in my bones,
 It's time, time for goodbye.'

'Where are you going?' they asked in alarm.
 'I'm going away,' he replied,
'I won't be back, but I'll see you again,
 If you know what I mean,' he smiled.

That said, he opened the doors of the barn
 And blessed its stores of grain.
*³'*Tá Dia maith*, you'll not want for food
 When I'm gone,' he repeated again.

Tired, though not yet quite finished,
 Columba sat down for a rest
On an old millstone by the side of the road.
 'Brother Diarmuid,' he said, 'Have you
guessed?'

'Guessed what, Brother?' Diarmuid his friend
asked,
 'I feel cross, yet I'm sad deep inside.
You talk of goodbye, of going away.
 What is it you're trying to hide?'

Just at that moment a *⁴*Sean-chapall Bán*
 With head drooping low in dismay,
Plodded along towards Columba, and stood
 Bereft of a whinney, or neigh.

Silent, he stood there, his mild mannered eyes
 Filled with sorrow intense.
He knew his old friend was going to die,
 Though how he knew – that baffles sense!

'Goodbye my Sean-chapall,' Columba said,
 'Surefooted, dependable friend.
On the broad of your back you carried me,
 *⁵*Beannacht Dé leat*. Amen.'

He stroked the old horse's forehead,
 Its eyes filled with tears to the brim.
They spilled over, rolled down its cheeks,
 And dropped from its quivering chin.

'Your tears are upsetting Columba,

Go away horse,' Diarmuid protested.
'Let him be!' said Columba, 'this dumb
creature knew,
 Though you have not even guessed it.

He senses that I am dying.
 I tell you, else you wouldn't know,
This creature's natural horse-sense
 Is a wonder God has bestowed.'

A last look to Ireland, then back to Iona,
 Where he had come to reside.
As the Sean-chapall turned and ambled away,
 Columba lay down – and died.

Columba just lay down and died
 At rest in peace. Amen.
Now this story has reached its beginning
 Because death is never the end.

*¹ Glory to God above.
 We praise you. We bless you, we thank you.
 We live out each day in your love.
*² Again and again
*³ God is good
*⁴ Old White Horse
*⁵ God bless you

Silence
*Here the teacher pauses to allow the children to
savour the richness of the story for themselves.*

PRAYERTIME

Sign of the Cross.

Teacher *(as the candle is lit)*
We remember saints who shared the light of
God's love in the world.
All over the world at this time of the year
people remember saints who are special to
them.
Many things and places are called after saints.
Our church is Saint _____. Our school is
called after Saint _____.
Today, as we remember the saints, we ask
them to pray for us.

All
Pray for us.

Teacher
Saint Brigid.

All
Pray for us.

Teacher
Saint Patrick.

All
Pray for us.

Teacher
Saint Margaret.

All
Pray for us.

Add to the above list the names of any local saints which are known to the children. Some children in the class may also know the names of other saints.

Teacher
Saint Columba (Saint Colmcille).

All
Pray for us.

Teacher
Glory be to the Father,
And to the Son,
And to the Holy Spirit.

All
As it was in the beginning,
Is now and ever shall be,
World without end. Amen.

Sign of the Cross.

Note: In the Artwork tomorrow the children will make simple 'story crosses'. On the crosses they will be asked to write the name of someone they know who has died. For homework tonight, ask the children to write down in a copy the name of someone they know, or have been told about, who has died. If possible encourage them to find out something about this person, e.g. where they lived/how old they were/what they looked like, etc.

Continue song: *Columba/Remember Them*

POEM

All Saints, All Souls

Remember those
Who kept the faith
Who always turned to pray,
Who showed the love of Jesus
In their lives from day to day.

Remember those
This special time
Who live with God above,
All Saints, All Souls,
And all our own
Who live with God in love.
Christy Kenneally

CHATTING

...about those who have died

The story of Columba tells us about the day he died. How do you think Columba felt that day? If you were Columba how would you feel? How did his friends feel? Perhaps someone you know has died. Tell us about them. Perhaps one of your relatives is dead. Do you remember them? Does your family remember them in any way? Do you think Columba's friends remembered him? How do you think his friends remembered him? Would they tell stories about him? Do you know stories about anyone who has died? Tell us a story. How do stories help us to remember people who have died? What would happen if we didn't tell stories about people who have died?

ART

The children will make a piece of artwork that will be a reminder of someone who has died. If they don't know anyone who has died, you might suggest a saint. This artwork may take two days to complete.

Making a Story Cross

You will need:

- Paper/card (if possible) for each child
- Adhesive
- Scissors
- Markers/crayons, etc.

To make the cross:

- Fold the paper/card in two, lengthways.
- Firmly press the fold and cut along the crease.
- Arrange the two strips of paper in the shape of a cross and glue securely.

Chat to the children about the person whose name they will write on the cross.

Ask the children to think about this person for a minute. What stories have you heard about this person? What do you know about them? Where did they live? What did they look like? What do you remember most about them? What do you like most about what you have been told about them?

When the children have thought sufficiently about the person, encourage them to draw pictures about the person on the cross.

To make a 'story cross'

- Using a strong colour, write the name of the dead person along the arm of the cross.
- Ask the children to draw pictures about the person along the shaft of the cross.
- Decorate the 'story cross' front and back.

PRAYERTIME

Sign of the Cross.

Teacher *(as the candle is lit)*
God the light of yesterday.
God the light of today.
God the light of tomorrow.

Today we ask God to be with all those who have died.
Like a mother cares for her child, like a father looks after his child, we ask God to care for those who have died. We know that they are with God.

All
May they rest in peace.

Teacher
For all the grandads and grannies who have died.

All
May they rest in peace.

Teacher
For all the dads and mums who have died.

All
May they rest in peace.

Teacher
For all the friends and neighbours who have died.

All
May they rest in peace.

Teacher
May God bless them and keep them.
Eternal rest grant unto them, O Lord.

All
May they rest in peace.

Song: *Remember Them*

Sign of the Cross.

Note: For the prayertime on Day Four you will need an autumn leaf for each child in the class. Ask the children to collect some autumn leaves and to bring them into school. The condition of the leaf is not important. If it is not feasible to ask the children to bring in an autumn leaf, ask them to draw a leaf at home tonight and to bring it to school with them tomorrow.

Day Four

Continue song: *Columba/Remember Them*

Continue art: *Making a story cross*

Recall story: *Columba*

CHATTING

...about the picture on page 7

The horse in the picture is crying. What do you think is going on in his mind? How do you think he feels? How do you think Columba is feeling? Have you ever felt as sad as this? Have you ever stroked a horse as Columba is doing? Have you ever felt sad about having to say 'Goodbye'? Look at Diarmuid's face. What do you think is going on in his mind? If you could go into the picture and talk to all three characters, what would you say to each one of them?

PRAYERTIME

Sign of the Cross.

Teacher
Today, as we light our candle, we remember that God is with us.
Hold the leaf gently in your hand. Look at the shape of the leaf. Look at all the different colours on the leaf. See the little marks or holes on your leaf. Feel the leaf. Maybe it feels hard. Maybe it feels crispy and dry. Your leaf wasn't always like this.

Let's close our eyes and remember...

In your mind imagine the springtime. Way back in spring this leaf was just a little bud, small and sticky. Then it pushed its way towards the sun and grew into a lovely fresh new leaf. Picture your leaf growing on the tree. The summer sun shines down on your leaf. Now notice your leaf changing colour. It is beginning to have lots and lots of different colours. Maybe it is turning brown or gold or rust or yellow. Your leaf wants to play with the wind. It doesn't want to hang on the tree anymore. Your leaf knows that it is time to leave the tree. Your leaf has left the tree. Winter has come and your leaf has died.

Open your eyes and ask God to bless the leaf as it curls up and dies.

Children hold up their leaf.

Bless this leaf, O God,
For sleep of winter now is here.
Bless this leaf, O God,
With the spring will come a new year.

Note: *Collect the leaves in a flower-pot and, if possible, cover them with a little potting compost/earth, or alternatively just place the leaves in a jar on the nature table.*

We pray together:

All
Glory be to the Father...

Sign of the Cross.

Day Five

WORKSHEET

If you wish to use the worksheet or workbook page which accompanies this lesson, this is an appropriate time to do so.

PRAYERTIME

Note: In preparation for the prayertime arrange the room so that there is space for the children to place their 'story crosses'. If possible, gather the children around this space. Children, in groups of five or six, will process with their crosses. Each child places his/her cross and calls out the name of the person who has died. (If this is too difficult or too sensitive for your class, just ask each child to place the cross down gently, to bow and return to her/his desk.)

This might be an opportunity to invite parents/guardians to join informally with the children as they pray for those who have died.

Sign of the Cross.

Teacher *(as the candle is lit)*
God the light of yesterday.
God the light of today.
God the light of tomorrow.

Today we are going to remember those who have died.

All
Song: *Remember Them*

Invite the children to come forward.

All *(after each group of children)*
Eternal rest grant unto them, O Lord.
May they rest in peace. Amen.

Teacher
We remember those who are feeling sad and lonely because someone they love has died. We ask God to remember all those who have died. Eternal rest grant unto them, O Lord.

All
May they rest in peace. Amen.

Poem: *All Saints, All Souls*

Sign of the Cross.

Note: When finished, you might like to display the crosses in the classroom using a title such as 'Our Crosses tell a Story' or 'We Remember', etc.

Columba

Patricia Hegarty

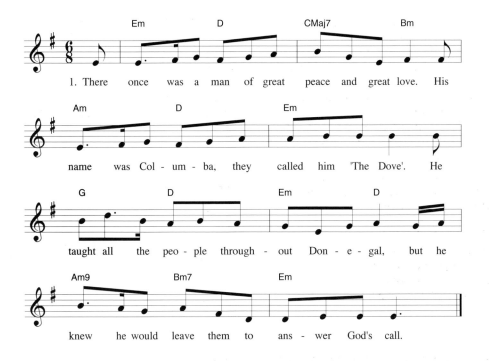

1. There once was a man of great peace and great love. His
name was Col - um - ba, they called him 'The Dove'. He
taught all the peo - ple through - out Don - e - gal, but he
knew he would leave them to ans - wer God's call.

2. When the time came to say his goodbyes,
   His friends gathered round him with tears in their eyes.
   'Do not be sad', he said. 'This you must know:
   My God will be with me wherever I go.'

3. Columba set sail and far did he roam,
   He came to Iona and made it his home.
   He lived there a long life of teaching and prayer
   And the people were happy Columba was there.

4. When the time came for Columba to die,
   His friends gathered round him with tears in their eyes.
   'Do not be sad', he said. 'This you must know:
   My God will be with me wherever I go.'

Remember Them

Words: Clare Maloney
Music: Patricia Hegarty

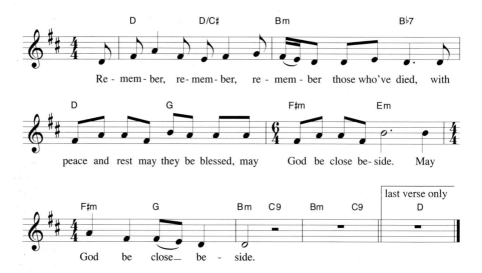

Re - mem - ber, re - mem - ber, re - mem - ber those who've died, with

peace and rest may they be blessed, may God be close be- side. May

God be close— be - side.

2. God keep them, God bless them,
God shine your love on them
Forever and forever, forever amen,
Forever more, amen.

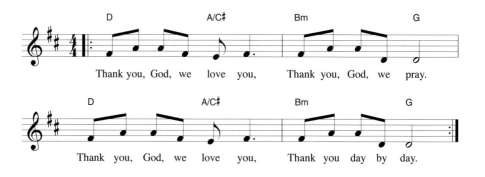

Thank you, God, we love you, Thank you, God, we pray.

Thank you, God, we love you, Thank you day by day.

Repeat Verse 1

Lesson 7: In Jesus' Time

And the Word became flesh
and lived among us.
(John 1:14)

And Jesus increased in wisdom and in years,
and in divine and human favour.
(Luke 2:52)

For the first time we introduce the children to the background of Jesus, his time and place. Not every child comes to school with a prior knowledge of Jesus and who he is. Apart from the Christmas and Easter stories in the infant classes, this may be the child's first real introduction to the historical Jesus.

Jesus is the 'image of the unseen God' *(Col 1:15)*. In his own life, in his deeds, in his attitudes towards people, Jesus shows us who God is and what God is like: loving, compassionate, embracing, forgiving, accepting. If we are to help children to have a real understanding of and relationship with Jesus we must begin by showing them Jesus as he walked, talked, ate and travelled with the people of his day. We must introduce them to the Jewish culture and way of life – a profoundly rich culture to which we as Christians are also heirs.

In these lessons then, we help the children to realise that Jesus grew up in Nazareth like any other Jewish child of his time. He lived in a typical Palestinian flat-roofed house, learned to read and write at the synagogue with the other Jewish boys, played the local games with his friends, joined in the Jewish festivals, and observed Jewish laws and customs. As he grew up he had many friends with whom he chatted, played, explored, shared, celebrated and travelled.

Jesus was steeped in all the religious and social traditions of the day. His immersion in the world of first-century Palestine enabled him to speak to people in images they understood and of situations they could identify with.

Much of what he learned in his early years about the Jewish way of life he would have learned from Mary and Joseph in the home. It is difficult for children in First Class/Primary Three to understand fully this historical and cultural background. In this lesson we focus on Jesus' everyday life as he grew up in Nazareth – the type of house he lived in; the games he played; the synagogue he went to, etc. These aspects of Jewish life are introduced to the children primarily through activities and songs.

FOR THE TEACHER:

I am a Jew because the faith of Israel demands of me no abdication of the mind.
I am a Jew because the faith of Israel requires of me all the devotion of my heart.
I am a Jew because in every place where suffering weeps, the Jew weeps.
I am a Jew because the promise of Israel is the universal promise.
I am a Jew because, for Israel, the world is not yet completed: we are completing it.
I am a Jew because, for Israel, humanity is not yet fully formed; humanity must perfect itself.
Edmond Fleg

Jesus Son of Mary

Jesus Son of Mary
    be born in us today.
Jesus lost in the Temple
    seek us when we pray.
Jesus living in Nazareth
    make our house your home.
Jesus in desert tempted
    forgive us when we roam.
Jesus making water wine
    fill us with your life divine.
Jesus light upon our way
    ever in our darkness shine.
Jesus healer of the sick
    make us strong and whole.
Jesus betrayed, denied
    protect our body and soul.

Jesus upon the cross
    our sure Saviour be.
Jesus risen from the dead
    give us life eternally.
Jesus, King, Ascended Lord
    evermore by us adored.
        David Adam

What am I trying to do?

To introduce the children to the historical Jesus who grew up, lived, and eventually ministered within a Jewish culture.

Why?

So that the children may begin to learn about the historical and cultural context within which Jesus lived and so lay the foundation for an ongoing understanding of the Incarnation.

Overview of the Week

Song: *The Passover Song*	Continue song			
	Did You Know?			
Did You Know?	Story: *The Passover*	Continue song	Continue song, art	Repeat poem
Chatting about houses	Chatting about the story	Chatting about school in Jesus' time	Chatting about food in Jesus' day	Worksheet
Activity: *This is the Way...*	Activity: *This is the Way...*	Art: *A Scroll*	Poem: *Jesus Growing Up*	Chatting about the picture
Prayertime	Prayertime	Prayertime	Prayertime	Prayertime

Day One

SONG

The Passover Song

DID YOU KNOW?

Jesus grew up in a town called Nazareth. In his day there was no electricity, no TV, no computers, no running water and no cars! People walked everywhere – they were great walkers. Sometimes people had donkeys, and if you were very well-off you might have a horse. The streets of Nazareth were narrow and full of people and clutter and noise. The houses didn't look like our houses today either – they were flat-roofed with no chimney. Usually the houses had one door and one room which was often divided in half, with the people living on one side of the room and their animals on the other! The flat roof on the house came in handy because people often kept their tools on the roof, e.g. a fisherman might keep his old nets on the roof, or a carpenter might keep his saw, his hammer and his adze on the roof. *(In the picture in the pupil's book, Jesus is holding an adze in his left hand.)* The women used the roof to spread out their washing to dry, and sometimes men slept there at night. The stairs was on the outside of the house and it led up to the roof. The women cooked the family meals in an oven that was often outside the house.

CHATTING

...about houses

On your way to school this morning what did you see? Let's see if we can make a list of all the things we saw. *Talk to the children about the roads/traffic lights/cars/houses/footpaths/street lighting/lampposts/factories, etc.* Who knows the name of the town where Jesus grew up? Let's look at our list. Would Jesus have seen any of the things on our list as he walked to school? What do you think? Let's make a list of what Jesus might have seen on his way to school.

Have you ever noticed the different types of roofs on houses? Show me with your hand the shape of the roof on your home. Have you ever seen a flat roof on a house? What would it be like to have the animals in your home with you all the time?

Does your home have a chimney? What is a chimney for? Why do you think there were no chimneys on the houses in Nazareth? Have you ever cooked outside? Would food taste different if it was cooked outside? Why? Why not? Have you ever slept in a sleeping-bag on the floor? Did you like it? Do you have a stairs in your home? Where is it? Would you like to live in a house like the one Jesus lived in? Why?

ACTIVITY

This is the Way...

This game seeks to introduce the children to a selection of activities that took place in Jesus' time.

For this game the words of the rhyme are sung to the tune 'This is the way we wash our face … on a cold and frosty morning'.

The children form a circle. The leader/teacher shouts out the name of an activity, then does the action for the others to imitate. The teacher can be the leader until the children become familiar with the actions and with the activity.

Sweeping the Floor
Chat a little about how the women in Jesus' day had to sweep the floor with a broom made from twigs. Chat about the action of sweeping the floor. Encourage all the children to do the actions.

* This is the way they swept the floor,
  Swept the floor, swept the floor,
  This is the way they swept the floor
  When Jesus was a boy.

Filling the Lamp
Chat about the fact that there was no electricity in Jesus' day so people used small lamps filled with olive oil to give them light. Chat about the actions of filling the lamp.

* This is the way they filled the lamp…

Grinding the Corn
Chat about how the women made the flour by grinding the grains of wheat between two big stones called a quern.
Chat about the actions of grinding the flour.

* This is the way they made the flour…

Making the Bread
Chat about how the women made the bread by hand and baked it in an oven which was usually outside the house.
Chat about the actions of bread-making.

* This is the way they baked the bread…

Sawing the Wood
Chat about how some men worked as carpenters. They made simple wooden furniture and wooden tools by hand.
Chat about the actions of cutting wood.

* This is the way they sawed the wood…

Rowing the Boats
Chat about how the fishermen caught fish which would be sold at the market.
Chat about the actions of rowing.

* This is the way they rowed the boat…

Carrying Water
Chat about the fact that in Jesus' day there was no running water in the houses. Women

had to carry water in large jars from the wells. They carried the water-jars on their heads. Chat about the actions of carrying water from the well.

- This is the way they carried the water...

PRAYERTIME

Sign of the Cross.

Teacher *(as the candle is lit)*
Holy are you,
Holy is your name,
O Lord, our God.

Let us ask God's blessing on all those who live today in the country where Jesus grew up.

All
Holy are you,
Holy is your name,
O Lord, our God.

Teacher
For those who bake bread.

All
Holy are you,
Holy is your name,
O Lord, our God.

Teacher
For those who row the boats.

All
Holy are you,
Holy is your name,
O Lord, our God.

Teacher
For all those who work in the home.

All
Holy are you,
Holy is your name,
O Lord, our God.

Teacher
For those who sweep the floors.

All
Holy are you,

Holy is your name,
O Lord, our God.

Teacher
For those who work with wood.

All
Holy are you,
Holy is your name,
O Lord, our God.

Sign of the Cross.

Note: For the artwork on Day Three you will need an 'empty' toilet roll for each child. Ask the children to start bringing them in.

Day Two

Continue song: *The Passover Song*

DID YOU KNOW?

The Passover is a very holy, happy feast. Each year the Jewish people celebrate this feast. They remember the meal eaten by Moses and his people before they escaped from Egypt where they were slaves. There are still lots of Jews in the world today. There are many Jews in our country.

STORY

The Passover

Moses and his people had been in a foreign country called Egypt for a long, long time. They had been captured and made to work as slaves. Now they wanted to go back to where they had come from. They wanted to go home. The Egyptians would not let them go home. The Egyptians wanted them to stay in Egypt and do all the work. Moses and his people were very unhappy. This was the same Moses who was left in the rushes as a baby and was watched over by Miriam. Moses grew up to be a great leader among his people.

One day he decided he would lead all his people out of Egypt and take them home to a place called the Promised Land.

First Moses talked to the King of Egypt and asked him to please let his people go home. The King said no. The King needed the people to do all the work.

After some time Moses tried again. This time the King said he would let Moses' people go. Moses and the people were happy. They were getting ready to leave when the King changed his mind. He sent his soldiers to stop them from going. Moses and his people were very disappointed.

'We have asked the King many times to let us go,' Moses said, 'but he will not. Now we will not ask him any more, we will just go.' But Moses also knew that they would have to be very careful. If the King found out that they were planning to run away, he would send his soldiers to stop them and bring them back. Moses and his people would have to make very careful plans.

Moses told the people to get ready. He told them to pack up whatever they needed. He said they couldn't take very much with them because they would have to travel quickly. They would sneak off in the middle of the night when all the Egyptians were fast asleep in their beds. They would travel all through the night and be as far away as they could by morning.

'We will not have time to stop and eat,' Moses told them, 'so, we must make a special meal before we go.' He told the people to kill a one-year-old lamb and cook it for the meal. He told them to bake some bread to eat as well.

'But Moses, if we make the kind of bread we always make,' said one woman, 'we will have to wait for the yeast in the bread to rise and that takes a long time.'

'This will be a special meal,' Moses said. 'We will have a special one-year-old lamb and we will have special bread too – unleavened bread. This bread will be different from all other bread. It will be new bread without any yeast, so we will not have to wait for it to rise. It will be flat.'

Then Moses said to the people, 'Now, remember, we must be ready to leave quickly, so you must not sit down to eat our special meal. You must eat it standing up with your coat on and your walking staff in your hand.'

The people did everything exactly as Moses had told them. As they were eating their meal, they prayed to God to bring them safely to the Promised Land. Then, in the darkness of the night, they set off; young children, old people, mothers, fathers, daughters and sons.

In the morning, by the time the King of Egypt woke up, they were gone! Moses and his people were glad to have left Egypt behind them.

CHATTING

...about the story

The people in the story were Jesus' people. They were his ancestors. Your ancestors are your gran, grandad, their mum, dad, gran and grandad, and so on. Do you think that would have anything to do with why Jesus would have liked the story so much? Do you know who any of your ancestors were? Do you think you'd like to hear stories about them? Perhaps you know some stories about them already. Jesus' ancestors had been living in a foreign country. Have you ever been in a foreign country? What was it like? Would you like to have stayed there for good? Why?

The people in the story wanted to go home. Why do you think they wanted to go home? Have you ever been somewhere and felt you wanted to go home? Would you like to tell us about it? Moses and his people were very unhappy. Imagine you were talking to some of Moses' people. Imagine you asked them what was making them unhappy. What do you think they would tell you?

The people had no choice but to sneak off in the night. Try to imagine that your family is there in Egypt with Moses' people. You are getting ready to have your meal. What are you going to eat? Why? Now that you have packed your things and eaten your meal you have to set off on a long journey. How do you feel about that? This special meal was called the Passover. Why do you think it was called this? Why do you think they had different bread that night? What does yeast do to bread? Have you ever eaten 'flat bread'?

ACTIVITY

**This is the way
...they played their games**

The following are some of the games that Jesus might have played as a young boy. They are games with which the children are already familiar – hide-and-seek, tug-of-war, blindman's-buff, tossing pebbles and catching them on the back of their hands, hop-scotch, marbles. You might like to choose one of these games, sing the rhyme and play the game with the children. Perhaps the children could make up a new game! These games could be played in the hall or alternatively the children could be encouraged to play them in the school yard at break-time. Chat to the children about the games. Chat about playing the games together.

- Leader/teacher shouts out the name of a game, e.g. hide-and-seek.
- This is the way they played hide-and-seek, played hide-and-seek, played hide-and-seek,
  this is the way they played hide-and-seek, when Jesus was a boy.
- Children then play the game.
- Leader/teacher could then shout out the name of another game, e.g. blindman's-buff/marbles/noughts and crosses, etc., sing the rhyme and play the game.

PRAYERTIME

Sign of the Cross.

Teacher (*as the candle is lit*)
Holy are you,
Holy is your name,
O Lord, our God.

You led your people out of Egypt.

All
Holy are you,
Holy is your name,
O Lord, our God.

Teacher
You gave them special bread to eat.

All
Holy are you,
Holy is your name,
O Lord, our God.

Teacher
You gave them special lamb.

All
Holy are you,
Holy is your name,
O Lord, our God.

Teacher
You were with them when they travelled.

All
Holy are you,
Holy is your name,
O Lord, our God.

Glory be to the Father...

Sign of the Cross.

Note: *Remind the children to bring in 'empty' toilet-rolls for the artwork on Day Three.*

Continue song: *The Passover Song*

CHATTING

...about school in Jesus' time

How do you think Jesus travelled to school? Would he have gone by car? What time does our school start at? Who brings you to school? What would Jesus have learned? Would he have learned to read? Would he have sat in tables and chairs like yours? How would he have sat on the floor? What would it be like to sit on the floor all day? What language do we speak? Jesus would have spoken a language called Aramaic. But Jesus read and wrote in a language called Hebrew. Jewish children today still learn to write in Hebrew. What sort of copies do you have? Show us one of your copies. How do you write on your copy? This is how Jesus would have written – from the right side of the page to the left! Often he would have written Hebrew on a piece of material called a scroll. He wouldn't have had a copy like you have. When he was finished with the scrolls he rolled them up neatly.

ART

A Scroll

Note: This art may take two days to complete. The scrolls will be used in the prayertime on Day Five.

Choose one of the following phrases/prayers for the children to write. Ask the children to copy the phrase from the blackboard onto their scroll.

'Peace be with you' in Hebrew = שׁ ל ו ם

or

A Jewish prayer:
Holy are you,
Holy is your name,
O Lord, our God.

or

A Passover prayer: We will praise our God forever.

For each child you will need:
- Two lollipop sticks/large cotton-buds, for both ends of the scroll
- A long strip of paper *(the size of the lollipop stick/cotton-bud will determine the width of the paper for the scroll.)*
- Crayons/markers
- Piece of brightly coloured wool
- One 'empty' toilet-roll for the scroll container.
- Adhesive tape
- Scissors

To make the scroll
Ask the children to copy the phrase onto their sheet. Decorate the page. Place a lollipop stick/cotton-bud on each end of the scroll. Secure the lollipop stick/cotton-bud to the strip of paper with adhesive tape and roll the two edges inwards to make a scroll. Tie the rolled-up scroll with a piece of wool. Decorate the scroll container (toilet-roll). Place the scroll in the container.

PRAYERTIME

Sign of the Cross.

Teacher *(as the candle is lit)*
We will praise our God for ever.

Close your eyes.
Place your hands gently on your lap.
Place your feet on the floor.
Listen to your heart beat.
Feel your breath travel gently in and out of your body.

As you sit comfortably in your seat you can go anywhere you like in your mind. Let's go back to Nazareth when Jesus was a young boy. Imagine that you are a child in Nazareth the same age as Jesus. One day you are outside your house playing by yourself. You hear someone calling your name. You look around. You wonder who it is. Look again. It's Jesus. See him standing there in the sun waiting for you to play with him. He tells you that he is waiting for you to play a game of hide-and-seek with him. This is your favourite game. You hide. Jesus chases and runs and searches for you. He finds you! Then it's Jesus' turn to hide. Look for him. Try in the house, maybe he is hiding on the flat roof, maybe he has gone to the well. Where is he? He must have found a really good hiding-place. Look! There he is hiding behind a big tree. Sneak up behind him quietly and tickle him. You both laugh and laugh. It feels good to be having such great fun with Jesus. Soon it's time to go home. Say goodbye to Jesus. Watch as he waves to you. Listen, he is calling. He is calling really loudly... 'Come back soon.' With your inside voice talk to Jesus. Thank him for the fun you have had with him.

Open your eyes... Stretch...

Sign of the Cross.

Day Four

Continue song: *The Passover Song*

Continue art: *A Scroll*

CHATTING

...about food in Jesus' day

What sort of food did Jesus eat, I wonder? What is your favourite food? How did they cook the food at the time of Jesus? Have you ever watched someone cook outside? Tell us about it. Jesus would have eaten outside. Have you ever eaten outside? Tell us about it. Jesus would have eaten cheese. Do you like cheese? What is your favourite cheese? What is cheese made from? What do you eat cheese with? Jesus would have loved eating fruit, especially figs and olives and grapes. What is your favourite fruit? Jesus would have had fresh water to drink from the well. When he grew up he would also have had wine. What is your favourite drink? Do you like milk? Do you usually drink water with your lunch? Why not? Jesus loved bread. When he ate bread it wasn't cut with a knife, it was always broken into pieces by hand. Have you ever broken bread with your hands. Tell us about a time when you might have broken bread with your hands – maybe it was when you had a picnic, maybe it was a time when there was no adult around to cut the bread with a knife. Do you like bread? What's your favourite type of bread?

POEM

Jesus Growing Up

Mary loved her little boy.
Joseph's heart was full of joy.
Rocked him in a cradle strong.
Rocked him to a desert song.

Rabbi taught the growing lad
Stories joyful, stories sad.
Rabbi loved him as a son,
God's anointed chosen one.

Helping Mary make a meal,
Helping Joseph mend a wheel.
Growing strong and growing tall,
Waiting for the Father's call.
Christy Kenneally

PRAYERTIME

Sign of the Cross.

Song: *The Passover Song*

Teacher *(as the candle is lit)*
Holy are you,
Holy is your name,
O Lord, our God.

You gave food to Moses and his people.
You gave food to Jesus and his people.
You give food to us today.
Let us give thanks to the Lord our God.

All
*Baruh atah adonai eloheinu.

Teacher
For the bread we eat.
Let us give thanks to the Lord our God.

All
Baruh atah adonai eloheinu.

Teacher
For the cheese we eat.
Let us give thanks to the Lord our God.

All
Baruh atah adonai eloheinu.

Teacher
For the fruit we eat.
Let us give thanks to the Lord our God.

All
Baruh atah adonai eloheinu.

Teacher
For the water and milk we drink.
Let us give thanks to the Lord our God.

All
Baruh atah adonai eloheinu.

Teacher
Let us thank God for the people who prepare
our food every day so that we can grow strong
and tall.

All
Our Father…

Sign of the Cross.

*Blessed are you Lord God.

Repeat poem: *Jesus Growing Up*

WORKSHEET

If you wish to use the worksheet or workbook
page which accompanies this lesson, this is an
appropriate time to do so.

CHATTING

…about the picture on pages 8 and 9

The people in this picture are busy working.
What are they doing? What is different about
how they are making the bread etc? Look at
their clothes. In what ways are their clothes
different from ours? Their home is different
too. How? If you could be in this picture, what
would you like to be doing? Imagine you
could go into the picture and bring all these
people home with you. What would they
think about your home? What would they
find strange or different?

PRAYERTIME

*Note: Ask the children to come forward and to
place their scrolls in a central position. If possible,
ask the children to form a circle around the scrolls.
In this prayertime the children will be introduced
to a 'prayer-round', using a simple prayer that
would have been known to Jesus. To begin the*

round the leader faces the child on her/his left, shakes the child's hand and says: ' Shalom.' The child responds: 'Shalom.' The same child then turns to the child on her/his left, and says: 'Shalom', shakes that child's hand, etc., and so the prayer-round continues until it comes back to the leader.

Sign of the Cross.

Song: *Passover*

Teacher *(as the candle is lit)*
Holy are you,
Holy is your name,
O Lord, our God.

When Jesus went to school he learned to pray. He loved to talk with God. Sometimes he talked to God with his inside voice that no one else could hear. Sometimes he talked out loud to God. He loved God very much. Jesus would have learned some of his prayers at school. This is one of the prayers that he would have learned. It's a very short prayer: 'Shalom.' It means 'Peace be with you'.

Today we are going to say this prayer.
We are going to offer each other the gift of peace.
We are going to use words and actions.

Leader
Turning to the left, offers a handshake of peace.
Shalom.

Child 1
Shalom.

Child 1
Turning to the left, offers a handshake of peace.
Shalom.

Child 2
Shalom.

Child 2
Turning to the left, offers a handshake of peace.
Shalom.

Child 3
Shalom.

Continue until each child has given and received a handshake of peace.

Leader
We have given to each other the gift of peace.
Now let us ask God to bless the world with peace.
For our families.

All
Peace be with them.

Teacher
For our friends in the neighbourhood.

All
Peace be with them.

Teacher
For all the classes in our school.

All
Peace be with them.

Teacher
For all the teachers in our school.

All
Peace be with them.

Teacher
For all people in our country.

All
Peace be with them.

Teacher
For all people throughout the world.

All
Peace be with them.

Teacher
Let us all hold hands and sing our song.

All
Sing: *The Passover Song*

Sign of the Cross.

The Passover Song

Clare Maloney

Refrain:

Ba - ruh a - tah a - don ai el - o - hei - nu,

el - o - hei - nu a - do - nai,

ba - ruh a - tah a - don - ai el - o - hei - nu,

el - o - hei - nu a - don - ai. 1. Re -

mem - ber the Pass - ov - er sto - ry. Re -

mem - ber the Pass - ov - er meal. Re -

mem - ber the jour - ney to free - dom.

Mos - es said 'Let my peo - ple go free.'

2. Remember the Passover story.
   Remember the Passover meal.
   Remember the eating of unleavened bread.
   'People! Make ready to flee!'

Lesson 8: Jesus – Journey Man

I am the Way, and the Truth, and the Life.
(John 14:6)

Journey is one of the great themes of human history and is echoed frequently in biblical narratives. Journey is used as a metaphor for the individual's path through life. The Church, too, taps into this imagery when describing the people of God as a pilgrim people – a people on the move, a people not yet arrived.

In this lesson we focus on the children's everyday experience of making journeys. The making of a journey, for anyone, be it long or short, familiar or unfamiliar, usually follows a particular sequence. First a decision is made, for whatever reason, to go on a journey. Then follows the preparations. Advice, information, directions, maps, instructions may, or indeed may not, be gathered! Finally, as we set off, the emotions that the particular journey calls forth – fear, excitement, joy, sadness, hope, love, expectation – travel along with us. Ultimately, we arrive. The journey is at its end. Completed.

As adults, it is easy to recognise this process and to see within it a mirror of life's journey. But children also make countless journeys and they can be encouraged to reflect on their own experiences. Children's journeys can be very familiar to them, as when they go to the shop for an ice-cream. They can also be unfamiliar, different, even frightening, as when they move to a new school or a new neighbourhood, or when they have to go to hospital, or visit the dentist. Their journeys can be short or long, happy or sad, made alone or with others. Sometimes they will know their way, at other times they may have to ask directions. They may even get lost. Unfortunately, children, and indeed adults, spend so much time focusing on the beginning or the end of a journey that the experience of the journey itself is often lost.

The Bible recounts many great journeys, epic stories of movement, displacement, trust, fear, hopes of new beginnings. Jesus himself lived a nomadic life. He never settled in one particular spot but travelled from place to place, from village to village. His life was framed by significant journeys. A journey from Nazareth to Bethlehem led to his birth. A journey to Egypt saved his life. A journey into Jerusalem marked his death. And a journey to Emmaus proclaimed his Resurrection.

FOR THE TEACHER:

A thought before beginning

Journey
O God,
who am I now?
Once I was secure
    in familiar territory
    in my sense of belonging
unquestioning of
    the norms of my culture
    the assumptions built into my language
    the values shared by my society.
But now you have called me out and away
    from home
and I do not know where you are leading.
I am empty, unsure, uncomfortable,
I have only a beckoning star to follow.
Journeying God,
pitch your tent with mine
so that I may not be deterred
by hardship, strangeness, doubt.
Show me the movement I must make
    toward a wealth not dependent on
    possessions,
    toward a wisdom not based on books,
    toward a strength not bolstered by might,
    toward a God not confined to heaven
but scandalously earthed, poor, unrecognised.
Help me to find myself
as I walk in others' shoes.
    Kate Compston

What am I trying to do?

To help the children to reflect on the different journeys that they make in their own lives.

Why?

So that they will become aware of the process of journeying in their own lives, realise that Jesus too took part in that process, and begin to lay down the foundation for a future understanding of the symbol of Life as Journey.

Overview of the Week

		Continue song	Continue song	
		Recall story	Story: *Jesus Goes to*	
Song: *We Go on a*	Continue song	Chatting about	*Jerusalem*	
Journey	Story: *Shortening the*	journeys with	*or*	Worksheet
Chatting about	*Road*	others/by myself	Poem: *Jesus is Lost*	Chatting about the
everyday journeys	Chatting about the	Poem: *Many Ways to*	Chatting about the	picture
Art: *Mapping it out*	story	*Travel*	story/poem	Bible Procession
Prayertime	Prayertime	Prayertime	Prayertime	Ritual

Day One

SONG

We Go on a Journey

Note: Throughout this week we will be reflecting with the children on their experiences of journeys. However, you might like to give them a here-and-now experience by bringing them on a journey as a class. This journey could be a routine one, like a trip to the hall, or it could be a special journey like a nature walk. On returning from their trip the children could then chat about what they saw etc.

CHATTING

...about everyday journeys

From Monday to Friday we all make a daily journey. Can you think what it is? How do you make that journey – by car, bus, on foot, etc? Do others make the journey with you? How long does it take? What streets/buildings/places, etc. do you pass by on your way? How do you feel when you make the journey to school? How do you feel on the way home from school? Which journey do you like best? Why? Would you describe your journey to and from school as a long journey or a short journey? Why? Sometimes on a journey there is a dangerous corner or a bad bend – do you know one of these? Sometimes on a journey there is a crossroad – do you know what a crossroad is? Sometimes on a journey there are signposts. Do you know any signposts? Sometimes on a journey there are other road signs – have you ever seen any of these?

Tell us about the longest journey you have ever been on. Where did you go? How did you travel? Who else travelled with you? How long did the journey take? Did you have to take anything with you on the journey? Can you remember the names of any places you passed through on your way? Which did you enjoy most, the journey there or the journey back? Why? What did you do to pass the time on the journey? Did you make any stops along the way? Looking back on that journey now, what did you like best about it? What did you not like about it? Which do you think seemed quickest, the journey away or the journey back? Why?

ART

Mapping It Out

Give each child a large sheet of drawing paper.
Invite them to draw their school in the
bottom left-hand corner.
Invite them to draw their home in the top
right-hand corner.
Invite them to draw a winding road between
the two.
Ask the children to look at their map, then to
close their eyes and think of some of the
things they see every day when travelling
between home and school.
When they have opened their eyes chat to the
children about the road signs/buildings/traffic
lights, etc. that can be seen on their journey to
school.
Now ask them to draw in anything they see
along the way as they make their journey
between home and school each day.

PRAYERTIME

Sign of the Cross.

Teacher
As we light our candle we ask God the Father,
Son and Holy Spirit to be with us on all the
journeys we make throughout the day. We ask
God to keep us safe as we travel between home
and school.

Teacher *(children repeating)*
Arise with me
in the morning.
Travel with me
through each day.
Welcome me
on my arrival.
God, be with me all the way.

All
May God be with us on our way.

Teacher
As we leave home to go to school.

All
May God be with us on our way.

Teacher
As we walk into the school yard in the
morning.

All
May God be with us on our way.

Teacher
As we go out to the playground at break-time.

All
May God be with us on our way.

Teacher
As we say goodbye to our teacher at the end of
the day.

All
May God be with us on our way.

Teacher
As we make our journey home in the
evenings.

All
May God be with us on our way.

Teacher *(children repeating)*
Arise with me
in the morning.
Travel with me
through each day.
Welcome me
on my arrival.
God, be with me all the way.

Sign of the Cross.

*Note: For the prayertime on Day Two you will
need Holy Water. For the Bible Procession Ritual
on Day Five of this and the following week you
will need a Bible and a candle. (Other additional
items like flowers, incense stick, some grains of
incense, a cloth, etc. may also be used.)*

Continue song: *We Go on a Journey*

STORY

Shortening the Road

One day the Goban Saor and his son set out on a long journey. When they had gone a little way the Goban Saor said, 'Son, shorten the road for me.'

The son thought his father was joking, but the Goban said again, 'Shorten the road for me son.' 'I cannot do that,' said the son. 'The road is as long as it is. No one can make it shorter.'

'If you cannot do a little thing like that,' said the Goban, 'we had better turn back home. Tomorrow we shall set out again. But I shall not finish the journey till you shorten the road for me.' So home they went.

The son's wife saw them coming, but she said nothing till they had eaten. Then she took the young man aside and asked, 'Why have you come back?' 'My father has set me a task that no one could do,' said the young man. 'He says he will not finish the journey till I shorten the road for him.' 'That is easy,' said his wife, 'Listen.' She whispered in his ear. The young man smiled.

Next morning the two set off at sunrise. When they had gone a little way the Goban said again: 'Son, shorten the road for me.'

'Once upon a time,' said the young man, 'there lived in Ireland a brave and mighty king,' and he began to tell his father a story.

It was a long story and a good story. The Goban and his son walked mile after mile and as the story went on they did not notice the journey going by and the road getting shorter. They were near the end of their journey before the story was finished. 'That was a fine story,' said the Goban. 'You shortened the road very nicely, my son.'

Traditional

CHATTING

...about the story

Where do you think the Goban Saor and his son might have been going? If you were the Goban Saor's son, what would you have thought he meant by 'Shorten the road for me son'? Why do you think the son's story-telling made the journey seem shorter? Do you like long journeys? Why? Why not? What makes a journey seem long? Do you think it would be easier and more enjoyable to make a long journey in a car or on a train? In a ship or on a plane? By bicycle or by foot?

PRAYERTIME

Note: Ideally this prayertime should take place at the end of the day as the children prepare to go home. You will need a Holy Water font or a small bowl and Holy Water. Place some Holy Water in the font or small bowl. You may like to put the small bowl of Holy Water/Holy Water font in a place where the children can reach it. The practice of blessing themselves as they come and go from the classroom could then be encouraged.

CHATTING

...about Holy Water

What is Holy Water? When do we use Holy Water? *Chat to the children about blessings.* We use Holy Water to bless people, places and things.

Hold up the Holy Water font or small bowl and

tell the children that this belongs to their classroom.

We will use it to bless ourselves as we leave the room. As we do, we will ask God to bless us as we go on our journey from the classroom at the end of the day.

Sign of the Cross.

Teacher
Today we are going to use the Holy Water from our font (or small bowl) to bless us all as we go home.
Our blessing will be:

All *(repeating after the teacher)*
Arise with me
in the morning.
Travel with me
through each day.
Welcome me
on my arrival.
God, be with me all the way.

As the children line up to go home, the teacher places Holy Water on the forehead of each child, saying:

Teacher
I bless you_____ on your journey home.

Child
God keep me safe.
This is continued for each child in the classroom.

All *(repeating after the teacher)*
Arise with me
in the morning.
Travel with me
through each day.
Welcome me
on my arrival.
God, be with me all the way.
Amen.

Sign of the Cross.

Day Three

Continue song: *We Go on a Journey*

Recall story: *Shortening the Road*

CHATTING

...about journeys with others/journeys by myself

What journeys can you make by yourself – to your friend's house? To the shop? To the park? To your neighbours? To school? On journeys that you make by yourself, you know the way. Can you tell me how to get from your home to your friend's home; from your home to the local shop; from your home to school, etc? Tell us what you have to be careful of when you make a journey by yourself?

Do you know a safe way to cross the road? Let's pretend we have a road through the middle of our classroom – let's see how you would cross the road. What journeys do you go on with your Mammy/Daddy/older brother/older sister/other adult? Why do you need a grown-up with you on these journeys? How does the grown-up look after you? Do they take your hand etc? Do grown-ups know the way? How do they know the way? What can they do if they don't know the way? Have you ever had to ask someone the way? Tell us about it. *(This might be a good point at which to revise relevant material from the School's Safety Awareness Programme or simply explain to children what to do if they get lost.)* Every journey has a beginning and every journey has an end. Tell us about an end or a beginning that you remember from one of your journeys.

POEM

Many Ways To Travel

There are many ways to travel
and one that I like
is to zoom down a hill
on a mountain bike.

There are many ways to travel
and another that's nice
is to slide on a sledge
on the snow and ice.

There are many ways to travel
and isn't it fun
to sail on the sea
in the wind and sun?

There are many ways to travel
but the best by far
is to ride on a rocket
to a distant star.

Tony Mitton

PRAYERTIME

Sign of the Cross.

Teacher
Travelling can be great fun. We can travel in
all sorts of ways. We can travel by car or by
bus, we can walk and skip, we can travel on
our bikes and on our rollerskates, we can travel
by boat or in the air. Let's ask God the Father,
Son and Holy Spirit to be with us as we travel
on our way.

All
God be with us all the way.

Teacher
When we travel by bus.

All
God be with us all the way.

Teacher
When we travel by foot.

All
God be with us all the way.

Teacher
When we travel in a wheelchair.

All
God be with us all the way.

Teacher
When we travel on our bikes.

All
God be with us all the way.

Teacher
When we travel on our own.

All
God be with us all the way.

Teacher
When we travel with others.

All
God be with us all the way.

Teacher
When we travel in our imaginations.

All
God be with us all the way.

Teacher
Now close your eyes and think of a really good
way to travel. We give praise and thanks to
God. Let us ask God the Father, Son and Holy
Spirit to be with us on all of our journeys.

All
Arise with me
in the morning.
Travel with me
through each day.
Welcome me
on my arrival.
God, be with me all the way.
Amen.

Sign of the Cross.

Day Four

Continue song: *We Go on a Journey*

STORY

Jesus Goes To Jerusalem
(Adapted from Luke 2:41-50)

Once, when Jesus was twelve years old, Mary and Joseph decided that they would take him to the city for the Passover celebration. Jesus was looking forward to the journey. It would take several days to get there. Many of the families from Nazareth would travel together. Many of his friends would be going too. Jesus was very excited.

When the morning came and everyone was ready, they all set off together. They sang songs along the way. They stopped every now and then for a rest and something to eat. Jesus was having a wonderful time. He loved going on journeys like this.

The city was very crowded. Lots of people had come for the Passover. Jesus saw one very big building. Joseph explained to him that this was the Temple where the Holy Men met together, and where people went to pray and listen to the stories from the Bible. Jesus wanted to go inside, but just then some of his friends called to him and he ran off.

Later, Jesus went back to the Temple. At first he was a little afraid. The Temple was a very big place, but he went in.

The Holy Men saw him. They were puzzled. They wondered what a child like this was doing in the Temple. They asked Jesus where he was from, where the rest of his family were, if he was a Jew, and lots more questions. They liked listening to Jesus and learning what he had to say about God.

Just then Mary and Joseph arrived. They had missed Jesus and had been searching everywhere for him. Joseph was cross. Mary was worried. They wanted to know why he had come to the Temple.

'My Father's business,' Jesus answered. No one was quite sure what he meant.

Mary and Joseph looked at each other. Then they took Jesus by the hand. Next day they followed all their friends on the long journey home to Nazareth.

POEM

Jesus is Lost

Note: As an alternative to the story Jesus Goes to Jerusalem, *you may like to read this poem to the children.*

'Where is that boy?' said Mary,
'I thought he was with you.'
'Well, I don't know,' said Joseph,
'I thought you had him too.
I was chatting for a minute
With old Matthew in the square.
When I looked around for Jesus,
He was gone, he wasn't there.'

'He's very bold,' said Mary,
'He knows he's not allowed
To run off playing on his own
In such a busy crowd.'
'Well, never mind,' said Joseph,
'It's no use giving out.
Let's go and try to find him,
He's somewhere hereabouts.'

They found him in the Temple
And Joseph said, 'Come, quick!
You're really very naughty,
Your mother's worried sick.'
But Mary simply hugged him.
'We'll go home now,' said she,
'It's good to have you back, you know,
Home's where we'd like to be!'
Finbar O'Connor

CHATTING

...about the story/poem

Have you ever set off on a journey to a special event? A party? A match? A celebration? A school tour? How did you feel as you set off? Tell us about the journey. Did you have fun? Did you go by yourself or with others? Would you like to have been on the journey Jesus went on? Have you ever been to a big city? What was it like? Did you ever get lost on a journey? How did you feel? Who found you? How did they feel?

How do you think Mary and Joseph felt when they couldn't find Jesus? How did they feel when they found him in the Temple? Do you know any building that you think might be a bit like the Temple?

PRAYERTIME

Sign of the Cross.

Teacher
We light our candle.

Close your eyes.
Place your hands gently on your lap and your feet on the floor.
God is with us in our heartbeat.
God is with us in our breath as it goes in and out of our lungs.

Feel your breath as it moves gently in and out of your body, bringing life to your whole body. Go into your inside world where it is dark and safe and quiet and peaceful. We can travel anywhere in our imagination.

When Jesus was twelve he went on a journey to Jerusalem. Imagine that you are going on this journey with Jesus. Mary and Joseph will be travelling too. Like Jesus, you are excited about going to the big city. You love journeys and you have never gone on this journey before. You set off along the road walking, as there were no cars in Jesus' time. When you feel tired you get a ride on the donkey. But mostly you play games with Jesus as you go along. Maybe you play 'I spy', or chasing games. It's good to be with Jesus.

Chat and talk with Jesus. Tell him some of your best stories. You know that Jesus loves you. Look, there is the big city – Jerusalem. You feel a little sad because the journey was fun. But all journeys come to an end and now it's time to say goodbye. Say goodbye to Jesus. Before you go, Jesus tells you how much he has enjoyed being with you. He tells you that he loves you and that you are very special to him. With your inside voice whisper something special in Jesus' ear. No one else can hear what you say. It is just between you and him. Jesus smiles.

Open your eyes.
Stretch.
Relax.

All
Arise with me
in the morning.
Travel with me
through each day.
Welcome me
on my arrival.
God, be with me all the way.
Amen.

Sign of the Cross.

Note: On Day Five the children are being introduced, for the first time, to the formal reading of the Word of God in the Bible. A child will be invited to read a short phrase from the Bible based on the story which is told in the lesson. The child who is to act as reader could be picked before the prayertime begins. To facilitate the reader, have the phrase, 'When Jesus was twelve years old he went on a journey', on a flashcard in advance of the prayertime. The flashcard could then be placed within the covers of the Bible so that the children will associate the phrase with the Bible.

It might be helpful to have a classroom Bible and to place it in a prominent position in the room. The children might help decide where best to place it. The Bible Procession Ritual can begin from there.

WORKSHEET

If you wish to use the worksheet or workbook page which accompanies this lesson, this is an appropriate time to do so.

CHATTING

...about the picture on pages 10 and 11

Can you find Joseph and Mary and Jesus in the picture? What do you think Jesus has in his bag? Do the people look happy? Do you think they are enjoying the journey? Have you ever gone on a journey like this? Would you like to? If you could be in the picture, who would you like to be? Would you like to ride on the camel? Would you like to be a bird in the basket? Perhaps they all sing songs to pass the journey. What might they sing? Perhaps they tell stories to shorten the road. What stories might they tell?

PRAYERTIME

Bible Procession Ritual

Take the Bible from its place in the classroom. Form a simple procession. As one child carries the Bible and another child carries the unlit candle (other items like flowers, incense stick, cloth, etc could also be carried in the procession), process to

a table where the Bible and the candle are placed reverently. Children bow and return to their seats.

Song: *We Go on a Journey*

Light the candle. You may also like to burn an incense stick or grains of incense.

Sign of the Cross.

Teacher
Note: If time allows, you might like to repeat the following and invite other children to come forward, raise the Bible and read the biblical phrase.

Jesus also went on a journey with Mary and Joseph one day.
_____ *(name reader)* will read the Word of God for us today.

The child is invited to come forward to read from the Bible.
The teacher takes the Bible from the table and ceremoniously hands it to the child.
The child faces the class, holding the Bible.

Teacher
We know that God is with us always. We know that God is with us in a special way when we read from the Bible. The Bible is God's story-book. This reading from the Bible is about a special journey that Jesus made with Mary and Joseph from Nazareth to Jerusalem. It was a very long journey. Jesus was a child. He loved going on journeys. Let's listen to God's word as we read from the Bible.

Reader
The Lord be with you.

All
And also with you.

Teacher
This reading is from the Gospel according to St Luke.

All
Glory to you, O Lord.

Reader
'When Jesus was twelve years old he went on a journey.'
The Gospel of the Lord *(raising the Bible)*.

All
Praise to you, Lord Jesus Christ.

Sign of the Cross.

We Go On A Journey

Kevin Farrell

1. Put on your seat — belt — sit back and smile. —

You're in the back — seat — here for a while.

We're on a jour - ney — mile af - ter mile —

and when we get — there — our jour - ney's worth - while.

Chorus:

Ev - 'ry day we go on diff - 'rent

jour - neys, some are short and some are —

long. Ev - 'ry day we go on diff - 'rent

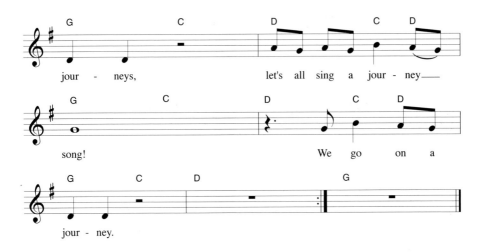

jour - neys,   let's all sing a jour - ney——

song!   We go on a

jour - ney.

2. Mary and Joseph walk hand in hand
   Searching for Jesus in a strange land,
   And when they find him, they turn and smile
   'Cos he's speaking and praying, their journey's worthwhile.

Lesson 9: Jesus – Story-teller

Jesus told the crowds all these things
in parables; without a parable
he told them nothing.
(Matthew 13:34)

Then they told their story
of what had happened...
(Luke 24:35)

Children love stories. They can listen enraptured to their favourite story being told over and over and over again. Even as adults we remember the magic of 'Once upon a time...', the excitement, the wonder as we got drawn into a world of fantasy and imagination. J.R.R. Tolkien once said that stories have the power to catch the breath and lift the heart. Their power should not be underestimated. They form our identity. They give expression to, and often shape, who we are as individuals, as family, as community, as nation. Indeed, when we are touched by the great mysteries of life and death, we often find someone to whom we can tell our story. Children are constantly hearing stories, some good, some bad. They hear them in chats at home with their families. They hear them when they gather in the playground with their friends. They hear them in the numerous cartoons and programmes they watch on television. Children are at ease with narrative language. In fact, they operate through its medium. Their fears, their angers, their hurts and their joys get told in story form.

The *seanchaí*, the *file*, and the bard, the professional story-keepers of the Celtic folklore tradition, were well aware of the importance of their role as story-tellers. Their function was to bring stories to life and to offer them to the listeners so that they could take shape in their hearts and in their consciousness.

Jesus grew up immersed in the great tales of his ancestors. As a child he would have heard stories time and time again about Abraham

and Sarah, about Moses and Miriam. He understood the power of story. 'Indeed, he would never speak to them except in parables' (Mt 13:34). He was story-teller *par excellence*. In language that was simple, in images that were familiar, in contexts that were ordinary, he wove his stories: about life and death, about despair and hope, about jealousy and love. In his story-telling he drew people face to face with the bountifulness of God's love and mercy. In Jesus, the story-teller, God's story continues.

In this lesson we introduce the children to the Parable of The Sower (Matthew 13:4-14), one of the many stories Jesus told. Parables are complex stories. Their language, however, is metaphorical and the images that are used are deeply symbolic. Young children are not ready to understand this abstract language, so we introduce them gradually to the richness of the parables by offering the stories to them in a manner appropriate to their age and development.

Several times during the school year we suggest that you might invite parents or guardians to take part in a Prayer Service in the classroom with their children. **This is optional. Each teacher will decide on its appropriateness for his or her own situation.** Inviting the parents/guardians in for these Prayer Services gives them the opportunity to see at first hand how children pray and to hear the prayer-language children use. It also provides them with insights into how the children are being taught to see themselves in relation to God and God in relation to them. A suitable time for the Prayer Service will vary from time to time and from place to place. One possibility is to invite the parents, guardians, or whoever is collecting the child on their behalf, to come twenty minutes earlier than usual. Obviously not all parents/guardians will be able to come. Grannies, grandads, minders, an older sister or brother might also be welcome to attend. If a particular child has no older person to accompany him or her to the Prayer Service, they can still take part. The teacher can herself or himself look after such children in a special way.

Should you decide to invite the parents/guardians, you may also wish to invite a priest or parish sister or another representative of the local parish team who may wish to lead or simply take part in the Prayer Service. This also provides the opportunity for the parish representative to take part in a meaningful way in the religious education of young children, and brings together the three agencies who are called on to work in partnership in the religious education of children: the school, the home and the parish.

What am I trying to do?

To help the children to reflect on their experience of hearing and telling stories and to introduce the children to the image of Jesus as story-teller by relating the Parable of The Sower.

Why?

So that the children may become aware of the importance of story-telling in people's lives, thus laying the foundation for a future understanding of the significance of the stories that Jesus told.

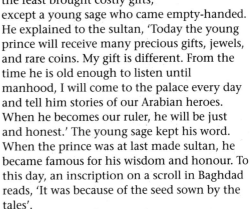

FOR THE TEACHER:

A thought before beginning

Many centuries ago, a rich sultan in Baghdad gave a banquet in honour of the birth of his son. All the nobility who partook of the feast brought costly gifts, except a young sage who came empty-handed. He explained to the sultan, 'Today the young prince will receive many precious gifts, jewels, and rare coins. My gift is different. From the time he is old enough to listen until manhood, I will come to the palace every day and tell him stories of our Arabian heroes. When he becomes our ruler, he will be just and honest.' The young sage kept his word. When the prince was at last made sultan, he became famous for his wisdom and honour. To this day, an inscription on a scroll in Baghdad reads, 'It was because of the seed sown by the tales'.

William J. Bausch

Overview of the Week

Song: *Once Upon a Time*			Continue song Activity: *My Favourite Story*	
Chatting about stories		Continue song Story: *The Parable of The Sower*	Picture-Book or Desk Mime: *Parable of The Sower*	
Story: *A Story Remembered*	Continue song Recall story	Chatting about the story	Worksheet	
Chatting about the story	Chatting about story-tellers	Poem: *Wait Till I Tell You*	Chatting about the picture	Bible Procession Ritual/Prayer Service
Prayertime	Activity: *Story Game* Prayertime	Prayertime	Prayertime	

Day One

Note: In advance of this week's work it might be helpful to have a copy of a Celtic story, one of Aesop's Fables, a Grimm's Fairy Tale, or a Hans Andersen story available.

SONG

Once Upon A Time

CHATTING

...about stories

Do you know any stories? What is your favourite story? Let's make a list of all the stories our class knows. Who told you these stories? Who else tells you stories? Tell us about someone who is good at telling stories. Tell us about someone who is very good at making up stories. Which do you like best: to read to yourself from a story-book, to listen to stories on a tape, or to have someone tell you a story? Why? Do you ever tell stories to others, to a baby sister or brother perhaps? Have you ever tried to make up a story of your own to tell? Sometimes it is difficult to make up a story; sometimes it is easy. Tell the person beside you the story of what you did when you went home from school yesterday, or a story about what you did when you were on holiday, or a story about when you were sick, etc.

STORY

A Story Remembered

Note: This story is adapted from The Táin

Once upon a time there were two very good friends called Eamonn and Morgan. They went to school together, where they spent seven years learning to be poets and story-tellers.

Eamonn and Morgan had a very good teacher whose name was Senchan. Senchan taught his pupils all the stories he knew. He would tell the story line by line and his pupils would repeat it after him. One day Senchan began to tell a story. Suddenly he stopped.

'What is the matter, teacher?' his pupils asked.

'Oh dear!' said Senchan, scratching his head, 'I cannot remember what comes next in the story. I have forgotten it. Oh dear, oh dear!' He started over again… and again.

But try as hard as he could, Senchan could not remember the rest of the story. He was very upset.

He called all the other poets and story-tellers in the land together to see if they could help him remember. But they were not much help. Some of them could remember some bits of the story and others could remember other bits, but between the lot of them they could not put the whole story together.

Then Senchan asked which of his pupils, in return for a blessing, would go in search of the whole story.

'We will gladly go,' said Eamonn and Morgan eagerly. And off they went.

They travelled many a long mile, on many a long road, for many a long day. They asked here and they asked there. They listened to many a story, but it was no use, they could not find the missing parts of the forgotten story. There was nothing more they could do. They would have to give up.

'It is getting dark now,' said Morgan, 'I will go and see if I can find a house where we can take shelter for the night.' And off he went.

When he was gone, Eamonn began to look around him. He saw a tall stone, about the size of a headstone. On it was written the name 'Fergus'. As he looked at the stone, some words sprang to Eamonn's mind. He spoke them to the stone. He said:

> If this rock could talk
> Fergus, what would it say?
> What memory would it unlock
> To send us on our way?

No sooner had Eamonn uttered the words than a great mist suddenly formed around him. For three days and three nights he could not be found. In the thick of the mist, the figure of Fergus approached Eamonn. He had a head of brown hair, he wore a green cloak, a red embroidered hooded tunic and bronze-coloured sandals. Fergus told Eamonn the whole story from start to finish, from beginning to end. As soon as he had finished, the mist cleared and Eamonn found Morgan waiting for him.

'Tell me where you have been,' said Morgan.

'It's a long story,' laughed Eamonn.

When they got home Eamonn told the teacher the whole story from beginning to end, just as Fergus had told it.

From that day on Eamonn and Morgan were blessed, they remembered every single word of every single story they ever heard. They never forgot anything.

CHATTING

...about the story

Do you think you would like a school without books? Did you ever learn anything off by heart? Can you say something you've learned by heart? Let's all say something together that we know off by heart. Would you like to go to a school like Eamonn's and Morgan's?

PRAYERTIME

Note: In preparation for this prayertime, place a selection of the children's favourite classroom story-books in a prominent position.

Sign of the Cross.

Teacher *(as the candle is lit)*
God our light.
Our light for all time.

It is good to have story-books to read. It is good to have someone to tell us stories. We all have our favourite story or our favourite story-book. We all have stories that we love to hear over and over again. Let us give thanks to God.

Close your eyes and think about your favourite story or your favourite story-book. Is your story a happy story or is it a sad story? Maybe it's a funny story. Maybe it's an exciting adventure story.

Today let's give praise to God for all our favourite stories.

All
We give praise to God for our favourite stories.

Teacher
Some stories make us laugh.
Who would like to name their favourite funny story?

For funny stories, we give praise to God.

All
We give praise to God for our favourite stories.

Teacher
Some stories make us sad.
Who would like to name their favourite sad story?

For sad stories, we give praise to God.

All
We give praise to God for our favourite stories.

Teacher
Some stories are exciting and thrilling.
Who would like to name their favourite adventure story?

91

For exciting stories, we give praise to God.

All
We give praise to God for our favourite stories.

Teacher
Let us praise God now for all the stories that
we have ever heard.
We pray to God.

All *(repeating after teacher)*
Praise
to God in the beginning,
in once upon a time.
Praise
to God ever after,
in word and story-line.
Amen.

Sign of the Cross.

Day Two

Continue song: *Once Upon a Time*

Recall story: *A Story Remembered*

CHATTING

...about story-tellers

Note: *During the following chat, it might be better
if the teacher told a brief version of some of the
stories suggested. Telling the stories rather than
reading them directly from a book can make the
story more immediate to the children and can take
less time.*

There are many famous story-tellers. Long ago
in Ireland the *seanchaí* told many stories. Here
are some of those stories... e.g. *The Children of
Lir, Diarmuid and Gráinne, The Goban Saor
(Shortening the Road).*

Aesop was a very famous story-teller. Aesop
told stories called fables. Have you heard of
*Town Mouse and Country Mouse, Swan Song,
How the Tortoise Got its Shell* and *The Jackdaw
who would be an Eagle.*

Hans Christian Anderson was a very famous
story-teller. You may have heard lots of his
stories: *The Princess and the Pea, Thumbelina,
The Emperor's New Clothes,* and one you
definitely all know – *The Ugly Duckling.*

There were also two brothers who were famous
story-tellers. They were the Grimm Brothers.
You have probably heard lots of their stories
too: *The Frog Prince, The Wolf and the Seven
Little Goats, Hansel and Gretel, Rapunzel,
Cinderella, The Musicians of Bremen* and
Rumpelstiltskin.

Would anyone like to be a story-teller and tell
one of these stories to the class?

ACTIVITY

Story Game

From the chatting above, choose a story with
which all the children are familiar.
Seat the children in a circle on the floor.

Take a soft ball.
The teacher rolls the ball towards one child.
That child begins to tell the story.
She/he tells a little of the story, then rolls the
ball towards someone else who must continue
the story, etc.

PRAYERTIME

Sign of the Cross.

Teacher *(as the candle is lit)*
God our light.
Our light for all time.

Let's be quiet and still and think about
somebody who tells you stories at home or
maybe at school, in the playground or maybe
on the bus.

Let us give praise to God for all the people

who tell us stories. Let us pray today for all story-tellers.

All
Praise God for story-tellers.

Teacher
Close your eyes and think. Who tells you stories in your home?
For story-tellers at home, we pray to God.

All
Praise God for story-tellers.

Teacher
Close your eyes and think. Who tells you stories in the classroom?
For story-tellers in the classroom, we pray to God.

All
Praise God for story-tellers.

Teacher
Sometimes story-tellers can be young. They have just a few stories to tell.
Sometimes story-tellers have been around for a long time. They have a lot of stories to tell.

All
Praise God for story-tellers.

Teacher
Thank you, God, for all story-tellers wherever they are.
Close your eyes for a moment. Think of someone who tells you stories. With your inside voice ask God to bless and care for that special story-teller.

Teacher *(children repeating)*
Praise
to God in the beginning,
in once upon a time.
Praise
to God ever after,
in word and story-line.
Amen.

Sign of the Cross.

Continue song: *Once Upon a Time*

STORY

Story-telling Ritual

The children can be encouraged to take up a special position for story-telling, e.g. in a circle. They might like to bring in a pillow or cushion to sit on as they listen to stories.

Sign of the Cross.

Teacher
For all the stories that we tell,
For all the stories that we read,
For all the stories that we hear,
We thank you, God. Amen.

The Parable of The Sower
(Based on Mt 13:4-10)

One day, a sower with a bag of seeds went out to sow. The sower scattered seeds here and scattered seeds there.

Some seeds fell at the side of the road. Hungry birds came and ate them all up.

Some seeds fell on stony ground where the soil was very shallow. These seeds sprouted very quickly. But their roots did not go deep, so the shoots soon withered and died.

Some seeds fell among the briars and thorns. As the thorns and briars grew bigger and stronger, they choked the sower's seeds, so that they did not have room to grow and they soon died.

Some seeds fell on good, rich soil. They put down deep roots. They sprouted and grew tall and strong. Here in the rich ground the sower's seeds produced a plentiful crop.

CHATTING

...about the story

What do you think the sower looked like? Have you ever seen anyone plant seeds? What sort of a bag do you think the sower had? Have you ever taken seeds out of a bag and planted them? What happened? The sower scattered the seeds here and scattered the seeds there – where did the seeds fall? Have you ever seen birds eat seeds that a farmer/gardener had planted? The seeds that fell near the stones didn't do too well. Why do you think that was? If you were a seed, would you like to grow among briars and thorns? Why? Why not? If you were a seed that fell on the nice rich soil, how would you feel?

POEM

This poem lends itself to being read all-in-one-breath, or two! According as children become more familiar with it, they may join in here and there.

Wait Till I Tell You

(or The Art Of Story-Telling)

First of all...
and then...
and then...
and second of all...
and then again...
and when...
and what...
and after that...
next thing you know...
and Lo!
and Oh!
and all of a sudden...
and quick as a wink...

just out of the blue...
and what d'ye think..
and I said nothing...
and she said 'No!'
and they said 'Never!'
and so...
and so...
the story goes
and grows and grows
and from that day to this
and so I'm told...
the story ran on...
and on to unfold...
and never before ...
and never again...
and ever after
and ever since then
that's the story...
and this...
is THE END!

PRAYERTIME

Sign of the Cross.

Teacher
Close your eyes.
Place your hands gently on your lap and your feet on the floor.
Listen to your heart beat.
Feel your breath as it moves gently in and out of your body, keeping you alive.

Go inside, into your inside world, where it is dark and safe and quiet and peaceful. In that inside place God is with you. Imagine that you have a big bag full of stories. In your bag there are some sad stories and some happy stories. Some of the stories in your bag are great adventure stories in far away places. Open your imaginary bag and look inside. Look at all the stories that you know. As you look into your bag, choose one story. Put it in your hand and take it out. Look at it. Now this story wants to be told. So imagine yourself sitting down in a nice, warm, sunny spot with your story. You feel safe. You know that God is always with you. You know that God is with you when you read stories. You know that God is with you when you tell stories. You know that God loves stories. Now with your special inside voice tell your story to God. *Pause.* You like telling God your story. God loves listening to your story. God has enjoyed your story! Thank God for listening to your story.

Open your eyes. Relax.

We pray together.

All
Thank you, God, we love you.
Thank you, God, we pray.
Thank you, God, we love you.
Thank you, day by day.
Amen.

Sign of the Cross.

Note: For prayertime on Day Four and Day Five you will need a Bible.

Day Four

Continue song: *Once Upon A Time*

ACTIVITY

Note: This activity may continue over two days.

My Favourite Story Picture-Book

You will need.
- Two A4 sheets of paper for each child
- Stapler

Give each child two A4 sheets of paper so that they can make a small story-book.
Fold each sheet of paper in two to make an eight-page book.
On the first page the children write 'My Favourite Story'.
Encourage the children to draw a series of six pictures on the story.
On the final page ask the children to write 'The End'.
Staple the book together for each child.

or

Desk Mime: Parable of The Sower

Divide the class into four groups of 'seeds':

Group 1   The seeds that fell by the roadside
Group 2   The seeds that fell on the stony soil
Group 3   The seeds that fell among the briars
Group 4   The seeds that fell on rich soil.

The teacher may like to take on the role of The Sower.

The teacher retells the story and, as the sower, he/she walks around the whole class scattering the seeds. As the seeds 'fall', all the children place their heads on their arms and go 'to sleep' on the desks.

Group One
Some seeds fell by the roadside.
Children begin to waken up *very slowly.*

Hungry birds came and ate them all up.
Children curl up on their chairs or disappear under the desks!

Group Two
Some seeds fell on stony ground.
Children begin to waken up *quickly,* raising their heads, stretching their arms up high.

But the roots did not go deep... they withered and died.
Children curl up *slowly* and 'die' by returning to their original position.

Group Three
Some seeds fell among the briars.
Children begin to awaken *slowly,* raising their heads, stretching their arms up high.

The thorns choked the sower's seed.
Children wrap their arms around themselves tightly, then begin to curl up slowly and 'die' by returning to their original position.

Group Four
Some seeds fell on good soil.
Children begin to awaken *slowly,* raising their heads, stretching their arms up high, swaying in the wind.

The seeds sprouted and grew tall and strong.
Children stand up tall, stretching high.

WORKSHEET

If you wish to use the worksheet or workbook page which accompanies this lesson, this is an appropriate time to do so.

CHATTING

...about the picture on page 13

What is in the sower's bag? What do you think of his hat? Look at the flower growing in his pocket. How do you think it got there? Does the sower remind you of anyone? Imagine the sower asked you to go in the picture and help him. What would you do? How would you help? Have you ever sown seeds? What did they grow into? What do you think the sower's seeds will grow into?

PRAYERTIME

Note: A Bible will be needed for this prayertime. Place the Bible on the table.

Sign of the Cross.

Teacher *(as the candle is lit)*
God the Father, Son and Holy Spirit.
God our light.
Our light for all time.

The Bible is a very special book. The Bible is the Word of God. It tells us a very special story. The Bible tells us how God loves all living creatures. In the Bible there are lots of God's stories.

Let us praise God for the stories we hear from the Bible.

As we raise the Bible we give praise to God for all the stories that are in it. *(Teacher holds up Bible.)*
The Lord be with you.

All
And also with you.

Teacher *(children repeating)*
Praise
to God in the beginning,
in once upon a time.
Praise
to God ever after,
in word and story-line.
Amen.

Sign of the Cross.

Note: In tomorrow's prayertime we celebrate story in a special way. We offer two choices here – a classroom prayertime (Bible Procession Ritual) and a Prayer Service. Choose whichever option is suitable to your class and circumstances. The Bible Procession Ritual is probably best suited for children celebrating First Penance and First Holy Communion, while the Prayer Service is most appropriate for children who are not celebrating the sacraments this year. The celebration could be held towards the end of the school day, before the children are collected. Ask the children who will be participating in the Prayer Service to bring a favourite story-book to school tomorrow.

We continue to provide the children with an opportunity to read from the Bible. A child will be invited to read a short phrase from the Bible based on the Parable of The Sower. The reader should be chosen before the prayertime begins. It might be helpful to have the phrase 'A sower went out to sow seeds' written on a flashcard in advance of the prayertime. The flashcard could then be placed within the covers of the Bible so that the children will associate the phrase with the Bible.

PRAYERTIME

Note: Choose one of the following prayertimes, depending on whether or not you have decided to invite the children's parents/guardians to join you.

Bible Procession Ritual
(for children preparing for First Communion/First Penance this year)

Take the Bible from its place in the classroom. Form a simple procession. As one child carries the Bible and another child carries the unlit candle (other items like flowers, incense stick, cloth, etc could also be carried in the procession), process to a table where the Bible and the candle are placed reverently.
Children bow and return to their seats.

Sing: *Once Upon a Time*

The teacher lights the candle (you may also like to burn an incense stick or grains of incense).

Sign of the Cross.

Teacher
Note: If time allows, you might like to repeat the following and invite other children to come forward, raise the Bible and read the biblical phrase.

Jesus told us a story about a sower who went out to sow seeds.

_____ *(name reader)* will read the Word of God for us today.

The child is invited to come forward.
The teacher takes the Bible from the table and ceremoniously hands it to the child.
The child faces the class, holding the Bible.

Teacher
As we read from the Bible we remember God's stories and we know that God is with us in a special way. Today we remember the story about the sower and the seeds.

Some seeds fell on the edge of the path.

Some seeds grew on patches of rock and withered.
Some seeds fell among thorns and the thorns choked them.
But some seeds fell on rich soil and produced a good crop.

Let us listen to the Word of God as we read it from the Bible.

Reader
The Lord be with you.

All
And also with you.

Teacher
This reading is from the Gospel according to St Matthew.

All
Glory to you, O Lord.

Reader
'A sower went out to sow seeds...'
The Gospel of the Lord *(raising the Bible).*

All
Praise to you, Lord Jesus Christ.

Teacher
For all God's stories that we tell,
For all God's stories that we read,
For all God's stories that we hear,
We thank you, God. Amen.

Sign of the Cross.

Prayer Service
(for classes where children are not celebrating First Penance or First Communion)

Celebration of Story
Prepare the room before the adults arrive. Arrange the chairs in a circle, if possible, so that each child may sit beside her/his parent(s)/guardian(s). The children whose parent(s)/guardian(s) are unable to attend can sit beside their friends.

Sign of the Cross.

Song: *Once Upon a Time*

Leader
The Lord be with you.

All
And also with you.

Leader
You are all very welcome to join us in our celebration of stories.
We have been talking about our stories during the week.
Today we want to thank God for all our stories.
Thank you, God, for stories to tell.
Thank you, God, for stories to read.
Thank you, God, for stories to hear.

Let us stand up with our story-books and give thanks to God.

All
For all the stories that we tell,
For all the stories that we read,
For all the stories that we hear,
We thank you, God. Amen.

Leader
We all have special stories that we like a lot.
We have special stories that we like to hear and tell again and again.
Let's tell someone about our special story now!

Invite the children to take their story-book and to talk to their parent/guardian/friend about the story/pictures. Children can talk to the teacher if an adult or friend is not available.

Leader
Did you enjoy hearing about the story?
Let's give our story-tellers a hug and a clap.
God loves stories too.
We read God's stories in the Bible.
Let us listen to a story from the Bible today.
Let us bring our Bible to the table so that we can hear the Word of God.

Form a simple procession. As one child carries the Bible and another child carries the unlit candle, process to a table where the Bible and the candle are placed reverently.

Children bow and return to their seats.

The teacher lights the candle (you may also like to light an incense stick).

Sign of the Cross.

Leader
Jesus told us a story about a sower who went out to sow seeds.
_____ (name reader) will read the Word of God for us today.

The child is invited to come forward.
The teacher takes the Bible from the table and ceremoniously hands it to the child.
The child faces the class, holding the Bible.

Leader
As we read from the Bible we remember God's stories and we know that God is with us in a special way. Today we remember the story about the sower and the seeds.

Some seeds fell on the edge of the path.
Some seeds grew on patches of rock and withered.
Some seeds fell among thorns and the thorns choked them.
But some seeds fell on rich soil and produced a good crop.

Let us listen to the Word of God as we read it from the Bible.

Reader
The Lord be with you.

All
And also with you.

Leader
This reading is from the Gospel according to St Matthew.

All
Glory to you, O Lord.

Reader
'A sower went out to sow seeds...'
The Gospel of the Lord *(raising the Bible).*

All
Praise to you, Lord Jesus Christ.

Leader
For all God's stories that we tell,
For all God's stories that we read,
For all God's stories that we hear,
We thank you, God. Amen.

You might like to invite a parent to read the reflection for parents provided at the end of this lesson.

All
Sing: *Once Upon A Time*

Sign of the Cross.

Once Upon a Time

Christy Kenneally

1. Tell a sto - ry, oh will you tell us please, why the tree wears a crown of gold - en leaves. Why do they curl up in aut - umn and let go to rus - tle down be - low? Let us hear it in once up - on a time.

2. Tell a story of Jesus long ago,
   And the stories he told so he could show his friends that
   Love is a special thing to share
   And in that love he's there.
   Let us hear it in once upon a time.

3. Tell the story how Jesus went to sow,
   How he scattered his words so we would know
   That love can grow from the smallest little seed
   Through every loving deed.
   Let us hear it in once upon a time.

Reflection for Parents

Sowing the Seed

The sower went out to sow his seed,
Remember the story? Yes indeed!
How well we saw his every throw
And wondered if the seeds would grow.

And some seeds fell on stony ground
And found no place to root.
And some seeds fell on arid clay
And never came to shoot.
The ones that fell on beaten paths
Were prey to passing feet,
And others fell on open plains
Where birds would see and eat.
And some seeds chose a bed
Of nettles to be born,
And found their light, their promise bright,
Was swallowed up by thorn.
And some seeds fell on fertile ground
Where earth was rich and true,
These stretched to grasp the light and air
And sturdily, they grew.

Our children will take wings one day
To fly the nest and go.
Like seeds, to sail the winds of life,
And scatter to and fro.
We pray that these, our precious seeds,
Who scatter from our hand,
Find fertile soil, prepared by God
To blossom where they land.
        Christy Kenneally

To what should I compare the
kingdom of God?
It is like yeast that a woman took and
mixed in with three measures of flour
until all of it was leavened.
(Luke 13: 20-21)

I am the Bread of life.
(John 6:35)

Bread is one of life's basic foods and is eaten
in many lands. It is the result of planted
seeds, harvested crops, milled grain. It is the
culmination of a long process involving the
skills and co-operation of many. Bread is the
work of human hands.

Bread-making is a ritual. The mixing, the
kneading, the shaping, has its own rhythm
often unique to the bread-maker. The smell of
the freshly baked bread evokes remembrances:
remembering the arrival of the breadman and
his van; remembering the bakerwoman, a
mother, a granny, a neighbour, as she carefully
took the hot bread from the oven;
remembering the kitchen table and how she
cut the bread, buttered it and shared it around;
remembering those no longer at the table, but
not forgotten. Bread is shared by human
hands.

Bread sustains and nourishes life. It is not
surprising then that it features a lot in the
Gospels. Indeed Jesus was deeply concerned
that his followers would have enough to eat.
'Have you anything to eat?' (Lk 24:42). Often
he fed them. Frequently he sat at their tables
and ate with them. He described himself as the
Bread of Life.

Children are very familiar with all kinds of
bread. It is part and parcel of their daily eating
routine. While not every child will experience
the ritual of making bread, they will none the
less experience other rituals surrounding
bread: mealtimes, school lunch, buying the
loaf, the making of sandwiches.

Children, this year, are being introduced for
the first time to the Eucharist, while some
children are preparing for their First Holy
Communion. It is important, therefore, to
explore with them an experience of bread as a
source of life and as a theme in life.

For the Teacher:

A thought before beginning

Sunlight

There was a sunlit absence,
the helmeted pump in the yard
heated its iron,
water honeyed

in the slung bucket
and the sun stood
like a griddle cooling
against the wall

of each long afternoon.
So, her hands scuffled
over the bakeboard,
the redding stove

sent its plaque of heat
against her where she stood
in a floury apron
by the window.

Now she dusts the board
with a goose's wing,
now sits, broad-lapped,
with whitened nails
and measling shins:
here is a space
again, the scone rising
to the tick of two clocks.

And here is love
like a tinsmith's scoop
sunk past its gleam
in the meal-bin.
Seamus Heaney

What am I trying to do?

To help the children to explore and reflect on their own experience of making, eating and sharing bread.
To introduce the children to the image of Jesus as breaker of bread.

Why?

So that they will become aware of the significance of eating and sharing bread with others and begin to lay down foundations for a future understanding of the concept of Jesus as the Bread of Life.

Overview of the Week

Song: *The Bread Song* Chatting about bread Story: *The Magic Loaf* Chatting about the story Prayertime	Continue song Recall story: *The Magic Loaf* Poem: *Farmer* Chatting about making bread Prayertime	Continue song Story: *Micah's Story* Chatting about the story Art: *Play-dough* or *Collage* Prayertime	Continue song, art Recall story: *Micah's Story* Activity: *Micah Chats at Home* Worksheet Chatting about the picture Prayertime	Bible Procession Ritual

Day One

Song

The Bread Song

Chatting

...about bread

Let's think about all the different kinds of bread there are. What is your favourite kind of bread? What is your favourite thing to put on bread? What is your favourite way to eat bread – toasted with marmalade/buttered with jam/bread pudding, etc? Where do you get the bread you eat at home? Do you know how bread is made? Let's talk about all the different

people who help in the making of bread. The farmer/the miller/the baker/the shopkeeper, etc.

Story

The Magic Loaf

Once upon a time in a faraway place the people were very hungry. They had no bread. The wicked fairy who lived at the top of the hill had stolen all the ears of wheat in the fields and now there was nothing left for the people to harvest.

'What will we do, we have no flour?' they said. 'How will we make bread?'

The wicked fairy laughed. It was a cruel, mean laugh. She would have all the bread for herself.

One day she decided to bake a loaf of bread. She put some flour and bread soda into her big mixing bowl. Then she stirred in the milk. She popped it in the oven and soon there was a delicious smell of baking bread. The smell filled the whole valley. The people got hungrier and hungrier. The children cried for bread.

The wicked fairy laughed to herself. 'All for me! All for me!' she cackled. Then she opened the oven door.

Suddenly the loaf started to grow. It grew and grew. It grew until it filled the whole oven. The wicked fairy tried to shut the oven door, but the magic loaf pushed its way out the door and grew to fill the whole kitchen. Then it pushed its way out of the kitchen, out of the house, and kept on growing until it filled the whole valley.

The people ran out of their houses. 'Bread!' they shouted gleefully, 'bread for everybody!'

They all came and took some bread. Old men with walking sticks, little children sucking their thumbs, even the dogs and cats and mice came running and helped themselves to the bread. There was plenty for everyone. No one need be hungry any more. The magic loaf would feed them all.

The wicked fairy danced and shrieked with rage.

'That's my bread! that's my bread!' she shouted. 'It's not fair, they're eating my bread.' But it was fair.

CHATTING

...about the story

Did you ever smell bread baking? Have you ever smelt other foods cooking? What is your favourite cooking smell? Does the smell of cooking make you feel hungry? How do you feel when you are hungry? How do you think the hungry people felt when they smelt the baking of the wicked fairy's bread? How did the people feel when the bread filled the whole valley?

Note: The prayertime on Days Two and Four of this week will focus on the sharing of bread. The children might eat their lunches during the prayertime. Encourage the children to bring some bread, in any form, as part of their lunch for these two days.

PRAYERTIME

Sign of the Cross.

Teacher *(as the candle is lit)*
God the Father, Son and Holy Spirit.
God our light.
Our light for all time.

Today we remember the times when we have eaten bread.
We give thanks to God for the bread that we eat.
We remember those who have no bread.
We remember those who don't have anyone to share their bread with.

We pray to God:
Give us this day our daily bread.

For the bread we eat at school.

All
Give us this day our daily bread.

Teacher
For the bread we make at home.

All
Give us this day our daily bread.

Teacher
For friends to eat our bread with.

All
Give us this day our daily bread.

Teacher
For those who have no bread to eat.

All
Give us this day our daily bread.

Teacher
Help us to be ready to share bread with others.

All
Give us this day our daily bread.

All
Our Father...

Sign of the Cross.

Day Two

Continue song: *The Bread Song*

STORY

Note: *Today you might recall the story of* The Magic Loaf *or, alternatively, you might like to tell any other similar story/fairytale/fable where bread/food is the focus of the story. Just as there are Bible stories from the Jewish tradition, Celtic stories from the Celtic tradition, etc. so there are also stories from the tradition which one might call 'cultural childhood'. It is important for children to hear these stories and thereby have the culture of childhood affirmed, in the context of a religion lesson.*

POEM

Farmer

'Farmer, is the harvest ready
For we must have bread?'
'Go and look in all my fields,'
Is what the farmer said.

So we ran and saw the wheat
Standing straight and tall.
'There's your bread,' the farmer said,
'Have no fear at all.'

'Miller, is the flour ready
For we must have bread?'
'Go and look in all my sacks,'
Is what the miller said.

So we ran and saw the flour
Soft and white as snow.
'There's your flour,' the miller said
As he turned to go.

'Baker, is the oven ready
For we must have bread?'
'Go and open wide the door,'
Is what the baker said.

So we ran and saw the loaves
Crisp and brown to see.
'There's your bread,' the baker said,
'Ready for your tea.'
        H. E. Wilkinson

CHATTING

...about making bread

Have you ever seen anyone making bread? Tell us about it. Let's pretend we are making a lovely cake of brown bread. What ingredients will we need? What else will we need – a bowl, etc. Let's put all the ingredients in the bowl. How much will we need? Let's try a handful of white flour and a fistful of brown flour and a little pinch of salt and a little milk and mix it round and round and all-in-together. Now let's roll it in a ball and put it out on the table and knead it and knead it and shape it and roll it and put a cross on the top and pop it in the oven and that's that!

That was fun! Perhaps someone at home will let you help them to make bread.

Who made your school sandwiches/packed lunch this morning? Let's see some of the different kinds of bread we have in our lunches. Can you remember a time when you forgot your lunch? Tell us about what happened then. If you could plan your favourite lunch, what would you put in it?

Why do we eat bread? Why don't we just eat cakes and bars and biscuits and goodies all the time?

Can you remember a time in your home when you ran out of bread? Let's talk about all the different times in the day when we eat bread – breakfast, lunch, supper, etc.

 PRAYERTIME

Prayer Ritual

Note: *Arrange the classroom, if possible, so that the children are gathered around the table. In preparation for the ritual invite the children to place the 'bread' part of their lunch on a table. You might like to begin by doing this yourself. Place a candle on the table.*

Here we continue to familiarise the children with some of the basic Eucharistic responses.

Sign of the Cross.

All
Sing: *The Bread Song*

Teacher *(as the candle is lit)*
The Lord be with you.

All
And also with you.

Teacher
Today as we light our candle we know that God is with us.
Bread nourishes us and keeps us healthy.
It helps us to grow strong limbs and bodies.
Blessed are you Lord, God of all creation.
Through your goodness we have this bread to eat.

All
Blessed be God forever.

Teacher
We remember all the people who made the bread that we are about to eat.

All
Blessed be God forever.

Teacher
Let's praise God for the land that grows the wheat, straight and tall.

All
Blessed be God forever.

Teacher
Let's praise God for the mill workers who make the flour, soft and white as snow.

All
Blessed be God forever.

Teacher
Let's praise God for the bakers who bake fresh bread every day, crisp and brown.

All
Blessed be God forever.

Teacher
We give praise to God for everyone who made the bread for our lunches that we are about to eat.
As we prepare ourselves to share in the eating of our bread today, we ask God to bless the bread and to bless us.

Blessed are you, God of all Creation,
Through your goodness we have this bread to offer,
Work of human hands.
Bless this bread.
May it make us strong.
May it remind us always to share with those who are hungry.
As we pray together:

All
Bless us, O God, as we sit together.
Bless the food we eat today.
Bless the hands that made the food.
Bless us, O God. Amen.

Each child in turn approaches the table and takes his/her bread. Each child waits in silence until everyone has a piece of bread, then each child eats their own piece. Perhaps some quiet music could be played in the background as this is happening.

When the children have finished eating the bread all say:

All
Thank you, God, for the food we have eaten.
Thank you, God, for all our friends.
Thank you, God, for everything.

Thank you, God. Amen.

Sing: *The Bread Song*

Sign of the Cross.

Note: Look at the alternatives for the artwork on Day Three. If you choose to do the collage, ask the children to bring in pictures of bread from old magazines and papers, or wrappings of various types of bread.

If you decide to make the 'play-dough', you will need the following ingredients: plain flour, oil, warm water and salt.

Day Three

Continue song: *The Bread Song*

 STORY

Note: This is one of the few stories in the New Testament where we meet a child. In this lesson the story is told from the perspective of the child, who is a central character in the biblical narrative, the one who gave Jesus the bread and fishes with which he fed the crowd.

Micah's Story
(Adapted from Luke 9:10-16)

Micah lived with his aunt and uncle. Every day his aunt made bread. Every day his uncle went to fish. Every day Micah went off to sell some of his aunt's bread and some of his uncle's fish so that they could have money to buy the things they needed.

One day Micah set off with his basket of loaves and fishes. He saw a large crowd of people. They looked as poor and as hungry as he did. They were following a man who was teaching them. Micah thought he might be able to sell them some of his food so he set off after them.

The man talked to the people. He told them

stories. After a while he realised that he had been talking for a long time and that the people had been listening, but now they were getting very hungry. He shouted out in a loud voice, 'Feed the people!' Suddenly Micah realised that all eyes were on him and his basket of loaves and fishes. The man came over to where Micah was sitting. He smiled at him and patted him on the head. 'Micah, you are heaven's messenger, a God-send,' he said. Then he took Micah's basket of bread and fish.

Micah sat and looked on as the man took the bread from the basket and blessed it and gave it to the hungry crowd. When they were finished eating and the scraps were gathered, there were twelve baskets full.

As Micah set off home, he looked back over his shoulder at the man who was teaching. He had never met anyone like him before. Micah thought about the man. He said to himself, 'That man has a way with food, and he knows my name!'

 CHATTING

...about the story

Have you ever had to give away something you didn't want to give away? Tell us how that felt. How do you think Micah felt when the man took his basket of loaves and fishes? How would you have felt if you had been Micah? Do you know who the man in the story was? What was he doing when Micah saw him first? What did Micah think about him? What do you think about him?

ART

Play-dough

Note: The quantity of the ingredients may be increased depending on the amount of play-dough you wish to make with the children. Either of these activities will probably take two days to complete.

How to make play-dough
You will need:
- Ten heaped tablespoons of plain flour
- Eight tablespoons of warm water
- Four tablespoons of oil
- One teaspoon of salt.

Mix the salt and flour in a bowl. Add the water a little at a time. Mix it together using your hand. Knead the dough until it holds together and is not too sticky. The play-dough could be coloured with cooking colouring if you wish. When a model is made, it can be baked in an oven to make it hard. If you wish to do this, bake the models at 350°F, 180°C, or gas mark 7, for thirty minutes. The models will keep for a long time if they are thoroughly dried.

or

Collage

In this activity we draw the children's attention to the range of bread that is available and help to foster a sense of wonder in them at the variety that exists, itself a reflection of the creativity that's possible through the 'work of human hands'.

Make a collage using the pictures and bread wrappings the children have brought in. Ask them to write suitable captions, e.g. 'Work of Human Hands', 'Thank you, God, for lovely bread', or 'Bread, bread, butter and bread', etc.

PRAYERTIME

Sign of the Cross.

Teacher
We light the candle.
God is with us right now.

Close your eyes.
Place your hands gently on your lap.
Place your feet on the floor.

God is with us in the beating of our hearts. Listen to your heart beat. God is with us in the air we breathe in and out of our lungs. Feel your breath as it goes in and out of your lungs, breathing life into every part of your body. Go into your inside world where it is dark and quiet and safe and peaceful. In this inside world we can imagine anything we like.

Imagine yourself in the middle of that crowd of people with Micah. The crowd is very big, there are people everywhere. It's fun to be with the crowd. Look all around you. Listen. Someone is talking, everyone seems to be listening. Listen again. Push your way through the crowd. There is a man chatting and telling stories. You love stories. Oh great! The man who is telling the stories is Jesus. You love listening to Jesus. He tells great stories. Sit down and listen to him. It's a lovely day. The sun is shining. You can feel the warmth of the sun on your face and on your arms and on your back. After a while you feel a bit hungry. Hear your tummy beginning to rumble. You haven't brought any food with you. Look around at the others. Nobody seems to have much food with them. You wonder what you will do. It's a long way home and now you are feeling very hungry. Just then you notice that Jesus has got some loaves of lovely fresh bread in his hands. They look delicious. Smell them. Watch Jesus carefully. See him bless the bread then break it into little pieces. He gives it out to some people. You hope that you will get some but the crowd is very big and you are small and everybody is pushing. But look, Jesus is coming towards you. He comes right up to you and asks you if you are hungry. Hold out your hand. Jesus gives you a big piece of your favourite bread. It tastes really good. You don't feel hungry anymore. What a day! With your special inside voice thank Jesus for the lovely fresh bread. Listen and see if Jesus says anything special back to you.

Open your eyes.
Stretch yourself.
Relax.

Sign of the Cross.

Day Four

Continue song: *The Bread Song*

Recall story: *Micah's Story*

Continue art *(if not already completed)*

ACTIVITY

Micah Chats At Home

Ask the children to form pairs. One child in each pair is Micah, the other child is someone who lives with Micah at home. The person who lives with him asks Micah questions about what happened that day. Micah tells the story.

Alternatively, invite one child to be Micah, while the class ask questions about what happened that day.

WORKSHEET

If you wish to use the worksheet or workbook page which accompanies this lesson, this is an appropriate time to do so.

CHATTING

...about the picture on pages 14 and 15

Look at the huge loaf. Have you ever seen a loaf this size? How many people and animals are eating from the magic hat? Do you recognise any of them? What do you think people in your home would say if this happened in your kitchen? Imagine it – spilling out the kitchen door, and the back door. Imagine all your neighbours and friends and pets. What would they do?

PRAYERTIME

Note: In this prayertime we focus on the children eating bread together.

Sign of the Cross.

Teacher *(as the candle is lit)*
We remember that God is with us now and always.
Ask the children to take out their lunches and to place them on their desks.

All
Bless us, O God, as we sit together.
Bless the food we eat today.
Bless the hands that made the food.
Bless us, O God. Amen.

Teacher
Let's listen to story of Micah again.

Encourage the class to tell the story, with volunteers telling bits of it as they remember it.

Who remembers the story? Who would like to begin to tell it to us?

Alternatively, the children could be asked to repeat the activity: 'Micah Chats at Home'.

Teacher

It's good to have food to eat. It's good to have people to eat our food with. It's good to be able to share our food with others.
Today we are going to ask God to bless our lunches.
Hold your lunch in your hands as we pray:

All

Blessed be God forever.

Teacher

Look at your lunch.
Look at all the different things you have to eat. We pray:

All

Blessed be God forever.

Teacher

Take up a bit of your lunch that you like a lot. Smell it. Enjoy the lovely smell of your favourite bit before you eat it. We pray:

All

Blessed be God forever.

Teacher

Who prepared your lunch for you today?
Let's think of the people who prepare food for us every day.
Would you like to say 'thank you' to God for someone who prepares food for you?

Invite the children to name someone if they wish to.

Let's ask God to bless them and to keep them safe and well.

All

Blessed be God forever.

Teacher

Now take a little taste of your lunch.
May we be nourished by this food
and filled with God's spirit.

All

Blessed be God forever.

Teacher and children eat their lunch together in the normal way.

All

Thank you, God, for the food we have eaten.
Thank you, God, for all our friends.
Thank you, God, for everything.
Thank you, God. Amen.

Sign of the Cross.

Note: The prayertime on Day Five continues to provide the children with an opportunity to read from the Bible. A child will be invited to read a short phrase from the Bible based on the story of the Loaves and Fishes. Choose the reader before the prayertime begins.

It will be helpful to have written the phrase 'Jesus blessed and broke the Bread' on a flashcard in advance of the prayertime.

The flashcard could then be placed within the covers of the Bible so that the children will associate the phrase with the Bible.

Day Five

PRAYERTIME

Bible Procession Ritual

Take the Bible from its place in the classroom. Form a simple procession. As one child carries the Bible and another child carries the unlit candle (other items like flowers, incense stick, cloth, etc could also be carried in the procession), process to a table where the Bible and the candle are placed reverently.
Children bow and return to their seats.

The teacher lights the candle. You may also like to burn an incense stick or some grains of incense.

Sign of the Cross.

Song: *The Bread Song*

Teacher

Note: If time allows, you might like to repeat the following and invite other children to come forward, raise the Bible and read the biblical phrase.

A crowd gathered around Jesus one day.

_____ *(name reader)* will read the Word of God for us today.

The child is invited to come forward to read from the Bible.

The teacher takes the Bible from the table and ceremoniously hands it to the child.
The child faces the class, holding the Bible.

As we read from the Bible we remember that the Bible is the Word of God. We know that God is with us. We know that God is with us in a special way when we read from the Bible. Today we hear a story about Jesus. People came from everywhere to hear Jesus. Many had made a long journey. They loved to hear him telling stories. They had listened to him all day. Now it was evening and it was time to eat.

Reader
The Lord be with you.

All
And also with you.

Reader
This reading is from the Gospel according to St Luke.

All
Glory to you, O Lord.

Reader
'Jesus blessed and broke the bread…'
The Gospel of the Lord *(raising the Bible)*.

All
Praise to you, Lord Jesus Christ.

Teacher
For all God's stories that we tell,
For all God's stories that we read,
For all God's stories that we hear,
We thank you, God. Amen.

Sign of the Cross.

Note: For artwork in Lesson 11, it is suggested that you make a rain-gauge. For this you will need:
- *an empty liquid-soap container*
- *strong sticky tape*
- *some small stones/bricks to secure the rain-gauge in the ground*

The Bread Song

Bernard Sexton

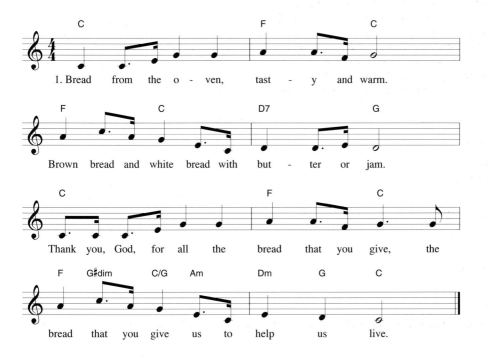

1. Bread from the o - ven, tast - y and warm.
Brown bread and white bread with but - ter or jam.
Thank you, God, for all the bread that you give, the
bread that you give us to help us live.

2. Pop goes the toaster, out pops the toast!
   Soft in the middle and outside a crust.
   Thank you, God, for all the bread that you give,
   The bread that you give us to help us live.

3. Cake for my birthday, cake for my tea,
   Cake on the table for you and for me.
   Thank you, God, for all the bread that you give,
   The bread that you give us to help us live.

Lesson 11: Jesus – Diviner

I will open rivers on the bare heights,
and fountains in the midst of valleys;
I will make the wilderness a pool of water,
and the dry land springs of water.
(Isaiah 41:18)

You make springs gush forth in the valleys;
they flow between the hills.
(Psalm 104:10)

All life depends on water. Water sustains life. Without water living things wither, shrivel and eventually die. Children relate to water on many levels. It gives them hours of fun and pleasure as they swim or paddle or splash about in it. It cleans and washes them, quenches their thirst, cools them on hot summer days and soaks them to the skin when it rains. Through painful experience, some children know its tragic dangers. Water, while it is to be enjoyed, must also be respected and treated with care.

Today, in many parts of the world, water is completely taken for granted rather than treated as a precious resource. It is indeed very difficult at times to raise the awareness of the significance of water with children who live in a country where it rains so much, and often too much! However, awareness of the connection between water and life is essential for the children's future appreciation of water as a symbol of life.

According to ancient tradition someone who discovers water is called a diviner. Such a person has the capacity to feel the energy flowing deep within the earth and to be drawn to the spot where water lies. A diviner leads people to the source of water. Divining is a gift to be shared. Until the diviner puts his or her finger on the right spot, the power of the water is trapped beneath the surface. Once it is tapped, it spurts forth with all its life-giving power and energy. Jesus was a diviner. He put his finger on the hidden riches and gifts inside those he met. Riches that were unknown were

called forth by Jesus. One such person who experienced the divining power of Jesus was the woman at the well in John's Gospel.

Water is the backdrop to the scene of Jesus and the woman at Jacob's Well. In this story Jesus and the woman meet at the well and there water is offered. In the interaction that takes place between that woman, whose name is unknown, and Jesus, much is discovered about water, about life, and about the woman's hidden capacity for love.

In a sense, the teacher is a diviner too, discovering and calling forth the hidden gifts and talents in the children, enabling them to become aware of their inner resources and to find ways of expressing them.

FOR THE TEACHER:

A thought before beginning

The Diviner

Cut from the green hedge a
    forked hazel stick
That he held tight by the arms
    of the V:
Circling the terrain, hunting the pluck
Of water, nervous, but professionally

Unfussed. The pluck came sharp as a sting.
The rod jerked down with precise convulsions,
Spring water suddenly broadcasting
Through a green aerial its secret stations.

The bystanders would ask to have a try.
He handed them the rod without a word.
It lay dead in their grasp till nonchalantly
He gripped expectant wrists. The hazel stirred.
Seamus Heaney

What am I trying to do?

To give the children an understanding of the gift of divining.

Why?

So that the children may respect water as a resource, develop an appreciation for the connection between water and life, and come to see Jesus as someone who tapped into the life-giving riches in the hearts of those he met.

Overview of the Week

			Continue song, art	
		Continue song	Recall story: *The*	
		Story: *The Woman at*	*Woman at the Well*	
Song: *Water Litany*	Continue song	*the Well*	Poem: *Granny's*	
Chatting about taps	Did You Know?	Chatting about the	*Finger* or *Water*	
and wells	Story: *Tojo's Garden*	story	Worksheet	
Activity: *Rain-Gauge*	Chatting about the	Art: *Diviner*	Chatting about the	Activity: *Rainmaker*
Did You Know?	story	*Collage/Diviner Rods*	picture	Bible Procession
Prayertime	Prayertime	Prayertime	Prayertime	Ritual

Day One

SONG

Water Litany

CHATTING

...about taps and wells

If you were thirsty and you wanted a drink of water, where would you get it? Where in your home do you have water-taps? Where in school do we have water-taps? How do you think we would manage if we had no water-taps at home or in school? Why do we usually have two water-taps together? What kinds of things do we use hot water for? What kinds of things do we use cold water for? As well as for drinking and cleaning, what other ways do we use water?

Years ago people did not have water-taps in their homes. You could ask someone at home or an older neighbour what it was like to live in a home without running water. In those days people had to go to the well or the pump and fill a bucket with water and bring it home. When the bucket was empty they would have to go back to the well or the pump again. What does a pump look like? Where might you find a pump? Have you ever seen a real pump? What do you have to do to get the water from the pump?

Wells are very deep. We need to take great care when we go to a well. Have you ever seen a well? Have you ever drunk water from a well or a pump? Tell us about it. (*If there is a special well or a Holy Well in the locality, you might like to visit it or talk about it during this week's lesson.*)

Rain-Gauge

You will need:
• An empty liquid-soap container
• Adhesive tape
• Some stones/bricks to stabilise the rain-gauge if it not being set into the ground

Take a liquid-soap container and cut off the top section.

Invert the top part and fasten with strips of adhesive tape.

If possible, sink the container into the ground (a flowerbed might be a good spot).

Alternatively, place the rain-guage on the ground where it is safe and is unlikely to be disturbed. Prop it up with bricks or stones to prevent it tipping over.

Perhaps you could ask a child to be responsible for checking on it each day.

DID YOU KNOW?

Years ago, when a person built a new home, they had to dig a well also to provide water for those who would live there. Water can be found deep, deep down under the ground. It gurgles away among the rocks and the earth under our feet. Most of the time we don't even see it, but it's there all the time. People often had to dig to find water for their homes. Sometimes they would have to dig a lot before they found anything. Sometimes they would be lucky – they would just dig one very deep hole and it would fill up with water and never be empty. This would be their well and they would get all the water they needed from it. Sometimes they would not be so lucky. They would dig several holes, but there would be no water in any of them. Then they would need help from a special person called a diviner.

A diviner has a special talent for finding water. The diviner would come to where the new home was to be built. He/she would have a special stick, shaped like a Y. The diviner would hold this forked stick in his/her hands and walk around. Soon the stick would begin to quiver and shake and its point would dip down towards the ground. When this happened, the diviner would know that the stick was pointing to where there was water underground. He/she would tell the digger that this was a good spot in which to dig a well. Even today, people sometimes need the help of a diviner to find water.

PRAYERTIME

Note: You may like to add some simple actions to the following prayer. For example – 'water that gurgles and gushes and goes' – move arms gently from side to side; 'water that trickles and tumbles and roars' – raise hands above the head, 'dance' fingers in downward direction for 'trickles and tumbles', make a wide sweeping gesture with both hands for 'roars'; 'water that splashes and sparkles and spouts' – move arms gently from side to side; 'water that flows gently in' – bring both arms in towards the body, and 'out' – open out both arms in an outward direction.

Sign of the Cross.

Teacher *(with children repeating)*
We give God thanks:
For water that gurgles and gushes and goes,
For water that trickles and tumbles and roars,
For water that splashes and sparkles and spouts,
For water that flows gently in and out.

We light our candle.

Close your eyes.
Place your hands gently on your lap and your feet on the floor.
Listen to your heart beat.
Feel your breath as it moves gently in and out of your body.

As you sit here with your friends you can go

anywhere you like in your imagination. Let's imagine now. Let's imagine that you are outside playing a game of hide-and-seek with your friends. It's a very hot day. You are running and chasing and laughing and messing. You are having great fun. You feel very hot. The sweat is trickling down your face. You feel thirsty and sticky. You wonder where you can get some water. You need water. Look around you. There at the back of your own house you see a tap. Turn on the tap. Water gushes from the tap. Put your hands under the running water. Hold the water between your hands. Splash the water on your arms. It feels lovely and cool. Splash some water on your face. Feel the water on your eyes and on your cheeks, on your nose and on your lips. It feels cool and refreshing. It's great to have water to cool us down. It's great to have water to refresh us. Thank you, God.

Open your eyes and stretch yourself.

We give God thanks:
For water that gurgles and gushes and goes,
For water that trickles and tumbles and roars,
For water that splashes and sparkles and spouts,
For water that flows gently in and out.

With arms still held in an outstretched position say:

Glory be to the Father…

Sign of the Cross.

Day Two

Continue song: *Water Litany*

DID YOU KNOW?

In Tojo's country the weather is hot and sunny almost all the time. Tojo likes rain. When it rains in Tojo's country the rain pours down for days. For days and days and weeks on end, it rains. Morning, noon and night, it rains. Tojo likes the rain because it fills up the lakes and rivers and wells. Three and sometimes four times every week Tojo goes on the long journey with her mother to the well. She carries a large water-jug on her head. She fills it with water for cooking and cleaning and drinking. Her mother does the same. Then she and Tojo carry the jars full of water all the way back to their home in the village. When the rain stops, Tojo knows it will not come back for a long time. Then she must hope that there will be enough water in the well to last until the rains return.

STORY

Tojo's Garden

Tojo loves school. She loves books and she particularly likes books with pictures. Her favourite book shows a little boy in his granny's garden. There are lots of flowers in his granny's garden. The little boy in the picture helps his granny to water the flowers so that they will grow tall and healthy. Tojo loves the picture of the garden full of flowers.

'Let's make a garden and grow flowers,' she said to her mother when she came home from school.

'Perhaps we can, some day,' her mother said, 'but in a very hot, sunny country like ours, flowers would have to be watered every day. That would mean we would have to walk all the way to the well and back every day to get water for them. The well is too far away for us to go there every day.'

Later, Tojo was turning the pages of her book. She came to the picture of Granny's garden. She looked at the tall sunflowers. They smiled at her. She loved them.

'Can we make a garden and grow flowers now?' she asked her mother when she came home from school. 'The little boy in the picture has a garden and he can grow flowers and he waters them. We can do the same as he does.'

'The little boy lives in a country where people have water-taps,' her mother told her. 'It is easy to water flowers every day when you have a water-tap close by.'

'A water-tap! What is a water-tap?' Tojo asked her mother.

'People have water-taps in their homes and when they turn them on, water comes out.'

'Don't they go to the well with water-jars like we do?' asked Tojo in surprise.

'No,' said her mother, 'they don't have to go to the well for water because the water comes to them.'

Tojo often thought about how lovely it would be to have a garden, but she began to think that she would never have one herself.

Then one day as she was walking home from school, she saw her mother running to meet her. Her mother was very excited.

'Come quickly, Tojo,' she called. 'Come and see.'

Tojo could hear a lot of noise. It was coming from the far side of the village. She ran with her mother. When she turned the corner where her own home was, she saw lots of big machines. There was a digger, a drill, lorries with trailers, and lots of people had gathered to watch.

'What is happening?' she asked her mother.

'We are going to have a water-tap right here in our village,' her mother cried. 'Look!'

Tojo saw a man with a strange-looking stick in his hands. It was shaped like a Y. He was walking around very slowly. Everything went quiet. The machines were switched off and the people stopped talking. Everyone was watching the man with the stick.

'Who is that man and what is he doing?' Tojo whispered to her mother.

'He is a water diviner. He can tell where there is lots of water underground,' her mother replied.

'How can he do that, he cannot see what is under the ground?' said Tojo.

'Sssh,' said her mother. The stick in the diviner's hands began to tremble. It pointed to a spot not far from Tojo's own home.

'Right here,' the man said. The machines moved in and bored a hole deep into the ground where the water diviner told them. The people clapped when they saw water fill up the hole.

'Hurrah!' they called.

The machines and the people worked hard. In a few short days there was a water-tap just outside Tojo's home. Everyone used it. They got water for drinking, for cooking, for cleaning, for watering their crops. They were very happy. The water-tap changed their lives. Now they did not have to walk miles and miles to the well anymore.

That night Tojo was tired out after all the excitement. She fell asleep as soon as her head hit the pillow. In her dreams she saw a garden of beautiful flowers right outside her window.

CHATTING

...about the story

Do you think Tojo's dream of having a garden can come true now? Why? Do you have a garden? Do you ever water flowers? How do you think life in Tojo's village will change now? What do you think some of Tojo's friends might like to do with the water, now that it is close to them? Would you like to be able to divine water? Why? Perhaps we could pretend to be water diviners. Let's make a diviner's stick with some construct-o-straws, or some pipe-cleaners. Perhaps you could take them out into the playground and see if you can divine water.

PRAYERTIME

Sign of the Cross.

All
Sing: *Water Litany*

Teacher
We know that we cannot live without water. Without it we would wither and die. We need water. It kills our thirst and helps things to grow. We are very lucky that we have plenty of water in this country. It is easy for us to get water. We can get water by turning on the taps. We can find water deep in a well. We can dig deep for water under the ground. Let's thank God for all the different ways we can get water. We light our candle.

All
Blessed be God forever.

Teacher
For taps that gush water into our sinks.

All
Blessed be God forever.

Teacher
For pipes that bring water into our homes.

All
Blessed be God forever.

Teacher
For water tanks that hold the water in our attics.

All
Blessed be God forever.

Teacher
For the diviner who finds water deep down under the ground.

All
Blessed be God forever.

Teacher
For wells that are full of cool, clear water.

All
Blessed be God forever.

Teacher
Bless the hands that turn the taps to get water. Bless the heads that carry home buckets of water.

All
Blessed be God forever.

Teacher moves around the children with a Holy Water font or with a small bowl of Holy Water.

Teacher
As we dip our hands in the water, we remember where it comes from. We remember the pumps and the wells, the taps and the buckets, the water tanks and the pipes. We remember those like Tojo who do not have enough water. We know that God the Father, Son and Holy Spirit is with us always and we ask God to bless us.

All
The children are invited to bless themselves with the Holy Water as they say:

In the name of the Father and of the Son and of the Holy Spirit. Amen.

Sign of the Cross.

Day Three

Continue song: *Water Litany*

STORY

The Woman at the Well
(Adapted from John 4:7-14)

Jesus had been walking for a long time. This part of the country was strange to him, he was very thirsty and he wanted to find some water. He walked quickly. Soon he came to a well called Jacob's Well. It was an old well and it was very deep. Jesus could not get a drink because he had no cup or jar or bucket to reach the water with. He sat down. He knew that wells were very important places. He knew that sooner or later everyone needed water. He knew that if he waited someone would come along and he would get a drink.

Sure enough, he had only just sat down when one of the local women came along. She did not know Jesus. She did not speak to him. She began to fill her water-jar.

Jesus said to her, 'Give me a drink please.'

The woman was surprised that this man whom she did not know spoke to her.

She did not answer 'yes' and she did not answer 'no'. She said, 'You have no bucket and the well is deep.' Then Jesus and the woman began to talk together. As they talked, the woman discovered that Jesus knew her very well. Indeed, she was amazed at how well he knew her.

They went on talking. The more they talked, the more she wondered how he knew so much about her. Then, without getting Jesus his drink from the well, she jumped up and ran off to the town to get her neighbours to come and meet this man. 'Come and see this man,' she told them, 'Come and see this man who has told me so much about myself.'

Her friends and neighbours came running to see if Jesus was who the woman thought he was. 'You are right,' they told her, 'we have seen him for ourselves and he really is who you said.' They were very excited to have Jesus there at their well, in their town. They invited him to stay there with them. Jesus stayed and talked to them and told them stories. In return, the woman and her neighbours looked after Jesus until it was time for him to travel on.

CHATTING

...about the story

Tell us about a time when you went on a long walk. Have you ever been on a long walk and been thirsty? What did you do? How does it

feel to be thirsty? Are there other times when you have felt thirsty – perhaps when you've been playing a football game or running a lot? Tell us about the things you do that can make you feel thirsty.

Has anyone ever asked you to get them a drink of water? Perhaps you have a little brother or sister who cannot reach the tap. Have you ever had to ask for a drink, perhaps when you were sick and had to stay in bed? Tell us about a time when you visited someone in hospital. Did they have water beside their bed?

In the story, Jesus and the woman who met at the well came to know each other. Why do you think the well was an important place in those days? Do you think a well would have been the kind of place where people would arrange to meet? Why? Tell us about a place in your neighbourhood where people go to meet each other?

How do people get to know each other? What kind of things would you tell someone so that they could get to know you better? What kind of questions would you ask someone if you wanted to get to know them better? Do you think Jesus and the woman at the well stayed friends even after Jesus moved on? Jesus stayed in the town for a few days. Can you think of any stories Jesus might have told the townspeople? How do you think the people would have looked after Jesus? Do you think they would have given him food and drink? What else would they have done for him?

ART

Diviner Collage/Diviner Rods

For each group you will need:
- old magazines/comics
- adhesive
- scissors
- a large sheet of paper with a 'Y' outline.

Arrange the children in groups of four or five.

Distribute the sheets of paper with the 'Y' outline. Invite the children to cut out pictures of water and any things that are associated with water, e.g. baths, buckets, umbrellas, etc. Stick the pictures on the 'Y'. Cut the 'Y' outline to make a diviner rod. These could then be mounted and displayed with a title like: *Our Diviner Collage* or *Our Diviner Rods/Sticks*.

PRAYERTIME

Sign of the Cross.

Teacher
As we light this candle we remember that God is always with us.
God loves us and takes care of us always.
One of the things which reminds us of God's great love for us is water. Water gives life, keeps the earth watered, helps us quench our thirst and keeps our bodies healthy.
We thank God for water.

All
For water that gurgles and gushes and goes,
For water that trickles and tumbles and roars,
For water that splashes and sparkles and spouts,
For water that flows gently in and out.

Sign of the Cross.

Continue song: *Water Litany*

Continue art: *Diviner Collage/Diviner Rods*

Recall story: *The Woman at the Well*

POEM

Granny's Finger

My Granny has one twiggy finger,
It has a life of its own.
It hovers in mid-air detecting
Underground Ticklish Zones.

It twitches and tweaks and hovers,
A diviner's rod gone berserk.
It darts; it starts then it's still,
But watch out for one sudden jerk!

My Granny has one twiggy finger,
It knows how to make tickles spout.
It's coming…it's coming…it's coming…
It dives in and laughter spurts out!

or

Water

Water has no taste at all,
Water has no smell;
Water's in the waterfall,
In pump, and tap, and well.

Water's everywhere about;
Water's in the rain,
In the bath, the pond, and out
At sea it's there again.

Water comes into my eyes
And down my cheek in tears,
When mother cries, 'Go back and try
To wash behind those ears.'
John R. Crossland

WORKSHEET

If you wish to use the worksheet or workbook page which accompanies this lesson, this is an appropriate time to do so.

CHATTING

...about the picture on page 16

Have you ever seen a well like this one? Who are the two people? What do you think the two birds are saying to each other? If you wanted a drink of water, would you go to a well? What would you do? What country do you think this well is in? How do you know that? Guess how deep this well is.

PRAYERTIME

Note: For this prayertime gather the children around the spot where the rain-gauge was put into the ground earlier in the week. Alternatively, take up the rain-gauge before the prayertime and place it on the table beside the candle. In this prayertime we continue the practice of gradually familiarising the children with the Eucharistic responses.

Sign of the Cross.

Teacher
As we gather around our rain-gauge let us thank God for water that falls as rain.

All
We praise you, we bless you, we thank you.

Teacher
Hold up the rain-gauge for all the class to see.

This is our rain-gauge which we placed in the ground to catch the rain that falls from the sky.

All
We praise you, we bless you, we thank you.

Invite a child to pour the water that has collected in the rain-gauge into a separate glass. A child can hold the glass up for all to see.

Teacher
This is the rain-water that fell from the sky and was collected in our rain-gauge during the week.

Or, in the case of a dry week:

We have no rain in our rain-gauge this week!

All
We praise you, we bless you, we thank you.

Teacher
Let us give thanks to God.
For drizzly rain that tickles our skin.

All
We praise you, we bless you, we thank you.

Teacher
For heavy rain that makes big puddles for us to splash in.

All
We praise you, we bless you, we thank you.

Teacher
For showers of rain that run down our window-panes.

All
We praise you, we bless you, we thank you.

Teacher
For soft summer rain that helps our flowers to grow.

All
We praise you, we bless you, we thank you.

Teacher
Glory be to the Father, and to the Son, and to the Holy Spirit.

All
As it was in the beginning, is now and ever shall be, world without end. Amen.

Sign of the Cross.

Note: In the prayertime on Day Five we continue to provide the children with an opportunity to read from the Bible. A child may be invited to read a short phrase from the Bible based on the story of the Woman at the Well. Choose the reader before the prayertime begins. It might also be helpful to have written the phrase: A woman came to draw water from the well, and Jesus said to her, 'Give me a drink of water please' *on a flashcard in advance of the prayertime. The flashcard could then be placed within the covers of the Bible so that the children will associate the phrase with the Bible.*

Day Five

ACTIVITY

Rainmaker

How to play
- Choose someone to act as the rainmaker of the storm.
- Players form a circle.
- Rainmaker stands in the centre of the circle facing the first child.
- Rainmaker starts by tapping her/his finger against the palm of the hand, copied by the first child.
- The action is passed on to the child on the left of the first child, who passes it on to the child on her/his left... and so on until they are all performing the action which sounds like gentle and increasingly heavy rainfall.
- The rainmaker then repeats the whole process with the same or a new hand-action (e.g. clapping hands), which makes the sound of the crescendo of the storm.
- The rainmaker decreases the volume of the storm by going through the above steps in reverse until the last child tapping her/his finger against the palm of the hand is silent.

PRAYERTIME

Bible Procession Ritual

Note: Take the Bible from its place in the classroom. Form a simple procession. As one child carries the Bible and another child carries the unlit candle (other items like flowers, incense stick, cloth, etc could also be carried in the procession), process to a table where the Bible and the candle are placed reverently.

Children bow and return to their seats.

The teacher lights the candle. You may also like to burn an incense stick or some grains of incense.

Sign of the Cross.

Sing: *Water Litany*

Teacher
Note: If time allows, you might like to repeat the following and invite other children to come forward, raise the Bible and read the biblical phrase.

One day Jesus met a woman at a well.
_____ *(name reader)* will read the Word of God for us today.

The child is invited to come forward to read from the Bible.
The teacher takes the Bible from the table and ceremoniously hands it to the child.
The child faces the class, holding the Bible.

Teacher
As we read from the Bible we remember that the Bible is God's Word. We know that God is with us. We know that God is with us in a special way when we read from the Bible. Imagine a woman beside Jacob's Well. It's a very hot day. She is drawing water from the well. She is using a water-jar. It is very hard work. She is thinking about how long it will take her to carry the water home on her head. She sees a man sitting by the well. She doesn't say anything to him. The man is Jesus.

Reader
The Lord be with you.

All
And also with you.

Teacher
We read from the holy Gospel according to
John.

All
Glory to you, O Lord.

Reader
A woman came to draw water from the well,
and Jesus said to her 'Give me a drink of water
please'.
The Gospel of the Lord *(raising the Bible)*.

All
Praise to you, Lord Jesus Christ.

All
For all God's stories that we tell,
For all God's stories that we read,
For all God's stories that we hear,
We thank you, God. Amen.

Sign of the Cross.

Water Litany

Bríd Ní Chatnáin

Capo 3: Play D

2. With water we all wash ourselves both morning time and night.
   It keeps us fresh, it keeps us safe, it helps us through our lives.

3. The water feeds the flowers too, it makes the grass look green.
   In nature if we look around its beauty can be seen.

Lesson 12: Jesus – Teacher

In the morning, while it was still very dark,
he got up and went out to a deserted place,
and there he prayed.
(Mark 1:35)

Jesus liked to be with people, to share his food, his stories and his life. However, there were times when he liked to be alone. The Gospels tell us how the Spirit frequently led Jesus into the desert to be by himself and to pray to God the Father. The apostles saw Jesus pray and noticed how central it was to his life. They were aware of the closeness of the relationship between Jesus and God. They observed the joy, peace and happiness Jesus experienced from speaking with the Father. They knew it was Jesus' relationship with God which enabled him to continue his work. So they asked him 'Lord, teach us to pray'. They were probably quite shocked when he told them 'Say this when you pray: Father (Abba)'. Jewish children used the word 'Abba' when speaking to their own father; it is an intimate, familial term, rather like our 'Dad'. The Jews at the time were scandalised that anyone would dare address God in such intimate terms. For them, God was a remote and distant God – a God to whom they offered homage.

By addressing God as 'Abba', Jesus opened up a whole new way of understanding our relationship with God. Jesus tells us that God wants to be addressed as 'Abba'. When we address God as 'Abba' we are not limiting our relationship with God to formal praise, adoration and thanksgiving. We are relating to God in a more intimate way, with the same confidence and trust that little children place in their fathers and mothers and those who love and care for them.

Through Baptism we are sisters and brothers of Jesus and we celebrate the fact that we are God's children. Because we are God's children, we too can share in the relationship of Jesus with God, we too can address God as 'Abba' or 'Father', just as Jesus did. It was the address of

God as 'Abba' that led people to ask 'Who is this man Jesus?' They were answered in the proclamation 'He is the Son of God'.

FOR THE TEACHER:

A thought before beginning

Lord, may your love play upon
    my voice,
and rest in my silence.
Let it pass through my heart,
into all that I do.
Let your love shine like stars in the darkness of
    my sleep,
and in the dawn at my awakening.
Let it burn in all the flames of my desires,
and flow in all the currents of my love.
Let me carry your love in my life,
as a harp does its music,
and give it back to you at last with my life.
    Donal Neary SJ,
    based on a poem by Tagore

What am I trying to do?

To help the children to become aware of the close relationship between Jesus and God the Father.

Why?

So as to deepen their understanding of God as a personal God, whom they can address as 'Abba'. So that they will deepen their awareness of the importance of prayer in their own lives.

Overview of the Week

	Continue song			
	Did You Know?			
	Story: *Jesus Prays*	Continue song		
Song: *Amen*	Chatting about the	Recall story	Continue song	
Chatting about	story	Poem: *When I Want*	Revise poem	
chatting	Activity: *Jesus*	*To Pray*	Continue art	
Activity: *Who?*	*Teaches His Friends*	Art: *Our Prayer*	Remember and Say	
Where? What?	*To Pray*	*Pictures*	Worksheet	Bible Procession
Prayertime	Prayertime	Prayertime	Prayertime	Ritual

Day One

SONG

Amen

CHATTING

...about chatting

When we sit together like this, we chat with one another. We chat about all sorts of things. Let's think of some of the things we chatted about in this class last week. Is it good to chat like this in class? Why? Why not? What do you like chatting about most?/least? Apart from chatting in class like this, who else do you chat with at school? What do you chat about? Would you chat about different things in different places, e.g. in the playground, in the PE hall, before class begins, when the day is over? Tell us about some of the things you might chat about in the playground/hall/on the way home from school. What is different about the sort of things you might chat about in class and the sort of things you might chat about outside of class? Who do you like to

chat with at home? Is it easy to chat when there is noise, like when the TV is on? Where do you go when you want a really good chat with somebody? What sort of things would you tell your mam/dad/guardian? If something was really bothering you, who would you tell? What sort of things do friends chat about? Tell us some things you would chat about with a friend. Would it be different to chatting with your man/dad/guardian? Why? Why not?

ACTIVITY

Who? Where? What?

If possible, get the children to sit in a circle for this activity. A soft ball will be passed from one child to another. The thrower of the ball names the child to whom the ball is to be passed and asks that child a question about chatting. The question must start with a Who? a Where? or a What? e.g. 'Mary, where do you like to chat?', 'Mary, who do you like to chat to?', 'Mary, what do you like to chat about?' The child answers the question and proceeds to pass (throw) the ball onto another child, asking him/her a Who? Where? What? question.

Continue the game until every child has been involved.

PRAYERTIME

Sign of the Cross.

Teacher *(as the candle is lit)*
Praise to the Father.
Praise to the Son.
Praise to the Spirit.
The Three in One.

Today let us thank God for all the times we spend chatting and talking to those we love.

All
Praise to the Father.
Praise to the Son.
Praise to the Spirit.
The Three in One.

Teacher
For our chats in the classroom.

All
Praise to the Father.
Praise to the Son.
Praise to the Spirit.
The Three in One.

Teacher
For our chats with our friends.

All
Praise to the Father.
Praise to the Son.
Praise to the Spirit.
The Three in One.

Teacher
For our chats at home.

All
Praise to the Father.
Praise to the Son.
Praise to the Spirit.
The Three in One.

Teacher
For all those who listen to us.

All
Praise to the Father.
Praise to the Son.
Praise to the Spirit.
The Three in One.

Teacher
For God who listens to us at all times.

All
Glory be to the Father…

Sign of the Cross.

Day Two

Continue song: *Amen*

DID YOU KNOW?

Jesus loved God the Father. He often prayed to God. He told his friends that they could talk to God too. He taught them the 'Our Father'. When we pray the 'Our Father' we talk to God too.

STORY

Jesus Prays

One day Jesus was very tired. He and his twelve apostles had worked hard all day. Crowds of people had come to him and by evening he was exhausted. He told his friends he wanted to be alone. He went off to a quiet place and stayed there for a long time. There he talked and listened to the Father.

Let's stop a minute and think about where Jesus might have gone…

Why do you think Jesus was tired? What makes you tired? Where do you go to when you are tired and you want to be by yourself? Where did Jesus go to? What kind of a quiet place do you think he found? Let's close our eyes and see if we can imagine Jesus going to this quiet place. Maybe he went into an empty room. Maybe he went into a desert. Maybe he went for a walk. Maybe he sat under a tree.

Imagine the place where you think he went. What do you think he talked to God about? Sometimes when Jesus talked with God he called God 'Abba' – it's a bit like our word 'Dad'. Why do you think he called God 'Abba'? Let's say the word together.

Let's finish our story...

Sometimes the apostles and Jesus' friends didn't know how Jesus could spend such a long time praying and chatting with God his Father. So one day while Jesus was off praying they talked amongst themselves.

'What a long time Jesus spends praying,' Andrew said to the other apostles. 'I couldn't pray for such a long time.' 'I couldn't either,' said Simon, 'I wouldn't know what to say.' 'Maybe,' said John, 'we could ask Jesus to teach us to pray.'

So when Jesus came back they said, 'Jesus, teach us to pray. Tell us what you say.' 'This is how I pray,' said Jesus. 'Our Father who art in heaven, hallowed be thy name. Thy kingdom come, thy will be done on earth as it is in heaven. Give us this day our daily bread and forgive us our trespasses, as we forgive those who trespass against us. And lead us not into temptation but deliver us from evil.'

But still the friends were not happy. 'But how can you spend such a long time praying?' James and Philip asked at the same time.

Jesus explained that when he prayed, he was not really alone. The Holy Spirit was there with him, helping him to remember Abba's love. When Jesus thought of God's great love, he felt like praising and thanking his Father.

CHATTING

...about the story

Jesus went to a quiet place to pray. Do you pray? When? Where do you go to pray? Who do you pray with? What do you talk to God about when you pray? What do you like about praying? Sometimes we light candles to help us to pray. What else helps you to pray? Does it help when we sing songs/close our eyes, etc?

Did Jesus' friends find it easy to pray? What did Jesus say when the apostles asked him how to pray? Do you think that his friends found it easy to pray for a long time? Why might it be hard to pray for a long time? Who helped Jesus to pray? Could the Holy Spirit help us to pray today? How?

ACTIVITY

Jesus Teaches His Friends To Pray

Ask the children to draw Jesus praying in the quiet place they imagined earlier in the lesson.

or

Draw a picture of Jesus sitting among his friends teaching them how to pray. Display the children's work under a caption, e.g. 'Jesus teaches us how to pray'.

PRAYERTIME

Note: This mirror-action prayer may be repeated if time allows.

Sign of the Cross.

Teacher *(as the candle is lit)*
Praise to the Father.
Praise to the Son.
Praise to the Spirit.
The Three in One.

Teacher
Our Father, who art in heaven *(arms crossed over chest)*

All
Our Father, who art in heaven *(arms crossed over chest)*

Teacher
Hallowed be thy name *(arms extended, level with shoulders)*

All
Hallowed be thy name *(arms extended, level with shoulders)*

Teacher
Thy Kingdom come *(arms extended high above head)*

All
Thy Kingdom come *(arms extended high above head)*

Teacher
Thy will be done on earth *(head bowed, hands together in front)*

All
Thy will be done on earth *(head bowed, hands together in front)*

Teacher
As it is in heaven *(arms extended, palms facing upwards)*

All
As it is in heaven *(arms extended, palms facing upwards)*

All
Praise to the Father.
Praise to the Son.
Praise to the Spirit.
The Three in One. Amen.

Sign of the Cross.

Day Three

Continue song: *Amen*

Recall story: *Jesus Prays*

POEM

When I Want To Pray

When I want to pray
I don't put on a face
Or search for a desert
Or other such place.
I can pray at my ease
Any place I can find,
Whether sitting or kneeling,
The Lord doesn't mind.
Christy Kenneally

ART

Our Prayer Pictures

Note: *This artwork may take two days to complete.*

For each child you will need:
*   paper/card
*   crayons/markers
*   puncher to make holes for the picture
*   a piece of wool/twine

Distribute paper/card to the children. Ask the children to write a simple prayer to God the Father, e.g. 'God our Father, we love you.' 'God our Father, thank you for loving me.' 'Abba, we know that you are always with us.' 'Abba, we pray to you.' etc.

Ask them to put a border/frame on their prayer picture and to decorate it. With a puncher make two holes at the top of the prayer picture. Distribute the wool/twine. Ask the children to loop the wool/twine through the holes and to secure it. The picture can now be hung.

If time allows, make a big collage of the word 'Amen'. Hang the children's prayer pictures around the 'Amen'.

PRAYERTIME

Note: You may like to repeat this mirror-prayer more than once if time allows.

Sign of the Cross.

Teacher *(as the candle is lit)*
Praise to the Father.
Praise to the Son.
Praise to the Spirit.
The Three in One.

Teacher
Give us this day our daily bread *(arms extended, beckoning actions towards body)*

All
Give us this day our daily bread *(arms extended, beckoning actions towards body)*

Teacher
And forgive us our trespasses *(head bowed, hand on heart)*

All
And forgive us our trespasses *(head bowed, hand on heart)*

Teacher
As we forgive those who trespass against us *(handshake of friendship towards child beside them)*

All
As we forgive those who trespass against us *(handshake of friendship towards child beside them)*

Teacher
And lead us not into temptation *(arms extended in front, hands making a 'pushing away' gesture)*

All
And lead us not into temptation *(arms extended in front, hands making a 'pushing away' gesture)*

Teacher
But deliver us from evil *(hands clasped in front, head bowed)*

All
But deliver us from evil *(hands clasped in front, head bowed)*

All
Praise to the Father.
Praise to the Son.
Praise to the Spirit.
The Three in One. Amen.

Sign of the Cross.

Day Four

Continue song: *Amen*

Revise poem: *When I Want to Pray*

Continue art *(if not already completed)*

REMEMBER AND SAY

Jesus taught us to call God 'Father'
And so we have the courage to say:
'Our Father who art in heaven,
Amen, Amen,' we pray.

WORKSHEET

If you wish to use the worksheet or workbook page which accompanies this lesson, this is an appropriate time to do so.

PRAYERTIME

Sign of the Cross.

Teacher *(as the candle is lit)*
Praise to the Father.
Praise to the Son.
Praise to the Spirit.
The Three in One.

As we gather to remember God's love for each one of us, we say the prayer Jesus taught his friends.

Our Father, who art in heaven *(arms crossed over chest)*

All
Hallowed be thy name *(arms extended, level with shoulders)*

Teacher
Thy Kingdom come *(arms extended high above head)*

All
Thy will be done on earth *(head bowed, hands together in front)*

Teacher
As it is in heaven *(arms extended, palms facing upwards)*

All
Give us this day our daily bread *(arms extended, beckoning actions towards body)*

Teacher
And forgive us our trespasses *(head bowed, hand on heart)*

All
As we forgive those who trespass against us *(handshake of friendship towards child beside them)*

Teacher
And lead us not into temptation *(arms extended in front, hands making a 'pushing away' gesture)*

All
But deliver us from evil *(hands clasped in front, head bowed)*

Amen *(hands outstretched, level with shoulders)*

All
Praise to the Father.
Praise to the Son.
Praise to the Spirit.
The Three in One.

Sign of the Cross.

Note: On Day Five the children will read the Word of God from the Bible. A child will be invited to read a short phrase from the Bible based on the story which is told in the lesson. The child who is to act as reader could be picked before the prayertime begins. To facilitate the reader, have the phrase 'Jesus got up and went to a deserted place and there he prayed' written on a flashcard in advance of the prayertime. The flashcard could then be placed within the covers of the Bible so that the children will associate the phrase with the Bible.

Day Five

PRAYERTIME

Bible Procession Ritual

Note: In preparation for the prayertime, display the artwork the children have done during the week.

Take the Bible from its place in the classroom. Form a simple procession. As one child carries the Bible and another child carries the unlit candle (other items like flowers, incense stick, cloth, etc could also be carried in the procession), process to a table where the Bible and the candle are placed reverently.

Children bow and return to their seats.

Song: *Amen*

The teacher lights the candle. You may also like to burn an incense stick or some grains of incense.

Sign of the Cross.

Teacher
Note: If time allows, you might like to repeat the following and invite other children to come forward, raise the Bible and read the biblical phrase.

In the morning while it was still very dark, Jesus got up and went out to a deserted place and there he prayed.

_____ *(name reader)* will read the Word of God for us today.

The child is invited to come forward to read from the Bible.
The teacher takes the Bible from the table and ceremoniously hands it to the child.
The child faces the class, holding the Bible.

Teacher
As we read from the Bible we remember that the Bible is the Word of God. We know that God is with us. We know that God is with us in a special way when we read from the Bible. Today we hear how Jesus loved to talk to God his Father. The Holy Spirit helped Jesus to remember God's love. Jesus knew that God always listened to him when he prayed. Let's listen to God's word as we read from the Bible.

Reader
The Lord be with you.

All
And also with you.

Teacher
This reading is from the Gospel according to St Mark.

All
Glory to you, O Lord.

Reader
'Jesus got up and went to a deserted place and there he prayed'.
The Gospel of the Lord *(raising the Bible)*.

All
Praise to you, Lord Jesus Christ.

Sign of the Cross.

Great Amen   Seoirse Bodley

A - men.— A - men. A - men. A - men.

Lesson 13: One Moment

In the sixth month
the angel Gabriel was sent by God
to a town in Galilee called Nazareth.
(Luke 1:26)

O ur lives are made up of a series of
moments. Some moments carry
immediate importance for us and they touch
us deeply. Other moments pass us by almost
unnoticed. Each of us, however, has
experienced moments that stand out from the
rest, times when the ordinary takes on an
extra-ordinary significance. For instance, a
meal may be simply a meal, but when eaten
with certain people to mark a particular event
or experience, it can become very significant.
Such experiences touch us deeply and we
'ponder them in our hearts'. Our everyday
experiences then hold within them
possibilities for reflection about ourselves, our
relationships, and our world. When preparing
for an event, the level of thoughtfulness with
which we attend to the preparation is a
measure of the importance in which we hold
the event. The recognition of such times as
being special brings with it the capacity to
enrich our lives.

Advent is a time when we can help the
children to prepare thoughtfully for
Christmas. In these three Advent lessons we
focus on the significant moments in the
children's own experiences as they prepare for
Christmas. How these possibilities unfold
during the Advent season will be different for
each child. For one child it may be the
moment the first Christmas card arrives, or
when the crib appears in the church; for
another it might be the moment when the
first Christmas carol is heard. For others it
might be the arrival of the Christmas tree or
the moment it sparkles with fairy lights. We
hope to heighten the children's sensitivities to
such moments. The greater their awareness of
such times as being special, the greater their
capacity to appreciate their richness.

We also recall the significant moments in the
Christmas biblical narratives as they move
towards the celebration of the birth of Jesus.
We begin by telling the children the story of
the Annunciation from the perspective of
Mary as she remembers the moment when the
angel Gabriel told her she was going to be the
mother of Jesus.

FOR THE TEACHER:

A thought before beginning

Mary

In order to welcome the gift of
the body of Jesus
    we must look more fully at
    the woman
    who conceived him
    and gave him birth –
    Mary.

For none like her
    enveloped his body,
    touched his body,
    loved his body,
    washed his body,
    venerated his body.
The body of Christ
    flowed from her body,
    the fruit of her womb.
    It was her body that nourished his body:
    her breasts gave
    him the energy and nourishment to grow;
    her touch protected him
    and revealed to him that he was loved;
    her presence made him sing with joy;
    the light in her eyes called forth the light
    in his.
Before she was touched and sanctified by his
words,
she had been touched and sanctified by his
body,
    the Temple of God,
    the sacred place where God resides.
                    Jean Vanier

What am I trying to do?

- To help the children to tap into the significant moments in their own experience as they prepare for Christmas.
- To introduce them to the story of the Annunciation, an event which marks a significant moment in the biblical infancy narrative.

Why?

So that their preparation for and celebration of Christmas will be more significant.
So that they will come to a deeper understanding of the significance of the birth of Jesus.

Note: To mark the period of preparation for Christmas, you may wish to have an Advent Wreath in the classroom. Instead of lighting the usual candle during prayertime, you might light the appropriate candle or candles on the Advent Wreath.

A simple wreath can be made as follows: Fill a circular tray with wet sand. Place four candles, three purple and one red, on the tray, secured by the sand. Arrange evergreen leaves around the edge of the tray. Intertwine a purple ribbon through the evergreen. It will be difficult to move this particular type of wreath from place to place, so find the most appropriate position for it in the classroom.

Alternatively, you may wish to make an Advent Wall Frieze. On a large sheet of chart paper (you might like to use a piece of wallpaper) paint a country scene with rolling hills, etc. Winding through the hills, paint a road/path. At the end of this road/path draw the empty stable. To represent the four weeks of Advent, mark out three 'stops' on the road to Bethlehem, the stable being the final and fourth stop. Make a cut-out picture of Mary and Joseph. Each week over the coming weeks, ask the children to 'move' Mary and Joseph towards Bethlehem.

Overview of the Week

	Continue song			
	Recall story	Continue song		
Song: *Mary*	Poem: *Mary's Song*	Poem: *A Few Little*	Continue song, art	
Story: *One Moment*	Did You Know?	*Moments*	Worksheet	Chatting about
Chatting about the	Activity: *String of*	Art: *Special*	Chatting about the	special moments at
story	*Bells*	*Christmas Letter*	picture	home
Prayertime	Prayertime	Prayertime	Prayertime	Prayertime

Day One

SONG

Mary

STORY

One Moment
(Adapted from Luke 1:26-38)

One very ordinary day Mary was in the kitchen. The sun was shining in the window and onto the table where she was baking bread. Mary felt happy. As she kneaded the

133

dough, she hummed a little song to herself. Then an unusual thing happened. She had turned around to get some more flour, when suddenly, out of nowhere, an angel stood in the kitchen doorway. Mary jumped.

'Oh!' she remembered saying, almost dropping the flour.

The angel smiled. 'Hello, Mary,' he said. 'My name is Gabriel. Do not be afraid. I have news for you!'

Mary remembered how surprised she was by what the angel had said. 'I hope it's good news,' she said, in a worried voice.

'Don't be afraid, it's wonderful news,' Gabriel replied.

Mary remembered listening to what the angel had to say.

'You are very special, Mary, and God loves you,' Gabriel continued. 'You are going to have a baby – a very special baby boy. His name will be Jesus. He will be God's son.'

Mary was amazed. For a moment she didn't know what to say. So the angel continued...

'And I have more news too, your cousin Elizabeth is also going to have a baby!'

Mary knew Elizabeth had wanted a baby for a long time. She knew Elizabeth would be overjoyed. She knew it would be lovely for her baby to have a little cousin.

She said, 'I know that God cares for me very much. God is very good. I will do whatever God asks.' Then the angel disappeared and Mary went on with her baking, singing her song.

Note: The children at this point could sing the song 'Mary'.

CHATTING

...about the story

Have you ever heard this story before? Tell us about when you heard it before. When Mary began to think back on the first moment, how do you think she felt? How did she feel at the end of the story? Do you think this was a special moment for Mary when she heard what the angel had to say? Why?

Have you ever heard a 'good-news' story? Would you like to tell us about it? Have you ever heard good news about a new baby? Would you like to tell us about that? When you go home today, you could ask those you live with if they ever heard a good-news story about a new baby going to be born.

Mary's new baby was to be called Jesus. Do you know how or why your name was chosen? Perhaps you can ask someone at home about it.

PRAYERTIME

Note: Today's prayertime focuses on the words of Mary and the angel Gabriel. Using the format of a simple prayer-round, the children will pass a blessing around the class. If possible, arrange the children in a circle. If this is not possible, ensure that the children can turn with ease to the child beside them in order to shake her/his hand.

Begin the blessing with the teacher turning to shake the hand of the child on her/his left and saying: 'You are very special (name child) and God loves you.' This child then responds with 'God cares for me. Thanks be to God', and then turns to the child on his/her left, etc, and so the blessing is passed around the whole group.

Sign of the Cross.

Teacher *(as the candle or the appropriate candle on the Advent Wreath is lit)*
In our winter darkness our Advent Candle lights the way.

The angel Gabriel blessed Mary when he said: 'You are very special, Mary, God loves you.' Mary thanked God for the blessing. She said: 'God is very good.' We are going to give God's blessing to the person beside us by saying: 'You are very special *(name of child)*, God loves you.' The answer to the blessing will be: 'God cares for me. Thanks be to God.'

Leader
Turning to shake the hand of the child on his/her left.
You are very special *(name)*, God loves you.

Child 1 *(with help from the teacher if necessary)*
God cares for me. Thanks be to God.

Child 1
Turning to shake the hand of the child on her/his left.
You are very special *(name)*, God loves you.

Child 2
God cares for me. Thanks be to God.

Child 2
Turning to shake the hand of the child on his/her left.
You are very special *(name)*, God loves you.

Continue until each child has given and received a blessing.

Teacher
Let us hold hands with the person beside us as we say together:

All
Hail Mary…

Sign of the Cross.

Continue song: *Mary*

Recall story: *One Moment*

 POEM

Mary's Song

I'm so full of joy
I could whistle and sing
For I've just been told
A most wonderful thing.
I'll soon have a baby –
A baby – just think!
A tiny wee fellow
All wrinkled and pink,
To hold and to cuddle,
And if he should cry,
To sing off to sleep
With a soft lullaby.
Finbar O'Connor

 DID YOU KNOW?

Mary would always remember the moment when the angel Gabriel told her she was going to have a baby and that the baby's name would be Jesus. It was a very special moment because it was such an important moment. We still remember it every day at Angelus time. The Angelus is a prayer which remembers the story of what happened when the angel came to Mary. Twice each day, at 12 o'clock and 6 o'clock, the church bell rings to remind us to pray the Angelus.

Did you ever hear a church bell? When might you hear a church bell? Who do you think might ring the church bell? Have you ever heard of the Angelus bell?

ACTIVITY

String of Bells

You will need:

- Paper for each child
- Crêpe paper (different colours)
- Adhesive
- Scissors

Distribute the paper. Ask each child to draw a bell and cut it out.

Then each child tears some crêpe paper into pieces and rolls them into balls. Using adhesive, stick them to the bell shapes. Make a string of bells by arranging several bells along the wall. If you wish, you might like to make a caption to go under the bells, e.g. 'My name is Gabriel. I have news for you.'

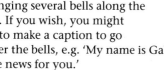

PRAYERTIME

Note: This is a good opportunity to introduce the children to the Angelus-time as a special moment of prayer. While the children are too young to understand the Angelus completely, they are ready to be introduced to the tradition of the Angelus-time. While the following prayer is not the Angelus as we know it, it focuses on the content of the prayer. If you can hear the Angelus bell you might make a point of praying at that time. If not, it may be possible to focus on 12 o'clock as the Angelus-time and to pray the following prayer. You may if you wish ring a bell before you begin the prayer.

Sign of the Cross.

Teacher *(as the candle, or the appropriate candle on the Advent Wreath, is lit)*
God is the light of our life.
The light of all time.

As we ring our bell we know that God is with us now.

Today we remember in prayer the story of the special moment when the angel Gabriel came to Mary. We will stand up and use our bodies along with our voices to pray to God.

Teacher *(with children repeating words and actions)*
Hail Mary, full of grace.
(Arms outstretched at the side, palms facing upwards)

The Lord is with thee.
(Arms lifted high above the head)

Blessed art though among women.
(Arms outstretched in front, palms facing upwards)

And blessed is the fruit of thy womb, Jesus.
(Cradle and gently rock the 'baby' in arms)

Sign of the Cross.

Note: For Art on Day Three (Special Christmas Letter) ask the children to bring in pieces of coloured string/wool. You will also need a fairly large box to collect the Special Christmas Letters, and some old Christmas cards/Christmas paper if you intend to decorate the outside of the box.

Day Three

Continue song: *Mary*

POEM

A Few Little Moments

The moment the angel appeared,
Mary grew worried, and yet,
The moment she first heard the news
Was a moment she'd never forget.

The moment she left on her journey,
Mary grew worried, and yet,
The moment Elizabeth hugged her
Was a moment she'd never forget.

ART

Special Christmas Letter

This is the time of the year when we 'take a moment' to reflect on and to acknowledge our appreciation for others in a way that we may not always do during the rest of the year. We do this in different ways, through sending cards, giving presents, etc. In this activity we want the children to take a moment to create something special for someone in the class and to reflect on that special moment. Each child will be given the name of another child in the class. The children will be asked to write a wish for that person. Each child will get a 'Special Christmas Letter' during prayertime on Day Five of Lesson 15.

This art may take two days to complete.

You will need:
- A4 sheet of paper for each child
- Adhesive
- Pieces of coloured string/wool
- A fairly large box for the Christmas Post-box.

Distribute the paper and ask the children to write their own name lengthways across the page. *If time allows, ask them to decorate their sheet.* When the children are ready, collect all the sheets from them, then redistributing these sheets give each child the name of another child in the class. *Turn the sheet face down on the desk so no one else will see the name.* Get the children to turn the sheet secretly and see what name they have got, then turn the sheet back. The children will write a Christmas wish for that person on this side of the sheet. Get them to close their eyes and think of the person. Now ask them to write their message, e.g. 'Happy Advent,' 'Happy Christmas', 'Have Fun', 'Advent Love', 'Advent Joy', 'Have a Great Time', etc. love _____ *(child signs her/his name)*. Decorate the Christmas wish.

To make the 'Letter', ask the children to fold the sheet, making sure that the name of the child to whom the message is being sent is clearly seen. Using adhesive, stick around the

edge of the 'Letter'. Tie a bow around the 'Special Christmas Letter' with the coloured string/wool.

Present/Prepare the 'Christmas Post-box'
If there is time, you could make the box special by helping the children to decorate it, e.g. by cutting out and sticking on pictures from old Christmas cards or wrapping paper.

PRAYERTIME

Sign of the Cross.

Teacher *(as the candle, or the appropriate candle on the Advent Wreath, is lit)*
In our winter darkness our Advent Candle lights the way.

During Advent we prepare to celebrate the birthday of Jesus. It's a special time. Today we wrote our good wishes for someone for Advent. God is with us as we send wishes to those we love.

Close your eyes.
Still your body.
Listen to your heart beat.
Listen to your breath as it goes in and out of your lungs, bringing God's gift of life to every part of your body.

Picture in your mind the person you are sending good wishes to. Think of the special message you have written. With your special inside voice that only you can hear, tell God the name of this person. Tell God what wish you made today. Ask God to take care of this person. Advent is a special time. It is a time when we prepare for Christmas by showing our love for others. Maybe you could watch to see if they have someone to play with at playtime, or maybe you could just say a friendly 'hello' to them, or maybe you could share a book with them. It could be anything you like. Ask God to be with you and to help you to remember to watch out for the person you are sending wishes to.

Open your eyes. Stretch.

Sign of the Cross.

Day Four

Continue song: *Mary*

Continue art *(if not already completed)*

WORKSHEET

If you wish to use the worksheet or workbook page which accompanies this lesson, this is an appropriate time to do so.

CHATTING

...about the picture on page 18

What is Mary doing? Have you ever made bread? Look at the little birds. They look surprised. Why? Mary looks surprised too. What has taken her by surprise? If you could go into the picture and talk to Mary, what would you say to her? Have you any questions you'd like to ask the angel while you're in there?

PRAYERTIME

Note: *Place the 'Christmas Post-box' in a prominent position where all the children can see it with ease.*

Sign of the Cross.

Teacher *(as the candle, or the appropriate candle on the Advent Wreath, is lit)*

In our winter darkness, our Advent Candle lights the way.

Let us ask God the Father, Son and Holy Spirit to be with us as we share our time and our love with others.

Ask the children to come forward one by one and to place their 'Special Christmas Letter' in the 'Christmas Post-box'. As each child places her/his letter in the box, the rest of the class can say:

All
Tidings of great joy,
The Lord is with us.

Teacher
God loves each one of us. God loves us like a mother loves her child. God loves us like a father who takes care of his child.
We ask God to take care of all the people we love.

Allow the children to mention a particular person if they wish.

Leave the box with the letters in a safe place in the classroom. The letters will be given out to the children during prayertime in Lesson 15, Day Five.

All
A Few Little Moments

The moment the angel appeared,
Mary grew worried, and yet,
The moment she first heard the news
Was a moment she'd never forget.

The moment she left on her journey,
Mary grew worried, and yet,
The moment Elizabeth hugged her
Was a moment she'd never forget.

Sign of the Cross.

CHATTING

PRAYERTIME

...about special moments at home

What preparations are being done at home at the moment? Tell us about some of them. What sort of things need to be done to prepare for Christmas? Who decorates the tree in your home? Have you sent any Christmas cards yet? Who might send a card to your home? Who prepares the food for Christmas Day? Do you help? What do you do? Getting ready for Christmas can be great fun. What is your favourite preparation? Getting ready for Christmas can also mean a lot of work for people. Who are the people who work hard to make Christmas special for others? What about the postperson who brings the Christmas cards? What about the shopkeepers who stay open long hours? Are there other people you can think of? Who in your home works hard to make Christmas a very special time? Tell us about them. Maybe we could do something to help make their preparation a little easier. Maybe we could give them a 'moment's rest'! Who would you like to do something special for? Maybe you could do it for your Dad/Mam, or maybe your Granny/Grandad, or maybe you could do something special for a brother or sister – it can be anyone at all who lives with you at home. Have you decided who it will be?

If time allows, you might like to get the children to draw about the special action they are going to do.

Sign of the Cross.

Song: *Mary*

Teacher (*as the candle, or the appropriate candle on the Advent Wreath, is lit*)
In our winter darkness, our Advent Candle lights the way.

Close your eyes.
Still your body.
Listen to your heart beat.

Picture in your imagination the person you have been thinking about. Now imagine the 'something special' you are going to do for them. Picture yourself at home. Are you on your own or are there other people there? What are the others doing? Picture yourself doing your 'special something'. You feel excited because you know that what you are doing is going to be a great help. You are surprised at how quickly you can do it. It doesn't take as long as you thought. It is a little hard but you are glad that you are doing it. You are nearly finished. Take one last look and see if you have forgotten anything.

Pause.

You feel very pleased with what you have done. You have done a good job. You hope that the person will be pleased too. With your special inside voice thank God for those who work to make Christmas a special time for you. Ask God to help you to make it a special time for others too.

Open your eyes.
Stretch.

All (*repeating after teacher*)
The moment the angel appeared,
Mary grew worried, and yet,
The moment she first heard the news
Was a moment she'd never forget.

The moment she left on her journey,
Mary grew worried, and yet,
The moment Elizabeth hugged her
Was a moment she'd never forget.

Sign of the Cross.

Mary

Christy Kenneally

1. Ma - ry will you take this ba - by boy?
Ma - ry will you take this ba - by boy? Will you
fill the world with love and joy? Will you
take this ba - by boy?

2. Mary, will you go to the little town?
   Mary, will you go to the little town?
   Will you find a manger to lay him down?
   Will you go to the little town?

3. Mary, will you show your little son?
   Mary, will you show your little son
   To the kings on whom the star has shone?
   Will you show your little son?

4. Mary, will you tell him we love him so?
   Mary, will you tell him we love him so?
   Will you tell him we would like to show
   That we love him, love him so?

Lesson 14: Watching, Waiting, Wondering

Where is the child who has been born king of the Jews? For we observed his star at its rising, and have come to pay him homage.
(Matthew 2:2)

Whenever times of deep significance are approaching we experience anticipation and excitement. The more important the event for us, the more time we are likely to invest in watching, waiting and wondering. This is a theme which resonates through the Old Testament. We hear about how the mother of Moses waited as the baby-basket floated down the river. Noah watched out for signs that the floods had ended. Abraham wondered how his descendants could be as numerous as the grains of sand on the shore. It was this momentum that gave life and hope to God's people as they waited for the coming of the Messiah.

Children have a great capacity for wonder as they wait for Christmas to arrive. They hear and see with awe the events of the Christmas stories as they unfold to them. In this lesson we help the children to become more attentive to the Christmas events by exploring the experiences of watching, waiting and wondering in their own lives, and in the story of the Three Kings.

FOR THE TEACHER:

A thought before beginning

The Advent

The events of history were controlled
for my coming to this world
no less than for the coming of the Saviour.
The time had to be ripe...
the place just right...
the circumstances ready...
before I could be born.
Anthony de Mello

What am I trying to do?

To provide an opportunity for the children to hear again the story of the Three Kings, with an emphasis on waiting, watching and wondering as the birth of Jesus approaches, and to focus the children on their own 'waiting' experiences as Christmas draws near.

Why?

So that they will come to a deeper understanding of the significance of Advent and Christmas.

Overview of the Week

Song: *Following a Star*	Continue song Story: *Watching, Waiting, Wondering*		Continue song Repeat poem	
Activity: *Musical Chairs* or *Pass the Ball*	Chatting about the story	Continue song Recall story	Art: *Silver Stars/Star Card*	Continue art
Chatting about the game	Activity: *I Wonder What Could it Be?*	Poem: *The Christmas Star*	Chatting about the picture	Worksheet
Prayertime	Poem: *Could It Be?* Prayertime	Prayertime	Prayertime	Prayertime

Day One

SONG

Following a Star

ACTIVITY

Musical Chairs

Note: The following games focus on observation. The aim of the games is to heighten the children's sense of watchfulness and attentiveness to themselves, to others, and to the situation.

How to play
- Form a large circle with everyone sitting on chairs.
- One 'extra' child stands inside the circle.
- Play some music.
- When the music plays, the children move and swap places.
- Whoever is left without a chair when the music stops becomes the 'extra' person.

The game continues.

or

Pass the Ball

Note: An object that makes a slight noise could also be passed round. The children would then need to watch and listen.

How to play
- Sit in a circle with everybody close together.
- Everyone sitting should have their hands behind their back.
- Choose one child to sit in the centre of the circle with his/her eyes closed.
- Someone goes around the outside of the circle and gives a ball to one of the children seated.

- The child in the centre uncovers his/her eyes.
- Seated children try to pass the ball around the circle, passing the ball to either the right or left, without the child in the middle seeing.
- The child in the middle has to try to guess who has the ball. They are allowed two guesses.
- Choose a new child for the middle and start again.

CHATTING

...about the game

Did you enjoy the game? Why? Why not? What did you have to watch out for? Was it difficult? Tell us about it. What other things in the game did you find it difficult to watch out for? Have you ever watched something carefully? What did you watch carefully? How did you feel while you were watching carefully? Did you learn anything from watching carefully? Do you think it is a good thing to watch carefully? Might there be things that it would not be good to watch? If you were not sure about whether you should watch something or not, what would you do? Is there a grown-up who could help you to decide? What kind of things do you enjoy watching? Have you ever missed something because you didn't watch carefully? Did you ever hear anyone tell you to 'watch out'? When? What are you watching out for as you wait for Christmas?

PRAYERTIME

Sign of the Cross.

Teacher *(as the candle, or appropriate candles on the Advent Wreath, is lit)*
In our winter darkness, our Advent Candle lights the way.

Let us think of some of the people who work hard to make Christmas special for us and thank God for what they do.

All *(with teacher)*
We watch and give thanks to God.

Teacher
Shopkeepers busy with their Christmas shop windows.

All
We watch and give thanks to God.

Teacher
Police busy directing the Christmas traffic.

All
We watch and give thanks to God.

Teacher
The postperson busy delivering the Christmas cards and parcels.

All
We watch and give thanks to God.

Teacher
Bakers busy making Christmas puddings and cakes.

All
We watch and give thanks to God.

Teacher
Carol singers as they sing Christmas songs.

All
We watch and give thanks to God.

Teacher
We thank God for all the people who work hard to make Christmas special for us all. Is there anyone special you would like to thank God for?

We pray that God the Father, Son and Holy Spirit will be with us as we prepare to celebrate Jesus' birthday.

All
Following a Star

Sign of the Cross.

Continue song: *Following a Star*

STORY

Watching, Waiting, Wondering
(Adapted from Matthew 2:1-3)

Once in the East there lived three kings. They were wise because they watched carefully, they waited endlessly, and they wondered at everything.

They watched the movements of the sun, the moon and the stars, they watched the changes in the weather and the ways of the animals. They looked deep into their own hearts and watched carefully to see what was happening inside themselves.

They waited patiently for those who were slow to move. They waited anxiously when there was nothing else they could do. But most of all, they waited eagerly for the right moment.

As they waited, they wondered. They wondered about the world. They wondered about life. They wondered about themselves.

'There is a new star in the sky tonight,' said Caspar.
'We see that,' said Balthasaar and Melchior.

They watched. They wondered.

'I wonder why there is a new star in the sky?' said Caspar.
'That's what I'm wondering too,' said Balthasaar.
'I wonder if it's a sign?' said Melchior, '…a star-sign.'

They watched. They waited. They wondered.

'Why are we waiting?' asked Balthasaar.
'Because we are wondering,' said Caspar.
'Waiting and wondering go well together,' said Melchior wisely.

They watched. They waited. They wondered.

Just at that moment the star began to move.

'Watch out!' said Melchior. 'The star is moving!'
'I see that,' said Caspar.
'I wonder why it's moving,' said Balthasaar.

They watched. They waited. They wondered.

'If something is moving, you can follow it,' said Caspar, wisely.
'True,' said Melchior. 'You cannot follow something that does not move.'
'Let's watch where this star goes and follow it,' suggested Balthasaar.

They stood up. They saddled their camels. They climbed on board.

'Ready …' said Caspar.
'Steady …' said Melchior.
'Go!' said Balthasaar.

And off they went to follow the star they had watched for, waited for, and wondered about – to follow wherever it would lead.

CHATTING

…about the story

The three people in the story were called 'wise' – do you think they were wise? Why? Do you know anyone whom you think is wise? Why would you call them wise? What kind of things did the wise people in the story do that showed their wisdom? Have you ever watched out for any of the things the wise people in the story watched for? Perhaps you could start today to watch out for some of the things they were interested in.

Have you ever had to wait? How do you feel when you are waiting for a surprise? A birthday? Christmas? An appointment at the clinic or the dentist? A visitor to your home? Your mum to come home from town? The wise ones were waiting for the star. We are waiting for that star too, in a way. We are waiting to celebrate the birth of the baby whom the star shone on. Do you think that the people in the story would have felt like we do – because we are all waiting for the same thing? They watched out for signs. We are watching for signs of Christmas too.

The people in the stories wondered about a lot of things. Do you ever wonder about anything? Have you ever wondered why Christmas is such a special time of the year? Let's wonder about it now.

ACTIVITY

I Wonder What Could it Be?

Let us play a game. Let us imagine that you could give any present you liked to your friend. I wonder what it would be! Close your eyes and imagine. Imagine the person. Now imagine what you might give to them.

Open your eyes again.
Let's say the poem *Could It Be?* and see if someone can guess what present is in your box.

Could it Be?

Teacher (*children repeating*)
Here is a box.
Make your hand into a fist.
Put on the lid.
Cover it with the other hand.
I wonder whatever inside it is hid.
Peek under the lid, by lifting your palm a little.
Could it be?
Take another look
Yes, without a doubt.
and another peep.
Open the box and let it come out.
Open your fist.
        Jean Chapman

Divide the children into pairs. Ask the children to face each other. One child says the poem while his/her partner listens. At the end of the poem the 'listener' guesses what is in the box. Then the other child says what he/she actually had. Repeat the exercise, reversing the roles.

Alternatively, a child could come to the top of the room and say the poem with the actions. The class could then guess what is in the box.

PRAYERTIME

Sign of the Cross.

Teacher *(as the candle, or appropriate candles on the Advent Wreath, is lit)*
In our winter darkness, our Advent Candle lights the way.

As we prepare for Christmas we wonder about a lot of things. We wonder if it will snow. We wonder if Santa will come. We wonder what presents we will get from others. We wonder what presents we can give to others. We wonder what cards we will make. We wonder about Mary and Joseph on that first Christmas night. We wonder what it must have been like.

I wonder, if you could have given a present to Jesus on that first Christmas night, what would it have been? Let's take a little time now to wonder what we would have given to Jesus.

Close your eyes.

Pause.

What have you got? Look at the present. It's a lovely present. Now imagine that you are going to give the present to Jesus. You can see Jesus, all snug and warm. He looks like he is waiting for you. Slowly you hand him the present. You wonder if he will like it. You wonder if he will make any sound. You watch to see his face as he looks at the present. You wait. Jesus looks up at you. He gives you a big smile. You feel very happy. You know that you are special to Jesus. You know that he loves you.

Open your eyes.
Stretch.

All
Could It Be? (with actions)

Sign of the Cross.

Continue song: *Following a Star*

Recall story: *Watching, Waiting, Wondering*

While retelling the story, invite the children to become involved in the telling. The children could say the words: 'They watched. They waited. They wondered.' Alternatively, the children could say the lines of Balthasaar, Caspar and Melchior.

POEM

The Christmas Star

A star looked down
from the frosty sky,
saw three lost kings
and winked its eye.

'Follow me,' it said
and blazed a trail
over sand and plain,
up-hill, down-dale.

'Here,' said the star
and faded from sight
as sun bathed the Baby
in clear morning light.
  Moira Andrew

PRAYERTIME

Sign of the Cross.

Teacher *(as the candle, or appropriate candles on the Advent Wreath, is lit)*
In our winter darkness, our Advent Candle lights the way.

Caspar, Melchior and Balthasaar were wise people. They were wise because they watched

145

and wondered and they waited for the right moment. We ask God to bless all the wise people we know, people who watch and care for us all the time. People who wonder each day if we are well, or how school went for us, or if we have eaten our meals, or if we are happy or sad.

Close your eyes and think of a wise person you know. Think of someone who cares for you. This person wonders how you are. They know the right time for things. This someone knows the right time for fun and for play. They know the right moment for meals and for bedtime. Picture the person in your mind.

Now let's thank God for all the wise people we know as we say: 'Thank you, God, for the people who watch and care for us.'

For mams and dads.

All
Thank you, God, for the people who watch and care for us.

Teacher
For our grans and grandads.

All
Thank you, God, for the people who watch and care for us.

Teacher
For those who live with us at home.

All
Thank you, God, for the people who watch and care for us.

Teacher
For our brothers and sisters.

All
Thank you, God, for the people who watch and care for us.

Teacher
For our friends at home and at school.

All
Thank you, God, for the people who watch and care for us.

Teacher
It is good to have someone who cares for you. It is good to know someone who is wise. With your special inside voice tell God about this person. Tell God what you like best about

what the wise person does or says. Maybe it's the way they hold your hand, maybe it's their smile. Tell God about her or him. Say 'Thank you' to God.

All
Thank you, God, for the people who watch and care for us.

Sign of the Cross.

Day Four

Continue song: *Following a Star*

Repeat poem: *The Christmas Star*

ART

Silver Stars

You will need:
- Stiff paper
- Aluminium foil
- Scissors
- Adhesive
- Thread
- Glitter
- Old Christmas Cards

To make the stars
Using the stiff paper, ask the children to draw and then to cut out several stars. Cover the stars with the aluminium foil. Put a few dabs of adhesive on the silver stars and shake some glitter over them. Some stars could have glitter on their tips only.

The children could be asked to bring the stars home and to hang them on the Christmas tree. Alternatively, the stars could be displayed in the classroom as a mobile or arranged on a black background as a night sky. In Senior Infants/Primary Two, Term One, Lesson 8, the children have already been introduced to some of the star formations, for example, The Plough, The Milky Way, The Great Bear, etc.

Perhaps some of the stars could be arranged in these formations.

or

Star Card

You will need:
- Paper for each child
- Old Christmas cards
- Adhesive
- Scissors
- Glitter

Fold the paper in two. Using scissors, make the edge of the card jagged like a star. Decorate the front of the card all over with stars – either drawn or cut out from old Christmas cards. Sprinkle some glitter around the edges to make the card sparkle. Write a message on the card. The card could be taken home and given to someone special.

CHATTING

...about the picture on pages 20 and 21

Which king do you think is Melchior, Balthasaar, Caspar? What are they doing? Why have they maps and rulers and pens? What are they looking for? Can you see a bright star in the sky? Can you see the map on the wall? Where do you think it's a map of? Can you name any of the instruments the kings might take on their journey to help them find their way?

PRAYERTIME

Sign of the Cross.

Teacher *(as the candle, or appropriate candles on the Advent Wreath, is lit)*
In our winter darkness, our Advent Candle lights the way.

The wise ones wondered about the bright star in the sky. But have you ever wondered about what we see all around us every day – about why the sky is blue, or why the snow falls softly, or where the wind comes from, or how the clouds are fluffy and soft? Have you ever wondered how it all seems to work so well? Today we will think and wonder as we say:

Teacher *(children repeating)*
We wonder at the world, O God.
How the stars don't seem to fall.

All
We wonder at the world, O God.

Teacher
How the trees stand straight and tall.

All
We wonder at the world, O God.

Teacher
How the birds know how to fly.

All
We wonder at the world, O God.

Teacher
How the wind blows through the sky.

All
We wonder at the world, O God.

Teacher
How frost makes all things white.

All
We wonder at the world, O God.

Teacher
Is there anything you wonder about?
Close your eyes and wonder.
It is good to be able to wonder.

All
Glory be to the Father...

Sign of the Cross.

Day Five

Continue art *(if not already completed)*

WORKSHEET

If you wish to use the worksheet or workbook page which accompanies this lesson, this is an appropriate time to do so.

PRAYERTIME

Sign of the Cross.

Song: *Following a Star*

Teacher *(as the candle, or appropriate candles on the Advent Wreath, is lit)*
In our winter darkness, our Advent candle lights the way.

Not everybody looks forward to Christmas. Let us ask God today to be with those people as we say: 'We pray to God.'

For those who don't look forward to Christmas.

All
We pray to God.

Teacher
For those who will be on their own this Christmas.

All
We pray to God.

Teacher
For those who won't get any presents on Christmas morning.

All
We pray to God.

Teacher
For those who will feel sad and lonely as they prepare for Christmas.

All
We pray to God.

Teacher
For those who will miss someone special this Christmas.

All
We pray to God.

Teacher
We pray to God for all people as Christmas comes near. We ask God the Father, Son and Holy Spirit especially to be with those who find Christmas-time hard. We think of them as we say:

All
Our Father…

Sign of the Cross.

Following a Star

Bernard Sexton

1. Why are we wait - ing here, why?——

Why are we wait - ing here, why?——

Wait - ing for the joy and hope the ba - by—— brings— to——

us and to the—— world.——

Chorus:

We are the wise men,——

Cas - par, Mel - chi - or and Bal - tha - saar.——

We are the wise men,——

fol - low - ing a—— star.——

2. Why are we watching here, why?
   Why are we watching here, why?
   Watching for a new star in the sky above
   To guide us on our way.

3. Why are we wondering here, why?
   Why are we wondering here, why?
   Wondering if the road we're on will ever end,
   If the new king will be there.

Lesson 15: The Moment They'd All Been Waiting For

And blessed is she who believed
that there would be
a fulfilment of what was spoken to her
by the Lord.
(Luke 1:45)

While they were there,
the time came for her to deliver her child.
And she gave birth to her firstborn son.
(Luke 2:6-7)

Like all good stories the Christmas story is told and retold, year after year. In its drama and wonder, its profundity, and yet its utter simplicity, it survives its telling and retelling. Each year the children will hear the story told in class. Each year we try to tell the story from a slightly different perspective. This year we help the children to begin to understand why the birth of Jesus was anxiously awaited by many. For years the Jewish people awaited the coming of the Messiah, the Promised One, the Anointed One. Long before the time of Jesus this was the great dream in the minds and hearts of the Jewish people.

For generations the Jews had yearned for a 'Son of David' who would restore them to a place of prominence in the world, who would lead them to victory over their enemies, who would bring them into an age of peace and prosperity. At this stage the children are too young to understand the complexities of this Jewish expectation. However, they are already familiar with the hopes and dreams of some Jewish people, e.g. Anna and Simeon who waited and watched all their lives for the special moment. Last week they heard how the wise men from the East watched and waited too. None knew exactly when the moment would arrive. But they each knew in their hearts that it would arrive and that they would recognise the moment when it came. For Christians, the celebration of the birth of Jesus at Christmas is the celebration of that long-awaited moment. Our Advent moments, pregnant with promise and expectation, come

to fruition in our celebration of the birth of Jesus at Christmas.

The Christmas crib is a lovely reminder of the first Christmas. Many of us remember, as children, the excitement of unwrapping and setting up the crib figures. For children today this can also be a very special moment. We try in this lesson, therefore, to provide the children with a focus for Christmas by centering on the nativity scene.

FOR THE TEACHER:

A thought before beginning

A woman holds a bundled baby sleeping quietly...
The husband looks so proud of his wife and newborn...
He turns to you... to welcome you... to lead you... to the mother and the baby...
Is there anything you want to say to him? Anything you want to do?

The mother leans against a thick pile of straw...
She holds the child close to her... cradled in her arms and wrapped in tattered strips of cloth...
Then she looks up into your eyes and smiles...
She is so very proud...
She lifts the cover from his face so you can see...
The baby... beautiful... happy... blinks... smiles...
And something deep within you knows that God has been born into the world...
Here... now... God has become human... become just like you...
God has been born... a new baby...

The light from the fire seems to make his face glow... so bright...
Then the mother invites you to come closer...
She raises her arms... offering the child to you...
She slides the newborn baby into your waiting arms...

You can feel the warmth... the softness... the
movement of gentle new life...
Life...
The life of God... in your arms... fragile and
alive... and so real...
Is there anything you want to say?
Anything you would like to do?

And the mother explains that she has been
asked... by God... to take care of Jesus...
She is to care for him... until he is old enough
to be given to the world...
To protect him... nurture him... and to love
him...
But she needs your help...
Can you? Can you help care for this child of
God?
Can you help God to grow... caring for him
with love?
Is there anything you want to say?
Anything you would like to do?

Mary gently... carefully... takes the baby back
into her arms...
She tells you that you also have God... within
you...
And God must grow there too...
Your task is to bring God to the world as
well...
And she can help you with that...

Mary asks if God can use your hands to help
others...
She takes your hands... kisses them softly...
making your hands holy...
Then she asks if God can use your ears to hear
the cry of others...
Then she gently kisses your ears... anointing
them...
She asks if God can use your heart to love
others...
And she softly touches your heart with her kiss
to consecrate your heart to God...
She hugs you in her arms with the infant
baby...
And thanks you...

She nods to you... and you now know... that
within you... rests Jesus...

Ready to grow...
Ready to use your hands...
To use your ears...
And to love others with your heart... Christ's
heart...

Be at peace...
Know that God will always remain within
you...
And will never leave...
God will always love others through you...
Know how sacred you are...
Feel the loving heart of God within you...
And be at peace...
And rest...
Thomas F. Catucci

What am I trying to do?

To deepen the children's appreciation of and love
for the Christmas event.

Why?

So that the children will come to a deeper
understanding of the birth of Jesus as the focus
of all the moments, preparations and waiting
which make up the Advent season.

*Note: For this lesson you will need a crib with
detachable figures.*

Directions to make a simple crib: *Get a box,
e.g. a shoe-box, and some old Christmas cards.
Decorate the box with Christmas paper. Using the
old Christmas cards, cut out the individual figures
of the crib – Mary, Joseph, etc. Paste the individual
cut-out figures onto a piece of cardboard a little
longer than the actual figures. Bend back the extra
bit of length and stick it to the crib base (use
something like velcro so that the figures can be
taken out). The figures can then be detached from
the crib if necessary (e.g. prayertime on Day Two).*

*Alternatively, you might like to ask the children to
make their own crib during class. In this case,
substitute the lesson's suggested activities with a
crib-making exercise.*

Overview of the Week

Song: *This is the Moment/Away in a Manger/Carol of the Journey*

Story: *The Moment They'd All Been Waiting For*	Continue song	Continue song	Continue song, art	
	Recall story	Poem: *A Few Little Moments*	Repeat poem	Prayertime
Chatting about the story	Poem: *The Crib Community*	Worksheet	Worksheet	Activity: *Special Christmas Letters*
Prayertime	Prayertime	Art: *Christmas Tree Decorations*	Chatting about the picture	Now We Know
		Prayertime	Prayertime	

Day One

SONG

This is the Moment/Away in a Manger/ Carol of the Journey

STORY

The Moment They'd All Been Waiting For

(Adapted from Luke 2:1-20)

A man called Caesar Augustus was a Roman emperor. He was 'in charge'. One day, he decided to count and see how many people he was in charge of. He sent soldiers throughout the land to give people this message. Every family must go to the town their ancestors had come from. There they must write the names of all those in their family into a special book. All the books in all the towns throughout the land were then to be collected and Caesar would count all the names. In this way he would find out how many people he was in charge of.

When Joseph heard the instructions he told Mary that the two of them would have to go from Nazareth to the town of his ancestor, King David. *(Do you remember the story of David from last year? The shepherd boy who became king of his people.)* Joseph's ancestors had lived in Bethlehem. As they travelled along the way to Bethlehem, Mary wondered whether Joseph would have two names or three names to write in Caesar's book. You see, Mary was going to have a baby. She wasn't sure of the exact moment her baby would be born, but she knew it would be soon.

When Mary and Joseph reached the city there was a long queue of people waiting to sign their names in Caesar's book.

As they stood in the queue, Mary and Joseph heard people talking and whispering. 'Some day we will have a true leader,' said a cross young woman, 'one of our own who will show everyone how to treat people fairly and justly.'

A young man beside her shook his head. 'We have been promised such a leader for a long time now,' he said bitterly, 'but there is no sign of him yet. How much longer do we have to wait?'

'Stop talking! Move along!' shouted the soldiers roughly.

'Well, whenever he comes, it will not be a moment too soon,' said the cross young woman.

Joseph and Mary signed their names in the book and went off to look for somewhere to stay. But with all the crowds in town, the only place they could find to stay in was a cave out on the hillside. It was getting closer and closer to the moment when Mary's baby would be born.

Out on the hills around Bethlehem some shepherds were rushing to gather their flocks together for the night. As they set about gathering their flocks they talked about the time when a new leader would come among them.

'But how will we know when this person that we have waited so long for has finally come?' asked Reuben, the youngest shepherd.

'There will be a sign,' said Isaac, the oldest shepherd. 'We do not know what kind of sign it will be, but when it comes, we will recognise it.'

At that very moment on a hillside outside Bethlehem, Mary's baby boy cried for the first time. The moment Mary and Joseph had been waiting for was finally here. The baby was born.

At that very same moment, the sign the shepherds had talked about was given; the sky above them was filled with the sound of angels singing. 'Go and see the new baby,' the angels told the shepherds.

And at that same moment the three wise ones mounted their camels and set off to follow a new star that had appeared in the sky. It brought them to a hillside where they found a cave. Inside the cave, shepherds were bowed down before a baby who lay in a manger. The baby's mother smiled at the three wise ones.

'You are just in time,' she said, showing them the new baby. 'This is the moment we have all been waiting for!'

around them. Can you remember why? How do you think you would have felt if you had been in that queue?

All of the people in the story had been waiting for someone special to come. They didn't know about Mary's baby. Can you imagine what kind of person they had in their minds when they talked about 'someone special' who had been promised? Mary knew her baby would be very special. He would be God's son.

Have you ever waited for a visitor – someone you had not met before? Perhaps you tried to imagine what they would be like. Can you remember doing this? Tell us what happened when you saw the person you had waited for. How were they different from/similar to how you had imagined them? Do you think Mary might have done the same as you? Do you think she might have imagined what her new baby would look like? Imagine you are Mary. Try to picture in your mind what the baby Jesus might look like. Perhaps you are like Mary. Perhaps you have tried to imagine what a new baby brother or sister would look like. Can you think back to a time like that? How do you think Mary and Joseph felt when they saw the new baby for the first time?

Lots of visitors came to see the new baby. Can you remember visitors coming to your home to see a new baby? How did you feel having visitors in your home? How did you feel having a new baby in your home? Did your home feel different in any way, e.g. people talking quietly so as not to wake the baby, etc? Does the Christmas celebration of Jesus' birth make your home seem any different? In what way? In how it looks, in how it feels, in the people who visit, in the food you eat, etc?

 CHATTING

...about the story

In the beginning some people in this story were not happy with what was going on

PRAYERTIME

Sign of the Cross.

Teacher *(as the candle, or appropriate candles on the Advent Wreath, is lit)*
Glory to God in the highest
And peace to his people on earth.

We watch, we wait, we wonder. We remember those who waited for the first Christmas.

Like Miriam.

All
We watch, we wait, we wonder.

Teacher
Like Moses.

All
We watch, we wait, we wonder.

Teacher
Like Anna.

All
We watch, we wait, we wonder.

Teacher
Like Simeon.

All
We watch, we wait, we wonder.

Teacher
Like Joseph.

All
We watch, we wait, we wonder.

Teacher
Like Mary.

All
We watch, we wait, we wonder.

Teacher
We think of all the people who are waiting for this Christmas.
We think of our mams and dads and those who live with us at home as they wait for Christmas.
We think of those who work in our shops and our factories and our hospitals as they wait for Christmas.

We think of everyone who waits for Christmas as we sing:

All
Sing: *Carol of the Journey*

Sign of the Cross.

Note: *For the prayertime on Day Two you will need a crib with detachable figures.*

Day Two

Continue song: *This is the Moment/Away in a Manger/Carol of the Journey*

Recall story: *The Moment They'd All Been Waiting For*

POEM

Note: *The picture in the pupil's book is an illustration of this poem. You might like to read it to the children.*

The Crib Community

Amidst all the tinsel and glitter
And fuss and bother and din,
To our house every Christmas
A whole community moves in.

Several men, one woman, one baby,
Where on earth will they fit?
Sheep, lambs, a cow and a donkey,
With a manger and straw – and that's it!

After settling their babe in the manger
They arrange themselves out before him,
Then spend Christmas Days, feasting their gaze;
It's obvious they simply adore him!

Amidst all the hustle and hassle
There's something so graceful about them,
Although they don't say or do anything,
It wouldn't be Christmas without them!

PRAYERTIME

Note: Place the empty crib in a prominent position.

Sign of the Cross.

Teacher *(as the candle, or appropriate candles on the Advent Wreath, is lit)*
Glory to God in the highest
And peace to his people on earth.

The crib reminds us of the first Christmas. Today we are going to ask God to bless our classroom crib as we remember the Christmas story.

Bless our crib, O God.
Our crib tells us the Christmas story about...

When Mary and Joseph could not find a place to stay in town.

All
Bless our crib, O God.

Teacher
How they found room in a cave.

The figures are placed in the crib by two children who then bow reverently and return to their seats.

All
Bless our crib, O God.

Teacher
How the animals kept them warm and safe.

Children come forward and place the animals in the crib, bow reverently and return to their seats.

All
Bless our crib, O God.

Song: *Away in a Manger*

Sign of the Cross.

Note: For art in Day Three you will need old Christmas magazines/cards, glitter, metal coat-hanger, Christmas tinsel. Ask the children to bring in some of the material that is needed.

Day Three

Continue song: *This is the Moment/Away in a Manger/Carol of the Journey*

POEM

A Few Little Moments

The moment the angel appeared,
Mary grew worried, and yet,
The moment she first heard the news
Was a moment she'd never forget.

The moment she left on her journey
Mary grew worried, and yet,
The moment Elizabeth hugged her
Was a moment she'd never forget.

The moment Joseph said 'Bethlehem',
Mary grew worried, and yet,
The moment he said 'I'll be with you',
Was a moment she'd never forget.

The moment the keeper said 'No room',
Mary grew worried, and yet,
The moment yon little lamb bleated
Was a moment she'd never forget.

The moment her baby first cried,
Mary grew worried, and yet,
The moment her baby first smiled
She thought, 'This is the best moment yet!'

ART

Christmas Tree Decorations

You will need:
- Paper circles (preferably made from card)
- Adhesive
- Glitter

- Old Christmas magazines/cards
- String/wool
- Metal coat-hangers and Christmas tinsel streamers.

Give the children a few paper circles.
Ask the children to think of some favourite Christmas moments. *(These could be moments from the story of the first Christmas or moments from their own preparation for Christmas.)*
Ask them to draw the moments on the paper circles, using both sides of the circle. *(Old Christmas cards/magazines could also be used.)*
The circles then become the Christmas tree decorations.
Sprinkle some glitter all around the edge of the circle to make the memory sparkle.

To display
- Divide the children into groups of four.
- Give a metal coat-hanger to each group of four children. *(Alternatively, the coat-hanger could be shaped into a circle.)*
- Wrap the tinsel around the coat-hanger, covering it completely.
- Tie the Christmas tree decorations to the coat-hanger. Use different lengths of string/wool so that the decorations hang unevenly.

P R A Y E R T I M E

Sign of the Cross.

Teacher *(as the candle, or appropriate candles on the Advent Wreath, is lit)*
Glory to God in the highest
And peace to his people on earth.

The crib reminds us of the first Christmas moment, the moment when God sent his Son Jesus into our world. We thank God Our Father for the gift of his Son Jesus. We ask God to be with us and to bless us in all our Christmas moments this year.

When we prepare our Christmas dinner.

All
God be with us and bless us.

Teacher
When we give presents to our family and friends.

All
God be with us and bless us.

Teacher
When we open our presents.

All
God be with us and bless us.

Teacher
When we visit the crib.

All
God be with us and bless us.

Teacher
When we pray together:

All
God be with us and bless us.

Sign of the Cross.

Day Four

Continue song: *This is the Moment/Away in a Manger/Carol of the Journey*

Continue art: *Christmas Tree Decorations*

Repeat poem: *The Crib Community/A Few Little Moments*

W O R K S H E E T

If you wish to use the worksheet or workbook page which accompanies this lesson, this is an appropriate time to do so.

CHATTING

...about the picture on pages 22 and 23

This is a very busy picture. What is everyone doing? Is your home like this? Even the crib community are busy. What are they doing? Can you find all the crib people and animals? Look at the cat. What might he be thinking about? How long do you think the crib people will stay?

PRAYERTIME

Sign of the Cross.

Teacher (*as the candle, or appropriate candles on the Advent Wreath, is lit*)
Glory to God in the highest
And peace to his people on earth.

We know that God is with us as we prepare for Christmas. Sometimes it is hard to wait. God is with us when we find waiting hard.

Close your eyes.
Still your body.
Listen to your heart beat.
Feel your breath as it moves in and out of your lungs, bringing life to every part of your body.

Imagine that first Christmas night. The sky was full of bright sparkling stars. This night feels different to any other night you have ever known. Feel the excitement in the air. You begin to feel excited too. You feel that something very special is going to happen. Look, a lot of people are on the move. Shepherds and sheep, even wise men with their camels. It all looks very strange. Follow them and see where they are going. They stop at a cave. It looks small but it also looks warm and inviting. Quietly creep in after the visitors. Now you see why you felt so excited –

a baby has just been born. Look at him snuggled up in the arms of Mary. She is keeping him warm and safe. Then you notice a man coming towards you. Is he going to give out to you for being here in his cave? But he takes you by the hand, you feel safe and happy, and he brings you right up to where Mary is with the baby. Mary leans forward and she places the little baby in your arms. Hold the baby carefully. You feel very special because you are holding a new baby. It's a wonderful feeling. Look at Mary, and as you hand back the baby, ask her: 'What have you called the baby?' Mary and Joseph answer together 'Jesus'. Give Jesus a little smile. With your special inside voice thank God for Jesus.

Open your eyes.
Stretch.

All
Song: *This is the Moment*

Sign of the Cross.

Day Five

Note: The Special Christmas Letter Box from Lesson 13 will be incorporated into today's Prayertime.

PRAYERTIME

Sign of the Cross.

Song: *This is the Moment*

ACTIVITY

Special Christmas Letters

Place the Christmas Post-box in a prominent position. The teacher dips into the box, chooses a letter and calls out a child's name. The child comes forward, and as he/she takes the letter the rest of the class could say (after the teacher until they become familiar with it):

All

Name is taking the letter to see what he/she will get. Perhaps it's a moment he/she will never forget.

The child then returns to his/her desk with the letter and waits until everyone else has their letter before opening it. This is repeated until each child in the class has received their letter. When everybody has received their letter and before the letters are opened, the class could say (after the teacher):

All

This is a moment we have been waiting for.

Teacher

We light our Christmas-week candle *(or the appropriate candle on the Advent Wreath)*. We remember that God is with us right now. God is with us at this special moment as we open our letters.

Open your letter carefully.
Look at the message.
Read the message silently to yourself.

Now close your eyes.
Picture the person who sent you the wish.
What does it feel like to have someone send you a good wish?
It is good to have people who care for us.
Can you remember anything nice that this person did for you over the last little while?
It is good to have people who watch out for us.
With your inside voice thank God Our Creator and Father for this moment.
Thank God Our Creator and Father for all those who care for you.

Thank you, God Our Creator and Father, for everyone in this classroom.
Thank you, God Our Creator and Father, for special moments that we will never forget.
Thank you, God Our Creator and Father, for your Son, Jesus.

All

A Few Little Moments
The moment the angel appeared,
Mary grew worried, and yet,
The moment she first heard the news
Was a moment she'd never forget.

The moment she left on her journey
Mary grew worried, and yet,
The moment Elizabeth hugged her
Was a moment she'd never forget.

The moment Joseph said 'Bethlehem',
Mary grew worried, and yet,
The moment he said 'I'll be with you',
Was a moment she'd never forget.

The moment the keeper said 'No room',
Mary grew worried, and yet,
The moment yon little lamb bleated
Was a moment she'd never forget.

The moment her baby first cried,
Mary grew worried, and yet,
The moment her baby first smiled
She thought, 'This is the best moment yet!'

Teacher

Glory to God in the highest.

All

And peace to his people on earth.

Sign of the Cross.

Note: *Encourage the children to visit their local church over the Christmas and to say a prayer at the crib.*

Now We Know

Q. On what day was Jesus Christ, the Son of God, born?

A. Jesus Christ, the Son of God, was born on Christmas Day.

This is the Moment

Kevin Farrell

1. Ma-ry and Jo-seph tried to find__ a place to stay in Beth-le-hem__ but they were turned a-way__ at ev - 'ry door. They set-tled in a sta - ble__ where ba - by Je-sus soon was born.__ 'This is the mo - ment we've wait - ed for.'

Chorus: As the star__ rose in the sky on that first Christ - mas night, Ma - ry took him in her arms and held him oh so tight. The mo - ment had ar - rived and he gave a lit - tle smile to the world__ a smile to the world.

2. The sound of angels filled the sky.
   Shepherds heard each word they sang.
   'Go see the baby and wait no more.'
   Three wise men in the morning light,
   Found that star, it was so bright.
   'This is the moment we've waited for.'

Away in a Manger

Traditional

Capo 3: Play D

A - way in a— man-ger no— crib for a bed, the— lit - tle Lord Je - sus lay— down his sweet head. The stars in the— bright sky looked— down where he lay, the— lit - tle Lord Je - sus a— sleep on the hay.

2. The cattle are lowing, the baby awakes,
   But little Lord Jesus, no crying he makes.
   I love you Lord Jesus look down from the sky
   And stay by my bedside 'til morning is nigh.

3. Be near me Lord Jesus, I ask you to stay
   Close by me forever and love me I pray.
   Bless all the dear children in thy tender care
   And fit us for heaven to live with you there.

Carol of the Journey

Bernard Sexton

2. Donkey on the dusty track, dusty track, dusty track,
   Now carries Mary on his back, on his back, on his back.

3. Journey of great hope and joy, hope and joy, hope and joy.
   Born this night is a baby boy, baby boy, baby boy.

4. Shepherds minding their sheep at night, sheep at night, sheep at night,
   See above them a shining light, shining light, shining light.

Refrain: *Angels singing 'Gloria, in excelsis Gloria'.*
                 Angels singing 'Gloria, in excelsis Gloria'.

5. Kings are travelling from afar, from afar, from afar,
   Guided by a special star, special star, special star.

Lesson 1: A Different Time

You in your great mercies did not
forsake them in the wilderness.
(Nehemiah 9:19)

Then Jesus was led by the Spirit into
the wilderness.
(Matthew 4:1)

We begin this term by focusing on the experience of being in the wilderness. At this time of year the aftermath of Christmas and the dreariness of the winter season can seem like a sort of wilderness. We help the children to explore this reality in terms of their own experience. We affirm for them the belief that God is with us at all times, even during the times of hardship, loneliness, struggle and emptiness that life thrusts upon us.

The story of Moses in the desert concretises this type of experience. Moses led the Israelites into the wilderness. To get to the Promised Land they had to journey through the wilderness for many years. They didn't want to be there. They became disgruntled. They said to Moses, 'Weren't there any graves in Egypt? Did you have to bring us out here in the desert to die?' (Exodus 16:3).

The Israelites' despair at having come to what seemed like the place of no return and no going forward, is characteristic of the desert or wilderness times in all our lives. We don't want to go into the desert. It's a place of barren emptiness. It can fill us with fear, anger and frustration. In fact, given a choice we would probably, like the Israelites, try to avoid it. However, our lives can be greatly enriched and renewed if we learn to embrace these times and work through them creatively. In this lesson, therefore, we help the children to recognise 'wilderness' times in their own lives, to see these experiences as part of life's journey and to lead them to an awareness that God is with them at all times, even in the 'wilderness' times. As a symbol of wilderness times the children will make a 'little wilderness' of sand,

stones and an empty vase (or flower-pot). The 'little wilderness' will be used during the prayertimes.

There is, however, another type of wilderness experience that is encapsulated in the story of Jesus entering the desert. In the Gospels of Matthew and Luke we hear how the Spirit led Jesus into the wilderness to pray. Jesus, turning away from the distractions of life around him, turned towards God in peace and solitude. Like Jesus, we too have times when we voluntarily withdraw from the busyness of our everyday lives and pause in reflection. In the liturgical year the Lenten Season offers us such an opportunity. Lesson Four picks up this theme of wilderness again but from a different perspective, as we explore the significance of the Lenten Season in the lives of the children. Once again the symbol of the 'little wilderness' will be used during the prayertimes.

FOR THE TEACHER:

A thought before beginning

...you neglect and belittle the
    desert.
The desert is not remote in the
    southern tropics,
The desert is not only around
    the corner,
The desert is squeezed in the tube-train next to
    you,
The desert is in the heart of your brother.
    T. S. Eliot

What am I trying to do?

To explore the reality of 'wilderness' as it occurs in the story of Moses and the Israelites in the desert and as it occurs in human life.

Why?

So that the children will see 'wilderness' times as part of their life's journey, and that they will know God is with them there and will lead them out.

Overview of the Week

		Continue song		
Song: *Christ Be Beside Me*	Continue song	Recall story		
Chatting about after Christmas	Story: *The People in the Wilderness*	Chatting about deserts		
Worksheet	Chatting about the story	Activity: *Little Wilderness*	Continue song	Art: *'God is with you' card*
Prayertime	Prayertime	Prayertime	Poem: *It'll be O-K*	Prayertime
			Prayertime	

Day One

SONG

Christ Be Beside Me

CHATTING

...about after Christmas

Do you remember the excitement we felt before the holidays? Why were we excited then? Now Christmas – 'the moment we had all been waiting for' – is over and long gone. How do you feel now? Are you sad/glad that it is all over? Would you like Christmas to have lasted longer? How long would you like it to last for? What about all the fuss and excitement – do you miss it or are you happy to see it go? Have you taken down your Christmas tree and all the decorations? Is that something you like doing? How does your home look when all the decorations have gone? Can you think of words to describe your home now that the decorations are gone – empty, quiet, bare, dull, plain, etc? Can you think of words to describe how you feel when all the decorations have been taken down and

the Christmas fun is over? The days and weeks after Christmas can seem like a wilderness after all the excitement and bright lights and glitter.

WORKSHEET

If you wish to use the worksheet or workbook page which accompanies this lesson, this is an appropriate time to do so.

PRAYERTIME

Sign of the Cross.

Teacher (*as the candle is lit*)
God is our light
In times of sadness,
In times of happiness,
In the wilderness.

When all the excitement and fuss is over. The Lord be with you.

All
And also with you.

Teacher
When everything looks bare and empty. The Lord be with you.

164

All
And also with you.

Teacher
When the moment we have been waiting for has come and gone. The Lord be with you.

All
And also with you.

Teacher
When we feel a little sad or lonely. The Lord be with you.

All
And also with you.

Teacher
God is with us during the quiet times. God is with us at all times.
Let us give God thanks and praise.

All
Glory be to the Father…

Sign of the Cross.

Day Two

Continue song: *Christ Be Beside Me*

STORY

The People In The Wilderness
(Adapted from Exodus 15:22-25)

After they had eaten their Passover meal, Moses and the people left as quickly as they could. Moses led them into the desert of Shur. The desert was an empty place, with very little in it except sand and rocks and hot sun. It was a wilderness. The people walked on and on.

They spent a long, long time walking in the desert. They began to grow tired and irritated. They became cross with Moses too.

'Why did you lead us out here into this wilderness?' they asked crossly. 'We should not have followed you, we should have stayed where we were. We have no food to eat and we have no water to drink. We have no home, nowhere that we can belong. What are we going to do?'

Moses answered them and said, 'Don't be afraid. Even in this wilderness, God is with us, God will look after us, you will see.'

Moses and his people wandered through the desert for many years. And while they were there, God was with them. God provided them with food and water. After wandering for many years, God brought them from the wilderness to a special place that they could call home.

Then the people were happy again. 'We will always remember God's goodness to us,' they said. And they did.

CHATTING

…about the story

Can you remember the story about the meal Moses and the people had to eat very quickly? Let's see if we can remember it together…

Moses led the people into the desert. What kind of a place is the desert? Have you ever seen pictures of a desert, or seen a desert on the television/film? Can you think of words to describe a desert? Why do you think the people followed Moses into the desert? If you had been there, would you have followed Moses? The people became cross with Moses. Why do you think that was? Have you ever felt yourself tired and irritated? Tell us about it. If you had been one of Moses' people, what would you have said to him? If you had been Moses, and the people were cross with you, what do you think you would have said back to them? What did Moses tell the people about God?

Do you think God was with them? How did the people know that God was with them? What made the people happy again? Where had God brought them by the end of the story? What did the people say about God now that they were home? When you are in 'bad form', or feeling a little bit down or cross or angry, what sort of things help to make you feel better again? Would you talk to God about how you feel?

PRAYERTIME

Note: To help the children connect with the wanderings of Moses and his people in the wilderness, you might like to ask them to walk around the classroom as they pray.

Sign of the Cross.

Teacher *(as the candle is lit)*
God is our light
In times of sadness,
In times of happiness,
In the wilderness.

Moses said: 'Don't be afraid, God is with you.'
The desert was hot and dry, but Moses said:

All
Don't be afraid, God is with you.

Teacher
The people walked for a long time but Moses said:

All
Don't be afraid, God is with you.

Teacher
The people grew tired, but Moses said:

All
Don't be afraid, God is with you.

Teacher
God was always with them.
Moses helped his people to feel God's presence with them in the desert.
When they came out of the desert the people always remembered God's goodness to them.
We know that God loves us too. We know that God is good to us.
Let us give praise to God as we say:

All
Glory be to the Father...

Sign of the Cross.

Day Three

Continue song: *Christ Be Beside Me*

Recall story: *The People in the Wilderness*

CHATTING

...about deserts

What would you find in a desert? Would you see any animals/birds in a desert? Does anyone know what you call the little place in a desert where you might find some water and you might see some trees? If you were in a desert and you saw an oasis, how would you feel? Do people live in the desert? Would you see houses there? How would you travel through a desert? Are deserts noisy places? Where do you go when you want to be quiet/to think? Where do you go when you feel sad? Lonely? Who do you talk to? Where do you go when you want to be by yourself?

ACTIVITY

Little Wilderness

Note: The making of the 'Little Wilderness' visualises for the children in a concrete way the concept of the wilderness. It is hoped that it will act as a symbol for the times in life when we experience emptiness, pain or struggle.

You will need:
- A tray or shallow container
- Sand
- Some stones
- Empty glass vase or flower-pot

Using a tray or shallow container, create a desert with the sand and stones. Place an empty glass vase or flower-pot in the desert.

Chat to the children about the desert – emptiness, little life, little water, hot, dry, no trees, lots of sand, etc.

PRAYERTIME

Note: Place the Little Wilderness in a prominent place.

Sign of the Cross.

Teacher *(as the candle is lit)*
God is our light
In times of sadness,
In times of happiness,
In the wilderness.

We know that God loves us and cares for us. Today, as we made a Little Wilderness, we chatted about the desert and about what you would find there. Let us now give praise to God our Creator for giving us quiet places like the desert.
We pray:

All
Praise to you, God our Creator.

Teacher
For deserts that are quiet and still.

All
Praise to you, God our Creator.

Teacher
For animals that live in the deserts.

All
Praise to you, God our Creator.

Teacher
For the golden sand.

All
Praise to you, God our Creator.

Teacher
For the oasis where water is found.

All
Praise to you, God our Creator.

Teacher
God our Creator, we ask you to be with all

people who live in or travel through deserts.
We pray:

All
Our Father…

Sign of the Cross.

Day Four

Continue song: *Christ Be Beside Me*

POEM

It'll Be O-K (Rap beat)

When Pharaoh let the people go
To cross the desert long ago,
The sand was hot, their throats were dry,
'Oh take us back, or else we'll die!'
But Moses said, 'It'll be okay.
It'll be okay, it'll be okay.
A fire by night, a cloud by day.
Just trust in God,' they heard him say,
'And it'll be O-K!'
So do not worry, 'What will I do?'
Remember God's great love for you.
Just live in love and learn to pray
And it'll be O-K!
                Christy Kenneally

PRAYERTIME

Note: Place the Little Wilderness in a prominent position. Place the candle beside it.

Sign of the Cross.

Teacher
As we light our candle we remember that God was with Moses and the people in the wilderness.

167

Close your eyes.
Still your hands on your lap.
Place your feet on the floor.
Listen to your breath as it goes in and out of your body.

Imagine you are one of the people Moses led into the desert. After all the excitement of leaving Egypt, you are in the wilderness. Look around you. There is sand everywhere… the sun is hot… you have been walking for a very long time… you feel tried and weary… and the sand goes on for ever and ever. You see Moses… you feel angry because it was his idea to go into the desert… you think of all the things you are going to say to him… you feel thirsty and hungry too… you go up to him. With your inside voice tell Moses how you are feeling. Moses listens… then he says, 'It will be all right. God has not forgotten us.' You stop for a while and you think… Moses is right. God loves us. God has not forgotten about us. God is with us. You feel God's presence beside you… you feel safe and happy… you know that things might be hard but you know that God is there. With your special inside voice thank God for being with you always.

Open your eyes.
Stretch.

All *(sing)*
Time and time and time again.
Praise God, praise God.

Sign of the Cross.

Day Five

'God is with you' card

For each child you will need:
• A sheet of paper
• Markers/crayons

Ask the children to think of someone they know who may be feeling tried/lonely/sick/frustrated/sad. Distribute the paper to each child and ask them to make a 'God is with you' card for that person. Ask the children to write the phrase 'God is with you' on the cover of the card. A message could then be written on the inside of the card. Ask the children to take the card home and give it to the person.

PRAYERTIME

Note: During this prayertime, if time allows, you might like to retell the story: The People in the Wilderness.

Sign of the Cross.

Song: *Christ Be Beside Me*

Teacher *(as the candle is lit)*
God is our light
In times of sadness,
In times of happiness,
In the wilderness.

Place your 'God is with you' card on the desk in front of you.
Let us think of the person we have made our 'God is with you' card for.

Close your eyes.
Picture that person in your imagination.
Now with your inside voice talk to God about this person.
Ask God to care for him/her. Ask God to be with him/her.

Open your eyes.
Let us hold hands together as we remember that God is with everyone. Let us hold hands as we remember that God is with the sick and the lonely. Let us hold hands as we remember that God is with us.
We say together.

All
Our Father…

Sign of the Cross.

Christ Be Beside Me

Traditional

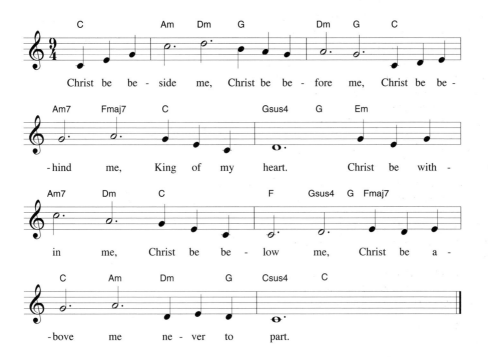

Christ be be - side me, Christ be be - fore me, Christ be be -
hind me, King of my heart. Christ be with -
in me, Christ be be - low me, Christ be a -
bove me ne - ver to part.

2. Christ on my right hand,
   Christ on my left hand,
   Christ all around me,
   Shield in the strife.
   Christ in my sleeping,
   Christ in my sitting,
   Christ in my rising,
   Light of my life.

3. Christ be in all hearts,
   Thinking about me,
   Christ be on all tongues,
   Telling of me.
   Christ be the vision,
   In eyes that see me,
   In ears that hear me
   Christ ever be.

At that time the disciples came to Jesus and asked, 'Who is the greatest in the kingdom of heaven?' He called a child, whom he put among them, and said, 'Truly I tell you, unless you change and become like children, you will never enter the kingdom of heaven'.
(Matthew 18:13)

Jesus affirmed the goodness of childhood when he placed a child before the disciples as an embodiment of the ideal required to enter the Kingdom of Heaven. Jesus invites us to wonder what the qualities of childhood are which can challenge our understanding of ourselves and of our world. The concerns of the disciples were about 'being the greatest'. Children's relationships are based on an ability for openness and spontaneity, and an ease with dependence and trust. This does not come so easily to adults.

As we begin to work with the children towards an understanding of the Sacrament of Penance, we affirm the goodness of childhood.

We provide opportunities for the children to look at themselves and, seeing who they are, to celebrate. We do this through the use of story. In this lesson the stories emphasise the positive nature of 'being' a child, of 'being' children. In each story the critical point is that it is through contact with children that the characters or 'Beings' are transformed. Children and childhood were valued by Jesus in a way not previously embodied in history. For example, in Jesus' world the dominant Roman power represented a society which placed value on the strong, the brave, the courageous, the masculine. Jesus turned such values on their head by insisting, 'Blessed are the meek'; 'unless you become as one of them', etc.

In these stories, therefore, the emphasis is on the 'natural', intrinsic nature of children. The stories concentrate on 'being' fun rather than having fun; on 'being' friendly rather than making friends; on 'being' surprising rather than getting a surprise – although often, of course, these things are inextricably linked. Consequently, the play on the word 'being' has characterised the central figure in each story as a little 'Being'.

The chats offer an opportunity to tease out some of the wisdoms in the stories, but the stories themselves try to offer a central image, one which encapsulates the essence of some aspect of childhood. Hopefully these images might nudge children towards an imaginative way of working with their experience and their childhood world at its best.

In the following stories, the main character is not a child but a 'little Being' which possesses many of the characteristics of a child. Nevertheless, the Beings are sufficiently different from the children who are listening to the story that they offer them the possibility of seeing themselves, or some aspects of themselves, projected safely at a distance.

The stories follow a certain format. Each story opens with the main character recognising itself as good and affirming for itself that sense of goodness. Then it gradually realises that something is missing, that all that might have been achieved has not as yet been realised in itself. What this is and how it can come about becomes clear when the little Being comes into contact with a group of children.

What am I trying to do?

To help the children to become aware of, to focus on, and to celebrate the goodness of childhood and the goodness of each of them as individuals.

Why?

So that they will have a sense of their own self-worth and begin to see themselves as being created, valued and loved by God.

FOR THE TEACHER:

A thought before beginning

Children who are truly loved, although in moments of pique they may consciously feel or proclaim that they are being neglected, unconsciously know themselves to be valued. This knowledge is worth more than any gold. For when children know that they are valued, when they truly feel valued in the deepest parts of themselves, then they feel valuable.

The feeling of being valuable – 'I am a valuable person' – is essential to mental health and is a cornerstone of self-discipline. It is a direct product of parental love. Such a conviction must be gained in childhood; it is extremely difficult to acquire it during adulthood. Conversely, when children have learned through the love of the adults around them to feel valuable, it is almost impossible for the vicissitudes of adulthood to destroy their spirit.

M. Scott Peck

Quick Tip: *Making Little Beings: If you are using Plasticine, cocktail sticks are useful. Stick one down through the beings head and into the body so that the head doesn't fall off.*

Overview of the Week

	Continue songs Chatting about being friends Story: *Being Friends* Chatting about the story			
Song: *Beings/We Thank You God, We Do* Activity: *I am Special* Chatting about being special Prayertime	Art: *Making a Little Being* Chatting about making a little Being Prayertime	Continue songs Activity: *I am Fun* Chatting about being fun Worksheet Prayertime	Continue songs Story: *Being Eager* Chatting about the story Art: *Bubbling Over* Prayertime	Art: *Symbolising* Chatting about the picture Prayertime

Day One

ACTIVITY

I Am Special

Spoken or sung to the air of **We Thank You God, We Do**

Solo child
I'm happy, I'm happy,
I'm happy through and through,

All join in
We thank God for happiness
And we thank God for you.

Repeat using:
2. I'm friendly
3. I'm clever

SONG

Beings

We Thank You God, We Do

Note: Today we help the children to acknowledge the fact that each one is unique and special, and to celebrate this. In doing this we will be revising some of the material already covered in the Junior Infants/Primary One and Senior Infants/Primary Two programmes.

4. I'm caring
5. I'm gentle
6. I'm quiet
7. I'm loving
8. I'm thoughtful, etc.

Last verse
We're children, we're children,
We're children through and through.
We thank God for childhood,
We thank you God, we do.

The teacher may supply other suitable verses. It is not necessary that each child have a different verse.

CHATTING

...about being special

Can you think of some of the things that are special about you? How is your voice special? How is your hair special? How are your hands special? Who are the people who have told you that you are special? What did they say was special about you? How does it feel when you know that you are special?

PRAYERTIME

Sign of the Cross.

Teacher
Today we are going to thank God for making each one of us special. We have here a bowl of Holy Water. Holy Water is special because it has been blessed. We ask God to bless us and to help us to continue to grow into the special people we are meant to be.

Ask each child to come forward in turn. They stand before the teacher who dips his/her thumb into the water and makes the Sign of the Cross on the forehead of the child.

Teacher
Thank you God for *(name)*, your special child. He/she is a special member of our class. We ask you to bless her/him. In the name of the Father, and of the Son and of the Holy Spirit. Amen.

The children can be encouraged to join in as appropriate.

Sign of the Cross.

Day Two

Continue songs: *Beings/We Thank You God, We Do*

Note: *Today we explore with the children their capacity to be friends. Most children are good at being friends. It is something they do without a lot of the inhibitions which often hold us back as adults. Their natural openness and spontaneity in this area is tempered only by the cautionary influence of adults.*

CHATTING

...about being friends

Who are you friendly with at home/at school/in your neighbourhood? Why do you think you are friends with these people? What kind of things can you do with your friends? Can you remember how you first made friends with them? Can you remember how you made friends on the first day you came to school? Have you any friends that you don't see often – perhaps when you go on holidays, or to the pool, or to dancing class, etc? Are you a good friend? What makes you a good friend? Do you like being a friend? Why?

Story

Being Friends

There are lots of different beings in the world. Here is a story about one little Being.

One day a little Being went for a walk by itself. As it walked it thought to itself, and as it thought it talked. This is what it said.

It said, 'I am pleased with myself. I have everything I need. I have a warm place in which to live. I have good food to eat. I have a safe place to sleep at night. I have things to do to keep me busy. What more could a Being ask for?' Then the little Being walked on.

As it walked it thought, and as it thought it talked, and this is what it said.

It said, 'I am pleased with myself. I have everything I could possibly want, but … it feels like something is missing. I wonder what it could be? I feel like a song, a lovely song, but there is only one note in this lovely song, and it is the note I sing. It would be a much better song if there were more notes in it. It is good to be me but I am by myself. It would be much better if I had friends. But,' said the little Being to itself, 'I don't know how to be friends.'

Just then the little Being heard a song. It was a very lively song. It looked up to see where the song was coming from. It saw a group of children. They were holding hands and singing at the tops of their voices. Some sang high notes, some sang low notes, and they all sang different notes. As they came towards the little Being they sang out, 'Sing little Being; join in and sing!' Before the little Being knew what was happening it was singing away at the top of its voice. It held hands with the children. It joined in. It sang its note in among the other notes. It became part of the song. It sang, 'You children are good friends.'

'Of course!' the children sang back. 'All children love to be friends. Children are good at being friends. We are friends with you,' they sang. And off they went still singing. The little Being walked on, thinking and talking and singing.

'I have learned something today and this is what it is. I have learned that the children are friends. They are friends with me and I am friends with them. I love being friends. It is wonderful to be me.' Then the little Being walked on.

Chatting

…about the story

What do you think the little Being in this story looked like? What do you look like? Tell us about how you look. This particular little Being was out walking. Have you ever gone out for a walk? This particular little Being was thinking and talking to itself. What kind of things was it thinking and talking about? What kind of things do you think and talk about? Do you like to think and talk to yourself sometimes? Let's think about us. We are doing what the little Being in the story was doing, we are thinking and talking too, but we are thinking and talking all together. Do you like to think and talk? Why? Can you remember what this Being was thinking about? Do you like to sing? Do you think you would like to sing a song with only one note in it? Why? Let's have a try and see what it would be like. Let's sing *Baa Baa Black Sheep* with only one note in it. What did you think of that? This little Being thought it was like a song with only one note because it was all alone. It had no friends. What do you think your life would be like if you had only yourself and no friends? Would you miss having friends? Why? The children in the story said that all children love to be friends. Do you agree with them? Why? Do you think children are good at being friends? Why? Are you good at being friends? How? Tell us about your friends in school/outside school.

173

ART

Making a little Being

Teachers on this occasion might consider giving the children new Plasticine or Play-dough so that the little Being will be extra special.

CHATTING

...about making a little Being

We are going to make a lot of little Beings using Plasticine or Play-dough. What do we need to do to make a little Being? What about eyes and ears? Can the little Being in the story see and hear? Can the little Being talk? How do you know? Will we need a head? Will we need a body? What about legs and arms? Does it have a name? Hold it up to your ear. Let it whisper to you. What does it say to you? Is it happy or does it think something is missing? Tell us what it says. Does it want to be your friend? Do you want it to be your friend? Perhaps your little Being and your friend's little Being would like to be friends. You can ask them. What do they say? Now we are all friends. How does that feel?

PRAYERTIME

Sign of the Cross.

Teacher
Today we thank God for all the ways in which we can be good friends. We ask God to help us always to be able to be a good friend. Our candle reminds us that God is always with us. God loves us and takes care of us. Just as we listen to our little Beings and to each other, God always listens to whatever we say. Place your little Being on the desk in front of you.

All
God, give us the gift of being good friends.

Teacher
We can be generous.

All
God, give us the gift of being good friends.

Teacher
We can be gentle.

All
God, give us the gift of being good friends.

Teacher
We can be caring.

All
God, give us the gift of being good friends.

Teacher
Now think of someone you like being a good friend to. Picture the person in your mind. Think of the last time you were with that person. Remember how you feel about that person. Now thank God for that person and ask God to bless her or him.

We pray together.

All
Our Father...

Sign of the Cross.

Day Three

Continue songs: *Beings/We Thank You God, We Do*

Note: *Children are most at home in the world of play. At play, children are free to allow their imaginations to run wild, to be spontaneous and open as they naturally tend to be. They relate with the freedom that characterises the world of play to their natural environment and to those around them. Children also love to be funny, to make others laugh. Today we explore some of the aspects of childhood that surround fun and play.*

ACTIVITY

I am Fun

You could ask the children to play any one of a variety of the following:

(a) **Ring a Ring o' Rosies**

(b) **Red Lights**

You will need to play this game either in the PE hall or in the playground. The teacher stands some distance away from the children and with his or her back turned towards them. The children must try to reach the place where the teacher is without the teacher spotting them move. Every few minutes the teacher turns around and says 'Red Lights'. Whoever is caught moving must return to the starting point again.

(c) Place the children in groups of about six. All, except one, are statues. They must neither move, nor speak, nor laugh. The one child must do funny things, for example, make funny faces, etc. to make the others laugh. As soon as one child laughs she/he takes the place of the one whose job it is to make the others laugh.

CHATTING

...about being fun

Did you enjoy the game(s)? Was it fun? What did you like best? When someone says to you 'You are great fun', what do you think they mean? When are you most funny? What makes you laugh? Who makes you laugh most? Do you make other people laugh? When? Make someone laugh now. Are there some people you know who are fun to be with? What do you do when you are with these people? What is your favourite fun game? What sort of fun do you have at home/at school/in the playground? Can you have fun by yourself? Can you remember a time when you had fun by yourself?

Are there places you know where it is fun to be? Has anyone ever said to you, 'It's fun to be with you'? Do you think you are fun to be with? Why? Why not?

WORKSHEET

If you wish to use the worksheet or workbook page which accompanies this lesson, this is an appropriate time to do so.

PRAYERTIME

Note: The response in this prayertime is the response used in the Eucharistic prayer for children. Its use here will help in preparing the children to take part in the Mass for their First Communion.

Sign of the Cross.

Teacher
God our Creator gave us the gift of fun.
Today we give thanks for the gift of fun.

For the fun in playing games with others.

All
We praise you, we bless you, we thank you.

Teacher
For the fun in playing by ourselves.

All
We praise you, we bless you, we thank you.

Teacher
For the fun of being at school.

All

We praise you, we bless you, we thank you.

Teacher

For the fun of being at home.

All

We praise you, we bless you, we thank you.

Teacher

For the fun on special days, like holidays.

All

We praise you, we bless you, we thank you.

Teacher

For the fun with our pets.

All

We praise you, we bless you, we thank you.

Teacher

For the fun inside ourselves.

All

We praise you, we bless you, we thank you.

Teacher

For the fun in making others laugh.

All

We praise you, we bless you, we thank you.

Teacher

Now tell God about a time you remember when you were very funny or when you made others laugh.

Encourage the children to tell a short story about such a time. For those who are preparing for First Penance, this exercise will help them to be ready to tell a story when they celebrate the sacrament.

Teacher

We pray together.

All

Praise the Father.
Praise the Son.
Praise the Spirit.
The Three in One.

Sign of the Cross.

Day Four

Continue songs: *Beings/We Thank You God, We Do*

Note: *Children never seem to get tired. They are always busy. They never think that it is time to go to bed, nor do they want to stay in bed in the morning. They are interested in everything, in exploring and in finding out about new things.*

 STORY

Being Eager

Here is another story about another little Being.

One day another little Being went for a walk. As it walked slowly along it thought, and as it thought it talked in a little voice, and this is what it said.

It said, 'I am fairly happy with myself. My food is all right. My work is not too hard. My days are enjoyable enough. Things could be a lot worse. All in all, it's nice to be me!' Then this little Being walked on.

As it walked it thought, and as it thought it talked. Then suddenly this little Being stopped. It sighed a heavy sigh. It thought for a moment. Then it spoke and this is what it said in its small little voice.

It said, 'Oh dear!' Then it sighed. 'Although there is nothing really wrong with me, I feel something is not quite right either. I wonder what it could be?' It sighed again.

It said in a hushed voice, 'I feel flat, like a can of fizzy drink that's got no fizzy bubbles rising up to the top, just bursting to pop, pop, pop all over the place.'

Just then the little Being saw a bubble go floating past. Then another and another. It looked to see where the bubbles were coming from. It saw some children. They were blowing bubbles, lots and lots of bubbles flowing out from the little hole in the wand. 'Catch, catch the bubbles, little Being,' the children shouted, and before the little Being knew what was happening, it was running here and there, reaching out trying to grasp a bubble, any bubble. 'OH!' exclaimed the little Being as it felt a beautiful bubble within its grasp. 'Hurrah!' it shouted in a big loud voice as it felt the bubble bursting with energy. Soon the little Being itself bubbled with eagerness to catch another and another and another. The children laughed and clapped and shouted 'Yes! Yes!' They followed the bubbles. The little Being walked on, thinking and shouting…

'I have learned something today and this is what it is. Children bubble. They bubble with energy. They laugh and jump and run. They say "Yes!" I am bubbling like the children. My life is a wonderful life.' Then this particular little Being walked on.

CHATTING

…about the story

Today we met another little Being who was thinking and talking. Can you remember anything of what it was thinking and talking about? Imagine you have a bottle or a can of fizzy drink. You open it up and you take a long drink. What is it like? Did you ever have a drink and the fizz went up your nose? What happened then? Have you seen bubbles in a bottle of lemonade? What do you think it would feel like to be a bubble? Have you ever had a tub of bubbles that you dip a little wand into and then blow? Sometimes you try your best to blow but the bubbles don't happen. How do you feel then? How do you think the little Being in the story was feeling before the bubbles came along? Have you ever felt 'flat', perhaps when you were sick? How do you feel when you are sick? How do you feel when you get well again? Have you ever chased bubbles? Has there ever been a time when you said 'Hurrah!'? Has there ever been a time when

you shouted 'Yes, Yes, YES!'? Have you ever felt yourself to be bubbling over with excitement; with energy; with readiness to go, go, go; with other happy feelings? Tell us about some of those times. Hold your little Being up to your ear. Listen. Is your little Being full of energy? Are there things it is bursting to do? What kind of things? Can you help it to do some of those things? Help it to run, jump, hop, skip, tumble, roll, etc. How does it feel to have so much energy? How does your little Being feel?

ART

Bubbling Over

You will need:
- Different coloured crayons for each child
- Paint of a thin, watery consistency

Using different coloured crayons, encourage the children to cover a whole page with circles of different colours and sizes. They can overlap, bump into each other, or even be contained inside each other. Then ask them to cover the page with a wash of very thin paint.

or

Pass a tub of bubbles around the class, giving each child time to blow some bubbles. Can your little Being catch the bubbles?

PRAYERTIME

Sign of the Cross.

Teacher
We light our candle and we remember that God is always with us. God who gives us life and energy.

Close your eyes.

Place your hands gently on your lap and your feet on the floor.
Listen to your heart beat.
Feel your breath as it travels gently in and out of your lungs.
Go inside, into your inside world.

In there it's dark and quiet and safe and peaceful. In there your heart is beating all day and all night. Your heartbeat sends blood flowing through your veins to every single part of your body, bringing life and oxygen and energy to your whole body.

Your energy, which comes from deep inside you, gives you the strength to move, to run, to jump, to play, to learn. Your energy keeps you from being tired. It's one of God's greatest gifts to you.

God our Creator gives you the gift of life and the gift of energy. With your inside voice, which no one else can hear, you can say thank you to God for the gift of life and the gift of energy.

Inside, in your inside world, you can meet your own little Being. You can ask your own little Being how it feels today. Maybe it is full of life and energy. Maybe it is tired. Maybe it is happy. Maybe it is sad. Your inside voice will tell you, if you listen very carefully.

Again you can say thank you to God for the gift of life and energy.

Open your eyes.

Together we pray.

All
Our Father…

Sign of the Cross.

ART

Symbolising

Invite one child to lie on the floor on a large sheet of paper – old wallpaper is very useful for this activity. Ask another child or some children to draw around him or her, and cut out the figure.

Lay the figure in the middle of the floor. The children, holding their little Beings (which are made of Plasticine or Play-dough), gather in a circle sitting around the cut-out.

The teacher then leads the children in a meditation based on the week's work, during which they identify with the little Beings in their hands.

CHATTING

…about the picture on page 25

Which type of little Being is your favourite? Why? They are all alike and yet each one is different – like you and your family. Can you think of any other things which might help describe the little Beings? For example, notes in a tune or puppies in a litter.

PRAYERTIME

Sign of the Cross.

Song: *Beings*

Teacher
We light our candle and we remember that God is always with us.
We thank God for making each one of us special and different.
We thank God for the goodness that is in each one of us.

Close your eyes.
Place your hands quietly on your lap and your feet on the floor.
Listen to your heart beat.
Feel your breath as it moves gently in and out of your body.

Go inside, into your inside world. In there it's dark and quiet and peaceful and safe. In there you are alone with your very special self.
Think about one of the ways that you are very special – your very special laugh, your very special face, your very special way of loving others. Or, you might think of something that no one else would ever be able to guess –

something special that you know about yourself.

With your inside voice, say thank you to God for your very special self. Say thank you to God, too, for the one thing that you have thought of that makes you a very special person.

Open your eyes.
Take your little Being in your hand. As you look at your little Being think of something good about your little Being.

Pause.

Way down deep inside you, in your little inside world, there are some good things about you that no one else knows about, like your goodness, your kindness, your love. Now tell your little Being about them.

Put your little Being somewhere on the cut-out figure.

Close your eyes again.
Say thank you to God for all the good things about yourself.
When you're ready, you can open your eyes.
Relax.

We sing together:

All
We Thank You, God, We Do

Sign of the Cross.

Beings

Words: Clare Maloney
Music: Patricia Hegarty

Refrain:

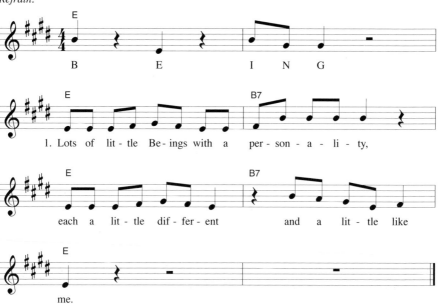

B E I N G

1. Lots of lit - tle Be - ings with a per - son - a - li - ty,
each a lit - tle dif - fer - ent and a lit - tle like
me.

2. Lots of little Beings like stars in the sky,
   Each one has a different little twinkle in its eye.

3. Lots of little Beings like leaves on a tree,
   Hanging all together in a Being family.

4. Lots of little Beings like peas in a pod,
   Beings all together, being loved by God.

We Thank You God, We Do

Words: Clare Maloney
Music: Ivor Redmond

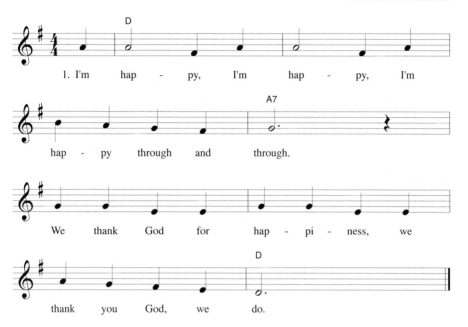

1. I'm hap - py, I'm hap - py, I'm
hap - py through and through.
We thank God for hap - pi - ness, we
thank you God, we do.

2. I'm friendly . . .
   We thank God for friendliness . . .

3. I'm clever . . .
   We thank God for cleverness . . .

4. I'm gentle . . .
   We thank God for gentleness . . .

5. I'm quiet . . .
   We thank God for quietness . . .

6. I'm thoughtful . . .
   We thank God for thoughtfulness . . .

7. We're children . . .
   We thank God for childhood . . .

An argument arose among them as to
which of them was the greatest. But
Jesus, aware of their inner thoughts,
took a little child to his side, and said
to them, 'Whoever welcomes this
child in my name welcomes me, and
whoever welcomes me welcomes the
one who sent me; for the least among
all of you is the greatest'.
(Luke 9:46)

When situated in the historical context of
the time, the stance that Jesus took
towards children was revolutionary. Children
were not seen as people with rights. They
were, like women and slaves, at the bottom of
the scale in terms of being valued and
important. Given this background, the answer
offered by Jesus to the disciples' question
about who is the greatest in God's Kingdom
would have been quite shocking. The
perspective on the Kingdom changes radically
when Jesus presents the child, excluded and
ignored in society, as an embodiment of the
ideal required to enter the Kingdom of
Heaven: 'For the least among all of you is the
greatest'.

We try to help the children to come to an
understanding of the qualities of childhood
which Jesus upheld as necessary for greatness
in God's Kingdom: qualities such as openness,
trustfulness, gentleness, etc. In doing this we
hope to put them in touch with their childlike
capacity for greatness, and to challenge them
to achieve some measure of that greatness.

Once again we suggest that you invite the
parents/guardians to take part in a simple
Prayer Service with the children. This Prayer
Service is probably more appropriate in
situations where the children are not
celebrating the sacraments. The Prayer Service
with the parents/guardians is optional. Each
teacher will decide on its appropriateness for
her/his own situation. We hope that these
opportunities will enable the
parents/guardians to come to a deeper
understanding of the way in which their
children are learning about God and being
helped to grow in relationship with God
through prayer. The Prayer Service can take
place in the classroom, in the school hall, in a
local parish hall or in the local church,
depending on what seems to be most
appropriate in each situation. If it takes place
in the classroom, one possibility is to invite
the parent, or whoever is collecting the child
on their behalf, to come ten minutes earlier
than usual. Obviously not all parents will be
able to come at that time. Grannies, grandads,
a child minder, an older sister or brother,
might also be welcome to attend. If a
particular child has no older person to
accompany her or him to the Prayer Service,
they can still be encouraged to take part. You
could, if you wished, invite an older brother or
sister from another class to take part. The
teacher might also take it on herself/himself to
look after these children in a special way.

*For the Prayer Service you will need: copies of the
reflection at the end of this lesson, a candle, the
children's baptismal candles, Holy Water.*

What am I trying to do?

To explore and to celebrate the particular
perspective on childhood which was given by
Jesus.

Why?

So that children will learn to acknowledge, to
express and to celebrate the goodness of
childhood and to find joy in it.

For the Teacher:

A thought before beginning

A Letter to Daniel

Hong Kong, February 1996
Daniel Patrick Keane was born on
4 February 1996

My dear son, it is six o'clock in the morning on the island of Hong Kong. You are asleep cradled in my left arm and I am learning the art of one-handed typing. Your mother, more tired yet more happy than I've ever known her, is sound asleep in the room next door and there is soft quiet in our apartment.

Since you've arrived, days have melted into night and back again and we are learning a new grammar, a long sentence whose punctuation marks are feeding and winding and nappy changing and these occasional moments of quiet.

When you're older we'll tell you that you were born in Britain's last Asian colony in the lunar year of the pig and that when we brought you home, the staff of our apartment block gathered to wish you well. 'It's a boy, so lucky, so lucky. We Chinese love boys,' they told us. One man said you were the first baby to be born in the block in the year of the pig. This, he told us, was good Feng Shui, in other words, a positive sign for the building and everyone who lived there.

Naturally your mother and I were only too happy to believe that. We had wanted you and waited for you, imagined you and dreamed about you, and now that you are here no dream can do justice to you. Outside the window, below us on the harbour, the ferries are ploughing back and forth to Kowloon. Millions are already up and moving about and the sun is slanting through the tower blocks and out on to the flat silver waters of the South China Sea. I can see the contrail of a jet over Lamma Island and, somewhere out there, the last stars flickering towards the other side of the world.

We have called you Daniel Patrick but I've been told by my Chinese friends that you should have a Chinese name as well and this glorious dawn sky makes me think we'll call you Son of the Eastern Star. So that later, when you and I are far from Asia, perhaps standing on a beach some evening, I can point at the sky and tell you of the Orient and the times and the people we knew there in the last years of the twentieth century.

Your coming has turned me upside down and inside out. So much that seemed essential to me has, in the past few days, taken on a different colour. Like many foreign correspondents I know, I have lived a life that, on occasion, has veered close to the edge: war zones, natural disasters, darkness in all its shapes and forms.

In a world of insecurity and ambition and ego, it's easy to be drawn in, to take chances with our lives, to believe that what we do and what people say about us is reason enough to gamble with death. Now, looking at your sleeping face, inches away from me, listening to your occasional sigh and gurgle, I wonder how I could have ever thought glory and prizes and praise were sweeter than life.

And it's also true that I am pained, perhaps haunted is a better word, by the memory, suddenly so vivid now, of each suffering child I have come across on my journeys. To tell you the truth, it's nearly too much to bear at this moment to even think of children being hurt and abused and killed. And yet looking at you, the images come flooding back. Ten-year-old Andi Mikail dying from napalm burns on a hillside in Eritrea, how his voice cried out, growing ever more faint when the wind blew dust on to his wounds. The two brothers, Domingo and Juste, in Menongue, southern Angola. Juste, two years old and blind, dying from malnutrition, being carried on seven-year-old Domingo's back. And Domingo's words to me, 'He was nice before, but now he has the hunger'.

Last October, in Afghanistan, when you were growing inside your mother, I met Sharja, aged twelve. Motherless, fatherless, guiding me through the grey ruins of her home, everything was gone, she told me. And I knew that, for all her tender years, she had learned more about loss than I would likely understand in a lifetime.

There is one last memory. Of Rwanda, and the

churchyard of the parish of Nyarabuye where, in a ransacked classroom, I found a mother and her three young children huddled together where they'd been beaten to death. The children had died holding on to their mother, that instinct we all learn from birth and in one way or another cling to until we die.

Daniel, these memories explain some of the fierce protectiveness I feel for you, the tenderness and the occasional moments of blind terror when I imagine anything happening to you. But there is something more, a story from long ago that I will tell you face to face, father to son, when you are older. It's a very personal story but it's part of the picture. It has to do with the long lines of blood and family, about our lives and how we can get lost in them and, if we're lucky, find our way out again into the sunlight.

It begins thirty-five years ago in a big city on a January morning with snow on the ground and a woman walking to hospital to have her first baby. She is in her early twenties and the city is still strange to her, bigger and noisier than the easy streets and gentle hills of her distant home. She's walking because there is no money and everything of value has been pawned to pay for the alcohol to which her husband has become addicted.

On the way, a taxi driver notices her sitting, exhausted and cold, in the doorway of a shop and he takes her to hospital for free. Later that day, she gives birth to a baby boy and, just as you are to me, he is the best thing she has ever seen. Her husband comes that night and weeps

with joy when he sees his son. He is truly happy. Hungover, broke, but in his own way happy, for they were both young and in love with each other and their son.

But, Daniel, time had some bad surprises in store for them. The cancer of alcoholism ate away at the man and he lost his family. This was not something he meant to do or wanted to do, it just was. When you are older, my son, you will learn about how complicated life becomes, how we can lose our way and how people get hurt inside and out. By the time his son had grown up, the man lived away from his family, on his own in a one-roomed flat, living and dying for the bottle.

He died on the fifth of January, one day before the anniversary of his son's birth, all those years before in that snowbound city. But his son was too far away to hear his last words, his final breath, and all the things they might have wished to say to one another were left unspoken.

Yet now, Daniel, I must tell you that when you let out your first powerful cry in the delivery room of the Adventist Hospital and I became a father, I thought of your grandfather and, foolish though it may seem, hoped that in some way he could hear, across the infinity between the living and the dead, your proud statement of arrival. For if he could hear, he would recognise the distinct voice of family, the sound of hope and new beginnings that you and all your innocence and freshness have brought to the world.

Fergal Keane

Overview of the Week

| Song: *We are the Greatest* Story: *We are the Greatest* Chatting about the story Worksheet Prayertime | Continue song Art: *Jesus and the Children* Prayertime | Continue song Recall story Poem: *Great!* Prayertime | Continue song Revise poem Chatting about the picture Art: *'We are the Greatest' Badges* Prayertime | Prayer Service Now We Know |

Day One

SONG

We are the Greatest

STORY

We are the Greatest
(Adapted from Matthew 18:1-5)

Today is Market Day. The children love Market Day. They go to the town square. All the grown-ups are there. There are men selling cheeses. There are women buying cloth. There are bakers selling bread. There are people buying spices and fruit. There are cows mooing and donkeys braying and goats baaing. The Market Place is busy. The Market Place is noisy. The Market Place is a busy place for the adults. It is a place of fun for the children. They love to run about and enjoy being with their friends. They play hide-and-seek among the adults.

Today a man comes to the Market Place. At first no one notices the man. He sits in the middle of the square where everyone will be able to see him. He speaks in a loud voice so that everyone will be able to hear him. He tells those who stop and listen about a kingdom. He calls it the Kingdom of God. He says that in God's kingdom everyone is happy. In God's kingdom everyone loves their friends as well as those who are not their friends.

'What kind of place is this kingdom,' say some of the grown-ups, 'where people love those who are not their friends?'

'How can we get to live in such a place?' say some others.

'God's kingdom is not any particular place,' says the man. 'Wherever people love one another, wherever people are kind and gentle, wherever people share with one another, that is where God's kingdom is. God's kingdom can be right here, right now.'

'I have a question for you,' says one man. 'In our community I am an important person. I would like to know who is the most important person in this Kingdom of God that you talk about.'

Now the Market Place grows quiet. The noise stops. The buying and selling stops. The children notice that everything has gone quiet too. The children go on playing. From where they are they can see the crowd of people gathered around the man.

'What's happening?' some of the children ask each other.

Just then the man comes over to the children. He says, 'Who will help me? I need one of you to help me teach the grown-ups something very important.'

'Me, me, me!' say the children. The man smiles. He takes the smallest child by the hand. He takes the child into the middle of the crowd. He wants everyone to notice the child.

'You ask me who is the most important person in God's kingdom,' says the man to the crowd. 'I will tell you now,' he says. 'Do you see this little child? I tell you, the child is the greatest in God's kingdom.'

A murmur of shock and surprise runs through the crowd of grown-ups. They can hardly believe their eyes. They can hardly believe their ears. The child! The child is the greatest in God's kingdom! They have never heard the like of this before!

When the man is finished the child runs back to the other children.

'What did the man want?'; 'What did the man say?'; 'What did the man teach the people?' they ask the child.

'He taught them that children are the greatest,' the child answers. The children clap and cheer.

'Who is this man?' the children ask.

'His name is Jesus,' the child answers.

'Hurrah for Jesus!' the children shout. 'Hurrah, hurrah, hurrah!'

CHATTING

...about the story

The children in the story like the Market Place. Why do you think they like it? Do you have a market place like that where you live? Tell us what kind of 'market place' you go to. Do you like to go there? Why? What is your favourite thing to see or do in your 'market place'? The children in the story were playing. What do you think they were playing? Why did no one notice the children? Can you remember a time when you were playing with your friends and no one noticed you?

The man in the story sat in the middle of the Market Place, where everyone could see him and hear what he wanted to tell them. Do you think he wanted the people to listen to him? Why? Can you remember what he was telling the people about? What kind of things do people do in the Kingdom of God? What kind of people do you think are in the Kingdom of God? Do you know anywhere that is like the Kingdom of God? When is your home like the Kingdom of God? Do people in your home love each other even during times when they have had a row and don't feel like being friends? Do you think being in our class could be like being in God's kingdom? How?

Jesus told the people that the children were the greatest in the Kingdom of God. What do you think about that – is that Good News to you? Why? What do you think it was that Jesus knew or saw that made him think that the children were the greatest? Why do you think the adults were surprised to hear this

news? What kind of person would think children are the greatest? Do you think Jesus loves children? Why?

WORKSHEET

If you wish to use the worksheet or workbook page which accompanies this lesson, this is an appropriate time to do so.

PRAYERTIME

Sign of the Cross.

Teacher
Today we are going to think about a time when other people saw that we were good and told us so. We light our candle.

Perhaps it was your Mam or Dad when you had been kind or helpful at home. Perhaps it happened in school. Jesus always saw the goodness in children. We will thank God for helping us to show our greatness to others.

For helping us to have fun with others.

All
O my God, I thank you for loving me.

Teacher
For helping us to be lively and full of energy.

All
O my God, I thank you for loving me.

Teacher
For helping us to be kind and helpful to others.

All
O my God, I thank you for loving me.

Teacher
For helping us to see when others need our help.

186

All

O my God, I thank you for loving me.

Teacher

Now think of a particular time when you did something great for someone at home, or at school, or when you were playing with your friends.

Encourage the children to think about the incident which they remember. Encourage them to tell the story. For those children who are preparing for First Penance, this will help them to prepare for the celebration of the sacrament. After each child has spoken, encourage the children to respond by saying, 'God our Creator, we give you thanks for (name) and for all his/her goodness'.

Teacher

We pray together.

All

Our Father...

Sign of the Cross.

Day Two

Continue song: *We are the Greatest*

 ART

Jesus and the Children

On a large sheet of paper (you might use a piece of wallpaper) draw a large circle in the centre surrounded by slightly smaller circles – one of these for each child in the class. Ask the children to fill in features of a face in the circle. The face in the middle belongs to Jesus.

Then, around the edge with coloured crayons, or markers, the children could write sentences describing themselves, e.g. I am friendly, I am funny, etc.

You could display this during the Prayer Service for the parents/guardians.

 PRAYERTIME

Sign of the Cross.

Teacher

We light our candle. It reminds us that God is always with us.
Jesus knows that you are the greatest.
Jesus knows each one of you by name.

Today we give thanks to God for Jesus who loves all children everywhere. God sent Jesus to show us how much he loves us.

Jesus says children are special.

All

Thank you, God, for Jesus.

Teacher

Jesus says children are good.

All

Thank you, God, for Jesus.

Teacher

Jesus says children are the greatest.

All

Thank you, God, for Jesus.

Invite each child to come forward by calling his or her name.

Teacher

Jesus says you are the greatest.

All

Thank you, God, for *(name)*.

Sign of the Cross.

Day Three

Continue song: *We are the Greatest*

Recall story: *We are the Greatest*

 POEM

Great!

'Grand' means – OK.
'Not bad!' means – good!
'Cool' means – better than most.
'Class!' means – Great!
'Wow!' means – Greater!
But as for the greatest –
That's us.

 PRAYERTIME

Sign of the Cross.

Teacher
We light our candle and we remember that
God is always with us.
Today we are going to imagine being there in
the crowd on the day that Jesus came to the
market.

Close your eyes.
Place your hands gently on your lap.
Put your feet on the floor.
Listen to your heart beat.
Feel your breath as it travels gently in and out
of your lungs, bringing life and energy to your
whole body.

Go inside, into your inside world, where it's
dark and quiet and safe and peaceful. Picture
yourself in the Market Place. Look at all the
people who are in the Market Place. Everyone
is listening to what Jesus is saying. The day is
warm. The sun is shining. The sky is blue.

Then Jesus looks at you and calls you into the
centre of the crowd. Imagine him putting his
hand on your shoulder and saying, 'Look at
this child. You must try to be like this child.'
Imagine how you feel when Jesus says these
words. Imagine that he bends down and tells
you that you are the greatest. Think what is it
about you that Jesus knows is great. Perhaps
he knows how much you love people at home,
or at school, or when you play with your
friends. Perhaps he sees you being kind.
Perhaps he knows that you are gentle with
others. Maybe he knows about the way you
share things with others. You would like to say
something back to Jesus. Remember, anytime
you wish, you can invite Jesus to come into
your inside world where you can listen to
what Jesus has to say to you, and you can say
whatever you wish to Jesus.

When you are ready, open your eyes.
Stretch.

We pray together.

All
Our Father…

Sign of the Cross.

Day Four

Continue song: *We are the Greatest*

Revise poem: *Great!*

 CHATTING

…about the picture on page 26

Can you name all the different things people
are buying and selling? If you were in the
picture, what would you like to buy? Can you
see the children? They are trying to get a look
in, but nobody notices them. Have you ever
been to a market like this? How many animals
can you find in the picture?

ART

'We are the Greatest!' Badges

For each child you will need:
- Coloured paper/card
- Safety pin
- Adhesive tape
- Crayons/markers
- Scissors

To make the badge
Distribute the paper. Ask the children to begin by cutting out a fairly large shape, e.g. star, circle, square, triangle. Then ask them to write 'We are the Greatest!' on the badge-shape. Decorate the badge. Using adhesive tape, secure the safety pin at the back of the badge.

The badges will be used in the prayertime on Day Five.

PRAYERTIME

Sign of the Cross

Teacher *(as the candle is lit)*
God is our light.
The light of the world.

Jesus saw the greatness in children. Let us pray today for all children.
For children in our families. Let us give thanks to God.

All
It is right to give God thanks and praise.

Teacher
For children in our school. Let us give thanks to God.

All
It is right to give God thanks and praise.

Teacher
For children all over the world. Let us give thanks to God.

All
It is right to give God thanks and praise.

Glory be to the Father...

Sign of the Cross.

Note: Remind the children to bring in their baptismal candles for tomorrow's Prayer Service.

Day Five

PRAYERTIME

Prayer Service

Note: For this prayertime the children will need the 'We are the Greatest!' badges. Place a lighted candle on a table in a central position in the room. Give each adult a copy of the reflection at the end of this lesson. Allow them a few moments to read and reflect on it.

Sign of the Cross.

Sing: *We are the Greatest*

Leader
When Jesus was asked who was the greatest he pointed to a child. Today we celebrate the greatness of children.

Each child has a baptismal candle. (You might like to use a simple night-light type candle if the baptismal candle is not available.)

The children come forward carrying their unlit candles, and the teacher lights them from the main candle.

Child *(with help from the teacher if necessary, while placing the candle around the main candle)*
I am a child.
Jesus said that children are the greatest in God's kingdom.

Reading
Story: *We are the Greatest*

Today is Market Day. The children love Market

Day. They go to the town square. All the grown-ups are there. There are men selling cheeses. There are women buying cloth. There are bakers selling bread. There are people buying spices and fruit. There are cows mooing and donkeys braying and goats baaing. The Market Place is busy. The Market Place is noisy. The Market Place is a busy place for the adults. It is a place of fun for the children. They love to run about and enjoy being with their friends. They play hide-and-seek among the adults.

Today a man comes to the Market Place. At first no one notices the man. He sits in the middle of the square where everyone will be able to see him. He speaks in a loud voice so that everyone will be able to hear him. He tells those who stop and listen about a kingdom. He calls it the Kingdom of God. He says that in God's kingdom everyone is happy. In God's kingdom everyone loves their friends as well as those who are not their friends.

'What kind of place is this kingdom,' say some of the grown-ups, 'where people love those who are not their friends?'

'How can we get to live in such a place?' say some others.

'God's kingdom is not any particular place,' says the man. 'God's kingdom can be anywhere. Wherever people love one another, wherever people are kind and gentle, wherever people share with one another, that is where God's kingdom is. God's kingdom can be right here, right now.'

'I have a question for you,' says one man. 'In our community I am an important person. I would like to know who is the most important person in this Kingdom of God that you talk about.'

Now the Market Place grows quiet. The noise stops. The buying and selling stops. The children notice that everything has gone quiet too. The children go on playing. From where they are they can see the crowd of people gathered around the man.

'What's happening?' some of the children ask each other.

Just then the man comes over to the children.

He says, 'Who will help me? I need one of you to help me teach the grown-ups something very important.'

'Me, me, me!' say the children. The man smiles. He takes the smallest child by the hand. He takes the child into the middle of the crowd. He wants everyone to notice the child.

'You ask me who is the most important person in God's kingdom,' says the man to the crowd. 'I will tell you now,' he says. 'Do you see this little child? I tell you, the child is the greatest in God's kingdom.'

A murmur of shock and surprise runs through the crowd of grown-ups. They can hardly believe their eyes. They can hardly believe their ears. The child! The child is the greatest in God's kingdom! They have never heard the like of this before!

When the man is finished the child runs back to the other children.

'What did the man want?'; 'What did the man say?'; 'What did the man teach the people?' they ask the child.

'He taught them that children are the greatest,' the child answers. The children clap and cheer.

'Who is this man?' the children ask.

'His name is Jesus,' the child answers.

'Hurrah for Jesus!' the children shout. 'Hurrah, hurrah, hurrah!'

All
Sing: *We are the Greatest*

Leader
We will now listen to the reflection.

You might like to invite a parent to read the reflection at the end of this lesson.

Leader
We now invite each child to go to her or his parent to hear why they are the greatest. Parents, you can whisper in your child's ear so no one else can hear. Then, bless your child, making the Sign of the Cross. Those whose parents are unable to be here can come to the teacher who will tell them why they are the greatest and bless them with Holy Water.

The children then go to the appropriate adult, who, having whispered in their ear why they are the greatest, makes the Sign of the Cross on their forehead with Holy Water.

Invite the children to put on their 'We are the Greatest!' badges.

Applause

Leader
We pray together.

All
Glory be to the Father...

Leader
As we go away from here we ask God to bless us and keep us safe.

All
May the Lord bless us and keep us.
May he let his face shine upon us and be gracious to us.

May he look upon us with kindness and give us his peace.
Amen.

Sign of the Cross.

NOW WE KNOW

Q. Why did God Our Father send his Son, Jesus?

A. God Our Father sent his Son, Jesus, to tell us that he loves us and wants us to be his children.

We are the Greatest

Words: Clare Maloney
Music: Fran Hegarty

1. Just the way— we— chil - dren are— is

just how we're hap - py to be—

full of life— and— full of fun—

just how we're hap - py to be— and

just in case there's an - y doubt—

we want you to know—

we are the great - est, yes we are— 'cos

192

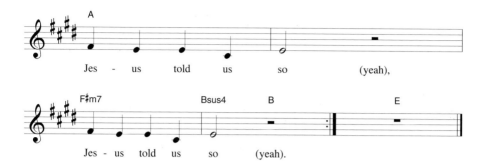

Jes - us told us so (yeah),

Jes - us told us so (yeah).

2. Just the way we children are
   Is just how we're happy to be,
   Full of surprises, full of love,
   Just how we're happy to be,
   And just in case there's any doubt
   We want you to know
   We are the greatest, yes we are
   'Cos Jesus told us so (yeah),
   Jesus told us so (yeah).

Reflection for Parents

Why is it, Lord?

Why is it, Lord,
That parents see puddles and think wellies
And our children see magic mirrors
Waiting for a pebble-plop
To ripple into smiles?

Why is it, Lord,
That parents see snow and think gloves
And our children see sleds and slides
And the tingle of a snowflake's farewell kiss
Upon the palm?

Why is it, Lord,
That parents see toys and think tidy
And our children see the endless possibilities
For fantasy and play?

Why is it that when we were growing up
We somehow grew away?
Away from all the joy and wonder
In the everyday?
From carefree to careful
From outgoing to anxious
From confident to concerned?
And unless we regain our vision of God
In the here and now
How shall we ever know Him then?

Help us to be humble.
To be led by our children
Into the small joys and special moments
Where miracles abound.
So that hand in hand
We may enter with them
The Kingdom of Heaven. Amen.
Christy Kenneally

Lesson 4: Lent – Turning Time

Then Jesus was led by the Spirit
into the wilderness.
(Matthew 4:1)

In the first lesson of this term we introduced the children to the concept of the wilderness as times of struggle, pain or emptiness that life thrusts upon us, often unpredictably. Together with the teacher the children created the 'Little wilderness' to symbolise such times in their lives. In this lesson we work again with the 'Little wilderness', this time allowing it to take on a different dimension, namely, that of freely seeking out the wilderness. This is concretised for us in the Gospel when we hear how 'Jesus was led by the Spirit in the wilderness' (Lk 4:1). In the solitude and stillness of his barren surroundings Jesus chose to withdraw and pray.

The season of Lent offers us an opportunity to enter voluntarily into this reality and to turn:
> Turn away, turn away from too-busy-ness.
> Be quiet, be still and pray.
> Turn towards God-in-the-wilderness.
> Turn, turn, day by day.

As we approach this Lenten Season, the Christian community enters a special time of reflection. At this point in the liturgical year Christians are encouraged to stop, to look at life, its rhythm and its direction. It is the time when the Church urges us to turn away and to step out of our usual pattern of life, to become more aware of where we are in terms of our relationship with others and with God. We focus on that which prevents us from realising our capacity for growth and turn towards that which is life-giving. It could be said that during Lent we are invited into a wilderness experience, a time to turn away from the distractions of everyday life and to turn once more towards God. People have always recognised the need for such times, hence the significance of pilgrimages to places such as Lough Derg, Croagh Patrick and Lourdes.

Six- and seven-year-olds' lives have been very short and their capacity for abstract reflection is limited. However, we can use this liturgical season to explore 'turning away' and 'turning towards' in the children's own lives, reflecting with them on that which holds them back from realising their full potential. We can build on their understanding of reconciliation, and reaffirm with them the all-sustaining love of God for each one of them. In this lesson we do this through ritual, story and the symbol of the 'Little wilderness'.

FOR THE TEACHER:

A thought before beginning

Incline your ear to me,
Answer me when I call.
Incline.

Lord, hear my prayer,
let my cry come unto you.
Answer me when I call.

Hide not your face from me
in the day when anguish takes hold.
Answer me when I call.

Lord, you reign for ever;
age after age recalls you.
Answer me when I call.

You will rise in pity for your People,
longing to show them your mercy.
Answer me when I call.
Taizé Prayer

Note: For prayertime on Day One you will need a small stone for each child (or where this is not appropriate use a small piece of Plasticine in the shape of a stone). These stones (pieces of Plasticine) will be used again during prayertime on Day Five.

What am I trying to do?

As the Lenten Season begins, to offer children an opportunity to explore – primarily through ritual and symbol – the experience of 'turning away' and 'turning towards', as a reflection of the Ash Wednesday call to 'Turn away from sin and embrace the Gospel'.

Why?

So that their understanding and awareness of Lent as a special liturgical season of conversion may be enhanced.

Overview of the Week

		Continue song		
		Aims of the Ritual		Continue song
		Preparation for the		Worksheet
Song: *Wilderness*		Ritual	Continue song	Preparation for the
Aims of the Ritual		Did You Know?	Preparation for the	Ritual
Preparation for the	Continue song	Chatting about Ash	Ritual	Chatting about
Ritual	Preparation for the	Wednesday	Did You Know?	doing something
Did You Know?	Ritual	Bible Procession	Chatting about bare	for Lent
Chatting about	Did You Know?	Ritual with the	feet	Activity: *My Special*
'Little wilderness'	Chatting about Lent	Distribution of	Activity: *Desert Foot*	*Promise For Lent*
Ritual	Ritual	Ashes	Ritual	Ritual

Day One

SONG

Wilderness

Aims of the Ritual

Lent is a time for reflection. We reflect best when we are in a quiet space free from outside distractions. When Jesus wanted to reflect, he withdrew to the desert to pray. In this ritual we hope to give the children an experience of creating a 'wilderness' within the classroom, a 'space' within which to reflect, a space that turns them away from everyday distractions. In this way we lay the foundation for a future understanding of Lent as a time of conversion.

Preparation for the Ritual

You will need the 'Little wilderness' and a small stone (Plasticine) for each child in the class.

Together with the class, decide how best to create a 'wilderness' space in your room. If possible, arrange the classroom furniture so that the children can be gathered around the space. To help the children enter into the experience of 'turning' it is suggested that each day, in preparation for the ritual, the 'wilderness' will be placed in four different parts of the room, e.g. the four corners of the classroom.

DID YOU KNOW?

Sometimes Jesus liked to be with friends and neighbours and family, to share his company with them. But sometimes he liked to be by himself too – to be quiet and still and thoughtful. Sometimes he would go to the desert or the wilderness because there was nothing to be busy about there. There wasn't much to see either and it was quiet and peaceful.

CHATTING

...about 'Little wilderness'

Most of the time, at home or at school or in the playground, we are surrounded by others, friends and family and neighbours. It is good to have people around us. Sometimes, too, it is nice to be on our own. Have you ever spent time all by yourself? When was it? How long did it last for? Where was it? What kinds of things do you like to do when you are on your own? Sometimes we can be on our own and still be very busy – too busy to have time to think. Have you ever found this? Sometimes we can be on our own and still have lots of noise around us. Do you like lots of noise when you are on your own? Why? Why not?

Let's look around our classroom. What is there to see? What is there to hear? What is there to do? Let's think about home. Imagine school is over for the day and you are at home. What is there to see? What is there to do? What is there to be heard? Imagine you are in the playground, in the school yard, or near where you live. Imagine it is full of children. What is there to see? What is to be heard? What is there to do?

Do you think that the place you go to, to be on your own, could be a bit like the desert that Jesus went to when he wanted to be by himself? What do you think Jesus might have thought about in the wilderness? What kind of things do you think he might have prayed about? Is there anything you feel you would think and pray about if you were in the wilderness now?

PRAYERTIME

Ritual

Sign of the Cross.

Teacher *(as the candle is lit)*
Turn away, turn away from too-busy-ness.
Be quiet, be still and pray.
Turn towards God-in-the-wilderness.
Turn, turn, day by day.

Today let us turn away for a little while from the busy day and turn towards the quietness of the desert.

Teacher *(Children repeating)*
Turn away, turn away from too-busy-ness. *(children begin to turn slowly)*
Be quiet, be still and pray. *(children pause)*
Turn towards God-in-the-wilderness. *(children continue turning until they see/face the 'Little wilderness')*
Turn, turn, day by day.

Teacher
We can stop being busy for a while. We can turn away from everything that is going on in the classroom right now and become quiet and still.

Invite each child to place a stone (or Plasticine) in the 'Little wilderness', and to turn away from the distractions of the classroom.
When each child has placed a stone (or Plasticine) in the 'Little wilderness':

All *(repeating after teacher if necessary)*
Turn away, turn away from too-busy-ness.
Be quiet, be still and pray.
Turn towards God-in-the-wilderness.
Turn, turn, day by day.

Teacher
Let us close our eyes and be quiet for a while.
Still your hands.
Place your feet on the floor.
Listen to your breath.

In your imagination go into the wilderness. You are by yourself. You want to get away from the noises and chatting. Look around you. Turn away from the noise and the chatter. You feel safe and warm and quiet and peaceful. Take a good long look around you again. Now, turn towards the wilderness. It is a big empty space. It is a good place to think. Maybe think about your friends... maybe about home... or school. Feel God in the wilderness with you. With your special inside voice tell God how you are feeling. Thank God for the space to wonder and to think. Thank God for the space to be still and quiet and peaceful.

Open your eyes.
Stretch.

All
Turn away, turn away from too-busy-ness.
Be quiet, be still and pray.
Turn towards God-in-the wilderness.
Turn, turn, day by day.

Sign of the Cross.

Day Two

Continue song: *Wilderness*

Preparation for the Ritual

 DID YOU KNOW?

Lent is a time when we can be quiet and still. Jesus went into the wilderness to be quiet and still. Lent can be a wilderness time for us, a special time when we can spend moments away from the busy day.

 CHATTING

...about Lent

Have you ever heard the word 'Lent'? Where have you heard it? Tell us what you know about Lent.

Sometimes it is good to be busy, but do you think it is good to be busy all of the time? Why? Why not? What kinds of things might you miss out on if you were always busy? What were you too busy to do? Did you ever see anyone else being too busy? How do you feel when someone is too busy for you? How do friends tell when you are too busy for them? What happens when you get too busy? If I began a 'TOO BUSY TO' list like this:

> Too busy to listen.
> Too busy to talk.
> Too busy to think.
> Too busy to take the time to...

...could you add on to the list? What kinds of things might keep you too busy to do the things on the list? For example, if I began another 'TOO BUSY' list like this:

> Too busy watching television.
> Too busy playing computer games.
> Too busy fighting.
> Too busy running around...

Could you think of other things that might go on our list?

 PRAYERTIME

Ritual

Teacher
First of all let's clear off our desks so that we won't be distracted. Let us place the 'Little wilderness'. *Discuss with the class where best to place the 'Little wilderness' today.*

Sign of the Cross.

Teacher *(as the candle is lit)*
Turn away, turn away from too-busy-ness.
Be quiet, be still and pray.
Turn towards God-in-the-wilderness.
Turn, turn, day by day.

Lent is a time when we can turn away from
busy times and turn to peaceful times.
As we face our 'Little wilderness' let us ask God
to help us to be quiet and still.

All *(as the children face the 'Little wilderness')*
Turn away, turn away from too-busy-ness.
(children begin to turn slowly)
Be quiet, be still and pray. *(children pause)*
Turn towards God-in-the-wilderness. *(children
continue turning until they face the 'Little
wilderness')*
Turn, turn, day by day.

Teacher
Close your eyes.

Let us take time to think of some of the things
we are just too busy for. Let us think of some
of the times when we are rushing about so
much we don't have time for others.
Let us tell God that we are sorry for the times
we don't make time for others. We say:

All
We are sorry God.

Teacher
For the times when we are too busy to listen.

All
We are sorry God.

Teacher
For the times when we are too busy watching
television.

All
We are sorry God.

Teacher
For the times when we are too busy shouting
and fighting.

All
We are sorry God.

Sign of the Cross.

Note: *As part of the prayertime on Day Three
there is a Bible Procession Ritual. A child will be*

invited to read the phrase 'One day Jesus went into
the desert'. It might be helpful to have the phrase
written onto a flashcard in advance of the
prayertime.

Day Three/Ash Wednesday

Continue song: *Wilderness*

Aims of the Ritual

By their participation in this ritual we hope
that the children will have a heightened
awareness of the significance of Ash
Wednesday and its place in the Lenten Season.
We continue to remind the children that Lent
is a special time when we turn away from the
distractions of every day and turn towards
God.

Preparation for the Ritual

 DID YOU KNOW?

On Ash Wednesday we wear ashes on our
forehead. Ashes remind us to:
Turn away, turn away from too-busy-ness.
Be quiet, be still and pray.
Turn towards God-in-the-wilderness.
Turn, turn, day by day.

 CHATTING

...about Ash Wednesday

Have you ever heard of Ash Wednesday? What
can you tell us about it? If you stopped being
too busy, what would you have time for?
What would be different? What would be
better? When do you become quiet and still?

What does it feel like? Tell us about a time when you were quiet and still. Did it feel different to being too busy? Was Jesus too busy for people? Why? Why not?

 PRAYERTIME

Bible Procession Ritual, with the Distribution of Ashes

Once again, put the 'Little wilderness' in a different place in the classroom. If possible, gather the children around the space. You might like to invite a priest to come and give ashes to the children. You might also like to bring in some palm and burn a little bit of it so that the children can see where the ashes have come from.

Take the Bible from its place in the classroom. Form a simple procession. Process to a table where the Bible and the candle are placed reverently. Children bow and return to their seats.

Song: *Wilderness*

The teacher lights the candle. You may also like to burn an incense stick or grains of incense.

Sign of the Cross.

Teacher
Note: *If time allows, you might like to repeat the following and invite other children to come forward, raise the Bible and read the biblical phrase.*

One day Jesus went into the desert.
_____ *(name reader)* will read the Word of God for us today.

The child is invited to come forward to read from the Bible.
The teacher takes the Bible from the altar and ceremoniously hands it to the child.
The child faces the class, holding the Bible.

Teacher
Jesus had many friends. He liked being with his friends. He liked eating with them and talking with them and sharing his life with them. Sometimes crowds of people would follow him. They wanted to hear what he had to say. They wanted to talk to him and tell him about how things were going for them. Jesus worked hard. The crowds of people often kept him busy. But he was never too busy to help those who needed him in any way.

One day Jesus decided that it would be good for him to go away and be on his own for a while. He wanted to go somewhere quiet, some place where there would be no distractions, some place where he could think and pray to God about his life, about his friends and about the world.

Then it dawned on him that the desert might be a good place for doing what he wanted to do. He went off and spent some time in the desert wilderness.

Let us listen to the Word of God as we read from the Bible.

Reader
The Lord be with you

All
And also with you.

Reader
This reading is from the Gospel according to St Mark.

All
Glory to you, O Lord.

Reader
'One day, Jesus went into the desert.'
The Gospel of the Lord *(raising Bible)*.

All
Praise to you, Lord Jesus Christ.

Priest *(holding ashes)*
Ash Wednesday is a special day. It marks the beginning of Lent.
The ashes help us to remember that it is important sometimes to turn away from being busy, to stop and to turn towards God.

Children come forward to receive the ashes.

Priest
_____ *(name)*, turn towards God.
In the name of the Father, and of the Son and of the Holy Spirit.

Child
Amen.

When each child has received his/her ashes:

All

Turn away, turn away from too-busy-ness.
Be quiet, be still and pray.
Turn towards God-in-the-wilderness.
Turn, turn, day by day.

Sign of the Cross.

Day Four

Continue song: *Wilderness*

Preparation for the Ritual

DID YOU KNOW?

Note: If there is a special place of local pilgrimage, e.g. well, Mass rock, mountain, chat to the children about this place rather than chatting to them about Lough Derg/Croagh Patrick.

There are some special places of prayer in Ireland where people go to pray. Sometimes they walk in their bare feet. One of these places is a small island on a lake called Lough Derg. Another place is a mountain called Croagh Patrick. People go to these places to pray and to be close to God. Taking off their shoes and walking in their bare feet is part of how they pray in a special way when they are in the wilderness.

CHATTING

...about bare feet

Have you ever taken off your shoes to walk/run about in your bare feet? Tell us about it. What is it like to paddle in your bare feet?

To walk in sand in your bare feet? To dance in your bare feet? Bare feet can be tickly. Have you ever had your bare feet tickled? What does that feel like?

What do you think it would be like to climb a mountain in your bare feet? Would it be hard or easy? Would you like to do it? Why do you think people might want to pray to God in their bare feet? Do you think it might help them to feel closer to God? What would it be like to walk in a desert in your bare feet?

At home tonight, ask your mam/dad/gran/grandad/guardian if they have ever heard about Lough Derg or Croagh Patrick (or any other special place of local pilgrimage).

ACTIVITY

Desert Foot

You will need:
- A large sheet of paper for each child
- Adhesive
- Scissors
- Sand

Distribute the paper.
Placing the paper on the floor, ask the children to put one foot (preferably bare) on it and to trace the outline of that foot. Alternatively, get them to work in pairs, with one child drawing the outline while the other child places his/her foot on the sheet of paper.
Ask the children to cut out the foot outline.
Ask the children to write their name on the foot and to decorate it.
Distribute a little sand from the 'Little wilderness' to each child. Alternatively, ask each child to take some sand from the 'Little wilderness' themselves.
Cover the foot with a thin layer of adhesive, then sprinkle the sand over the foot.

PRAYERTIME

Ritual

In preparation for the ritual and in discussion with the class, once again create a space for the 'Little wilderness'. If possible, gather the children around this space.

Ask the children to place the foot on the desk in front of them.

Sign of the Cross.

Teacher *(as the candle is lit)*
Turn away, turn away from too-busy-ness.
Be quiet, be still and pray.
Turn towards God-in-the-wilderness.
Turn, turn, day by day.

For holy places to walk in.

All
We praise you, O God, and we bless you.

Teacher
For Croagh Patrick.

All
We praise you, O God, and we bless you.

Teacher
For Lough Derg.

All
We praise you, O God, and we bless you.

Teacher
For holy wells.

All
We praise you, O God, and we bless you.

Teacher
For the wilderness.

All
We praise you, O God, and we bless you.

Invite the children to place their desert foot near or around the 'Little wilderness'.

All
Praise the Father.
Praise the Son.
Praise the Spirit.
The Three in One.

Sign of the Cross.

Continue song: *Wilderness*

WORKSHEET

If you wish to use the worksheet or workbook page which accompanies this lesson, this is an appropriate time to do so.

Preparation for the Ritual

CHATTING

...about doing something for Lent

Have you ever heard anyone say 'what are you doing for Lent'? What do you think they might mean by this? What sort of things do people do? People do things during Lent because it helps them feel closer to God. Sometimes during Lent people decide to go to Mass every day, sometimes they do other things like keeping their bedroom tidy or being kind to someone they know.

Do you think we could do something during Lent? Let's think about what we could do. Let's see if we could make a list: we could try to be tidier; we could be kind to someone; we could do the dishes in the evening; we could remember our Trócaire boxes, etc.

ACTIVITY

My Special Promise for Lent

You will need a special piece of paper for each child.
Ask the children to draw about one thing that they will try to do during Lent. When they have finished, ask them to fold it carefully. Their promise is between themselves and God.

PRAYERTIME

Ritual

In preparation for today's ritual, put the 'Little wilderness' in the centre of the classroom. If possible, gather the children around the 'Little wilderness'. To further highlight the significance of being in the wilderness you might like to ask each child to take a stone (Plasticine) from the 'Little wilderness' and to arrange the stones in a wide circle around the 'Little wilderness'. The children could then sit within the circle of stones

(Plasticine). As the children participate in this ritual they could chant 'Turn away, turn away...' quietly.

Sign of the Cross.

Song: *Wilderness*

Teacher
We light our candle.
We remember that Lent is a time when we turn away from the busy day and turn to God.

All
Turn away, turn away from too-busy-ness.
Be quiet, be still and pray.
Turn towards God-in-the-wilderness.
Turn, turn, day by day.

Teacher
Each of us has made a little promise to God for Lent. We offer these promises to God now.

Invite the children to come forward and place their promise in the 'Little wilderness'.

We have placed our promise before you God. We ask you to be with us as we try to keep our promise. We know that you love us. We know that you are with us always.

All
Turn away, turn away from too-busy-ness.
Be quiet, be still and pray.
Turn towards God-in-the wilderness.
Turn, turn, day by day.

Sign of the Cross.

Wilderness

Fran Hegarty

Take time to turn a - way___ to___

leave be - hind this bu - sy world___

Take time out on our own___ in a

wil - der - ness a - lone.___ 1. In the

wil - der - ness___ that's all a - round___ just

turn and see what's to___ be found. ___

Close your eyes___ and see what you___ can

see.

Think of all— the friends you know— and

let the love in your— heart grow.—

Be the ve - ry best that you— can

be.

2 In the wilderness you just might find
That when you turn and take the time,
You see things in a very different way
Think of all the friends you know
And let the love in your heart grow.
Be the very best that you can be.

Lesson 5: The Good Shepherd

Rejoice with me,
for I have found my sheep that was lost.
(Luke 15:6)

We introduce the children to the story of the lost sheep. This story offers the possibility of exploring the experiences of being lost and of being found. In a sense, when children cease to show the goodness that is potentially theirs, they too are lost or separated from their truest self, which is the image of God. In the case of a child, the experience of being lost in, for instance, a supermarket or a railway station, can be a particularly terrifying one. It may be equally terrifying for children to find themselves, for example, in a fit of temper and thus separated from the way they are familiar with and from those whom they love.

In this lesson we reflect on the experience of the sheep and of the shepherd. In the Bible sheep represented the chief wealth and total livelihood of pastoral peoples, providing food to eat, milk to drink, wool for making cloth, and hides and bones for other uses. In addition, the sheep was a medium of exchange and a sacrificial animal. Allusions to sheep and to sheep-raising are numerous in the Bible and the care of sheep is a rich source of theological imagery. The sheep must be protected from wild animals, theft and inclement weather. The shepherd leads the sheep to water in a land where springs are scarce. In bad weather the sheep are sheltered in folds and an injured sheep or lamb is carried to protection by the shepherd. The central imagery of sheep in the Bible is that of an animal who is gentle and submissive and in constant need of guidance and care. In the Old Testament God chose shepherds to be leaders on more than one occasion, for instance, Moses, Abraham and Amos. In the New Testament there are many figurative references to sheep and to Jesus as shepherd. Sheep need to be led and the shepherd goes to great trouble to find the sheep that has strayed. This is an image which helps us to explore the care of God for the sinner. The resurrected Christ told the apostle Peter to 'feed my lambs' and 'tend my sheep' (Jn 21:15-17). Acknowledging this background, we use the experience of the sheep and of the shepherd as a starting point for a reflection on the child's own experience of being lost or of being found. We focus on the story of the Parable of the Good Shepherd.

Parables are complex stories. Their language is metaphorical and the images that are used are deeply symbolic. Young children are not ready to understand this abstract language. So we introduce them gradually to the richness of the parables by offering the stories to them in a manner appropriate to their age and development. During the week we offer the children an opportunity to make and play with sheep and a shepherd.

What am I trying to do?

To help the children reflect on their experience of being lost and on the experience of being found as told in the story of the lost sheep.

Why?

So that they will be able to recognise, in their own lives, moments of being lost, and become aware of the experience of being found.

FOR THE TEACHER:

A thought before beginning

And a woman who held a babe
    against her bosom said,
Speak to us of children.
And he said:
Your children are not your
    children.
They are the sons and daughters of Life's
    longing for itself.
They come through you but not from you,
And though they are with you yet they belong
    not to you.

You may give them your love but not your
  thoughts,
For they have their own thoughts.
You may house their bodies but not their
  souls,
For their souls dwell in the house of tomorrow,
  which you cannot visit, not even in your
  dreams.

You may strive to be like them, but seek not to
  make them like you.
For life goes not backward nor tarries with
  yesterday.
You are the bows from which your children as
  living arrows are sent forth.

The Archer sees the mark upon the path of the
  infinite, and He bends you with His might
  that His arrows may go swift and far.
Let your bending in the Archer's hand be for
  gladness;
For even as He loves the arrow that flies, so He
  loves also the bow that is stable.
    Kahlil Gibran

Reference: *The Good Shepherd & The Child,*
Sofia Cavelletti, Patricia Coulter, Gianna
Gobbi & Silvana W. Montanaro MD. New
York: Don Bosco Multimedia, 1993.

Overview of the Week

			Continue song	Art: *Picture the*
Song: *The Lost Sheep*	Continue song		Story: *The Lost*	*Situation*
Chatting about	Story: *The Good*	Continue song	*Sheep's Story*	Chatting about the
sheep	*Shepherd*	Art: *Making Sheep*	Worksheet	picture
Prayertime	Prayertime	Prayertime	Prayertime	Prayertime

Day One

SONG

The Lost Sheep

CHATTING

...about sheep

Have you ever seen a sheep? What does a
sheep look like? What do sheep do all day
long? Do you know what a mammy/daddy/
baby sheep is called? What kind of coat has a
sheep? Who looks after the sheep? Why do
you think sheep might need someone to look
after them? How does the farmer/shepherd
look after his/her sheep? Sheep all look alike
to us; do you think the farmer knows each
separate sheep? Do you think the farmer can
tell the difference between them? Do you
think you could tell the difference between all
the sheep in one flock? Do you think the
shepherd has a name for each one of the
sheep? If you had a sheep, what would you
call it? Let's try and think of names for sheep.
When it's springtime and the weather is
getting warmer, the farmer shears the sheep.
Do you know what that means? What does
the farmer do with the wool? At what time of
the year do you wear woolly clothes?

P R A Y E R T I M E

Sign of the Cross.

Teacher *(as the candle is lit)*
God is our light. The light of our world.

Close your eyes.
Place your hands gently on your lap and your feet on the floor.
Listen to your heart beating.
Feel your breath as it moves gently in and out of your body, bringing air and oxygen and life to every single part of your body.

Go inside, into your inside world. In there it's dark and quiet and safe and peaceful. Imagine yourself looking at a field full of sheep. There are white sheep with white faces and white sheep with black faces. There are big sheep and some little lambs. Some of them are grazing. Some are just standing and some of them are running to and fro. Some are making no sound at all and some of them are making a lot of noise. You can wonder what they are saying. As you look at your imaginary field full of sheep, choose one. This can be your own sheep. You can give it a name. Name your sheep. Let your sheep know that you care for it. Imagine yourself sitting on the grass with your sheep in your arms. Stroke your sheep and cuddle it. Talk to your sheep. Imagine how it feels to hold your sheep gently in your arms. When you feel it wriggle, you can let it go. Off it goes into the middle of all the sheep in the field. As you watch it run and jump, you can say thank you to God for the sheep and for all animals.

Open your eyes. Relax.

We pray together.

All
Time and time and time again.
Praise God, praise God.

Sign of the Cross.

Continue song: *The Lost Sheep*

STORY

The Good Shepherd
(Adapted from Luke 15:3-7)

Once there was a shepherd, a good shepherd. He had one hundred sheep. He loved every single one of the sheep in his flock. He knew the name of each one of his sheep. In the morning when he took his sheep out to graze for the day, he would call each one of them by name. The good shepherd always walked ahead of his sheep. The sheep knew that their shepherd loved them and would never let them come to harm. They followed him day after day, up hill and down.

One day the good shepherd was out with his flock. He found a place for them to graze. He made sure the sheep were all happy, then he sat down to watch over them. He wanted to make sure that they were all safe, so he began to count to see if his sheep were all there. When he had finished he realised that one sheep was missing. He was very worried. He looked all around. He called the lost sheep's name. There was no answer. He called again. There was still no answer.

The good shepherd loved his lost sheep. He wanted to find it. He was unhappy for it to be separated from him and the rest of his flock. He decided he must go and look for it. He made the rest of the sheep gather in together so that they would keep each other company while he went off to look for the one lost sheep. The sheep knew he would come back to them. So off he went in search of his lost sheep.

He searched and searched. He called and called. He travelled up hill and down. He looked everywhere. Then, he heard something. He looked closer. There it was. His lost sheep, he had found it. He called its name. He ran to it and when he got there he picked the sheep up. He checked to see if it was all right and to make sure that it wasn't hurt in any way. Then he carried it on his shoulders back to the flock. Now the good shepherd was very happy again.

That evening he led all his flock back home. Then, when they were all safe and sound for the night, he went around to his friends' houses. He told them, 'A terrible thing happened today. I lost one of my sheep. I was so worried. I was so sad and lonely. Even though I have ninety-nine other sheep, I love each one of them. So I went to look for my sheep and found it. Now I am so happy again. I want to invite you all to come to my house tonight and celebrate with me. My lost sheep is found. Thank goodness.'

 PRAYERTIME

Sign of the Cross.

Teacher *(as the candle is lit)*
God is our light.
The light of our world.

Today we think of the way in which the shepherd in the story loved the sheep and cared for them. We give thanks for all those who love and care for us like the shepherd cared for the sheep.

Think of someone special who loves you at home. Your mam or your dad, your gran or your grandad. Close your eyes for a moment and picture that person.

Think of one time when that person showed you how much they love you, by caring for you, by looking after you, by getting you the things you need. Silently, deep in your heart, ask God to bless and care for that person who loves you so much. Open your eyes and we will pray together.

All *(sing or say)*
Time and time and time again.
Praise God, praise God.

Teacher
Now think of someone else in your family who loves you and cares for you but does not live at home. It may be your older brother or sister, your gran or your grandad, your aunt or uncle. Remember some particular time when they took care of you, which shows how much they love you. Or a time when they got you something you needed. Once again close your eyes and picture that person. With your inside voice ask God to bless that person and to take care of her or him. As you open your eyes, we pray together.

All
Time and time and time again.
Praise God, praise God.

Teacher
Now think of someone else in school who loves you and cares for you. It may be one of the teachers. Or it may be one of your friends who plays with you and perhaps shows you how to do things when you need help. Close your eyes and picture that person. Think of a time when that person showed you how much she or he cares for you by helping you or by giving you something you needed. With your inside voice ask God to bless that person and to care for her or him always. As you open your eyes, we pray together.

All
Time and time and time again.
Praise God, praise God.

Teacher
Now remember that there is someone else who loves us and cares for us always, no matter what. That someone is God. God loves us like a loving mother loves her child. God cares for us like a loving father cares for his child. Together we pray.

All
Time and time and time again.
Praise God, praise God.

Sign of the Cross.

Day Three

Continue song: *The Lost Sheep*

ART

Making Sheep

Give each child a piece of cotton wool, a piece of black paper, a piece of chalk and a pair of scissors.

Ask the children to draw an outline of a sheep on the black paper.
Draw the sheep's face.

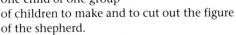

Invite the children to cut around the outline and to stick on the cotton wool to make the sheep's body. Ask one child or one group of children to make and to cut out the figure of the shepherd.

Playing with the Sheep
Using a piece of wool, or a chalk line, mark out an area of the classroom floor as a field.

1. Give the children some time to play freely with the sheep and the shepherd, moving the figures about as they think appropriate. They can talk freely to one another as they go about what they are doing. The role of the teacher in this activity is to observe what is taking place in an effort to assist his or her understanding of the children's perception of the story.

2. Invite the children to put their sheep somewhere in the field. Where will we put the shepherd? Does the shepherd need to see all of the sheep? Why?

Some children can take turns in getting their sheep 'lost'. The others ask that child about the sheep: how it got separated from the rest; what

it is feeling now that it is lost; what it is doing wherever it is. Then the child whose sheep is lost must look for it, find it, and carry it back.

Now the teacher may talk to the children, asking them how they feel now that the lost sheep is found; what the shepherd can do to celebrate the 'finding' of the lost sheep; what advice they might give the sheep who was lost so that it won't get lost again, etc. The teacher might also ask the sheep's owner how he/she feels about finding the sheep. Is she/he cross with it for having got lost? Will he/she punish it, and if so why? If not, why not? The teacher might direct them to reflect on the behaviour of the shepherd in the story in this regard.

PRAYERTIME

Sign of the Cross.

Teacher
As we light this candle we remember again that God is always with us, always listening to us.

Close your eyes.
Place your hands gently on your lap and your feet on the floor.
Listen to your heart beat.
Feel your breath as it moves gently in and out of your body, bringing life and oxygen to your whole body.

Go inside, into your inside world, where it is dark and safe and quiet and peaceful. Imagine that you are the sheep who got lost. You left the other sheep and went away by yourself. Imagine why you might have done that. Imagine how you felt when you realised that you were lost. You couldn't see the shepherd, you couldn't think where you should go. Imagine how you felt. Maybe you felt lonely, maybe you felt afraid, maybe you felt sorry that you had gone away by yourself. Then imagine that you see the shepherd coming to find you. First you see the shepherd in the distance. Imagine what you might do. Maybe you wait for the shepherd or maybe you run to meet the shepherd. Then imagine what it feels like when the shepherd gathers you up and carries you safely back to the others. Remember that God cares for you like the shepherd cares for the sheep. God wants to find you whenever you are lost. With your inside voice you can talk to God and say anything you wish. We pray together.

All
Time and time and time again.
Praise God, praise God.

Sign of the Cross.

Day Four

Continue song: *The Lost Sheep*

STORY

The Lost Sheep's Story

I am a sheep. I have a black face, two long ears, two bright eyes, and lots and lots of lovely wool all over me keeping me warm. I live in a flock with ninety-nine other sheep. The other sheep look like me but we are all different. We are all friends too. We have one very special friend. He is our shepherd. He is a good shepherd. He looks after us. He loves us. He has a name for each one of us and each morning when we go out to graze, our shepherd calls us by our name. I don't know how he remembers all our names, but he does.

Nearly every day we do the same thing: we go out to graze in the morning and we come home again in the evening. But one day was not the same as the other days, it was very different. I will tell you about it.

All of us sheep were following our shepherd in the morning. He always leads and we follow him wherever he goes. You see we trust our shepherd. We know he loves us and he will give us what we need, and wherever we go he keeps us safe. This particular day though, I got lost! Yes, LOST! One minute I was there following with the others, then, I looked around and, whatever happened, I was all by myself.

At first I wasn't worried. In fact I thought to myself, 'I'm a clever sheep, I can manage to find what I need by myself. I will go a different way. I will do things my way. I don't need others.' That was all very well for a while. But as time went on I began to realise I was all by myself. I had no friends now to talk to, to walk with, to be close to. I had no friends to care about me and no shepherd to love me. I thought to myself, 'I am still a clever sheep, but even clever sheep can do foolish things. I should return to my shepherd and my flock.' And off I went, but, oh dear, I couldn't find them. I was sad and lonely. I didn't know what to do. I kept calling and calling and then I heard a voice answer. The voice was calling my name. I listened. It was the voice of my shepherd. I began to run towards him. Then I saw him. He ran to me, and do you know what he did? He picked me up. He looked carefully at me to see if I was hurt. He carried me on his shoulders all the way back to my flock! I was so happy. I have such a good shepherd. I love my shepherd and he loves me. I bet you would love to be a sheep and have a good shepherd like I have!

WORKSHEET

If you wish to use the worksheet or workbook page which accompanies this lesson, this is an appropriate time to do so.

PRAYERTIME

Sign of the Cross.

Teacher
We light our candle and we know that you are always with us.
When we are lost, you search and find us.

When we have no one to play with and we feel lost and lonely.
Let's ask God to take care of us. We pray together:

Teacher and children
You search and find us, O God.

Teacher
When we have had a row with our friend and we feel lost and lonely.
Let us ask God to take care of us. We pray together:

Teacher and children
You search and find us, O God.

Teacher
When we have done something which upset our mam or dad or someone at home and we feel lost and lonely.
Let us ask God to take care of us. We pray together:

Teacher and children
You search and find us, O God.

Teacher
When we lose our mam or dad in the supermarket and we feel lost and lonely.
Let us ask God to take care of us. We pray together:

Teacher and children
You search and find us, O God.

Sign of the Cross.

ART

Picture the Situation

Note: The aim of this exercise is to help the children to take a broader perspective of the Parable of the Lost Sheep.

Give each child a page and some markers or crayons.

Invite them, in silence, to draw a picture of the story. You might like to play some background music while they are doing this.

As they are doing so, you might walk around and try to interpret what you see being drawn. You might watch out for certain things which will help you to become aware of the children's understanding of the various elements of the story. You might note where the lost sheep is in relation to the other sheep; in relation to the shepherd; if there is a fence around the sheep and, if so, what it might represent in terms of the child's ability to distinguish between togetherness and separateness; whether or not one sheep stands out from the others, and if this sheep is the sheep the child named in the story; where it is in relation to others in the story; the size of the good shepherd in relation to the size of the sheep; if a child has drawn a particular part of the story, e.g. the lost sheep on its own, what the significance of this might be for this particular child.

These are only hints as to some of the things you might look for and wonder about and chat about with the children.

Invite the children to talk to the others at their table about their picture for two or three minutes.

CHATTING

...about the picture on page 28

How many sheep can you find in the picture? Do they remind you of the little Beings? The sheep are all alike and yet each one is different. Can you see the shepherd on the hill? What is he looking for? Which sheep do you think was the lost sheep who has been found? Why? Look at the shepherd's face as he carries his sheep. What is he thinking?

PRAYERTIME

Sign of the Cross.

Sing: *The Lost Sheep*

Teacher
We light our candle and we remember that God is always with us and is always caring for us. Let us think about some of the times when we feel God's love for us and give thanks to God.

We feel God's love for us when our mam or dad show us that they love us. Think of a time when you felt like that. *(Pause)*

All
Time and time and time again.
Praise God, praise God.

Teacher
We feel God's love for us on days when we are having fun with our friends or with our family. Think of a time when you felt like that. *(Pause)*

All
Time and time and time again.
Praise God, praise God.

Teacher
We feel God's love for us when someone is kind or caring or loving to us when we feel sad. Think of a time when you felt like that. *(Pause)*

All
Time and time and time again.
Praise God, praise God.

Encourage the children to mention times in their own experience when they felt that God loved them. The rest of the class can respond as above.

Teacher
We pray together.

All
Praise to the Father.
Praise to the Son.
Praise to the Spirit.
The Three in One.

Sign of the Cross.

The Lost Sheep

Finbar O'Connor

1. The poor lit - tle sheep, he start - ed to weep, all

lost and a - lone in the wood, he

did - n't cry 'Mum - my', he did - n't cry 'Mum', he

just start - ed bleat - ing as loud as he could,

'Baa, baa, baa, I've lost my Ma -

ma, maa, maa,

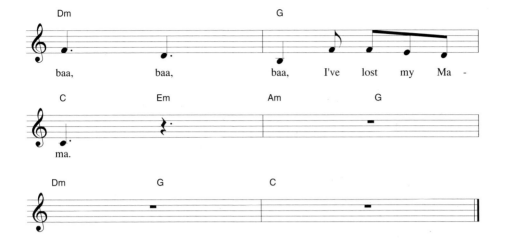

baa, baa, baa, I've lost my Ma -

ma.

2. Back home in the shed, the mother sheep said,
   'My baby is not by my side.'
   She didn't cry 'Sonny', she didn't cry 'son',
   She just started bleating and here's what she cried,
   'Maa, maa, maa, I've lost my baba, baa, baa.
   Maa, maa, maa, I've lost my baba.'

3. The shepherd came in and said with a grin,
   'See mother, I've brought home your boy!'
   He didn't cry 'Mummy', she didn't cry 'Son',
   They just started bleating aloud in their joy,
   'Maa, maa, maa, I've found my baba, baa, baa,
   Baa, baa, baa, I've found my mama.'

Lesson 6: Losing My Way

If we say that we have no sin,
we deceive ourselves,
and the truth is not in us.
(I John 1:8)

In the lesson entitled *My Goodness* we tried to put the children in touch with their own individual goodness, with the collective goodness of childhood, and with the goodness that is at the heart of human nature. Made in the image and likeness of God, we reflect something of the goodness of God.

Jesus is the one who, above all, embodied and reflected the full potential of that human goodness in himself, in his own life and actions. He also showed us what the goodness of God is like. From this starting point we help the children to become aware of, and to reflect on, the fact that there are times when they embody and express in their behaviour less than the good that is potentially theirs.

The goodness of the children was clearly obvious to Jesus. This is evident when we read the Gospel story about Jesus and the children. There are times, however, when, because of their behaviour, the innate goodness of childhood is not shown to others as clearly as it might be. We lead the children to review in a critical way some aspects of their behaviour. We offer them the opportunity to focus on particular moments when they didn't live up to the goodness that Jesus saw in children.

In this lesson the little Being character appears in a series of situations that are deliberately unspecific. These situations focus on the essence of the wrongdoing rather than on the specific content, i.e. they show the little Being in a temper but deliberately do not say how the temper came about. This leaves open the possibility of reflecting on the stories with the children in such a way that they are helped to look at similar situations in their own experience.

In each one, the central character, the little Being, is clearly not exactly like the children but not too different either. In the context of the relationships between the little Being and the significant adult, e.g. a parent, the little Being in each case comes to recognise that what it has done is wrong. The adult, who has made it clear that he/she loves the little Being, enables it to recognise its wrongdoing and come to the point of saying sorry.

Through the chat and prayertime the children are then helped to recognise similar moments in their own experience, to reflect on what they have done and on its consequences. In doing this the children will use the little Beings they made in a previous lesson.

FOR THE TEACHER:

A thought before beginning

Listen to what God is saying to us:
You are my child.
You are written in the palm of my hand.
You are hidden in the shadow of my hand.
I have moulded you in the secret of the earth.
I have knitted you together in your mother's womb.
You belong to me.
I am yours. You are mine.
I have called you from eternity and you are the one who is held safe and embraced in love from eternity to eternity.
You belong to me. And I am holding you safe and I want you to know that whatever happens to you, I am always there. I was always there; I am always there; I always will be there and hold you in my embrace.
You are mine. You are my child. You belong to my home. You belong to my intimate life and I will never let you go. I will be faithful to you.
Henri J. M. Nouwen

What am I trying to do?

To help the children to identify types of behaviour which do not show the goodness that is potentially theirs, to reflect on the consequences of this behaviour, to recognise that it is wrong and to say sorry.

Why?

So that they will become more aware of and be able to articulate stories of times when they did not show the goodness that they are capable of.

Begin to teach the children the following prayers. These will be used in the prayertimes during the week.

Act of Sorrow
O my God, I thank you for loving me.
I am sorry for all my sins, for not loving
others and not loving you.
Help me to live like Jesus and not sin again. Amen.

Prayer for Forgiveness
O my God, help me to remember the times
when I didn't live as Jesus asked me to live.
Help me to be sorry and to try again. Amen.

Prayer after Forgiveness
O my God, thank you for forgiving me.
Help me to love others.
Help me to live as Jesus asked me to. Amen.

These prayers are particularly relevant to those children preparing for First Penance.

Note: In the lessons following, material contained within boxes is for classes where the children are celebrating First Penance and First Communion.

Overview of the Week

		Continue song	Continue song,
Song: *I'm Sorry*		Story: *Being Violent*	poem
Story: *Being*		Chatting about the	Recall story
Destructive	Continue song	story	Activity: *God Can Be*
Chatting about the	Recall story	Chatting about	*Glad*	Worksheet
story	Prayertime	friends	Prayertime	Chatting about the
Did You Know?	Art: *Let's Draw for*	Poem: *One Day*	Art: *Let's Draw for*	picture
Prayertime	*Home*	Prayertime	*Home*	Prayertime

217

Day One

SONG

I'm Sorry

Note: If the original little Being has not survived, you might like to begin this lesson by asking the children to make a new little Being.

STORY

Being Destructive

First of all this little Being poked a hole in something. In the beginning it was just a tiny hole. As it poked at the tiny hole the little Being thought to itself, 'I don't think I should be doing this but…'

Then the little Being poked its finger through the hole. Now it was a bigger hole. Now it took a marker and scribbled all over it. As it scribbled, the little Being thought to itself, 'I don't really think I should be doing this but…'

The little Being began to bend it. It bent it over and back and over and back until, oh dear, it broke off. Now there was a big hole in part of it, some of it was scribbled on, and a piece of it was broken off. The little Being stood and looked at it.

Now it was in bits. Now it was destroyed. Now it was no use any more. Just then the little Being's dad came along. He looked at the little Being. He looked at what the little Being had done.

CHATTING

…about the story

What do you think it might have been that the little Being destroyed? Have you ever seen something being destroyed? Have you ever had just a little hole in something, and then it got bigger? How did the hole get bigger? Could you make a little hole bigger? How would you do that? Have you ever made a hole in something? Have you ever made a hole or a tear or a rip worse than it was? Can you remember what the little Being did with the markers? When you have markers you need something to draw on – what do you like to draw on? There are some things that it is not good to draw on – can you think of something it is not good to draw on? Why? Have you ever scribbled on something like that?

Sometimes things get broken. Sometimes they get broken by accident. Have you ever seen something get broken by accident? Do you think the little Being broke the thing in the story by accident? How do you know it was not an accident? Do you think the little Being in the story knew it was doing something wrong? What makes you think it knew? Would you know if you were doing something wrong? What might you be doing that would be wrong? Can you remember a time when you did something and you knew it was wrong? Ask your little Being why the Being in the story scribbled on and broke the thing it had. What would you do if you were in the story and you were the little Being's dad? Why would you do that? Let's see what the little Being's dad does.

Continuing the story…

Dad looked at the little Being. He looked at the broken piece and the hole and the scribbles. 'Oh dear,' he said. 'Now it is broken. Now it does not look good. Now it cannot work. Now it cannot be what it should be.'

218

The little Being felt sad. 'We will get a new one, Dad,' it said.

'We could get a new one,' said Dad, 'but that will not make this one better. It is destroyed. I feel sad about it.'

'We can fix it,' said the little Being.

'No,' said Dad. 'It cannot be mended. It is useless now.'

The little Being looked sad.

'What is the matter, little Being?' Dad asked. 'You look sad.'

'I am sad because it is no use now. It is broken. I should not have broken it.'

Dad put his arms around his little Being. 'I love you little Being,' he said.

The little Being felt its dad's arms and its dad's love around it. It said, 'I am sorry for destroying it, Dad.'

CHATTING

...about the story

Did you ever break something in your home and then you got a new one? Sometimes if something gets broken we can get it fixed – did this ever happen in your home? In the story, the little Being's dad says they won't get a new one and they cannot fix the one they have. Why? How does the little Being feel about that? How would you feel if you destroyed something and it couldn't be fixed? Has anything like that ever happened to you? Have you ever destroyed something and then you were sorry you did it? Can you remember what the little Being's dad did/said? Were you surprised at what the little Being's dad did/said? Why? Do you think the dad loved his little Being? How can you tell this? Why was the little Being's dad sad? The thing was a good thing in the beginning. Was it still a good thing when the little Being was finished with it? Why not? Do you think the little Being learned

anything from what happened? If you could talk to that little Being now, what would you say to it? Do you think the little Being might do something which would make up for what it has done? Can you suggest some way it could make up for what it has done? Have you ever tried to make up for being destructive? Do you think your little Being has learnt anything from this story? Ask it. What does it say to you?

DID YOU KNOW?

The world we live in is a good world. It is full of the good things God our Creator has given us. It is wrong when good things get destroyed. But God our Creator loves us, even when we do wrong and destroy things. God loves us so much that he wants us to grow and to change and to be as good as we can possibly be. The little Being's dad still loved it even though it had done something wrong. Your mam/dad/guardian still love you even if you do something wrong. You can show them that you are glad they love you, by saying sorry. When you do something wrong, you can say sorry.

PRAYERTIME

Sign of the Cross.

Teacher
As we light our candle we remember that God is always with us. God loves us always. When we are destructive we are not being the way God wants us to be. We tell God that we are sorry for all those times.

All *(repeating after teacher)*
Act of Sorrow
O my God, I thank you for loving me.
I am sorry for all my sins, for not loving others and not loving you.

Help me to live like Jesus and not sin again.
Amen.

Teacher
We ask God to help us to love others always.
When we say sorry, God always forgives us for
the wrong things we do. We thank God.

All *(repeating after teacher)*
Prayer after Forgiveness
O my God, thank you for forgiving me.
Help me to love others.
Help me to live as Jesus asked me to. Amen.

Sign of the Cross.

Day Two

Continue song: *I'm Sorry*

Recall story: *Being Destructive*

P R A Y E R T I M E

Note: *During the prayertime invite the children to
place their little Being in front of them.*

Sign of the Cross.

Teacher
We light our candle and we remember that
God is always with us. We know that God
loves us even more than a loving mother and
even more than a loving father.
Today we are going to remember the times
when we destroyed things and we are going to
tell God that we are sorry.
It might be that we got cross and broke
something.
Maybe we did it in a fit of temper.
Can you remember a time when that
happened to you?

Close your eyes and think. *(Pause)*
Now, tell God that you are sorry.

We pray together.

All
Act of Sorrow

Teacher
It could also be that we were careless and by
not handling something with care caused it to
get broken.
Can you remember a time when that
happened to you?

Close your eyes and think. (Pause)
Now, tell God that you are sorry.

We pray together.

All
Act of Sorrow

Teacher
It may be that we did things which destroyed
the place around where we live, by damaging
trees or walls or hedges, or by thoughtlessly
leaving papers or rubbish around.
Can you remember a time when that
happened to you?

Close your eyes and think. *(Pause)*
Now, tell God that you are sorry.

We pray together.

All
Act of Sorrow

Teacher
Let us have a moment's silence.

All
Act of Sorrow

Sign of the Cross.

ART

Let's Draw for Home

Ask the children to choose one of the
moments from their own experience which
they thought about and to draw a picture of it.
Encourage them to tell their little Being about
the picture. Encourage them to take the
picture home and to tell the story of what
they did to their parents/guardians.

Day Three

Continue song: *I'm Sorry*

STORY

Being Violent

Today a little Being is fighting. It kicks with its feet. It thumps with its fists. It pulls hair and it gives slaps with its hands. It pushes and shoves with all its might. It makes nasty faces with its tongue and its eyes and its mouth. It calls horrible names with its voice. This little Being is using its whole body to be violent. It uses its whole self to cause hurt and pain. It goes KICK, THUMP, BEAT, HURT. This little Being has a friend. Its friend sees what is happening.

CHATTING

...about the story

Why do you think this little Being is fighting? Ask your little Being – perhaps it knows why. What did it say? Tell us about a time when you saw someone fighting. Have you ever seen anyone fighting like this little Being? Have you ever been in a fight like this?

Let's think about all the good things we can do with our feet/hands/fingers/faces/voices/whole bodies. These are the good things. Why are they good things? How do you feel when you do good things with your body? Sometimes we can do bad things with our bodies too. The little Being showed us some of them. Can you think of others as well? Why are these bad things? Have you ever had a

kick/slap, etc. that hurt you? Did it make you cry? Did you ever do anything like the little Being in the story? Do you know why you did it? How did you feel when you were doing it? How did you feel when it was over? Do you think fighting is a good thing? What do you think the little Being's friend will say? What do you think it will do? Would your little Being like to say something to the little Being in the story? What does it want to say? If you could go into the story and talk to the little Being, what would you say/what would you do?

Continuing the story...

The little Being's friend looked cross. 'Why are you being violent? Why are you hitting and thumping and calling names?' it asked.

'I'm not the one who started it,' the little Being answered.

'It doesn't matter who started it,' the friend replied. 'You are hurting another little Being. That is not good.'

'You are supposed to be my friend,' the little Being said back. 'You should be helping me if you are really my friend.'

'I am your friend, but I am sad. I am sad to see my friend using its feet to kick and hurt, using its hands to punch and cause pain, and using its voice to call names and say nasty things. Your feet are good, your hands and face and voice are good. You can use them to do good things and make everyone happy. But you are using them to hurt another Being. I am your friend, but I am a very sad friend.'

The little Being listened to its friend. 'You are right, friend,' it said. 'You are a good friend. You have shown me that what I am doing is wrong.' The little Being reached out. This time it did not punch. This time it used its hands to shake hands; it used its voice to say sorry; it used its face to smile, and it used its two arms to put around its friend and the little Being that was getting hurt. Now they are all friends.

CHATTING

...about friends

Have you got a friend? Have you got a good friend? If you were fighting with someone, would you expect your friend to help you? If you saw your friend fighting, what would you do? The little Being told its friends that it hadn't started the fight, but the friend said... Can you remember what the friend said? Do you agree with the friend? Why? The little Being's friend was sad. Why was it sad? But even though it was not happy and not pleased with the little Being, it was still its friend. How could that be? Do you think you could show friendship to your friends if they did something that made you unhappy? Would it be difficult to stay as their friend? Have you ever tried to make up to your friend when you did something which hurt her or him? What did you do? Is your little Being your friend? Is it a good friend? Why? Pick it up and tell it why it is a good friend.

POEM

One Day

One day I felt so angry
I flew into a temper,
I kicked and yelled and thumped and lashed
For as long as I can remember.

Then, I felt so sad that
I'd said some hurtful things.
I had no room left inside
To feel the love God brings.

PRAYERTIME

Sign of the Cross.

Teacher
As we light our candle we remember that God is always with us. God loves us always.
When we are destructive we are not being the way God wants us to be.
We tell God that we are sorry for all those times.

All
Act of Sorrow
O my God, I thank you for loving me.
I am sorry for all my sins, for not loving others and not loving you.
Help me to live like Jesus and not sin again.
Amen.

Teacher
We ask God to help us to love others always.
When we say sorry, God always forgives us for the wrong things we do. We thank God.

All
Prayer after Forgiveness
O my God, thank you for forgiving me.
Help me to love others.
Help me to live as Jesus asked me to. Amen.

Sign of the Cross.

Day Four

Continue song: *I'm Sorry*

Continue poem: *One Day*

Recall story: *Being Violent*

ACTIVITY

God Can Be Glad

Ask the children to form pairs. Number them 1 and 2. Say the following chant with the appropriate actions.

All: Sad *(frown)* can be glad *(smile)* when you say

1s: I'm sorry.

All: Sad *(frown)* can be glad *(smile)* when you say

2s: I forgive.

All: Sad *(frown)* can be glad *(smile)* when you say

1s: I still like you.

All: Sad *(frown)* can be glad *(smile)* when you say

2s: We're still friends. *(all shake hands)*
　　　Carole MacClennan

PRAYERTIME

Note: *During the prayertime, invite the children to place their little Being in front of them.*

Sign of the Cross.

Teacher
We light our candle and we remember that God loves us no matter what.
Today let's think about our bodies.

It is fun to have a body. We can do all sorts of things with our bodies.
We often do good things with our bodies.
Think of some of the good things you can do with your body.
Let's now think of some of the good things you do with your hands.

Close your eyes and think. *(Pause)*

We pray together.

All *(Teacher, with children repeating)*
Thank you, God, for kind hands.
Thank you, God, for gentle hands.
Thank you, God, for helping hands.
Thank you, God, for caring hands.

Teacher
Sometimes we do things with our hands which are not good.
Now think of some of the things you do with your hands which are not good.

Close your eyes and think. *(Pause)*

Now let's tell God that we are sorry.

All *(repeating after teacher)*
Prayer for Forgiveness
O my God, help me to remember the times when I didn't live as Jesus asked me to live.
Help me to be sorry and to try again. Amen.

Teacher
Sometimes we do good things with our feet.
Think of some of the good things you do with your feet.

Close your eyes and think. *(Pause)*

We pray together.

All
Thank you, God, for feet to walk and run and jump and play.

Teacher
Sometimes we do things with our feet which are not good.
We use our feet to hurt people or to damage things.
Now think of some of the things you do with your feet which are not good.

Close your eyes and think. *(Pause)*

Let's tell God that we are sorry.
We pray together.

All *(repeating after teacher)*
Prayer for Forgiveness
O my God, help me to remember the times
when I didn't live as Jesus asked me to live.
Help me to be sorry and to try again. Amen.

Teacher
Sometimes we do good things with our voices.
Let's think of some of the good things we do.

Close your eyes and think. *(Pause)*

We pray together:

All *(teacher, with children repeating)*
Thank you, God, for kind words.
Thank you, God, for gentle words.
Thank you, God, for the songs we sing.

Teacher
Sometimes we do things with our voices
which are not good.
Now think of some of the things you did with
your voice which were not good. *(Pause)*
Let's tell God we are sorry.

Let us have a moment's silence.

All
Act of Sorrow
O my God, I thank you for loving me.
I am sorry for all my sins, for not loving
others and not loving you.
Help me to live like Jesus and not sin again.
Amen.

Sign of the Cross.

ART

Let's Draw for Home

Ask the children to draw a picture of a time
when they were fighting and hurt somebody.
Encourage them to tell their little Being about
the picture.
Encourage them to take their pictures home
and to tell the story to their parents/guardians.

Day Five

WORKSHEET

If you wish to use the worksheet or workbook
page which accompanies this lesson, this is an
appropriate time to do so.

CHATTING

...about the picture on page 30

Do these people remind you of any little
Beings? Which ones? Why? If you could go
into the picture, what would you say to each
of them? What might they say to you? Has
anything like this ever happened to you? Look
at the faces. What is going on behind those
faces? Perhaps you could show these pictures
to your little Being. What does it think about
what's going on here?

PRAYERTIME

Sign of the Cross.

Song: *I'm Sorry*

Teacher
We light our candle and we remember that
God loves us no matter what.
Sometimes we fight and shout, but God still
loves us.
Sometimes we say things that are not good,
but God still loves us.

Sometimes we destroy things or lose our temper, but God still loves us.

Let us tell God that we are sorry for all the times when we are not what God wants us to be.

All
Act of Sorrow
O my God, I thank you for loving me.
I am sorry for all my sins, for not loving others and not loving you.
Help me to live like Jesus and not sin again. Amen.

Teacher
We know that God loves each one of us.

We know that we are good.
We know that God wants us to show our goodness to others.
We know that God forgives us when we say sorry.

Let us thank God.

All
Prayer after Forgiveness
O my God, thank you for forgiving me.
Help me to love others.
Help me to live as Jesus asked me to. Amen.

Sign of the Cross.

I'm Sorry

Geraldine Doggett

Refrain:

G — D — G
I'm sor-ry, I'm sor-ry, I'm real-ly ve-ry sor-ry. I

D — G — D — G
hurt your feel-ings, caused you pain, I'd like to be your friend a-gain. I'm

— D — G
sor-ry, I'm sor-ry, I'm ve-ry, ve-ry sor-ry.

G D/F♯ Em Em/D C9 G/B Am7 D
1. Some-times when we play our games I get an-gry, I call you names.

Em B7/D♯ G/D Em/C♯ C9 G/B Am7 D
I know I should not act this way, That is why I'd like to say—

2. Sometimes I tell tales on you,
   I make up stories that are not true.
   I know I should not act this way,
   That is why I'd like to say . . .

3. Sometimes I won't let you play,
   I turn my back till you go away.
   I know I should not act this way,
   That is why I'd like to say . . .

Lesson 7: Time To Change

Be kind to one another, tenderhearted,
forgiving one another,
as God in Christ has forgiven you.
(Ephesians 4:32)

In this lesson we develop the theme of the goodness of childhood and we reaffirm the possibility for goodness that is at the heart of human life. We continue to enable the children to identify within their own experience types of behaviour which do not reflect their potential goodness. We help them to explore particular times when they did not live up to the goodness that Jesus recognised in children. We explore with them the need to say sorry and the process whereby reconciliation takes place.

FOR THE TEACHER:

A thought before beginning

Psalm 139:13-18

For it was you who formed my inward parts;
you knit me together in my mother's womb.
I praise you, for I am fearfully and wonderfully made.
Wonderful are your works; that I know very well.
My frame was not hidden from you,
when I was being made in secret,
intricately woven in the depths of the earth.
Your eyes beheld my unformed substance.
In your book were written all the days that were formed for me,
when none of them as yet existed.
How weighty to me are your thoughts, O God!
How vast is the sum of them!
I try to count them – they are more than the sand;
I come to the end – I am still with you.

What am I trying to do?

To help the children to identify types of behaviour which do not show the goodness that is potentially theirs; to reflect on the consequences of this behaviour; to recognise that it is wrong and to say sorry.

Why?

So that they will become more aware of and be able to articulate stories of times when they did not show the goodness that they are capable of.

---

*We continue to teach the children the **Act of Sorrow**, the **Prayer for Forgiveness** and the **Prayer after Forgiveness**. Begin to teach the children the **Confiteor**.*

Confiteor
I confess to almighty God,
And to you, my brothers and
sisters,
That I have sinned through my
own fault,
In my thoughts and in my
words,
In what I have done,
And in what I have failed to do;
And I ask blessed Mary, ever
virgin,
All the angels and saints
And you, my brothers and
sisters,
To pray for me to the Lord our
God.

These prayers are particularly relevant to those preparing for First Penance.

Overview of the Week

			Continue song	
			Recall story	
			Worksheet	Story: *Being Jealous*
Song: *I'm Sorry God*	Continue song,		Chatting about the	Chatting about the
Story: *The Lost*	story	Continue song	picture	story
Temper	Poem: *Sulk*	Story: *Being Selfish*	Poem: *Huff*	Did You Know?
Chatting about the	Prayertime	Chatting about the	Prayertime	Prayertime
story	Art: *Let's Draw for*	story	Art: *Let's Draw for*	Art: *Let's Draw for*
Prayertime	*Home*	Prayertime	*Home*	*Home*

Day One

SONG

I'm Sorry God

STORY

The Lost Temper

Today a little Being sits in an armchair in its home. It has a frown on its face. Its arms are folded tightly. Its eyes do not look at anyone. They stare crossly at the floor. This little Being is in a temper.

As it sits there it thinks to itself and as it thinks it feels. Deep down in its insides it feels a shout beginning to happen. The shout rises up and up until the little Being opens its mouth. It shouts, 'NO!' It shouts, 'I won't. I don't like you.' It shouts, 'Go away.'

And as it shouts it feels angrier, and as it feels angrier, it screams, 'I could just shake this whole world!', and as it shouts, it jumps up and stamps its feet hard on the floor, STAMP, STAMP, STAMP! It bangs its fists on the chair, BATTER, BATTER, BATTER!

As it thumps and batters, it grinds its teeth. It feels very cross now. It feels as if there is a balloon deep down inside it, a balloon that is blowing up bigger and bigger and bigger until... just as the little Being feels that the balloon is going to burst, it flings the room door open wide and SLAMS it shut with a mighty BANG! This little Being has lost its temper.

The little Being's mam hears the bang. She comes into the room. She says, 'What's the matter little Being, why have you lost your temper?'

The little Being is in a huff. It says nothing.

CHATTING

...about the story

Can you think of any reasons why this little Being has lost its temper? Ask your little Being – it might know why. What does it say? Has anything like this ever happened to someone you know? Has anything like this ever happened to you? Did you feel any of the feelings the little Being felt? Did you feel like shouting? What did you shout? Did you feel like stamping your feet or battering with your fists or slamming the door? Were there other people there when this was happening to you? How do you think they would have felt when you were losing your temper? Do you think it is good to lose your temper? Why not? If the little Being in the story was in our classroom now, what would you say to it? What would your little Being say to it? Ask it. What do you think the little Being's mam will say? What do you think she will do?

Continuing the story...

Mam looked at her little Being. She loved it even if it was in a temper. Very gently, she put her arms around it. 'Don't be angry,' she said in a soft voice. 'It is not good to be in a temper. When you're whole little being is full up with temper, there is no room left inside to feel love. I am sad when you have no room left inside to feel my love for you and your love for me.'

The little Being listens to its mam. It knows she is right. It says, 'You are right, Mam. I am sorry for losing my temper. I love you.'

CHATTING

...about the the story

Do you think Mam did the right thing by putting her arms around the little Being and talking gently? Why? Can you remember what Mam told her little Being? Do you think what Mam says is true? Why? Why do you think the little Being said sorry? Have you ever said sorry to someone? Ask your little Being if it has ever said sorry. What does it say? Do you think it is good to say sorry? Has anyone ever said sorry to you? What does it feel like when someone says sorry to you?

As well as saying sorry, do you think the little Being might do something which would make up for what it has done? Can you suggest some way it could make amends? Have you ever tried to make up for losing your temper?

Do you think God loves you like the mam loved her little Being? Do you think God loves you like your mam/dad/guardian loves you?

In the Sacrament of Penance, God's love is like Mam's/Dad's/Guardian's arms wrapped gently around us. God speaks gently to us. We know that God loves us even when we lose our temper. God loves us so much that he wants us to become as good as we can possibly be. When we lose our temper, and tell God we are sorry, God always forgives us.

PRAYERTIME

Sign of the Cross.

Teacher
God loves us always, even when we are not being the way God wants us to be.
We tell God that we are sorry for all those times.

All (repeating after teacher)
Act of Sorrow
O my God, I thank you for loving me.
I am sorry for all my sins, for not loving others and not loving you.
Help me to live like Jesus and not sin again. Amen.

Teacher
We ask God to help us to love others always.
When we say sorry, God always forgives us for the wrong things we do. We thank God.

All (repeating after teacher)
Prayer after Forgiveness
O my God, thank you for forgiving me.
Help me to love others.
Help me to live as Jesus asked me to. Amen.

Sign of the Cross.

Continue song: *I'm Sorry God*

Recall story: *The Lost Temper*

POEM

Sulk

I scuff
   my feet along
And puff
   my lower lip
I sip my milk
   in slurps
And huff
And frown
And stamp around
And tip my chair
   back from the table
Nearly fall down
   but I don't care
I scuff
And puff
And frown
And huff
And stamp
And pout
Till I forget
What it's about.
       Felice Holman

PRAYERTIME

Note: *During the prayertime, invite the children to place their little Beings in front of them.*

Sign of the Cross.

Teacher
As we light our candle we remember that God is always with us, God who loves us and cares for us always.

Sometimes we all lose our tempers. When we do, we can hurt other people. We don't think carefully about what we do and say when we lose our temper.

Can you remember a time when you lost your temper?

Close your eyes and think.

(Pause)

What happened that caused you to lose your temper?

What did you do when you lost your temper?

Do you think that you hurt anyone else?

Now, let's tell God that we are sorry.

Let us have a moment's silence.

(Pause)

All
Prayer for Forgiveness
O my God, help me to remember the times when I didn't live as Jesus asked me to.
Help me to be sorry and to try again.

Sign of the Cross.

ART

Let's Draw for Home

Ask the children to draw a picture of a time when they lost their temper. Encourage them to tell their little Being about the picture. Encourage them to take the picture home and to tell the story of what happened to their parents/guardians.

Continue song: *I'm Sorry God*

STORY

Being Selfish

One day a little Being sat down to think. 'What shall I think about today?' it said to itself. 'I know – I will think about me!' And that is what it did. And as it thought about itself, it talked to itself, and this is what it said.

It said, 'Me, me, me. What a good word "me" is. It is better than any other word I know because it means "ME". It is better than the word "you" or "him" or "her" or "them". The word "ME" is the most important word I can think of because it is all about ME! Everything is all about ME!' And as it sat there thinking only about itself, the little Being kept saying 'me, me, me: always ME!'

Just then the little Being's family came and sat down too. 'What are you doing, little Being?' they asked.

'I am thinking,' the little Being replied. 'I am thinking about me, me, me. I like thinking about me.'

'Won't you think about us too? We are your family and we love you.'

'Oh No,' replied the little Being. 'I just want to think about myself.'

The little Being's family and friends wondered what they could do. 'We may as well just go away,' they said, 'because there is no room for us in little Being's thoughts. This little Being's thoughts are all about itself.'

'You can sit here and think all about me too,' suggested the little Being.

The little Being's family and friends looked at each other.

CHATTING

...about the story

What do you think the little Being's friends and family could do? Ask your little Being what it thinks they could do. What does it say? What would you do if you were in the story? What kind of things do you think the little Being is thinking about itself? What do you think it would be like to have this little Being for a friend? What do you think would happen if you wanted to play a game with this little Being? What do you think would happen if you wanted to borrow something from it? What do you think it would do if it had sweets? What do you think would happen if its mam or dad or guardian wanted the little Being to do something for them? Do you think this little Being likes to get everything its own way? What do you think it would do if it didn't get its own way – in a game perhaps, or in a supermarket where it wanted sweets, or at a friend's house when it wanted a certain toy, etc? Do you think it would be easy to like this little Being? Why? Does this little Being remind you of anyone? Does it remind you of yourself? Can you think of words to describe the kind of being this little one is? *(In the course of exploring words to describe the little Being, the teacher may introduce the word 'selfish'.)* What kind of person is a selfish person? What do you think would be the opposite of a selfish person? Sometimes we are very UNselfish. Can you think of ways or times when you were unselfish? Sometimes we can be selfish and think only about ourselves and what we want. Can you remember a time when you were like that? Let's go back to the little Being and see what happens to it.

Continuing the story...

The little Being's family and friends looked at each other. 'We are sad, little Being,' they said. 'We would like to stay here with you because we love you, but you are being selfish. You think only about yourself. You have no room in your thoughts for us. As long as you are selfish, there is no room for us. We cannot stay with you because you have squeezed us out.'

Then the little Being's family and friends put their arms around it. Now the little Being could feel their love. Now it knew it had been selfish. The little Being said, 'All of you are right. I have been selfish. I have been thinking only about myself. I have not wanted to think about you, but you have thought about me. I was wrong. I am sorry.' The little Being hugged its family and friends. Now everyone is happy.

CHATTING

...about the story

What do you think about what the little Being's family and friends said? Do you agree with them? Does your little Being agree with them? Ask it. What helped the little Being to realise that it had been selfish? Do you think it is good to think about yourself all the time? Why not? Do you think it is good to say sorry like the little Being did? Why? Do you think you could help the little Being to think of some way it could make up for having been selfish? Perhaps you can tell us about how you have made up at times when you were selfish.

God loves us like our family and friends do. God wants to be part of our lives and part of our thoughts. But when I think only about myself – about what I want to do; what I want to play; what I want to have; when I always want to have things MY way – then there is no room for God or anyone else in my life.

God loves us always. God loves us more than our family and friends. In the Sacrament of Penance we celebrate God's love and tell God that we are sorry.

PRAYERTIME

Sign of the Cross.

Teacher
As we light our candle we remember that God is always with us. God loves us always, even when we are not being the way God wants us to be.
We tell God that we are sorry for all those times.

All
Act of Sorrow
O my God, I thank you for loving me.
I am sorry for all my sins, for not loving others and not loving you.
Help me to live like Jesus and not sin again.
Amen.

Teacher
We ask God to help us to love others always.
When we say sorry, God always forgives us for the wrong things we do. We thank God.

All
Prayer after Forgiveness
O my God, thank you for forgiving me.
Help me to love others.
Help me to live as Jesus asked me to. Amen.

Sign of the Cross.

Day Four

Continue song: *I'm Sorry God*

Recall story: *The Lost Temper*

WORKSHEET

If you wish to use the worksheet or workbook page which accompanies this lesson, this is an appropriate time to do so.

CHATTING

...about the picture on page 31

Look at the faces in these pictures. How are they different from the last faces? What is happening in these pictures? What do you think these people might be saying to each other? Perhaps your little Being knows what it feels like to say sorry. Perhaps you know too. Do you?

POEM

Huff

I am in a tremendous huff –
Really, really bad,
It isn't any ordinary huff –
It's one of the best I've had.

I plan to keep it up for a month
Or maybe for a year
And you needn't think you can make me smile
Or talk to you. No fear.

I can do without you and her and them –
Too late to make amends.
I'll think deep thoughts on my own for a while,
Then find some better friends.

And they'll be wise and kind and good
And bright enough to see
That they should behave with proper respect
Towards somebody like me.

Perhaps I'll give them another chance,
Now I'm feeling stronger,
But they'd better watch out – my next big huff
Could last much, much, much longer.
Wendy Cope

PRAYERTIME

Note: During the prayertime, invite the children to place their little Beings in front of them.

Sign of the Cross.

Teacher
We light our candle and we remember that God is always with us, God who loves us and cares for us always.
Sometimes we are very unselfish. When we are unselfish we think about other people. We do things to help other people. We wonder about what other people need.
Think about times when you were unselfish.

Close your eyes. *(Pause)*
Think about what you did.
Think of the people who were happy because of what you did.
That was a good thing to do.

Now we pray together:

All *(Children repeating after the teacher)*
Thank you, God, for times when we were unselfish.
When we did something to help someone else.
When we shared something with someone else.

Teacher
Now we will think of times when we were selfish.
Can you think of times when you only thought about yourself and about what you wanted for yourself?

Close your eyes. *(Pause)*
Let's tell God that we are sorry.
Let us have a moment's silence.

All
Prayer for Forgiveness
O my God, help me to remember the times when I didn't live as Jesus asked me to live.
Help me to be sorry and to try again. Amen.

Sign of the Cross.

ART

Let's Draw for Home

Ask the children to draw pictures of times when they were selfish. Encourage them to tell their little Being about the picture. Encourage them to talk to their parents/guardians about their pictures.

Day Five

STORY

Being Jealous

One day a little Being went out walking. As it walked it thought, and as it thought it talked, and this is what it said.

'There are other Beings who are better than I am. I am jealous of them. They are better than I am because they can do things that I cannot do and they have things that I do not have.' As it thought about all the things the other Beings could do that it could not do and all the things they had that it did not have, this little Being became angry.

Just then its friend came along the road. 'Good day little Being,' said the friend.

'I wish I were you. I do not like being me. You can do things that I cannot do. You have things that I like and I want to have. I do not like you for being able to do things that I cannot do,' said the little Being in a cross voice. And without another word it walked off and left its friend standing there.

CHATTING

...about the story

Can you think why the little Being thought other Beings were better than it? Have you ever thought others were better than you? Why? What could they do that you would have liked to be able to do? What does your little Being think about the other Beings in the class? Does it think some of them are better than it is? What does it say? How do you feel when someone does things better than you can – does it make you feel jealous? How do you feel when someone has things that you don't have, like a toy or some sweets? Is feeling jealous a good feeling? What do you think it was that the little Being's friend could do better than it? How do you think the friend feels about what the little Being said? How would you feel if you were the friend? If you could go into the story, what would you say to the little Being? What would you say to the friend? Why? Let's see what happens next.

Continuing the story...

As it walked on, the little Being thought, and as it thought it talked, and this is what it said.

'There are lots of other Beings who are better than I am. Even if they don't DO some things better, they are still better than me just as they are! I feel jealous of them.'

Just then the little Being's big sister came along.

'Good day little Being,' said the big sister.

'I wish I was you. I do not like being me. You are older than I am. I do not like you for being older than me,' said the little Being in a cross voice. And without another word it walked off and left its sister standing there.

CHATTING

...about the story

Why is the little Being jealous of its big sister? Do you have a big sister or brother? Tell us about her/him/them. Would you like to be her/him? Why? Do you ever think that they might like to be you? Why/Why not? Can you think of other things that people are that you would like to be, e.g. clever; tall; curly-haired; a good singer, etc.? Does that mean you shouldn't like them for being that way? Why? Have you ever felt that you don't like someone because they are what you would like to be? How do you think the big sister in the story feels? If you could talk to her right now, what would you say to her? If you could talk to the little Being right now, what would you say to it? What would your little Being say to it? Ask it. Let's see what happens now.

Continuing the story...

The little Being walked on. Its friend and its sister walked after it. They were very concerned. Soon they caught up with it. 'We like you just the way you are, little Being,' said the friend. 'But you feel jealous. It is not good to be jealous,' said the big sister. 'Your jealousy is keeping you from loving yourself just as you are and from loving us as we are, no matter what we have or what we can do,' said its neighbour.

The little Being thought about what they said. It answered, 'I am happy that you love me just as I am. Now I must not be jealous any more.' Then it said to its friend, 'I am happy that you can do things I cannot do and that you have things that I don't have.' It said to its big sister, 'I am happy for you to be older than I am.'

The friend and the sister hugged the little Being. It felt their love all around it. It whispered to them, 'I am glad that you love me. I am sorry for being jealous.'

CHATTING

...about the story

If you were in the story now and could talk to the little Being, what would you say to it? Do you think the little Being has learned anything? Do you think you can learn something from the little Being and its friends? Is there anything in the story that you think it would be good to remember if you feel jealous some time? Can you think of any way in which you could make up for having been jealous? Talk to your little Being. Would you like to make up for being jealous? How do you think the little Being would feel after making amends? How have you felt when you've done something to make up for thinking or acting jealously?

DID YOU KNOW?

Remember that God loves you just the way you are. God loves you no matter what you do. God loves you no matter what you have or have not got. God loves you and he wants you to love yourself too. God loves you so much that he wants you to be the best boy or girl you can possibly be. You can tell God you are sorry for being jealous.

PRAYERTIME

Note: During the prayertime, ask the children to place their little Being in front of them.

Sign of the Cross.

Sing: *I'm Sorry God*

Teacher
As we light our candle we remember that God is with us. God loves us always.

Can you think of times when you were happy because someone else got something special, won a prize or had a birthday?
Close your eyes and think. *(Pause)*

We pray together.

All
Thank you, God, for times when we are happy with others.

Teacher
Sometimes we get jealous of others.
Think of the things that make you feel jealous.
Now close your eyes and try to remember one time when you felt jealous of someone else.

Why did you feel jealous?
What did you do?
Do you think you might have done something which hurt someone else's feelings?
You can now tell God that you are sorry.

Let us have a moment's silence.

All
Prayer for Forgiveness
O my God, thank you for forgiving me.
Help me to love others.
Help me to live as Jesus asked me to. Amen.

Sign of the Cross.

ART

Let's Draw for Home

Ask the children to draw pictures of times when they felt jealous and of things that they did. Encourage them to tell their little Being about the picture. Encourage them to take the pictures home and to tell the story to their parents/guardians.

I'm Sorry God

Mary Amond O'Brien

Refrain:

God wraps us in his love each day,— speaks
gent - ly to us on our way.—
Ev - en when we dis - ob - ey— God's
love is al - ways there, God
loves us ev - 'ry day.

1. Some - times God I do not care,— I'm
sel - fish and I do not share.— I'm

sor - ry God,

Now I've come to know.

2. Sometimes God I tell a lie
   Or hurt my friends and make them cry
   I'm sorry God,
   Now I've come to know...

3. When I'm angry, God, I shout
   I scream, I stamp and I give out,
   I'm sorry God,
   Now I've come to know...

Lesson 8: I Was Lost, I Am Found

If we confess our sins,
he who is faithful and just will forgive us our
sins and cleanse us from all unrighteousness.
(1 John 1:9)

People were bringing even infants to
him that he might touch them;
and when the disciples saw it, they
sternly ordered them not to do it.
But Jesus called for them and said, 'Let
the little children come to me…'.
(Luke 18:15-16)

During the past weeks we have led the
children on a particular journey, through
which we have helped them to recognise their
essential goodness, to rejoice in it, to be aware
of their failures and to say sorry for the times
when their behaviour has been destructive or
has caused pain or hurt.

We have, through the stories, tried to help
them to recognise the sense of failure, the
sense of being lost within themselves, and to
be aware of the steps necessary for
reconciliation. We have also helped the
children to be aware of the never-ending love
of God for each of them, in spite of any failure
on their part.

These lessons come to a close with a
celebration of God's love. For those children
who will be celebrating their First
Communion/First Penance this year, this
celebration will be their first celebration of the
Sacrament of Penance. Parents/guardians and
godparents are invited to participate in the
service, which could take place in the local
church. It was the parents/guardians in the
presence of the Christian community who
first brought their child to be baptised. The
initiation of the child into the membership of
the Church began then. In the Sacrament of
Penance the parents/guardians accompany
their child on another step in that faith
journey. To highlight the importance of this
journey, the celebrant will welcome the
parents/guardians, godparents and children at
the church door. From here they will 'journey'
to the place where the Liturgy of the Word will
take place. The children will then be asked to
'journey' into the wilderness – a place of quiet
and reflection. Finally, the parents/guardians
will be asked to hand a lighted candle to their
child, symbolising the child's movement from
the wilderness into the light.

The children who are not celebrating their
First Penance this year will participate in a
Blessing Ritual, which will celebrate the life
and goodness of children. This celebration
could take place in the classroom.

FOR THE TEACHER:

A thought before beginning

Lord, we heard that you were
  hungry
And we did not share our food.
Forgive us, Lord, forgive.

Lord, we heard that you were
  thirsty
And we kept our drink to ourselves.
Forgive us, Lord, forgive.

Lord, we saw you as a stranger
And we closed our door and our heart.
Forgive us, Lord, forgive.

Lord, we saw you go naked
And we fussed about our clothes.
Forgive us, Lord, forgive.

Lord, we discovered that you were sick
And we avoided contact with you.
Forgive us, Lord, forgive.

Lord, we heard that you were in prison
And we pretended we did not know you.
Forgive us, Lord, forgive.

Lord, you came to us again and again
And we were closed up in ourselves.
Forgive us, Lord, forgive.
David Adam

What am I trying to do?

To develop the children's understanding of the never-ending love of God for each one of them in spite of any wrongdoing on their part, and to celebrate the life and goodness of children.

Why?

So that they will be able to appreciate and celebrate God's love and forgiveness.

Overview of the Week

Song: *The King of Love*	Continue song			Sacrament of Penance
Worksheet	Chatting about the picture	Preparation for Celebration of	Preparation for Celebration of	Rite 1 and Rite 2
Recall Story: *We are the Greatest*	Recall story: *The Good Shepherd*	God's Blessing/ Sacrament of	God's Blessing/ Sacrament of	Blessing Ritual
Prayertime	Prayertime	Penance	Penance	Now We Know

Day One

SONG

The King of Love

WORKSHEET

If you wish to use the worksheet or workbook page which accompanies this lesson, this is an appropriate time to do so.

For those preparing for First Penance, revise the Act of Sorrow, the Prayer for Forgiveness and the Prayer after Forgiveness.

Recall story: *We are the Greatest.*

Note: *In recalling 'We are the Greatest' the teacher could read the story and, following the indications in the text, may involve the children in making a*

tableau of the story. There are four groups of characters – sellers, buyers, children and grown-ups – as well as the character of Jesus. Appoint different groups of children to take up the roles of the sellers, the buyers, the children and the grown-ups. One child can take the role of Jesus. The teacher as narrator can tell the story, indicating as necessary where and when the children should move to make the tableau.

STORY

We are the Greatest
(Adapted from Matthew 18:1-5)

Today is Market Day. The children love Market Day. *A group of children leave their seats and form a circle in a corner of the room.* They go to the town square. All the grown-ups are there. There are men selling cheeses. There are women buying cloth. There are bakers selling bread. *A group of sellers leave their seats and form a circle in the centre of the room.* There are people buying spices and fruit. There are cows mooing and donkeys braying and goats baaing. The Market Place is busy. The Market Place is noisy. But most of all, the Market Place is fun! The grown-ups are so hard at work that they have no time for the children. *A group of 'grown-ups' leave their seats and form a circle around the sellers.* They do not notice the children. They do not see how the children play. They do not hear how the children sing. Right now the grown-ups have other things to think about.

Today a man comes to the Market Place. At first no one notices the man. He sits in the middle of the square where everyone will be able to see him. He speaks in a loud voice so that everyone will be able to hear him. *Jesus slips quietly out of the seat and makes his/her way to the centre of the classroom. He/she stands on a chair so he/she can be seen.* He tells those who stop and listen about a kingdom. He calls it the Kingdom of God. He says that in God's kingdom everyone is happy. In God's kingdom everyone loves their friends as well as those who are not their friends.

Some of the sellers gather around Jesus. 'What kind of place is this kingdom,' say some of the grown-ups, 'where people love those who are not their friends?'

Some of the buyers join the sellers gathered around Jesus. 'How can we get to live in such a place?' say some others.

'God's kingdom is not any particular place,' says the man. 'God's kingdom can be anywhere. Wherever people love one another, wherever people are kind and gentle, wherever people share with one another, that is where God's kingdom is. God's kingdom can be right here, right now.'

'I have a question for you,' says one man. 'In our community I am an important person. I would like to know who is the most important person in this Kingdom of God that you talk about.'

Now the Market Place grows quiet. The noise stops. The buying and selling stops. The children notice that everything has gone quiet too. The children go on playing. From where they are they can see the crowd of people gathered around the man.

'What's happening?' some of the children ask each other.

Just then the man comes over to the children.

Jesus approaches the children in the corner. He says, 'Who will help me? I need one of you to help me teach the grown-ups something very important.'

'Me, me, me!', say the children. The man smiles. He takes the smallest child by the hand. *One child goes with Jesus.* He takes the child into the middle of the crowd. He wants everyone to notice the child.

'You ask me who is the most important person in God's kingdom,' says the man to the crowd. 'I will tell you now,' he says. 'Do you see this little child? I tell you, the child is the greatest in God's kingdom.'

A murmur of shock and surprise runs through the crowd of grown-ups. They can hardly believe their eyes. They can hardly believe their ears. The child! The child is the greatest in God's kingdom! They have never heard the like of this before! They wondered what it was about the child – was the child kind, or loving, or gentle, or was the child just full of life and joy as children are?

When the man is finished the child runs back to the other children. *Child returns to children's circle and buyers/sellers return to their circles. Jesus returns to his/her seat.*

'What did the man want?'; 'What did the man say?'; 'What did the man teach the people?', they ask the child.

'He taught them that children are the greatest,' the child answers. The children clap and cheer.

'Who is this man?' the children ask.

'His name is Jesus,' the child answers.

'Hurrah for Jesus,' the children shout. 'Hurrah, hurrah, hurrah!' *Children's circle shout. The whole class shout.*

PRAYERTIME

Sign of the Cross.

Teacher
God is always with us. God loves us like a loving father. God cares for us like a loving mother. God is always listening to us. We light our candle to help us to remember these things.

Close your eyes.
Place your hands gently on your lap and your feet on the floor.
Listen to your heart beat.
Feel your breath as it moves gently in and out of your lungs, bringing oxygen and life to every part of your body.

Go inside, into your inside world where it is dark and quiet and safe and peaceful. Remember the story about Jesus and the children. Imagine yourself there in the crowd. Jesus takes you by the hand and brings you into the centre of the crowd. He speaks to the crowd. Then he bends down and tells you that you are the greatest. What is it about you that Jesus thinks is great? Softly, so as no one else can hear, you can say something to Jesus. What would you like to say to Jesus? With your little inside voice you can say anything you wish to Jesus.

Open your eyes.

We pray together:

All
Praise to the Father.
Praise to the Son.
Praise to the Spirit.
The Three in One.

Sign of the Cross.

Continue song: *The King of Love*

CHATTING

...about the picture on page 32

Can you think of a name for each child? Look at their faces. Do you think they enjoy being with Jesus? Imagine you are in the picture too. What would you say to Jesus? What would Jesus say to you?

Recall story: *The Good Shepherd*

Note: You might do this by retelling the story as it appears in Lesson 5. Alternatively, you might like to do the following version which suggests a way in which the children can be invited to 'enter into' the story. Before reading the story the teacher might ask the children to think of a name they would call a sheep. It may be that each child would call the sheep by his or her own name.

STORY

The Good Shepherd
(Adapted from Luke 15:3-7)

Once there was a shepherd. This shepherd was a good shepherd. He had one hundred sheep in his flock. He knew the name of every single one of his sheep. In the morning when he took his sheep out to graze on the hillsides, he would call each one by their name. He would call... What do you think the names of some of his sheep might be? Let's try to think of one name each... *Allow the children a moment to think of a name. After repeating 'In the morning*

242

when he took his sheep out to graze on the hillsides, he would call each sheep by its name', invite each child to call out their sheep's name.

The shepherd walked ahead of his sheep so that if there was any danger, they could hide safely behind him and come to no harm. The good shepherd walked ahead and his sheep followed behind. They followed him up hill and down hill and up hill and down hill. *The teacher may walk around the classroom weaving her or his way in and out between the desks as the children follow. She/he could halt the flock now and again and allow 'imaginary dangers' to pass by, e.g. a big rock rolling down the hillside across their path; a wolf in the bushes, etc.*

One day the good shepherd was out with his flock. He found a place for them to graze. He sat down to watch over them. As he sat he counted to make sure all his sheep were there. He counted his sheep by name. *The teacher counts the sheep, pointing to a different child on each number. As the teacher calls each number, a child calls out the name of their sheep and makes a 'baa' sound in response to being counted.*

Soon the shepherd realised that one of his sheep was missing. He looked all around. He called the lost sheep's name. *The teacher calls a name. Maybe a child who's absent from the class or maybe an extra name which the teacher thinks of, representing 'the missing sheep'. The rest of the flock stand around in the middle of the floor.* There was no answer. He called again. *Call name.* Still there was no answer.

The good shepherd was very worried. 'What shall I do? What shall I do?' he cried. 'My precious sheep _____ is missing.'

As the children stand there wondering what has happened, the teacher might engage them in a conversation similar to the following:

How do you think the good shepherd feels when he discovers that _____ is missing? Can you think why _____ is missing? Where do you think _____ might be? What do you think _____ might be doing right now? Do you think _____ is all alone? How do you think _____ might be feeling? How are you all feeling now that _____ is separated from you? How do you think the good shepherd is feeling right now? Why is he feeling that way? What

should the good shepherd do? Let's continue the story and see what he does.

The good shepherd told all his sheep to wait on the hillside. *The children sit down to wait.* He told them that he did not want to be separated from _____. He told the rest of his flock that he would go and find the one lost sheep and bring it back into the flock. Then he set off. He walked up hill and down hill and up hill and down, calling the lost sheep's name.

After searching long and hard the good shepherd found the lost sheep and brought it carefully back to the flock. He was so happy to have all his flock back together. He led them home. *The children return to their seats.* That night the shepherd went round to all his friends' houses. He told his friends the terrible thing that had happened when he lost one sheep. But now that he had found it again he was very happy. He was so happy he was going to have a party to celebrate. He asked all of his friends to come to the party and celebrate the finding of the lost sheep in the wilderness.

Would you like to celebrate with the good shepherd? What could we do to celebrate the lost sheep being found? What kind of feelings would the people at the party have? Do you think they might know what it feels like to have something go missing and then to find it again? Have you ever been separated from your mam or dad or from your friends? How did that make you feel? Tell us what happened. How did you feel when you were found again? How did your friends feel when you were found? Imagine God, the Good Shepherd, coming to find you, to carry you back to your friends and your family and all those who love you. (Pause)

In the Sacrament of Penance we celebrate because we know that God will always search and find us when we feel that we are lost.

P R A Y E R T I M E

Sign of the Cross.

Teacher
We know that God is always with us. We know that God loves us more than a loving mother. We know that God cares for us more than a loving father. We light our candle to help us always to remember these things. Like the shepherd in the story, God cares for us. God loves us. God searches for us when we are lost.

Close your eyes.
Place your hands gently on your lap.
Place your feet on the floor.
Listen to your heart beat.
Feel your breath as it moves gently in and out of your lungs, bringing oxygen and life to every part of your body.

Remember a time when you felt lost, because you were afraid, because you had a row with your friend or with your mam or dad, because you were lonely. Remember how you felt.

Now imagine God, the Good Shepherd, coming to find you... searching, searching. Then imagine that God, the Good Shepherd, sees you and gathers you up in his arms. He looks carefully at you to make sure that you are not hurt or injured in any way.
Imagine that God, the Good Shepherd, carries you safely in his arms, back to your family and friends and to all those who love you.
You don't feel lost and lonely and frightened any longer. You are happy to be with those who love you. We know that God will always search for us whenever we are lost or lonely.

Open your eyes.
We pray together.

All
Our Father...

Sign of the Cross.

Days Three and Four

Days Three and Four will be spent in preparation for the Sacrament of Penance and the Blessing Ritual.

Day Five

P R A Y E R T I M E

Rite for Reconciliation – Rite 2

Note: *Before the celebration of the Sacrament of Penance, prepare the place where it is to happen so that it will be 'child friendly'. Around the lectern place banners, artwork or posters which reflect the content of the lessons the children have done recently. In another part of the sanctuary place the 'Little Wilderness' which was used earlier in this term. 'Little Wilderness' symbolises 'turning away' and 'turning towards' God. Gathering around the Little Wilderness the children will engage in quiet reflection on the ways in which they have failed to show the goodness that is potentially theirs.*

The children may use a picture as they did in Lessons 6 and 7 to help them to remember times when they did not show their goodness.

INTRODUCTION: RECEPTION OF THE CHILDREN

The celebrant greets the parents/guardians and godparents at the church door. He speaks briefly to them of the joy of this occasion. He reminds them why they have come together.

Celebrant
When you brought your child to the church to be baptised, you accepted the responsibility of accompanying your child on her/his journey of faith. Today your child takes a further step on that journey.

What do you ask of God's Church for your children?

Parents/Guardians

The celebration of God's forgiveness in the Sacrament of Penance.

All

Song: *The King of Love*

Children, parents/guardians and godparents, together with the priest, process to the place where the Liturgy of the Word will take place.

WORDS OF WELCOME

Sign of the Cross.

Celebrant

Welcome to this celebration of the love and forgiveness of God. Even if we sometimes forget God, God never forgets us. Even when we don't love others, God still loves us. Today we want to praise and thank God for loving us. Let us sing our praise and thanks.

All

Sing: *The Lost Sheep*

Celebrant

Today we are going to remember the times when we weren't so good, the times when we were selfish, when we were destructive, when we were careless about people and things, when we did or said things which hurt others. The times when we lost our way or strayed. We are going to ask God to search for us, to find and forgive us, as the Good Shepherd found the sheep that was lost. We will listen again to the story of the Good Shepherd.

THE GOOD SHEPHERD

Note: The celebrant might like to use the version of The Good Shepherd in the Teacher's Book, in which the children are involved in the retelling.

Once there was a shepherd, a good shepherd. He had one hundred sheep. He loved every single one of the sheep in his flock. He knew the name of each one of his sheep. In the morning when he took his sheep out to graze for the day, he would call each one of them by name. The good shepherd always walked ahead of his sheep so that if there was any danger they could hide behind him. The sheep knew that their shepherd loved them and would never let them come to harm. They followed him day after day, up hill and down.

One day, the good shepherd was out with his flock. He found a place for them to graze. He made sure the sheep were all happy, then he sat down to watch over them. He wanted to make sure that they were all safe so he began to count to see if his sheep were all there. When he had finished he realised that one sheep was missing. He was very worried. He looked all around. He called the lost sheep's name. There was no answer. He called again. There was still no answer.

The good shepherd loved his lost sheep. He wanted to find it. He was unhappy for it to be separated from him and the rest of his flock. He decided he must go and look for it. He made the rest of the sheep gather in together so that they would keep each other company while he went off to look for the one lost sheep. He told them he would come back. Then off he went in search of his lost sheep.

He searched and searched. He called and called. He travelled up hill and down. He looked everywhere. Then, he heard something. He looked closer. There it was. His lost sheep, he had found it. He called its name. He ran to it and when he got there he picked the sheep up and carried it on his shoulders back to the flock. Now the good shepherd was very happy again.

That evening he led his flock back home. Then when they were all safe and sound for the night he went around to his friends' houses. He told them, 'A terrible thing happened today. I lost one of my sheep. I was so worried. I was so sad and lonely. Even though I have ninety-nine other sheep, I love each one of them. So I went to look for my sheep and found it. Now I am so happy again. I want to invite you all to come to my house tonight and celebrate with me. My lost sheep is found. Thank goodness.'

HOMILY

Celebrant

The good shepherd searched for the lost sheep. When he found the sheep that was lost he was so happy that he called his friends to celebrate. God is like the good shepherd. When we get lost God comes to find us. We will now tell God who loves us like a loving mother, who cares for us like a loving father, about the times when we were lost. To do this we will gather around the 'Little Wilderness'. We will ask God to find us and bring us back, to forgive us for the wrong things we have done.

When Jesus wanted to be quiet and still, the Spirit led him into the wilderness. Let us now journey to the 'Little Wilderness' and become quiet and still. Here we can think for a while.

Children proceed to gather around the Little Wilderness.

Celebrant
God, help me to remember the times when I didn't share the goodness that is deep within me with others. Help me to be sorry and to try again.

EXAMINATION OF CONSCIENCE

Celebrant
We thank God for making each one of us special. We thank God for the goodness that is in each one of us. Jesus recognised the goodness that is in children. But sometimes we don't live up to the goodness that Jesus saw in all children.

Close your eyes.
Place your hands gently on your lap.
Still your body.
Feel your breath as it moves in and out of your body.

Go into your inside world. In there it is dark and quiet and peaceful and safe. In there you are alone with your very special self. God loves you. God knows the goodness that is deep inside you. Sometimes we share this goodness with others. You share your goodness by being kind to those around you. You share your goodness by being gentle. You share your goodness by being a good listener and by trying to understand others.

With your inside voice, that no one else can hear, tell God about a time when you were gentle and kind and loving. Maybe you helped someone at school. Maybe you said nice things to someone at home. Maybe you washed the dishes after dinner. Maybe you tidied your bedroom without being asked. Tell God about some of these times. Thank God for the goodness within you.

Pause.

Sometimes we don't live up to the goodness

that Jesus saw in all children. We don't share our goodness when we lose our temper or when we are destructive or when we are selfish. Can you think of a time when you weren't being gentle and kind and loving? Maybe you lost your temper at home. Maybe you were rough and violent in the playground. Maybe you hurt someone by saying or doing something that wasn't nice. Maybe you felt jealous of someone.

Pause.

ACT OF REPENTANCE

All
Song: *I am Sorry*

The celebrant invites the children to remember, in silence, the times when they have not loved God. He asks them to remember the times when they have not shown their goodness and when they have not loved others. They may use their picture to help them to do this.

Pause.

All
O my God, I thank you for loving me.
I am sorry for all my sins,
For not loving others and not loving you.
Help me to live like Jesus and not sin again.

INDIVIDUAL CONFESSION AND ABSOLUTION

The children are then invited to approach the priest or one of the priests present.

Teacher/Reader
We realise that we have not always loved God and others. We have not always been good. We know that God never stops loving us. And so we come to Father _____ to celebrate the Sacrament of Penance. *(Silence)*

Each child acknowledges his or her sinfulness and expresses his or her sorrow before the priest. They might tell the priest the story of what happened. Again, they may use their picture to help them to do this.

Celebrant
Extending hands over the head of the child, says: God Our Father forgives you. *He then makes the Sign of the Cross over the child as he concludes the words of absolution:* I absolve you from your sins, in the name of the Father and of the Son and of the Holy Spirit. Amen.

The children return to their seats and give a hug to their parents as a sign of their sorrow and of the parents' forgiveness. All say together the Prayer after Forgiveness.

All
O my God, thank you for forgiving me.
Help me to love others.
Help me to live as Jesus asked me to.

The celebrant invites the parents/guardians/ godparents to come forward and receive a lighted candle on behalf of their child. They return to their seats where they hand the candle to their child and bless the child.

Celebrant

I invite you *(parent/guardian/godparent)* now to bless your child on the ears and the mouth as was done on the day they were baptised.

We pray:

The Lord Jesus made the deaf hear and the dumb speak. May he touch your eyes to receive his word, and your mouth to proclaim his faith, to the praise and glory of God.

All
Amen.

CONCLUSION

Celebrant
May God bless all those who care for and love these children.
We thank God for the gift of children.

All
Amen.

Celebrant
May God bless all those who accompany these children on their faith journey.
We thank God for the gift of children.

DISMISSAL

Celebrant
Go in peace to live like Jesus.

All
Amen.

Celebrant
Go in peace to love one another.

All
Amen.

Celebrant
May Almighty God bless you all, the Father, the Son and the Holy Spirit.

All
Amen.

Concluding Hymn
Sing: *We are the Greatest*

Sign of the Cross.

Rite for Reconciliation – Rite 1

If the children are celebrating the Sacrament of Penance according to Rite 1, they might still have a communal preparation in the form of a penance service which could take place in the church.

RITE FOR RECONCILIATION OF INDIVIDUAL PENITENTS

The following rite is used when there is no penance service. The location in the church may be the reconciliation room or the confessional. It is important that the children be familiarised with the place where the sacrament will be celebrated.

The structure is as follows:
- reception of the penitent;
- reading of the Word of God;
- confession of sin and expression of sorrow;
- Act of Sorrow;
- absolution;
- proclamation of praise of God and dismissal.

Celebrant
Before beginning, the celebrant might encourage the child to say:

Turn away, turn away from too-busy-ness.
Be quiet, be still and pray.
Turn towards God-in-the-wilderness.
Turn, turn, day by day.

Jesus welcomes you and blesses you. Let us listen to the words of Jesus. Jesus said: 'Rejoice with me, for I have found my sheep that was lost' (Luke 15:6).

The celebrant invites the child to acknowledge that it is his/her first confession, to acknowledge that he/she didn't always live up to the goodness that Jesus saw in children, and to say sorry.

Each child acknowledges her/his sorrow. Encourage the children to tell their own story in their own words and in whatever way they are capable of doing. The following are some examples of how the children might concretely express their wrongdoing and their sorrow.

- I wasn't being kind when I hit my friend and hurt her/him.
  God, I am sorry.
- I wasn't being fair when Mam/Dad/Teacher asked me to share the sweets with my sisters/brothers and I ate them all myself.
  God, I am sorry.

The celebrant encourages the child to live in the way Jesus asks and then proposes a suitable act of penance. The act of penance should correspond, as far as possible, to the seriousness and nature of the wrongdoings the child has mentioned. Thus the act of penance for a child might take the form of a prayer, an act of self-denial, or an act of kindness.

ACT OF SORROW

O my God, I thank you for loving me.
I am sorry for all my sins, for not loving others and not loving you.
Help me to live like Jesus and not sin again.
Amen.

ABSOLUTION

The celebrant extends his hands over the child's head (or he extends his right hand) and says the words of absolution.

Celebrant
Extending his hands over the head of the child says:
God forgives you.

He then makes the Sign of the Cross over the child as he concludes the words of absolution:
I absolve you from your sins, in the name of the Father and of the Son and of the Holy Spirit. Amen.

PROCLAMATION OF PRAISE OF GOD AND DISMISSAL

Celebrant
Give thanks to the Lord for he is good!

All
Amen.

Celebrant
Go in peace to live like Jesus.

All
Amen.

To symbolise the movement into the light of God's

love and forgiveness, you might like to give the children a lighted candle and ask them to place it on the altar. Alternatively, you might encourage the children, with their parents/guardians, to light a candle at one of the shrines in the church.

Blessing Ritual
(For classes who will not be celebrating their First Penance this year)

PREPARATION
Days Three and Four will be spent preparing for the ritual which will take place on Day Five. Involve the children in the preparation for this ritual. Selecting what is appropriate for your class, encourage the children to do some of the following:

- Draw the Good Shepherd carrying a sheep. The children put their own name on the sheep.
- Draw Jesus surrounded by pictures of children from all around the world (these can be cut out from magazines).
- Make some banners/posters/collage of a few phrases like:
  Jesus loves children.
  Jesus said: 'We are the Greatest.'
  It's good to be us!
  It's good to be a child!
  May God bless us and keep us.
- Make 'Thank You' cards to Jesus, e.g. 'Thank you, Jesus, for loving me.'
  or
  Make 'God Bless You _____' cards, e.g. 'God Bless Mam/Dad/Gran/Grandad.'
  Encourage the children to give the card to someone at home.
- Write out some simple bidding prayers, e.g. Thank you, God, for our class; Bless our class, O God.

PRAYERTIME BLESSING RITUAL

For this prayertime you will need Holy Water and oil. During the prayertime, the teacher will bless the children with Holy Water. The teacher and children will then bless each other with oil. Place the Holy Water and the oil in containers on a table in the centre of the room. If possible, cover the table with a cloth and place the lighted candle beside the Holy Water and the oil.

Sign of the Cross.

Teacher

God, you know each one of us inside out.
You know the goodness that is deep within us.
Today we ask you to bless us and to bless all
children around the world.

All

Sing: *We are the Greatest*

Teacher

As we light our candle today we remember
that God is with us.
To help us remember that God is with us in a
very special way I am going to bless you all
using this Holy Water.

As I sprinkle the water over you, we will say:
Bless us and keep us, we pray.

*As the teacher sprinkles the child with Holy Water,
she/he says:*

God knows the goodness that is within us.

All

Bless us and keep us, we pray.

Teacher (*as she/he sprinkles the child with Holy
Water*)
God knows the goodness that is within
everyone in this class.

All

Bless us and keep us, we pray.

Teacher (*as she/he sprinkles the child with Holy
Water*)
God knows the goodness that is within all
children everywhere.

All

Bless us and keep us, we pray.

Teacher

Let's hear again the story in the Bible where
Jesus tells the people that children are the
greatest.

We are the Greatest

Today is Market Day. The children love Market
Day. They go to the town square. All the
grown-ups are there. There are men selling
cheeses. There are women buying cloth. There
are bakers selling bread. There are people
buying spices and fruit. There are cows
mooing and donkeys braying and goats
baaing. The Market Place is busy. The Market
Place is noisy. But most of all, the Market
Place is fun! The grown-ups are so hard at work that
they have no time for the children. They do
not notice the children. They do not see how
the children play. They do not hear how the
children sing. Right now the grown-ups have
other things to think about.

Today a man comes to the Market Place. At
first no one notices the man. He sits in the
middle of the square where everyone will be
able to see him. He speaks in a loud voice so
that everyone will be able to hear him. He tells
those who stop and listen about a kingdom.
He calls it the Kingdom of God. He says that
in God's kingdom everyone is happy. In God's
kingdom everyone loves their friends as well
as those who are not their friends.

'What kind of place is this kingdom,' say some
of the grown-ups, 'where people love those
who are not their friends?'

'How can we get to live in such a place?' say
some others.

'God's kingdom is not any particular place,'
says the man. 'God's kingdom can be
anywhere. Wherever people love one another,
wherever people are kind and gentle, wherever
people share with one another, that is where
God's kingdom is. God's kingdom can be right
here, right now.'

'I have a question for you,' says one man. 'In
our community I am an important person. I
would like to know who is the most important
person in this Kingdom of God that you talk
about.'

Now the Market Place grows quiet. The noise
stops. The buying and selling stops. The
children notice that everything has gone quiet
too. The children go on playing. From where
they are they can see the crowd of people
gathered around the man.

'What's happening?' some of the children ask
each other.

Just then the man comes over to the children.
He says, 'Who will help me? I need one of you
to help me teach the grown-ups something
very important.'

'Me, me, me!' say the children. The man
smiles. He takes the smallest child by the
hand. He takes the child into the middle of

the crowd. He wants everyone to notice the child.

'You ask me who is the most important person in God's kingdom,' says the man to the crowd. 'I will tell you now,' he says. 'Do you see this little child? I tell you, the child is the greatest in God's kingdom.'

A murmur of shock and surprise runs through the crowd of grown-ups. They can hardly believe their eyes. They can hardly believe their ears. The child! The child is the greatest in God's kingdom! They have never heard the like of this before!

When the man is finished the child runs back to the other children.

'What did the man want?'; 'What did the man say?'; 'What did the man teach the people?', they ask the child.

'He taught them that children are the greatest,' the child answers. The children clap and cheer.

'Who is this man?' the children ask.

'His name is Jesus,' the child answers.

'Hurrah for Jesus!' the children shout. 'Hurrah, hurrah, hurrah!'

Teacher
When Jesus was asked who was the greatest, he pointed to a child.
Today we celebrate the greatness of children.

Let us pray:

Alternatively, use the bidding prayers that the children have made up themselves.

Child
We have fun.

All
Blessed be God.

Child
We pray together.

All
Blessed be God.

Child
We laugh and cry.

All
Blessed be God.

Child
We sing and dance.

All
Blessed be God.

Teacher
We don't always live up to the goodness that Jesus saw in children.
Sometimes we do selfish things.

All
We ask God to forgive us.

Teacher
Sometimes we don't show our goodness to others.
Let us ask God's forgiveness for these times.

All
We ask God to forgive us.

Teacher
Sometimes we lose our tempers and shout and yell.

All
We ask God to forgive us.

Teacher
Sometimes we are destructive and break things.

All
We ask God to forgive us.

Prayer after Forgiveness
O my God, thank you for forgiving me.
Help me to love others.
Help me to live as Jesus asked me to.

Teacher
When we were babies we were brought to the church to be baptised.
The priest blessed us with oil.
Today we are going to bless one another with oil.
As we do, we know that God is blessing us.

Teacher blesses the first child by making the Sign of the Cross with oil on her/his forehead. The child then does likewise for the teacher. Each say 'In the name of the Father and of the Son and of the Holy Spirit'. The children then come forward, in pairs, and do the same. To maintain the attention of the rest of the class the teacher may say, as each pair comes forward, 'We will now ask God silently to bless Ann and John', etc.

All

Sing: *We are the Greatest*

Glory be to the Father...

Sign of the Cross.

Now We Know

Q. What does God Our Father do for us in the Sacrament of Penance?

A. In the Sacrament of Penance God Our Father forgives us.

The King of Love

Traditional

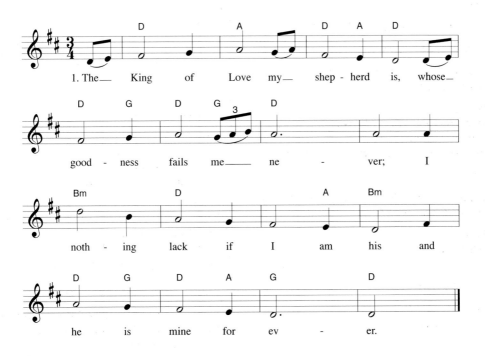

1. The— King of Love my— shep - herd is, whose— good - ness fails me— ne - ver; I noth - ing lack if I am his and he is mine for ev - er.

2. Where streams of living water flow
To rest my soul he leads me.
Where fresh and fertile pastures grow
With heavenly food he feeds me.

Lesson 9: Time For Joy

Why do you look for the living
among the dead?
He is not here, but has risen.
(Luke 24:5)

Easter is the Christian celebration of light and new life. Children in First Class/ Primary Three are still too young to understand many of the concepts contained in the story of the Death and Resurrection of Jesus. As adults, one of the ways in which we grapple with the mysteries of the Passion, Death and Resurrection of Jesus is through the ritual of the liturgies of Holy Week and Easter Sunday. Initially, children enter ritual not by understanding it at an intellectual level but by physically taking part in it. This process was begun with the children in Senior Infants/ Primary Two.

This year we continue to provide opportunities for the children to take part in a series of simple rituals. The Last Supper ritual focuses on the sharing of unleavened bread. In the Good Friday ritual the children follow the Way of the Cross with Jesus. The Resurrection ritual focuses on the story of the women at the tomb. The children participate in these rituals in a variety of ways – standing, sitting, singing, eating, being silent, praying, etc.

The type of learning that we hope for from this lesson is significantly different from much of the learning that has taken place during the year. Therefore, the structure of the lesson deviates from the normal format.

Note: During the prayertime throughout the year the children have frequently meditated on passages from the Bible, entering into the scenes and imagining themselves within them, and meeting God in the silence of their hearts. In this lesson, for the first time, we introduce the children to a form of contemplative prayer.

Because the children are very young, entering a

total silence may be difficult for them. For this reason we begin by teaching them the use of a mantra. A mantra is a short phrase, e.g. 'Come Lord Jesus', that is repeated silently several times by the person. The frequent repetition of the phrase calms the mind and stills the heart. It is important to recognise that like any form of prayer it takes time to learn.

You may like to practise this form of prayer with the children first. Start by asking them to say a phrase gently out loud a few times. Then, as their voices gradually become lower and lower and more and more quiet, ask the children to say the phrase with their inside voice, i.e. completely silently.

FOR THE TEACHER:

A thought before beginning

I say to myself each night, 'The dawn will come and all this dark will be gone'. I watch the tide's far ebb and whisper, 'it will flow'. In the mid of winter I cry to my heart, 'Soon the green banners of spring will blow through the land'. Yet surer still I am that Thou art my friend. Thou has wrought a miracle in my thought.
Thou has changed faith to knowledge, and hope to sight.
    Alaistair Maclean

What am I trying to do?

To provide opportunities for the children to take part in a series of simple rituals which celebrate some of the events in the stories of the Passion, Death and Resurrection of Jesus.

Why?

So that they may be helped to come to a deeper understanding of the story of the Passion, Death and Resurrection of Jesus and thereby begin to learn to enter into the Church's liturgical events at Easter.

Overview of the Week

	Worksheet		Aims of the Ritual	
	Aims of the Ritual		Preparation for the	Aims of the Ritual
	Preparation for the	Poem: *Jesus Stumbles*	Ritual	Preparation for the
	Ritual	Prayertime	Did you Know?	Ritual
Song: *Alleluia*	Ritual: *The Last*	Art: *Our Four Stations*	Ritual: *Stations of the*	Ritual: *An Easter*
Prayertime	*Supper*	*of the Cross*	*Cross*	*Surprise*

Day One

SONG

Alleluia

PRAYERTIME

Sign of the Cross.

All *(Sing)*
Time and time and time again.
Praise God, praise God.

If possible, create a special reflective atmosphere in which the Holy Week stories can be heard. Instead of the normal chatting about the story, the children will remain silent. This silence will be followed by a short meditation.

Teacher
We light our candle. We know that God is with us as we listen to the story of how Jesus shared the Last Supper with his friends.

The Last Supper
(Adapted from Luke 22:7-20)

On the first day of the Passover celebration, Jesus, his friends and his followers discussed the preparations they would have to make for the Passover meal. Jesus sent some of them to a house that he knew in the city of Jerusalem. There they prepared a big room and food for the meal. They were very busy. They set out the room. They had to get some herbs and a one-year-old lamb. They had to make some unleavened bread and buy some red wine. When Jesus and the others arrived, everything was ready.

When evening came, everyone sat down to eat the Passover meal. They said special prayers, they shared their special story about Moses leading the people out of Egypt, and they shared their special memory of things that had happened to their people in times past. This Passover was the same as every other Passover until, as they were sharing the special food and wine, Jesus did something that was very different to every other Passover. He took the unleavened bread and blessed it and broke it and shared it out among his friends and followers, and he said, 'This is my body, take and eat it.' Then he took the cup of wine. He blessed it and said, 'This is my blood, take and drink it.'

Jesus' friends and followers had never seen this done, or heard these words spoken, at a Passover meal before. This was new. At first they weren't sure what Jesus meant, but he said to them, 'Do this in memory of me.'

When the supper was over, Jesus and his friends went off to a hill nearby called The Mount of Olives to pray.

Teacher
Let us pause awhile and be still for a while.

We pray.

Let us spend a little quiet time today to

253

remember what Jesus said to his friends on the night of the Last Supper. He said, 'Do this in memory of me.'

All

Do this in memory of me.

Teacher

Note: You may like to practise this form of prayer with the children first. Start by asking them to say a phrase gently out loud a few times. Then, as their voices gradually become lower and lower and more and more quiet, ask the children to say the phrase with their inside voice, i.e. completely silently.

To help us to be still and quiet, we will say 'Do this in memory of me' with our inside voice. We will repeat the words quietly and gently, over and over again.

Play some quiet music.

Close your eyes.
Still your hands.
Place your feet on the floor.
Feel your heart beat.
Feel your breath as it goes in and out, bringing life to every part of your body.

Now with your inside voice that no one else can hear, repeat the phrase 'Do this in memory of me' quietly and gently.

Silence.

Teacher *(When the children are ready)*
May God the Father, Son and Holy Spirit bless us and keep us always.

All

Amen.

Sign of the Cross.

Day Two

WORKSHEET

If you wish to use the worksheet or workbook page which accompanies this lesson, this is an appropriate time to do so.

Aims of the Ritual

The aims of this ritual are to help the children to focus on the Last Supper. During the meal Jesus blessed, broke and shared unleavened bread with his friends. Through the ritual we hope to lay the foundation for the children's future understanding of the significance of what Jesus did at the Last Supper and also for their own future participation in the Eucharist.

Preparation for the Ritual

Note: In Term One the children have already had an experience of sharing bread. In this lesson we focus particularly on unleavened bread. This was the bread that was broken and shared by Jesus at the Last Supper. In participating in this ritual, we hope that the children may come to a fuller awareness of the significance of Jesus' actions as he sat with his friends for his last supper.

We suggest that during this week you have a prayertime with the children which involves blessing and sharing bread. For this, you might like to make some unleavened bread. You will need: 200 gms flour; 50 gms fat or olive oil (we add fat so that the bread will keep moist and fresh, but it is not strictly necessary); pinch of salt, and enough water to mix all these ingredients into a stiff dough. Make small balls of the dough and press flat. Cook in a hot oven for ten minutes.

It will be quite brittle and easy to break but will give the children the opportunity of handling and tasting a type of bread which would otherswise be outside of their experience. Alternatively, you could simply bring in a cake of brown bread, or a portion of a cake, depending on the number of children in your class, which can be shared among them during the prayertime.

You will need sufficient bread to allow each child to have a piece.
Arrange the room so that the children are sitting as if around a big table.

PRAYERTIME

Ritual: The Last Supper

Note: Settle the class around the table. Have the unleavened bread in a basket or on a tray. Place the basket/tray on the table with the candle.

Sign of the Cross.

Sing (or play tape/CD): *Alleluia*

Teacher
We light the candle. We know that God Our Creator and Father is with us today as we share unleavened bread with one another. Today we remember all the times we share bread with others, at school, at home, at special celebrations.

All
Blessed be God forever.

Teacher
We remember all the people who bake bread.

All
Blessed be God forever.

Teacher
We remember that God our Creator gives us life.

All
Blessed be God forever.

Teacher
Jesus often shared bread with his friends.
At the Last Supper Jesus shared unleavened bread in a special way. This week, all over the world, people are remembering the meal that Jesus had with his friends the night before he died.

All
Blessed be God forever.

Teacher
We prepare now to share our unleavened bread.
We remember how Jesus took bread and gave God thanks and praise.
Then Jesus broke the bread and gave it to his friends. We pray:

All
Jesus blessed, Jesus broke, Jesus shared bread.

Teacher *(holding the unleavened bread)*
Invite the children to raise their hands in the air.
God our Creator, you made us to live for you and for each other. Bless this bread. May it nourish us, body and soul. May it remind us to share food with those who are hungry.

Pass the basket/tray around the class. Ask each child to break off a piece of bread, hand it to the child on her/his left and say:

Child
Jesus blessed, Jesus broke and Jesus shared the bread.

All
Bless us, O God, as we sit together.
Bless the food we eat today.
Bless the hands that made the food.
Bless us, O God. Amen.

Each child waits in silence until everyone has a piece of bread. Then they eat.

Teacher
We pray together:

All
Thank you, God, for the food we have eaten.
Thank you, God, for all our friends.
Thank you, God, for everything.
Thank you, God. Amen.

Sign of the Cross.

POEM

Jesus Stumbles

Jesus stumbles,
Falls, and then,
Stumbles on
And falls again.
Jesus on the dusty road,
Falls beneath his heavy load.

Mary stands
That dreadful day,
Friends and comrades
Ran away.
Only John remains to cry,
Only one to say goodbye.

Soldiers ask
'Why did he die?'
Loving Son
Of God most high.
Loving people great and small
Giving up his life for all.
Christy Kenneally

PRAYERTIME

Sign of the Cross.

Teacher
We light our candle.
We know that God is with us as we listen to the story of how Jesus died.

Jesus Dies on the Cross

After Jesus had eaten the Last Supper with his friends and apostles, he went into a garden called Gethsemane to pray. While he was there, the Roman soldiers came and took him away. They were cruel to Jesus. They gave him a big heavy wooden cross to carry to the top of a hill. The cross was so heavy and Jesus was so tired that he got weak and he fell. The soldiers ordered him to get up and to go on. He struggled to his feet and carried the cross a little further. But he fell a second time. Still the soldiers would not take pity on him. They simply shouted louder at him until he managed to get up again. Carrying the cross on his back, he walked on. He was very tired now. As he paused to catch his breath, he stumbled and fell a third time. The Roman soldiers made him carry the cross all the way to the hill called Calvary.

When he reached the top of the hill, Jesus was crucified.

Teacher
This is the Word of the Lord.

All
Thanks be to God.

Sign of the Cross.

ART

Our Four Stations of the Cross

You will need:
* Paper for each group
* Crayons/markers

Divide the class into groups. Ask each child in the group to draw one of the following scenes:
* Jesus falls the first time.
* Jesus falls the second time.
* Jesus falls the third time.
* Jesus dies on the cross.

Day Four

Note: You might like to encourage the children to visit their local church and look at the Stations of the Cross. Alternatively, you might like to bring them on a visit to the church and point the Stations out to them.

Aims of the Ritual

The aims of this ritual are to help the children to focus on the great love that God has for each one of us. In memory of Jesus' Death on the Cross we will enact a simple Stations of the Cross.

We hope to lay down a foundation for the children's future understanding of the Death of Jesus on the Cross as one of the signs of God's love for all.

Preparation for the Ritual

DID YOU KNOW?

In every church there are fourteen pictures hanging around the walls which tell the story of the Passion and Death of Jesus. Each picture tells of something which happened on the way to Calvary. They are pictures of fourteen different moments on that journey. Today we are going to remember four of these moments: they are the third, seventh, ninth and twelfth Stations.

On the walls of the classroom, put up the children's artwork of Jesus' journey to Calvary: Jesus falls the first time; Jesus falls the second time; Jesus falls the third time; Jesus dies on the cross. Leave a space between each four sets of pictures – these become the Stations of the Cross. Arrange the classroom furniture so that it is possible to walk around the room to pause at the four Stations. You will need a crucifix and a candle. During the ritual the teacher (carrying the lighted candle) and a child (carrying the crucifix) will walk around the room and stop at each of the four Stations of the Cross.

PRAYERTIME

Ritual: Stations of the Cross

Sign of the Cross.

All *(sing)*
Time and time and time again.
Praise God, praise God.

Teacher
We light our candle.
God loves us and cares for us all the time.
All through his life Jesus loved those who lived and shared their life with him. He also loved God and knew that God loved him. Jesus died on the cross rather than stop loving God or his friends.

Today we will carry a crucifix and a candle and we will follow the Way of the Cross. We will remember four special moments on the journey that Jesus made on the day he died. We will remember his love for us all. We will stop four times. Each time we will say:

All *(repeating after teacher)*
Jesus, we bless you and adore you.

Teacher
Let us stand and face our first Station: Jesus Falls the First Time.
We remember how Jesus carried a big heavy wooden cross all the way to the top of the hill of Calvary.

Jesus stumbles,
Falls, and then,
Stumbles on
And falls again.
Jesus on the dusty road,
Falls beneath his heavy load.

Let us pause in silence for a moment.
Let us bow our heads.
Let us pray.

All
Jesus, we bless you and adore you.

Teacher
Let us turn and face our second Station of the Cross: Jesus Falls a Second Time. We remember

257

how Jesus carried a big wooden cross all the way to the top of the hill of Calvary.

Jesus stumbles,
Falls, and then,
Stumbles on
And falls again.
Jesus on the dusty road,
Falls beneath his heavy load.

Let us pause in silence for a moment.
Let us bow our heads.
Let us pray.

All
Jesus, we bless you and adore you.

Teacher
Let us turn and face our third Station of the Cross: Jesus Falls a Third Time. We remember how Jesus carried a big wooden cross all the way to the top of the hill of Calvary.

Jesus stumbles,
Falls, and then,
Stumbles on
And falls again.
Jesus on the dusty road,
Falls beneath his heavy load.

Let us pause in silence for a moment.
Let us bow our heads.
Let us pray.

All
Jesus, we bless you and adore you.

Teacher
Let us turn and face our fourth Station of the Cross: Jesus Dies on the Cross. We remember how Jesus died on the cross. We remember how Mary, his mother, and John, his friend, stood by.

Mary stands
That dreadful day,
Friends and comrades
Ran away.
Only John remains to cry,
Only one to say goodbye.

Soldiers ask
'Why did he die?'
Loving Son
Of God most high.
Loving people great and small
Giving up his life for all.

Let us pause in silence for a moment.
Let us bow our heads.
Let us pray.

All
Jesus, we bless you and adore you.

Teacher (*placing crucifix and lighted candle on the table*)
Let us stand. God sent Jesus into the world. Most clearly of all, Jesus shows us how much God loves us and cares for us. We give thanks to God.

All (*sing*)
Time and time and time again.
Praise God, praise God.

Sign of the Cross.

Invite the children to take their pictures of the Stations of the Cross home with them.

Day Five

Aims of the Ritual

On this day we help the children to celebrate the Resurrection of Jesus. The emphasis in the ritual is on the telling of the story of the empty tomb.

Preparation for the Ritual

Decorate a table with a yellow cloth or yellow paper. Place the 'Little Wilderness' on the table. In or beside the 'Little Wilderness' place the candle. You might like to put some spring flowers or whatever is available in the 'Little Wilderness' also.

 PRAYERTIME

Ritual: An Easter Surprise

Sign of the Cross.

Teacher
Women searching in the gloom
Find a silent empty tomb.

258

'Do not fear,' the angel said,
He is not among the dead.

Today we celebrate the Resurrection of Jesus. Every Easter a special candle is lit in the church. It is called the Paschal Candle and it is lit to remind us that God has raised Jesus to new life.
Today we light this special candle to remind us that God has raised Jesus to new life.

As we do, we pray together:

Teacher lights the candle.

All *(Sing)*
Alleluia.

Teacher
We will stand up as we listen to the story of the Resurrection. Before we do, we will make the Sign of the Cross on our foreheads, on our lips and on our hearts.

An Easter Surprise
(Adapted from Luke 24:1-10)

Jesus died on the cross. His friends took his body down from the cross and laid it in the tomb. They left the tomb and went home. They were very sad because Jesus was no longer with them. They didn't talk or laugh or sing.

There was a woman called Mary, who was one of the friends of Jesus, who came from a place called Magdala. Because it was getting late, Mary and her friends didn't have time to finish taking care of the body of their friend Jesus. They decided they would come back and finish their work the next day. That is why, on Easter Sunday morning, they got up very, very early. They set off walking to the tomb where Jesus' body had been laid. They brought special oils and ointments and creams with them for the body.

'Oh dear,' said Mary, stopping suddenly. 'We have forgotten something.'

'What?' asked her friends.

'The huge stone,' said Mary. 'We forgot about the huge stone they rolled in front of the tomb where Jesus' body is.'

'That's right,' the others said. 'What shall we do?'

'We will never be able to roll it away from the entrance by ourselves,' said Mary, in a very worried voice.

'It would be much too heavy,' the others agreed.

'We will just have to think of something,' said Mary, as she continued determinedly on her way.

'Perhaps there will be someone there already who will help us,' said one of the friends.

'I don't think so,' said another, 'it is much too early in the morning for anyone else to be awake.'

'We'll be okay, you'll see, we will think of something,' said Mary.

But when they got to the tomb they could hardly believe their eyes. They were very surprised indeed. The huge stone was not there! It had been rolled away. The women were very glad.

They took their oils and ointments and went inside to where the body lay. But the body was not there! Now the women were very upset.

'Where's the body of our friend Jesus?' said Mary.

'Perhaps someone has taken it away,' said the others.

'Jesus is not here, he is risen,' said a voice behind them. The women turned around and saw a young person standing there in shining bright clothes. 'Jesus is not here, he is risen. You must go and tell everyone the good news that Jesus is risen from the dead.'

Mary and her friends were very happy. They ran off to tell everyone what had happened.

Teacher
We sing together:

All *(Sing)*
Alleluia.

Teacher
'Jesus is not here. He is risen.' That was the message that the women were given.
Turn to the person on either side and give that person the message that Jesus is risen. Tell them 'Jesus is not here. He is risen'.

Encourage the children to spread the good news to each other.

We sing together once again:

All *(sing and dance)*
Alleluia.

Sign of the Cross.

NOW WE KNOW

Q. What happened on Good Friday?

A. On Good Friday Jesus died on the Cross.

Q. What happened on Easter Sunday?

A. On Easter Sunday God Our Father raised Jesus to new life.

Alleluia

Bernard Sexton

Al - le - lu - ia, al - le - lu - ia, al - le - lu - ia,

al - le - lu - ia, al - le - lu - ia, al - le - lu - ia.

Je - sus is ri - sen, he has saved his peo - ple,

sing out your prai - ses, al - le - lu - ia.

Al - le - lu - ia, al - le - lu - ia, al - le - lu - ia,

al - le - lu - ia, al - le - lu - ia, al - le - lu - ia.

Lesson 1: Mary's Joy

From now on
all generations will call me blessed;
for the Mighty One
has done great things for me.
(Luke 1:48-49)

We honour Mary, the mother of Jesus. The months of May and October are special times of devotion to Mary. Liturgically, we celebrate special feasts in her honour: the Immaculate Conception of Mary free from sin on 8 December; the feast of the Birthday of Our Lady on 8 September; the Annunciation to Mary that she was to be the mother of God on 25 March; the Visitation of Our Blessed Lady to her cousin Elizabeth on 31 May. We honour her when we say the Rosary and meditate on the Joyful, Sorrowful and Glorious Mysteries.

We honour Mary because she is the mother of Jesus. She loved and cared for Jesus when he was a baby. She watched him as he grew up in Nazareth and as he set off on his public ministry. She was at his side as he died on the cross. The Gospels tell us little about Mary's life. Like most mothers, Mary's life was punctuated with moments of great joy and moments of great sorrow.

When we pray the Rosary we honour Mary in a particular way as the mother of Jesus and our mother too. In this lesson we introduce the children to the Joyful Mysteries of the Rosary: The Annunciation, The Visitation, The Birth

of Our Lord, The Presentation, The Finding of the Child Jesus in the Temple. The children are already familiar with these five stories. In this lesson we help them to recall the stories either by hearing them told again or by telling them themselves with help from the teacher and from one another. Having done this, we then help them to meditate on each of the stories in prayer.

Note: While this lesson appears in the text immediately after Easter, the ideal time to do it in class is during the first week of May.

FOR THE TEACHER:

A thought before beginning

She was a woman who did not hesitate to proclaim that God vindicates the humble and the oppressed, and removes the powerful people of this world from their privileged positions ... a woman of strength, who experienced poverty and suffering, flight and exile.
    Paul VI, Marialis cullus, 37

What am I trying to do?

To introduce the children to the Joyful Mysteries of the Rosary and to encourage in them a devotion to Mary.

Why?

So that the children may honour Mary as the mother of God's son, and as our mother too.

Overview of the Week

			Continue song	
			Chatting about	
Song: *Mary, Our*			blessings	
Mother		Continue song	Recall story: *Anna*	Continue song
Did You Know?	Continue song	Chatting about	*and Simeon*	Chatting about the
Chatting about	Chatting about	those who look	Activity: *One-Decade*	journey to
Mary	Mary and Elizabeth	after us	*Rosary Beads*	Jerusalem
Recall story: *One*	Recall story: *Two*	Recall story: *The*	Worksheet	Recall story: *Jesus*
Moment	*Cousins*	*Moment They'd All*	Chatting about the	*Goes to Jerusalem*
Activity: *Making a*	Activity: *Mary was*	*Been Waiting For*	pictures	Activity: *One-Decade*
May Altar	*full of joy*	Activity: *Mary Card*	Prayertime	*Rosary Beads*
Prayertime	Prayertime	Prayertime		Prayertime

Day One

SONG

Mary, Our Mother

DID YOU KNOW?

May is the month in which we remember Mary. May is Mary's month. We pray to her in a special way during this month. Mary was the person who was closest to Jesus. We remember the things she did. We make May altars. We say the Rosary. The Rosary is a special prayer to Mary.

CHATTING

...about Mary

What was Jesus' mother's name? What do you think she was like? What sort of things do you think she might have done all day long? What sort of clothes would she have worn? Do you remember any stories about her? Does anyone know in which months of the year we think about Mary in a special way? Do you know any special prayers to Mary? Does anyone remember the story about the time before Jesus was born – when the Angel Gabriel came to Mary?

STORY

One Moment
(Adapted from Luke 1:26-38)

In remembering the story with the children, focus on Mary's happiness, excitement and joy at hearing the good news from the Angel Gabriel.

One very ordinary day Mary was in the kitchen. The sun was shining in the window and onto the table where she was baking bread. Mary felt happy. As she kneaded the dough, she hummed a little song to herself. Then an unusual thing happened. She had turned around to get some more flour, when suddenly, out of nowhere, an angel stood in the kitchen doorway. Mary jumped.

'Oh!' she remembered saying, almost dropping the flour.

The angel smiled. 'Hello, Mary,' he said. 'My name is Gabriel. Do not be afraid. I have news for you!'

Mary remembered how surprised she was by what the angel had said. 'I hope it's good news,' she said, in a worried voice.

'Don't be afraid, it's wonderful news,' Gabriel replied.

Mary remembered listening to what the angel had to say.

'You are very special, Mary, and God loves you,' Gabriel continued. 'You are going to have a baby – a very special baby boy. His name will be Jesus. He will be God's son.'

Mary was amazed. For a moment she didn't know what to say. So the angel continued...

'And I have more news too. Your cousin Elizabeth is also going to have a baby!'

Mary knew Elizabeth had wanted a baby for a long time. She knew Elizabeth would be overjoyed. She knew it would be lovely for her baby to have a little cousin.

She said, 'I know that God cares for me very much. God is very good. I will do whatever God asks.' Then the angel disappeared and Mary went on with her baking, singing her song.

ACTIVITY

Making a May Altar

Note: As a focal point to the May altar, you will need a picture/icon/statue of Mary. Over the week, use a variety of modern images of Mary from religious and church art. You may like to involve the children in the setting up of the May altar. The following suggestions may be helpful.

Discuss with the children how they could make a May altar/corner in their classroom. For the May altar the children might like to:
- draw pictures of Mary;
- write phrases, e.g. Hail Mary, Mary is Jesus' mother, Mary is our mother;
- make a collage of the name 'Mary' or 'Mary we love you';
- make 'Happy month of May' cards;
- bring in flowers or leaves or branches for decorating the altar.

Alternatively, you could get the children to make some paper flowers. Ask the children to draw a variety of simple flower shapes/outlines. Then ask them to fill in the shapes with scraps of coloured paper/sugar paper. You might like to ask the children to cut out the flower shapes and to arrange them on chart paper.

PRAYERTIME

Sign of the Cross.

Teacher *(as the candle is lit)*
Hail Mary, full of grace.

Today we remember that special moment when the Angel Gabriel came to Mary.

We pray to Mary: *(children repeat after teacher)*

Mother of Jesus, blessed are you.
Mother of Jesus, my mother too.
Help me to live like Jesus
And help me to live like you.

Close your eyes.
Place your hands gently on your lap.
Place your feet on the floor.

Imagine that day when Mary heard the wonderful news that she was to be the mother of Jesus. Imagine how she felt when the Angel Gabriel spoke with her. Imagine her excitement. With your inside voice ask Mary how she felt... Now tell Mary you are glad that she became Jesus' mother. Tell her you are glad that she is our mother too.

Open your eyes.
Let us pray.

Our Father, who art in heaven
Hallowed be thy name.
Thy kingdom come,
Thy will be done on earth as it is in heaven.

All
Give us this day our daily bread
And forgive us our trespasses
As we forgive those who trespass against us.
And lead us not into temptation
But deliver us from evil. Amen.

Teacher
Hail Mary, full of grace,
The Lord is with thee.
Blessed art thou among women
And blessed is the fruit of thy womb, Jesus.

All
Holy Mary, Mother of God,
Pray for us sinners,
Now, and at the hour of our death. Amen.

Teacher
Glory be to the Father,
And to the Son,
And to the Holy Spirit.

All
As it was in the beginning,
Is now and ever shall be,
World without end. Amen.

Sign of the Cross.

Day Two

Continue song: *Mary, Our Mother*

CHATTING

...about Mary and Elizabeth

Do you remember who Elizabeth was? When did Mary visit Elizabeth? Why do you think she visited Elizabeth? How do you think Mary and Elizabeth got on together? What good news did they have? Do you have any good news you would like to tell us today? Let's see if we remember the story about Mary's visit to Elizabeth.

STORY

Two Cousins
(Adapted from Luke 1:39-56)

In remembering the story with the children, focus on the good news Mary had to tell Elizabeth, the two women chatting and laughing together, their joy and excitement because they were both going to have a baby.

The two cousins, Mary and Elizabeth, had good news – they were each going to have a new baby.

'I shall go on a journey and visit my cousin Elizabeth,' said Mary. 'Elizabeth and I have a lot to chat and talk about, so I will stay in her house for a while. Now, let me see, what do I need to take with me?'

Mary sat down and drew up a list of all the preparations she would have to make.

'Now,' said Mary, when she had finished all her preparations, 'I think that is everything. Oh, I almost forgot – I must get a present for Elizabeth's baby.'

Mary was very excited as she went on her journey. Elizabeth was very excited at the news that her cousin Mary was coming to visit. 'I must get a present to give Mary for her new baby', she said to Zechariah.

Elizabeth could hardly wait for her cousin Mary to arrive. 'It's such a long time since I saw Mary. I wonder what she'll look like now that she's going to have a new baby?' thought Elizabeth, smiling to herself.

Next thing she saw her Cousin Mary coming up the path. She ran to meet her, shouting, 'Mary, Mary, it's so good to see you.'

Mary ran up the path towards Elizabeth. Mary was delighted to see her cousin. 'Elizabeth, Elizabeth, I'm here, hurrah, hurrah!'

The two cousins hugged and kissed and put their arms around each other. Then they went inside. Mary took off her coat and opened the bag she had packed.

'I've brought a present for your new baby when it comes,' said Mary smiling, as she handed the present to her cousin.

Elizabeth laughed. 'I've bought a present for your new baby when it comes too!'

The two cousins opened their presents and held them up.

ACTIVITY

Mary was full of joy

Nobody really knows exactly what Mary looked like. We have no photos of her to tell us. But she probably wore the same sort of clothes that other women in Nazareth wore at that time. Mary loved to share her excitement and good news with others.

Ask the children to draw a picture of Mary telling some good news to someone else.
Ask the children to cut out the pictures and make a big collage – 'Mary was full of joy'.

PRAYERTIME

Sign of the Cross.

Teacher
This is the month in which we remember Mary.
We light our candle at the May altar.
We pray in movement as well as in word.

Teacher *(with actions)*
Hail Mary, full of grace.
(Arms outstretched at the side, palms facing upwards.)

All
(Repeat using the same actions.)

Teacher
The Lord is with thee.
(Arms lifted high above the head.)

All
(Repeat using the same actions.)

Teacher
Blessed art thou among women.
(Arms outstretched in front, palms facing upwards.)

All
(Repeat using the same actions.)

Teacher
And blessed is the fruit of thy womb, Jesus.
(Cradle and gently rock the 'baby' in arms.)

All
(Repeat using the same actions.)

Teacher
Holy Mary, Mother of God.
(Arms lifted high above the head again.)

All
(Repeat using the same actions.)

Teacher
Pray for us sinners now, and at the hour of our death.
(Head bowed, hands joined together.)

All
(Repeat using the same actions.)

Teacher
Amen.
(Hands raised high over head, palms facing upwards.)

All
(Repeat using the same actions.)

Sign of the Cross.

Day Three

Continue song: *Mary, Our Mother*

CHATTING

...about those who look after us

Who are the people at home who look after you? What do they do to show you that they love you? What do you do to show them that you love them? Did anyone ever tell you about the day your were born? Do you know what weight you were? Who decided what you would be called? How do people feel when a new baby is born? Does anyone have a new baby sister or brother? How do you think Mary felt when Jesus was born? When was he born? How did Mary show him that she loved him?

Do you think Mary was a good mother? If you met Mary, what sort of questions would you like to ask her? Who remembers the story about when Jesus was born? Let's see if we can remember any of it.

STORY

The Moment They'd All Been Waiting For
(Adapted from Matthew 2:1-3)

When remembering the story with the children, focus on Mary's joy and excitement at Jesus' birth, how she shared that joy and good news with the shepherds and the kings.

A man called Caesar Augustus was a Roman emperor. He was 'in charge'. One day, he decided to count and see how many people he was in charge of. He sent soldiers throughout the land to give people this message. Every family must go to the town their ancestors had come from. There they must write the names of all those in their family into a special book. All the books in all the towns throughout the land were then to be collected and Caesar would count all the names. In this way he would find out how many people he was in charge of.

When Joseph heard the instructions he told Mary that the two of them would have to go from Nazareth to the town of his ancestor, King David. *(Do you remember the story of David from last year? The shepherd boy who became king of his people.)* Joseph's ancestors had lived in Bethlehem. As they travelled along the way to Bethlehem, Mary wondered whether Joseph would have two names or three names to write in Caesar's book. You see, Mary was going to have a baby. She wasn't sure of the exact moment her baby would be born, but she knew it would be soon.

When Mary and Joseph reached the city there was a long queue of people waiting to sign their names in Caesar's book.

As they stood in the queue, Mary and Joseph heard people talking and whispering. 'Some day we will have a true leader,' said a cross young woman, 'one of our own who will show everyone how to treat people fairly and justly.'

A young man beside her shook his head. 'We have been promised such a leader for a long time now,' he said bitterly, 'but there is no sign of him yet. How much longer do we have to wait?'

'Stop talking! Move along!' shouted the soldiers roughly.

'Well, whenever he comes, it will not be a moment too soon,' said the cross young woman.

Joseph and Mary signed their names in the book and went off to look for somewhere to stay. But with all the crowds in town, the only place they could find to stay in was a cave out on the hillside. It was getting closer and closer to the moment when Mary's baby would be born.

Out on the hills around Bethlehem some shepherds were rushing to gather their flocks together for the night. As they set about gathering their flocks they talked about the time when a new leader would come among them.

'But how will we know when this person that we have waited so long for has finally come?' asked Reuben, the youngest shepherd.

'There will be a sign,' said Isaac, the oldest shepherd. 'We do not know what kind of sign it will be, but when it comes, we will recognise it.'

At that very moment on a hillside outside Bethlehem, Mary's baby boy cried for the first time. The moment Mary and Joseph had been waiting for was finally here. The baby was born.

At that very same moment, the sign the shepherds had talked about was given; the sky above them was filled with the sound of angels singing. 'Go and see the new baby,' the angels told the shepherds.

And at that same moment the three wise ones mounted their camels and set off to follow a new star that had appeared in the sky. It brought them to a hillside where they found a cave. Inside the cave, shepherds were bowed down before a baby who lay in a manger. The baby's mother smiled at the three wise ones.

'You are just in time,' she said, showing them the new baby. 'This is the moment we have all been waiting for!'

ACTIVITY

Mary Card

Mary was Jesus' mother.
She is very special. We love her as our mother too.
Ask the children to make a card to Mary (use blue paper if possible).
On the outside write 'Mary is Our Mother' or 'Hail Mary, Full of Grace'.
On the inside write, e.g. 'We love you, Mary', 'You are very special', 'The Lord is with you', etc.
Decorate the card.
Encourage the children to give the card to someone special at home.

PRAYERTIME

Sign of the Cross.

Teacher *(as the candle is lit)*
Mother of Jesus, blessed are you.
Mother of Jesus, my mother too.
Help me to live like Jesus
And help me to live like you.

Today we remember in a special way the story of the birth of Jesus.

Close your eyes.
Place your hands on your lap.
Place your feet on the floor.

Imagine that night in Bethlehem. Imagine the joy that Mary must have felt when Jesus was born, a lovely baby boy. Imagine what she might have said to Joseph. With your inside voice ask Mary how she felt that night. Tell her you are glad that she is the mother of Jesus and our mother too.

Open your eyes.

Today, as we say the *Hail Mary*, we will remember the story of that night in Bethlehem when Jesus was born.

Hail Mary, full of grace,
The Lord is with thee.
Blessed art thou among women
And blessed is the fruit of thy womb, Jesus.

All
Holy Mary, Mother of God,
Pray for us sinners,
Now, and at the hour of our death. Amen.

Teacher
Glory be to the Father,
And to the Son,
And to the Holy Spirit.

All
As it was in the beginning,
Is now and ever shall be,
World without end. Amen.

Sign of the Cross.

Note: For the art on Day Four the children will be making a simple one-decade Rosary beads. Ask them to bring in twelve penne pasta shapes and some wool/twine.

Day Four

Continue song: *Mary, Our Mother*

CHATTING

...about blessings

When you were a little baby, did your family bring you to the church? Why did they bring you to church? Do you know any story about the day you were baptised? Who were your godparents? What does the priest do? Has anyone ever been at a baptism? When Jesus was a baby, did Mary and Joseph bring him to the Temple to be blessed? Who remembers the story? Who did they meet there? Who was Anna? Who was Simeon? Let's see how much of the story we remember.

STORY

Anna and Simeon
(Adapted from Luke 2:22-29)

When remembering the story, focus on Mary and Joseph's joy at having Jesus blessed. Mary shared her joy with Anna and Simeon. They were very excited too.

When Anna and Simeon were young, they were very happy about something.

They weren't quite sure YET what it was they were happy about. The only thing they did know about whatever it was, was that they had to wait for it.

Every day and every week and for a whole year, they waited. And do you think, after all that time, they gave up waiting? No, they did not.

Another year went by and another ten years went by and another twenty years went by. Still they waited. They went to the Temple and prayed.

Then they became old, but still they waited.

When they went to the Temple they said a special prayer that God would let them see the very important thing they had waited for before it was time for them to die.

One day as they prayed in the Temple, Simeon asked Anna, 'How long have you been waiting?'

'I have been waiting all my life,' she answered.

'Me too,' said Simeon.

Then they stopped talking and each one of them went off to a different part of the Temple to pray some more.

Before long the doors of the Temple opened. Anna looked up. Simeon looked up. Simeon and Anna walked towards the doors. Simeon held out his arms. Anna smiled with joy. It had come. God had kept his word. At long, long last their waiting was over.

'Praise to you, Lord,' said Anna.

'Blessed be God forever,' said Simeon, and he took the baby in his arms.

And do you know who that very special baby was?

It was baby Jesus.

ACTIVITY

One-Decade Rosary Beads: Part I

You will need:
*   Twelve pasta shapes (penne)
*   Paints to colour the pasta shapes
*   Paintbrushes

Distribute a variety of paint colours to each group. Ask the children to begin to decorate their pasta shapes. Encourage them to use bright colours. Ask the children to paint two of the pasta shapes a completely different colour to any of the other ten pasta shapes. *(These will become the first and last bead.)* Leave the shapes aside to dry.

WORKSHEET

If you wish to use the worksheet or workbook page which accompanies this lesson, this is an appropriate time to do so.

CHATTING

...about the pictures on pages 34, 35 and 37

The Annunciation: Have you seen a picture like this before? Can you remember where? How do you think the milk came to be spilled? How would you describe the look on Mary's face? Imagine you can see what Mary sees. Tell us about it.

The Visitation: Have you seen this picture before? Can you remember where? Who are these two women? Which is Mary and which is Elizabeth? How can you tell? Why are they hugging each other? Imagine you can hear them talking. What are they saying to each other?

The Birth of Jesus: Who are the people in this picture? Why do you think baby Jesus is in Mary's bed? Do you think the baby likes being there? Why? When you go home, ask your mother if she took you into bed beside her when you were born. Do you think the baby looks like his mother? Who do you look like?

The Presentation: Who do you think the old man in the picture is? How would you describe the look on his face? How do you think Simeon feels as he holds the baby? Have you ever waited a long time for something? How did you feel when it finally arrived? How does the baby feel? Do you think he will 'make strange'/be frightened by the old man?

The Finding of the Child Jesus in the Temple: What age do you think Jesus is here? Look at the faces of the men. What might they be thinking? Look at Jesus' face. What might he be thinking? Who do you think the two people in the background are? Why have they come to the Temple?

PRAYERTIME

Sign of the Cross.

Teacher *(as the candle is lit)*
Mother of Jesus, blessed are you.
Mother of Jesus, my mother too.
Help me to live like Jesus
And help me to live like you.

We remember how Mary and Joseph brought Jesus to the Temple to be blessed.
Today, let us ask Mary to pray for us and those we love.

For those we live with at home.

All
Holy Mary, Mother of God,
Pray for us sinners,
Now and at the hour of our death. Amen.

Teacher
For those we work with in school.

All
Holy Mary, Mother of God,
Pray for us sinners,
Now and at the hour of our death. Amen.

Teacher
For our friends.

All
Holy Mary, Mother of God,
Pray for us sinners,
Now and at the hour of our death. Amen.

Teacher
For those who are sick or lonely.

All
Holy Mary, Mother of God,
Pray for us sinners,
Now and at the hour of our death. Amen.

Teacher
Mary, mother of Jesus and our mother too, watch over us and care for us always.

All *(repeating actions after teacher if necessary)*
Hail Mary, full of grace.
(Arms outstretched at the side, palms facing upwards.)

The Lord is with thee.
(Arms lifted high above the head.)

Blessed art thou among women.
(Arms outstretched in front, palms facing upwards.)

And blessed is the fruit of thy womb, Jesus.
(Cradle and gently rock the 'baby' in arms.)

Holy Mary, Mother of God.
(Arms lifted high above the head again.)

Pray for us sinners now, and at the hour of our death.
(Head bowed, hands joined together.)

Amen.
(Hands raised high over head, palms facing upwards.)

Sign of the Cross.

Day Five

Continue song: *Mary, Our Mother*

Chatting

...about the journey to Jerusalem

Have you ever been lost? What happened? How did you feel? Who found you? What did they say when they found you? How do you think they felt? How did you feel then?

Who remembers the story about when Mary, Joseph and Jesus went to Jerusalem, and Jesus got lost? Why did they go? What happened? Where did they find Jesus? What did Mary and Joseph say? Let's see if we can remember the story.

Story

Jesus Goes to Jerusalem
(Adapted from Luke 2:41-50)

When remembering the story, focus on Mary's feelings when she found Jesus – relief, happiness, joy.

Once, when Jesus was twelve years old, Mary and Joseph decided that they would take him to the city for the Passover celebration. Jesus was very excited. The city of Jerusalem was a long way from Nazareth where he lived. Jesus was looking forward to the journey. It would take several days to get there. Many of the families from Nazareth would travel together. Many of his friends would be going too. They could play and have fun along the way. They would sleep out at night. Jesus was very excited.

When the morning came for them to go, Mary and Joseph and Jesus met up with their neighbours at the well in the village square. When everyone was ready, they all set off together. They sang songs along the way. They chatted and talked about other long journeys they had been on, and other Passovers they had celebrated. They stopped every now and then for a rest and something to eat. Jesus was having a wonderful time. He loved going on journeys like this one.

When they reached the city, it was very crowded. Lots of people had come for the Passover. There was noise and bustle everywhere. There were merchants selling food and cloth and spices. There were farmers selling noisy animals. There were people shopping and children playing in the streets. There was one very big building in the city. Joseph explained to Jesus that it was the Temple where the Holy Men met together, and where people went to pray and listen to the stories from the Bible – stories about Moses and Miriam and others. The Temple was the biggest building Jesus had ever seen. He wanted to go inside, but just then some of his friends called to him and he ran off. But he knew he needed to go back to see it.

When the Passover feast was over, Mary, Joseph and all their friends from Nazareth set off on the long journey home. Jesus, however, had decided to stay in Jerusalem. He set off for the Temple.

At first he was a little afraid. The Temple was a very big place. The Holy Men might be cross with him for going in there. But he ran all the way, through side streets and back streets. By the time he reached the Temple he was out of breath. He looked up to the very top of the Temple. There were lots of pigeons roosting on a ledge high up on the Temple wall. They were all asleep except one. It fluttered its wings and looked at Jesus. He thought this little bird was telling him not to be afraid, that he belonged in the Temple too, just as the Holy Men did. He pushed open the door and, holding his breath, he tiptoed inside.

It was dark and warm and quiet and welcoming. 'I'm in! I'm in!' Jesus said to himself as he raised his hands in the air. 'Amen. Amen,' he said.

The Holy Men saw him. They were puzzled. They wondered what a child like this was doing in the Temple. They asked Jesus where he was from, where the rest of his family were, if he was a Jew, and lots more questions. They liked listening to Jesus and learning what he had to say about God.

Just then Mary and Joseph arrived. They had missed Jesus and had been searching everywhere for him. Joseph was cross. Mary was worried. They wanted to know why he had come to the Temple.

'My Father's business,' Jesus answered. No one was quite sure what he meant.

Mary and Joseph looked at each other. Then they took Jesus by the hand. Next day they followed all their friends on the long journey home to Nazareth.

ACTIVITY

One-Decade Rosary Beads: Part II

Each child will need:
- Twelve coloured pasta (penne) shapes
- String/wool (30 ins/75 cms approx.)

Ask the children to begin to string the coloured pasta shapes together, beginning and ending with the pasta shapes that are coloured differently to the other ten shapes. Finally, ask the children to knot the two ends together securely. Do not cut off the ends of the string.

Note: If time allows, you might like to ask the children to make a simple cross for the beads.

For each child you will need:
- A strip of paper/card
- Scissors
- Markers/crayons

Ask the children to draw the outline of a cross (3-4 ins/8-10 cms). Decorate both sides and cut it out.

To attach the cross to the beads:
- Make a small hole at the top of the cross.
- Using the remaining string at the end of the beads, attach and secure the cross.
- Tidy up any stray pieces of string.

PRAYERTIME

Sign of the Cross.

Song: *Mary, Our Mother*

Teacher (*as the candle is lit*)
Mother of Jesus, blessed are you.
Mother of Jesus, my mother too.
Help me to live like Jesus
And help me to live like you.

Today let us pray one decade of the Rosary.

Children could use their beads if they are finished. Divide the class into ten groups and ask each group to call out the Hail Mary while the rest of the class respond.

As we pray the Rosary we remember Mary's joy at being the mother of Jesus. We remember how she shared her good news with other people.

Our Father, who art in heaven
Hallowed be thy name.
Thy kingdom come,
Thy will be done on earth as it is in heaven.

All
Give us this day our daily bread
And forgive us our trespasses
As we forgive those who trespass against us.
And lead us not into temptation
But deliver us from evil. Amen.

Teacher
Hail Mary, full of grace,
The Lord is with thee.

Blessed art thou among women
And blessed is the fruit of thy womb, Jesus.

All
Holy Mary, Mother of God,
Pray for us sinners,
Now, and at the hour of our death. Amen.

(Repeat ten times in all)

Teacher
Glory be to the Father,
And to the Son,
And to the Holy Spirit.

All
As it was in the beginning,
Is now and ever shall be.
World without end. Amen.

Sign of the Cross.

Mary, Our Mother

Patricia Hegarty

Capo 3: Play D

Refrain:

Ma - ry, our moth - er, the Lord is with you.

Final refrain only

Guide us, pro - tect us in all that we do.

1. Ang - el Ga - bri - el said to you,

'You will be moth - er of Je - sus.'

2. With Elizabeth you rejoiced, 'I will be mother of Jesus.'

3. In a manger in Bethlehem you became mother of Jesus.

4. In the temple your baby was blessed, glad to be mother of Jesus.

5. In the temple you found your son, proud to be mother of Jesus.

He did not speak to them except in parables, but he explained everything in private to his disciples.
(Mark 4:34)

The following four lessons focus on laying the foundation for the children's understanding of Eucharist. Catechesis on the Eucharist, however, is not confined to these lessons. In a subtle way, throughout the entire programme, we endeavour to explore with the children the human values and attitudes which are central to an understanding of, and meaningful participation in, Eucharistic celebration, namely: a sense of their own goodness; a sense of being with others; a sense of the meaning of celebration; a sense of listening to others; a capacity to forgive and to be forgiven; a sense of ritual and symbol; a sense of gratitude and thankfulness.

To help the children to understand the ritual and significance of the Eucharist, we focus on four fundamental aspects of the celebration:
shared story – the risen Jesus is with us as we gather with our own stories and listen to the words of Jesus;
shared meal – the risen Jesus gives us the Bread of Life, which is himself;
shared memory – the risen Jesus is with us as we remember his Life, Death and Resurrection;
shared living – the risen Jesus is with us as we gather together in families and communities to live as Jesus asks us to. The Eucharist is a meal in which we remember the Life, Death and Resurrection of Jesus. When we eat the Bread of Life together, we make present the Risen Jesus among us.

In this lesson we focus on Shared Story. Telling stories is an integral part of human living. No matter what the context, be it a wedding, a birthday party or Christmas dinner, when people gather together for a festive occasion, stories get told and retold. Indeed, few stories within our own families would be remembered were it not for such events. We

need to know and to tell the stories of our families, our communities, our culture. People's stories give them meaning and identity; a country's stories shape how it sees itself and others. As followers of Jesus, the stories about Jesus, the stories he told, the things he did and said shape our identity as a Christian community. We need to hear them told and retold.

The Liturgy of the Word is the natural story-telling part of the Eucharistic celebration. In the biblical readings we hear the stories of God's relationship with his people and we are reminded of the life and teachings of Jesus. In the Bible Procession Rituals we prepare the children to understand the importance of the Bible, to take part in a series of rituals, and to begin to appreciate the significance of the Bible as the Word of God.

The children have already been introduced, in a simple way, to the power and importance of language and of story in the lesson *I Want A Word* in the Senior Infants/Primary Two programme, and in the lesson *Jesus – Story-teller* in Term One of this programme. Throughout the year children have heard stories about Jesus and stories that Jesus told. They have listened to the words of Jesus – words of friendship, forgiveness, truth, love, peace – and hopefully have begun to put some of those words into practice in their daily lives. In the Eucharist we hear again some of these stories. We lead the children to an awareness of the Risen Jesus speaking to us in the scripture reading and in the Eucharistic Prayers.

What am I trying to do?

To help the children to recall some of the stories they have already heard about Jesus and to deepen their awareness of the importance of these stories for his followers.

Why?

So that the children will begin to understand the importance of the Liturgy of the Word at Mass as a means of keeping the stories of Jesus alive.

For the Teacher:

A thought before beginning

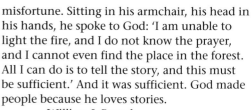

When the great Rabbi Israel Shem Tov saw misfortune threatening the Jews, it was his custom to go into a certain part of the forest to meditate. There he would light a fire, say a special prayer, and the miracle would be accomplished and the misfortune averted. Later, when his disciple, the celebrated Magid of Mezritch, had occasion, for the same reason, to intercede with heaven, he would go to the same place in the forest and say: 'Master of the Universe, listen! I do not know how to light the fire, but I am still able to say the prayer', and again the miracle would be accomplished. Still later, Rabbi Moshe-leib of Sasov, in order to save his people once more, would go into the forest and say, 'I do not know how to light the fire. I do not know the prayer, but I know the place and this must be sufficient.' It was sufficient and the miracle was accomplished. Then it fell to Rabbi Israel of Rizhyn to overcome misfortune. Sitting in his armchair, his head in his hands, he spoke to God: 'I am unable to light the fire, and I do not know the prayer, and I cannot even find the place in the forest. All I can do is to tell the story, and this must be sufficient.' And it was sufficient. God made people because he loves stories.

William J. Bausch

Note: These lessons prepare the children who will be celebrating their First Communion this year for this celebration. Material specifically for the sacramental classes is presented within a closed box. Throughout the prayertimes each day we familiarise the children with the responses at Mass.

Note: During the Bible Procession Ritual on Day One, a child will be invited to read a short phrase from the Bible. It might be helpful to have 'Jesus said, "Whoever welcomes this child welcomes me"' written on a flashcard in advance of the prayertime. The flashcard could then be placed between the covers of the Bible.

Begin to teach the children the responses at Mass.

'The Lord be with you.'
'And also with you.'

'A reading from the Holy Gospel according to_____.'
'Glory to you, O Lord.'

'This is the Gospel of the Lord.'
'Praise to you, Lord Jesus Christ.'

'The Lord be with you.'
'And also with you.'

'Lift up your hearts.'
'We lift them up to the Lord.'

'Let us give thanks to the Lord our God.'
'It is right to give him thanks and praise.'

These prayers are particularly relevant to those preparing for First Communion.

Overview of the Week

Song: *Once Upon a Time/Happy in the Presence*
Activity: *Favourite stories about Jesus*
Recall story: *The Market-Place*
Chatting about the story
Remember and Say
Bible Procession
Ritual

Continue song
Recall story
Poem: *Let the Children Come*
Art: *Story-line*
Prayertime

Continue song, art
Recall story: *The Parable of the Sower*
Prayertime

Continue song
Recall story: *The Good Shepherd*
Worksheet
Prayertime

Bible Procession
Ritual
Now We Know

Day One

SONG

Once Upon a Time

ACTIVITY

Favourite stories about Jesus

This activity asks the children to remember and name favourite stories about Jesus and to describe the story in one word. In this way the children progress from a simple naming of the story to an identification with it from within their own experience. This activity may continue for two or three days.

- Ask the children to tell the class their favourite story about Jesus.
- Ask the children to describe, using one word, what kind of story their favourite story is, e.g. it's a story about love/friendship/families/food/children/bread.
- Encourage the class to choose, from the

stories which have been heard, the favourite class story.

or

Make a graph of the children's favourite stories about Jesus.

Recall story: *The Market-Place*

STORY

The Market-Place
(Adapted from Luke 9:46-48)

Every Market Day the children went off to town with the grown-ups. It was their favourite day of the week. On Market Day the town square was full of the noise of goats and sheep with their little kids and lambs, and shepherds. It was packed with bright coloured stalls selling everything from cloth and wool, to furniture, to footwear, to bright coloured baubles and knick-knacks. The air was heavy with the scent of everything from spices and perfumes, to huge round smelly old cheeses.

Today is Market Day for Reuben and Rachel and their friends. They have arranged to meet together in the square beside the well. The grown-ups have little time for the children on Market Day. The grown-up men are buying and selling and making deals. Today Reuben and Rachel and their friends wander around, exploring everything, wondering at everything, laughing, chatting, playing and making the very most of every moment of their day in the busy market-place.

Today a different man comes to the market-place. The grown-ups are so engrossed in their work that they do not notice him at first. The children spot him sitting in the middle of the square, watching and wondering at all that is going on around him. After a moment or two he stands up and begins to speak in a loud voice. It takes some time before the grown-ups become aware of him. Those who stop to listen, hear him speak about a kingdom – 'The Kingdom of God' he calls it. He says that in this kingdom, as well as loving their friends, people love those who are not their friends. In this kingdom everyone is happy, everyone is treated fairly. He says that there is peace everywhere throughout this kingdom. Now more people begin to listen attentively.

'I'd like to live in such a kingdom. Where is it? How can I get there?' asks one merchant.

'The Kingdom of God is not like other kingdoms,' this unusual man says. 'It is not any particular place. God's kingdom exists anywhere and everywhere where people love each other, forgive each other, treat each other fairly and live together in peace.'

'That sounds like a strange place indeed,' says a woman from the crowd. 'Who rules there, who is the boss, who is the greatest in this kingdom?'

At this, the man steps outside of the crowd which has encircled him. He walks over to where Reuben and Rachel and their friends are playing happily together, unnoticed by anyone except the man. 'Will you come with me for a moment?' he asks, 'I need your help.' The children stop their game and take his hands. He leads them into the middle of the crowd of grown-ups.

'You ask me who is the greatest in God's Kingdom,' he says. 'I tell you,' – the whole market-place falls silent and waits for his answer – 'Children are the greatest in God's Kingdom.' The grown-ups are stunned. The children laugh and run back to their game.

CHATTING

...about the story

You have heard this story before – can you remember when? Do you like hearing some stories again and again? This is a story about a man who was different. Do you know who that unusual man was? You have heard other stories about Jesus. Can you remember any of them, or bits of them? Let's tell some other stories about Jesus. When we go to Mass we hear stories about Jesus. Can you remember any story or part of a story that you heard being read from the Bible at Mass? Why do you think we keep telling stories about Jesus every time we go to Mass? What do you think would happen to all these stories if we stopped telling them, and reading them, and listening to them? Perhaps stories that are never told or read or listened to die – is it possible for stories to die? If stories are things that can die, then they must also be able to live. Would you agree or disagree? Why? How do you think a story could be kept alive? Do you think that telling and reading and listening and sharing stories about Jesus might have something to do with keeping them alive? Can you think why we would want to keep these special stories alive?

> Jesus was a story-teller. At Mass
> we tell and listen to his stories.

Remember and Say

Sharing stories, remembering stories,
Telling and listening too.
Jesus did this all of his life;
At Mass, it's what you and I do.

PRAYERTIME

Bible Procession Ritual

Take the Bible from its place in the classroom. Form a simple procession and process to a table where the Bible and the candle are placed reverently. Children bow and return to their seats.

Song: *Once Upon a Time (sing or listen to tape/CD)*

The teacher lights the candle.

Sign of the Cross.

Teacher
Note: If time allows, you might like to repeat the following and invite other children to come forward, raise the Bible and read the biblical phrase.

Jesus loved to tell stories. One day a large crowd gathered around him.
————— *(name reader)* will read the Word of God for us today.

The teacher takes the Bible from the table and ceremoniously hands it to the child.
The child faces the class, holding the Bible.

Teacher
We know that God is with us when we read from the Bible at Mass. We listen to God's word in the Bible. God is talking to us in the words we hear from the Bible. Imagine Jesus standing there talking to the big crowd. He is telling stories about God's kingdom. People don't fully understand what he means. He stops to see how he will explain what he is saying. Imagine him looking around and noticing the children.
Today as we read from our class Bible we know that God is with us in a special way.

Reader
The Lord be with you.

All
And also with you.

Teacher
A reading from the Holy Gospel according to St Luke.

All
Glory to you , O Lord.

Reader
Jesus said: 'Whoever welcomes this child welcomes me.'
The Gospel of the Lord *(raising the Bible).*

All
Praise to you, Lord Jesus Christ.

For all God's stories that we tell,
For all God's stories that we read,
For all God's stories that we hear,
We thank you, God. Amen.

Sign of the Cross.

Day Two

Continue song: *Once Upon a Time*

Recall story: *The Market-Place*

POEM

Let the Children Come

Once upon a time
We were very, very small
And all the other kids at school
Were very, very tall.
Our teacher told a story
Of a seed who grew and grew
And we listened, and we wondered,
If we would grow up too.

Once upon a time
In a land so far away
The grown-ups told the children 'go',
But Jesus told them 'stay'.
'Let the children come,' he said,
And drying up their tears,
He told them all that God had made
Was wonderful, and theirs.
Christy Kenneally

ART

Story-Line

Note: This artwork may take two days to complete.

Ask the children to remember their favourite stories about Jesus which they were chatting about yesterday and to imagine some character in one of the stories. What did she/he look like? What was his/her name?

Each child will need:
- Sheet of stiff paper
- Selection of scraps of old material, wool, etc.
- Adhesive
- Crayons/markers/paints

Ask the children to draw any character out of one of the stories about Jesus. Cut out the outline.
Using the material available to them, decorate the character.
Write the character's name on the back.

To display
Make a simple line with twine, onto which the children's characters will be attached/hung/pegged.
When the children are finished making their story-character, ask each child to come forward and to name the character for the rest of the class as the teacher places each character on the 'Story-Line'.

or

Ask the children to draw a picture or to make a poster telling people about their favourite 'Jesus' story.

PRAYERTIME

Sign of the Cross.

Teacher (*as the candle is lit*)
God is our light.
The light of our lives.

Today let us give thanks to God for all the stories about Jesus that we have heard.
As we say: Time and time and time again.
Praise God, praise God.

For the story about the woman at the well.

All
Time and time and time again.
Praise God, praise God.

Teacher
For the story about the sower.

All
Time and time and time again.
Praise God, praise God.

Teacher
For the story about the market-place.

All
Time and time and time again.
Praise God, praise God.

Teacher
For all Jesus' stories.

All
Time and time and time again.
Praise God, praise God.

Teacher
Close your eyes. Remember your favourite story about Jesus. Think of what your story was about. With your special inside voice tell God the name of your story.

We pray together:

All
For all the stories that we tell,
For all the stories that we read,
For all the stories that we hear,
We thank you, God. Amen.

Sign of the Cross.

Day Three

Continue song: *Once Upon a Time*

Continue art: *Story-Line (if not already completed)*

Recall story: *The Parable of the Sower*

STORY

The Parable of the Sower
(Adapted from Matthew 13:4-10)

One day, a sower with a bag of seeds went out to sow. The sower scattered seeds here and scattered seeds there.

Some seeds fell at the side of the road. Hungry birds came and ate them all up.

Some seeds fell on stony ground where the soil was very shallow. These seeds sprouted very quickly. But their roots did not go deep, so the shoots soon withered and died.

Some seeds fell among the briars and thorns. As the thorns and briars grew bigger and stronger, they choked the sower's seeds, so that they did not have room to grow and they soon died.

Some seeds fell on good, rich soil. They put down deep roots. They sprouted and grew tall and strong. Here in the rich ground the sower's seeds produced a plentiful crop.

PRAYERTIME

Meditation

Sign of the Cross.

Teacher
Close your eyes.

Place your hands gently on your lap and your feet on the floor.
Listen to your heart beat.

Imagine that you are in a library full of all kinds of books – big books, thin books, small books, heavy books. As you wander around the library you recognise some storybooks. You have heard some of these stories lots of times. Pick up one of these storybooks. You see by the little sticker inside the book that the book has been borrowed from the library by a lot of people. You are glad because you know that stories love to be read and told! Then you notice some very dusty books … they look rather old. You go on your tippeytoes and you take one down. It's very dusty. Carefully you open the cover … this story hasn't been borrowed for a very, very long time. You feel sad … maybe this story has died because nobody has told it recently. As you wonder if it has died, you begin to read the story for yourself … each page pulls you into it, begging you to read on and on and on. It's a wonderful story. What story do you think it might be? Decide upon one from all the stories that you know. You want to keep this story alive. You wonder what you can do. Then you think 'I know, I'll tell it to someone'. Think of someone you know who would love this story. You run out of the library and you take this person by the hand. You sit down together and you tell the story. Imagine yourself telling the story.

With your special inside voice thank God for your lost story.
Let us thank God for all stories that are kept alive by being told.

Open your eyes.
Relax.

Sign of the Cross.

Day Four

Continue song: *Once Upon a Time*

WORKSHEET

If you wish to use the worksheet or workbook page which accompanies this lesson, this is an appropriate time to do so.

Recall story: *The Good Shepherd*

STORY

The Good Shepherd
(Adapted from Luke 15:3-7)

Once there was a shepherd, a good shepherd. He had one hundred sheep. He loved every single one of the sheep in his flock. He knew the name of each one of his sheep. In the morning when he took his sheep out to graze for the day, he would call each one of them by name. The good shepherd always walked ahead of his sheep so that if there was any danger they could hide behind him. The sheep knew that their shepherd loved them and would never let them come to harm. They followed him day after day, up hill and down.

One day the good shepherd was out with his flock. He found a place for them to graze. He made sure the sheep were all happy, then he sat down to watch over them. He wanted to make sure that they were all safe so he began to count to see if his sheep were all there. When he had finished he realised that one sheep was missing. He was very worried. He looked all around. He called the lost sheep's name. There was no answer. He called again. There was still no answer.

The good shepherd loved his lost sheep. He wanted to find it. He was unhappy for it to be separated from him and the rest of his flock. He decided he must go and look for it. He made the rest of the sheep gather in together so that they would keep each other company while he went off to look for the one lost sheep. The sheep knew he would come back to them. So off he went in search of his lost sheep.

He searched and searched. He called and called. He travelled up hill and down. He looked everywhere. Then, he saw something. He looked closer. There it was. His lost sheep, he had found it. He called its name. He ran to it and when he got there he picked the sheep up. He checked to see if it was all right and to make sure that it wasn't hurt in any way. Then he carried it on his shoulders back to the flock. Now the good shepherd was very happy again.

That evening he led all his flock back home. Then when they were all safe and sound for the night he went around to his friends' houses. He told them, 'A terrible thing happened today. I lost one of my sheep. I was so worried. I was so sad and lonely. Even though I have ninety-nine other sheep, I love each one of them. So I went to look for my sheep and found it. Now I am so happy again. I want to invite you all to come to my house tonight and celebrate with me. My lost sheep is found. Thank goodness.'

PRAYERTIME

Sign of the Cross.

Teacher
Today we light our candle.
The Bible is God's Word. When we listen to the Word of God from the Bible we listen to God. We know that God is with us when we listen to stories in the Bible.
We ask God's blessing as we share stories with others.

All
For all God's stories that we tell.

Teacher
May almighty God bless us.

All
For all God's stories that we read.

Teacher
May almighty God bless us.

All
For all God's stories that we hear.

Teacher *(using a simple open-hand gesture)*
May almighty God bless us.
The Father, the Son and the Holy Spirit. Amen.

Sign of the Cross.

Day Five

PRAYERTIME

Bible Procession Ritual

Take the Bible from its place in the classroom. Form a simple procession. As one child carries the Bible and another child carries the unlit candle (other items like flowers, incense stick, cloth, etc could also be carried in the procession), process to a table where the Bible and the candle are placed reverently. Children bow and return to their seats.

The teacher lights the candle. You may also like to burn an incense stick or some grains of incense.

Sign of the Cross.

Song: *Once Upon a Time*

Teacher
Note: If time allows, you might like to repeat the following and invite other children to come forward, raise the Bible and read the biblical phrase.

A crowd gathered around Jesus one day as he told a story.
_____ *(name reader)* will read the Word of God for us today.

The child is invited to come forward to read from the Bible.
The teacher takes the Bible from the table and ceremoniously hands it to the child.
The child faces the class, holding the Bible.

As we read from the Bible we remember that the Bible is the Word of God. We know that God is with us. We know that God is with us in a special way when we read from the Bible. Today we listen to a story that Jesus told. People came from everywhere to hear Jesus. They loved to hear him telling stories. One day he told a story about a shepherd who lost one of his sheep. The Good Shepherd searched and searched until he found the lost sheep. Then he carried it home, called in all his friends and celebrated.

Reader
The Lord be with you.

All
And also with you.

Reader
This reading is from the Gospel according to St Luke.

All
Glory to you, O Lord.

Reader
'Rejoice with me for I have found my sheep that was lost.'
The Gospel of the Lord *(raising the Bible)*.

All
Praise to you, Lord Jesus Christ.

Teacher
For all God's stories that we tell,
For all God's stories that we read,
For all God's stories that we hear,
We thank you, God. Amen.

Sign of the Cross.

NOW WE KNOW

Q. What do we listen to at Mass?

A. At Mass we listen to the words of Jesus.

Once Upon a Time

Christy Kenneally

1. Tell a sto - ry, oh will you tell us please, why the tree wears a crown of gold - en leaves. Why do they curl up in aut - umn and let go to rus - tle down be - low? Let us hear it in once up- on a time.

2. Tell a story of Jesus long ago,
   And the stories he told so he could show his friends that
   Love is a special thing to share
   And in that love he's there.
   Let us hear it in once upon a time.

3. Tell the story how Jesus went to sow,
   How he scattered his words so we would know
   That love can grow from the smallest little seed
   Through every loving deed.
   Let us hear it in once upon a time.

Happy in the Presence

Bernard Sexton

Capo 2: Play D

Hap-py in the pres-ence of the Lord. We
come and sing— our praise to lord Je - sus,
Hap-py in the pres-ence of the Lord. We
come and sing— our praise to the Lord— of
all.
1. Come and share the bread— of life,—
bread that will feed— us, help and pro - tect— us,

285

come and share the sto-ries of old,——

sto-ries of Je - sus, his work and his world.——

2. Come to share the mem'-ries we've had,——

Hap-py days, sad days, days full of joy,——

Come to tell the Lord that we love——

We'll live the life—— he told us to live.——

Lesson 3: A Time To Share Meals

Then he took a loaf of bread,
and when he had given thanks, he broke it
and gave it to them, saying,
'This is my body, which is given for you.
Do this in remembrance of me.'
He did the same with the cup
after supper, saying,
'This cup that is poured out for you
is the new covenant in my blood.'
(Luke 22:19-20)

In this lesson we explore the children's experience of sharing meals as opposed to simply eating food. Nowadays, while much attention is given to food and consumption, sharing meals is often neglected. A shared meal is a sign of friendship, trust, hospitality, unity and love. A shared meal strengthens and deepens the relationship between people. People come together to share meals when they wish to celebrate important events in their lives. To do so, they turn to what is familiar. Old rituals take on a new meaning when a significant experience is brought to them. Children naturally and spontaneously enter into such rituals, for instance, when they celebrate birthdays with their families and friends. They experience the joy of such celebrations: looking forward to the event, giving and receiving presents, the shared experience, the happiness of being together, the memories.

Family celebrations provide children with experiences which, when reflected upon, provide them with a framework for a basic understanding of the Eucharist. In family celebrations the people come together; they focus on and remember the event they are celebrating; they tell stories; they remember those who are absent; they share food; they sing.

For Jesus, the sharing of food with others was significant throughout his entire life. In his sharing of meals a space was created where people found themselves loved, accepted,

forgiven. There was always enough for everyone and no one was left out. It was in the context of a shared meal that he gave himself to his apostles in bread and wine and promised that he would be with them always. When we come together to celebrate the Eucharist, the Risen Jesus is present in a very special way. The presence of Jesus in the bread and wine is called the real presence. The bread and wine are changed into the body and blood of Jesus. They become Jesus himself. When we come together to celebrate the Eucharist, we are doing what Jesus asked his disciples to do, and in so doing we share his real presence in the bread and wine.

Once again it is suggested that, where appropriate, you invite the parents or guardians of the children, the school chaplain, or the priest or other parish representative, to take part in the Prayer Service (Shared Meals Celebration) at the end of the week. How, where and when this Prayer Service will take place depends upon what best suits you in your own circumstances.

If you decide to have the service, you will need to invite the various people who will be attending. Decide who will be the leader; it may be you, the school principal or one of the priests or pastoral representatives who will be attending.

What am I trying to do?

To explore the children's experience of food and of eating and to differentiate between simply eating food and sharing meals.

Why?

So that we might awaken in the children an awareness of the Eucharistic symbols and ritual overtones of every shared meal. In doing this we lay down a foundation from which they can begin to understand the real presence of Jesus in the consecrated bread and wine and the significance of what we do when we celebrate the Eucharist.

FOR THE TEACHER:

A thought before beginning

The Promise

I imagine the scene of the Last
    Supper...
as if I am present there myself.

I observe Jesus as he takes bread in his hands,
blesses and distributes it.
When I receive it from his hands
I think what I want this bread to be for me...

Then Jesus speaks with us, his disciples.
His words are an essential part
of the eating of that bread,
so I listen carefully:

He first gives us a new command
– to love one another as he has loved us.
I pray that this bread will increase
my capacity to love...
and I think what love has come to mean for
    me
and what place I give it in my life...

If we eat this bread,
this body which is broken,
we shall necessarily share
in the passion and death of Jesus.
I hear him prophesy that we will be
    persecuted,
even by our own...
So I pray for the courage that sustained the
    martyrs
and the strength to live and speak as he did...

He makes a gift at this holy meal: Peace.
Not the peace of the world, he says,
but his peace.
I ponder on the meaning of those words...
and I ask for that gift for me
and for those I love...

Jesus speaks long and late into the night.
Supper is finally over.
Now he takes a cup of wine.
I listen to the words he utters over it...
The cup is passed from hand to hand
and when it is my turn to drink
I pray that I shall be intoxicated
and lose myself in love...
    Anthony de Mello SJ

*We continue to teach the responses
at Mass. Begin to teach the children
the responses at Communion and
the Communion Prayers:*

'The Body of Christ.'
Amen.

Prayer before Communion
Lord Jesus, come to me.
Lord Jesus, give me your love.
Lord Jesus, come to me and give
    me yourself.

Lord Jesus, friend of children,
    come to me.
Lord Jesus, you are my Lord and
    my God.
Praise to you, Lord Jesus Christ.

Prayer after Communion
Lord Jesus, I love and adore you.
You're a special friend to me.
Welcome, Lord Jesus, O
    welcome.
Thank you for coming to me.

Thank you, Lord Jesus, O thank
    you
For giving yourself to me.
Make me strong to show your
    love
Wherever I may be.

Be near me, Lord Jesus, I ask you
    to stay
Close by me forever and love
    me, I pray.
Bless all of us children in your
    loving care
And bring us to heaven to live
    with you there.

I'm ready now, Lord Jesus,
To show how much I care.
I'm ready now to give your love
At home and everywhere.

*These prayers are particularly
relevant to those children preparing
for First Communion.*

Overview of the Week

Song: *Eat This Bread/Céad Míle Fáilte Romhat*
Activity: *Shared Meals Album*
Story: *Names in the Pot*
Chatting about the story
Prayertime

Continue song
Recall story
Chatting about the story continued
Worksheet
Activity: *Shared Meals Album*
Prayertime

Continue song
Chatting about breakfast- and dinner-times
Recall story: *The Last Supper*
Remember and Say
Activity: *Shared Meals Album*
Prayertime

Continue song
Chatting about special meals
Chatting about the picture
Poem: *Sharing Meals*
Art: *Jesus is the Bread of Life*
Prayertime

Shared Meals Celebration
Now We Know

Day One

SONG

Eat This Bread

Céad Míle Fáilte Romhat

ACTIVITY

Shared Meals Album

Ask the children to begin to bring in photos (alternatively, they could draw pictures) of their favourite meals which they have shared with others. As the week goes by, use a scrapbook to create a class album of favourite shared meals, adding to it gradually. As each picture is added, the child to whom it belongs could be asked to tell the class about the meal. Where, when, and why it happened? Who was there? Was it a happy time? Why? etc.

STORY

Note: This story captures something of the essence of sharing meals. The challenge Jesus puts to us is that we make an effort to use what we have in such a way that no one is left wanting. The woman in the story does not appear to have much food, but using it as she does, she makes enough for everybody.

Names In The Pot

Old Mother Hubbard
Went to the cupboard
– Everyone knows for what!
It wasn't quite bare
But all that was there
Was a bag of potatoes – and that's that!

Mother Hubbard took out a small pot and began to wash the potatoes.
'One potato, two potatoes,
Three potatoes, four –
Two for Doggy, two for me
And one potato more!' she counted.

Just as she was setting two places, one at the table and one beside it, who should arrive into her kitchen but Jack and Jackie Spratt. Although they differed over what sort of meat they ate, both of them loved potatoes. They saw the pot and they saw the potatoes.
'Put our names in the pot too,' they said, and sat down.

289

'Six potatoes, seven potatoes,
Drop them in the pot,
Along with all the others
And surely, that's the lot,' Mother Hubbard
counted.

She had just finished setting two more places
at the table when who should arrive but the
Knave and Queen of Hearts. The Queen's tarts
were all gone, so when she and the Knave saw
the pot and the potatoes they said, 'Put our
names in the pot too.'

'Eight potatoes, nine potatoes,
Ten potatoes, oh dear,
I'll need to use a bigger pot
If anyone else eats here,' Mother Hubbard
counted.

She had just finished setting two more places
at the table when who should arrive but Little
Tommy Tucker. He saw the pot and he saw the
potatoes. 'I can sing for my supper,' he said,
'but I can sing even better for my dinner. Put
my name in the pot too,' he sang at the top of
his voice.

Mother Hubbard took all the potatoes out of
the small pot and put them in her middle-
sized pot. She counted:

'One potato, two potatoes,
Three potatoes, four –
Two for Doggy, two for me,
And one potato more.
Six potatoes, seven potatoes,
Eight potatoes, nine –
The list of names in this old pot
Grows longer all the time.
Ten potatoes, eleven potatoes,
Twelve potatoes, stop!
Not another single spud
Will fit inside this pot!'

She had just finished setting a place for
Tommy Tucker when who should arrive
into her kitchen but The Old Shoe Woman
and all her children. They were very
hungry, they hadn't eaten since supper the
night before, and even that was – well, you
know what it was, don't you? They saw the
pot and they saw the potatoes. 'Put my
name in the pot,' said one, 'and mine... and
mine... and mine,' they all said one after
the other. Mother Hubbard took out her

biggest pot. She counted from the
beginning again:

'One potato, two potatoes,
Three potatoes, four –
Two for Doggy, two for me,
And one potato more.
Six potatoes, seven potatoes,
Eight potatoes, nine –
The list of names in this old pot
Grows longer all the time.
Ten potatoes, eleven potatoes,
Twelve potatoes, stop!'
Not another single spud
Would fit in the middle-sized pot.
'Thirteen potatoes, fifteen potatoes,
Eighteen potatoes, twenty –
Oh here,' she said, as she tipped in the lot,
'Might as well have plenty!'

Mother Hubbard tipped every last potato into
the sink, washed them and crammed the lot
into her giant-sized pot. She set out every last
knife and fork and plate in the house. When
the potatoes were boiled she piled them on a
huge plate in the middle of the table. You have
never seen such a mountain of potatoes!
Everyone ate their hearty fill. As they ate, they
chatted and laughed and talked, remembering
old times and old stories. Such a feast they
had.

CHATTING

...about the story

Why do you think Mother Hubbard's
cupboard always tends to be bare, or almost
bare? What does this tell you about Mother
Hubbard? She is called 'Mother' Hubbard, yet
she only seems to have her dog for company –
why might that be? If there were others in her
family, where do you think they might be
now? How do you think she might feel if her
dog wasn't around? Does Mother Hubbard
remind you of anyone?

Mother Hubbard has lots of company in this
story. How do you think she feels about

having so many visitors just at dinner-time? Have you ever had unexpected visitors arrive into your home at dinner or another meal-time? What happened? What do you think about Mother Hubbard using her whole bag of potatoes to share with her neighbours and friends? Which do you think Mother Hubbard would enjoy best – eating all her potatoes by herself, or sharing them among her neighbours and friends? Why? Do you think she enjoys sharing a meal, talking and chatting, sharing her news, listening to the stories the others might tell, remembering other times they met and ate together, etc? Which would you prefer? Why? Do you do all of these things at times during the meals in your home? Tell us about them.

Since there were so many people to be fed all at once, why do you think they didn't go into different rooms? Why did she set all the places around the table?

If there was no food in the cupboards in your home, what would happen? How do you think people who have empty cupboards and no money to buy more food manage? Do you think there are any people who have no money to buy food? Why is that? What do you think Mother Hubbard will do when dinnertime comes the next day?

PRAYERTIME

Sign of the Cross.

Teacher *(as the candle is lit)*
God is our light.
The light of our lives.

Today we thank God for the food we have to eat that helps us to grow and keeps us alive and healthy. We pray:

Teacher *(children repeating)*
For food to eat
And food to share,
We thank you, God,
For your love and care.
Amen.

Sign of the Cross.

Continue song: *Eat This Bread/Céad Míle Fáilte Romhat*

Recall story: *Names in the Pot*

CHATTING

...about the story continued

Do you think the people in Mother Hubbard's house that day would have known each other or do you think Mother Hubbard would have had to introduce them? Have you ever sat down to a table where there were people you did not know? Where was that – at a wedding or a party? Tell us about it. Perhaps you didn't know them when the meal began, but by the time it was over you had got to know them? When people share a meal they sit down together. But as well as eating the food, what else do they do? What kind of things might they talk about?

Do you think there is a difference between 'eating food' and 'sharing a meal'? For example, imagine you went to town with your family one day, you did your shopping and then you went somewhere to get something to eat. Imagine the place was very busy. Imagine you had to share a table with people you did not know. You eat your food and they eat their food. You do not talk to each other – there is no need. Then you could say, 'I am eating food with other people, but I am not sharing a meal.' Would you agree? How do you think you would know when you were simply 'eating food' with others and when you were actually 'sharing a meal with others'? Do you think the people in the story were eating food with each other or sharing a meal together? Why?

WORKSHEET

If you wish to use the worksheet or workbook page which accompanies this lesson, this is an appropriate time to do so.

ACTIVITY

Continue to work on the Shared Meals Album. Invite the children to add their photo/picture and to chat about it with the class.

PRAYERTIME

Sign of the Cross.

Teacher (*as the candle is lit*)
God is our light.
The light of our lives.

Meal times can be special times. Times when we sit down with others, eat our food and listen and chat to one another. Let us thank God for these times today as we pray:

All
Blessed be God forever.

Teacher
Blessed are you, Lord, God of all creation.
In your goodness you give us all the food we eat.
We bless you for all the food that comes from the earth.
We ask you to bless the people who make and prepare our food.
Bless us and all the people we share our food with.

All
Blessed be God forever.

Teacher
Blessed are you, Lord, God of all creation.
In your goodness you give us all we drink.
Bless us and all the people we share our drinks with.

All
Blessed be God forever.

Teacher
For the people who share food and drink with us.
Close your eyes. Think of some of the people you have shared food and drink with this week. With your inside voice name these people. Thank God for them.
We ask God to bless them.

All
Blessed be God forever. Amen.

Sign of the Cross.

Day Three

Continue song: *Eat This Bread/Céad Míle Fáilte Romhat*

CHATTING

...about breakfast- and dinner-times

What is your first meal of the day? Have some of your family already left for the day by the time you get up? Who eats breakfast with you? Do you talk and chat with anyone while you are eating? Where do you eat breakfast? Do you have time to sit at the table or do you tend to be in too much of a hurry? Why might you be in a hurry? Is breakfast-time different on the days when you aren't rushing out to school – like on Saturdays or during the holidays? Tell us about those breakfast-times. Which of these two kinds of breakfast-times do you enjoy most? Why?

When do the people in your home have 'the dinner'? Tell me about the dinner in your home? Do you sit at a table? What is on the table? Have you ever set a table? What do you need to set the table? Do you sit down to eat dinner? What happens while you are eating? Do you talk? What kind of things might you talk about? Eating and chatting seem to go together? Why do you think that is? Do you have dinner every day in your home? Perhaps there are days now and again when no one feels like having dinner. What might you have instead? Have you ever had a take-away? Are there other things your family might do on days when there is no dinner?

Who generally makes the dinner in your home? Who clears up afterwards? Tell me about a time you helped with the preparing or the clearing-up. When you go home today, talk to your mammy or daddy or whoever makes the dinner. Ask them to tell you what it is like to make a dinner every day; about how they choose what to make for the dinner; if they ever get tired making dinners; if they think dinner is important. Thank them for all the dinners they have made for you.

Recall story: *The Last Supper*

STORY

The Last Supper

On the first day of the Passover celebration, Jesus, his friends and his followers discussed the preparations they would have to make for the Passover meal. Jesus sent some of them to a house that he knew in the city of Jerusalem. There they prepared a big room and food for the meal. They were very busy. They set out the room. They had to get some herbs and a one-year-old lamb. They had to make some unleavened bread and buy some red wine. When Jesus and the others arrived, everything was ready.

When evening came, everyone sat down to eat the Passover meal. They said special prayers, they shared their special story about Moses leading the people out of Egypt, and they shared their special memory of things that had happened to their people in times past. This Passover was the same as every other Passover until, as they were sharing the special food and wine, Jesus did something that was very different to every other Passover. He took the unleavened bread *(bread which hasn't risen)* and blessed it and broke it and shared it out among his friends and followers, and he said, 'This is my body, take and eat it.' Then he took the cup of wine. He blessed it and then he said, 'This is my blood, take and drink it.'

Jesus' friends and followers had never seen this done, or heard these words spoken, at a Passover meal before. This was new. At first they weren't sure what Jesus meant, but he said to them, 'Do this in memory of me.'

When the supper was over, Jesus and his friends went off to a hill nearby, called The Mount of Olives, to pray.

At Mass, we don't just eat food together. We share a meal, we share food – the Bread of Life which is the Risen Jesus. We also share our lives, our thoughts and our worries by praying for each other; we share stories and memories about the Life, Death and Resurrection of Jesus; we give thanks for all our gifts; and as we leave we offer to share peace with one another and amongst our community and our world.

Remember and Say

Jesus is the Bread of Life
We eat at Mass together.
Jesus gives his life for us
Always and forever.

ACTIVITY

Continue to work on the Shared Meals Album.
Invite the children to add their photo/picture
and to chat with the class about it.

PRAYERTIME

Sign of the Cross.

Teacher *(as the candle is lit)*
God is our light.
The light of our lives.

We thank God for all the food we have eaten
and for the people who prepared the food.

Close your eyes.
Think of the person who makes dinners for
you day after day after day. *(Pause)*
Think of the person who calls you when your
dinner is ready. *(Pause)*
Think of the person who washes all the dishes
when your dinner is over. *(Pause)*

We thank God for the food we have to share
every day.
In our inside world we thank God for all the
people we have thought about.
We ask God to bless them and keep them safe.
As we say together:

All
For food to eat
And food to share,
We thank you, God,
For your love and care.
Amen.

Sign of the Cross.

Continue song: *Eat This Bread/Céad Míle Fáilte
Romhat*

CHATTING

...about special meals

We have different kinds of meals every day.
Sometimes we might have a little nibble or a
piece of bread by ourselves; sometimes we eat
a snack or a meal with others; sometimes we
sit down to a set table and eat with friends or
family; and sometimes, particularly on special
occasions, we go out for a meal. Tell us about a
time when you have gone out for a meal.
What was the special occasion – a wedding, a
christening, a birthday, an anniversary, some
special celebration? Why do you think we
often celebrate special occasions with a shared
meal? When you are eating with your family
this evening, perhaps you could ask them why
meals and chat and special occasions seem to
'go together'. Perhaps as you are eating you
can remember special meals and special
occasions your family have shared together.

CHATTING

...about the picture on page 39

Can you name any of the people round the
table? How many potatoes do you think are in
the pot altogether? Do you think there will be
enough for everyone? Imagine you are among
the children looking in the window. What are
they saying? What do you think the people
round the table are talking about?

POEM

Sharing Meals

Light the candles. Blow them out.
Happy Birthday. Hear them shout.
Cut a slice for everyone,
Birthday treats are so much fun.

Gathered round the candlelight
Happy faces, shining bright.
Christmas dinner, Christmas tree,
Memories for you and me.

At a table, long ago,
Friends of Jesus, sad and low,
Jesus gently sharing bread.
'Remember me this way,' he said.
Christy Kenneally

ART

Jesus is the Bread of Life

Make banners for the classroom with the words 'Jesus is the Bread of Life'. Ask each child to make one letter of the phrase. Ask the children to use big letters, to colour them in and cut the letters out. Stick all the letters together to make the banner. You may like to make more than one banner.

PRAYERTIME

Note: *Place the Shared Meals Album in a prominent position.*

Meditation

Sign of the Cross.

Teacher
Close your eyes.
Place your hands on your lap.
Listen to your breath as it goes gently in and out of your body.

Imagine that you are alive, there in the land where Jesus lived. It's evening time. You are walking along the road. As you do you see some people going into a house. They seem to be carrying some food. Perhaps they are going to have a meal. You wait and watch and wonder.

You watch the lamps being lit in the house. You go to the window. The people are sitting around a table. You recognise Jesus. Yes, and you recognise his friends. You've seen them together before. You hear them say the prayers. You've heard those prayers before. You've heard your family pray those prayers on special nights. Then as the meal goes on Jesus takes bread. He blesses it and breaks it and gives it to them to eat. They eat it. He then takes some wine, blesses that and gives it to them to drink. They drink it.

They talk together. They seem to be sad. You're not sure why but you know that this must be a very special meal. As you turn to go you know that you will always remember what you've seen.

Open your eyes.
Stretch.

Teacher *(raising the Shared Meals Album)*
We thank God for the meals we have shared.
We ask God to bless all the people we have shared meals with.
We think of those who are hungry and have no food.
We ask God to help us to share with others.
We pray:

All
Our Father…

Sign of the Cross.

Day Five

PRAYERTIME

Read meditation Part on previous page. P

Shared Meals Celebration

Hang the banners that the children have made around the classroom. Place the table with the lighted candle in a central position. Place the children's 'Shared Meals Album' beside the candle.

In preparation for the ritual, place some bread or a portion of cake on the table. If possible, arrange the classroom so that the children and their parents/guardians are gathered around the table.

Sign of the Cross.

All
Sing: *Eat this Bread*

Teacher *(as the candle is lit)*
The Lord be with you.

All
And also with you.

Teacher
Story: *The Last Supper*

You are all very welcome here today as we gather together to share bread with one another. Bread nourishes us and keeps us healthy. It helps us to grow strong limbs and bodies. Today we ask God to be with us as we come to share this bread with one another:

Leader holds the cake of bread in his/her hands.

Blessed are you, Lord, God of all creation. Through your goodness we have this bread to offer.
Work of human hands.
Bless this bread. May it make us strong. May it remind us always to share with those who are hungry.

All
Bless us, O God, as we sit together.
Bless the food we eat today.
Bless the hands that made the food.
Bless us, O God. Amen.

Teacher
On the night before he died, Jesus blessed the bread and broke it and gave it to his disciples. Today as we cut/break our cake of bread, we give thanks to God.

Teacher cuts/breaks the bread.

All
We praise you, we bless you, we thank you.

Teacher
Today we share bread with one another.
As we prepare to share our food today we ask God to bless the food and to bless us as we share it.
Bless this food. May it nourish us body and soul.

Teacher invites the children to come forward and he/she hands each of them a piece of bread. Each child returns and breaks the bread with his/her parents/guardians. Each person waits until all have a piece before eating.

All eat the bread together.

All
Thank you, God, for the food we have eaten.
Thank you, God, for all our friends.
Thank you, God, for everything.
Thank you, God. Amen.

Teacher
May we be nourished by the food we have eaten.

You might like to invite a parent to read the reflection for parents provided at the end of this lesson.

All
Amen.

Teacher
May God bless us and keep us safe now and always.

All
Amen.

Song: *Eat This Bread*

Sign of the Cross.

NOW WE KNOW

Q. Who comes to us in Holy Communion?

A. The Lord Jesus comes to us in Holy Communion.

Céad Míle Fáilte Romhat

2. Glóir agus moladh duit, a Íosa, a Íosa,
    Glóir agus moladh duit, a Íosa,
    Glóir agus moladh duit, a Shlánaitheoir,
    Glóir, moladh agus buíochas duit, a Íosa, a Íosa.

Eat This Bread

Jacques Berthier

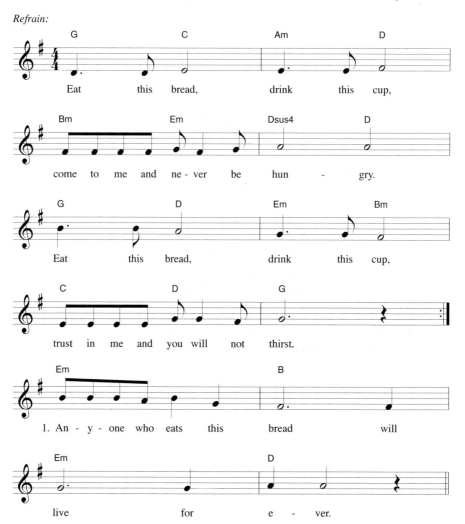

Refrain:

Eat this bread, drink this cup,
come to me and ne-ver be hun - gry.
Eat this bread, drink this cup,
trust in me and you will not thirst.

1. An - y - one who eats this bread will
live for e - ver.

Reflection for Parents

The Table

The chosen ones prepare to fly,
The promise shines in every eye.
'No time for feasts, unleavened bread,
And stand to eat,' the leaders said.
'Bear staff in hand, and stay awake.
Let Israel Pharaoh's land forsake.'

An upper room, a table plain,
'If you would heaven's table gain.
Now take the cup, the broken bread,
And share this supper,' Jesus said.
'And if you would your love renew
Then do as I have done for you.'

Our lives are full of rush and fuss,
Of 'tie your laces', 'catch the bus',
Of wondering, 'Did I pay that bill?'
A thousand things to do, and still,
We show our love as best we're able
When sitting 'round the kitchen table.
Christy Kenneally

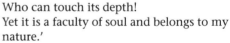

For I received from the Lord what I also handed on to you, that the Lord Jesus on the night when he was betrayed took a loaf of bread, and when he had given thanks, he broke it and said, 'This is my body that is for you. Do this in remembrance of me.' In the same way he took the cup also, after supper, saying, 'This cup is the new covenant in my blood. Do this, as often as you drink it, in remembrance of me.' For as often as you eat this bread and drink the cup, you proclaim the Lord's death until he comes.

(1 Corinthians 11:23)

Our memory is a connection between something back there and a moment right now. There is a deeply felt human need to remember the things from our past which are important. We need to remember the people and the events which have had a significant or normative influence on us as individuals, as members of families and communities, as people belonging to a particular cultural or religious background.

We remember in different ways: by telling and listening to stories, by talking or looking at pictures or photographs, by celebrating and re-enacting the original event in ritual and festivity. As followers of Jesus we remember his Life, Death and Resurrection. We need to remember the things he did and said so that we can keep alive the connectedness which we need to feel between those original events which shaped the Christian community to which we belong, and our present-day experiences of being part of that community.

We do this by remembering and telling stories about Jesus. Most importantly, we do it in the Eucharist by remembering and making present what he did at the Last Supper. This summed up all that he had done and said. It left his followers with his vision for them and for their future, and with his presence to enable

them to live as he had asked them to. When we come together to celebrate the Eucharist, the Risen Jesus is present to us in a very special way and given to us as the Bread of Life. He is present in his word as it is read from the Bible. He is present in the bread and wine, blessed and broken. He is present in the minister and in the community gathered together.

In the Eucharist Jesus continues to offer himself to the Father, as he did at the Last Supper and on the cross. In the Eucharist, we too offer Jesus to the Father and, united with him by the Holy Spirit, we offer ourselves along with him to the Father. At this age, children cannot fully understand the sacrificial aspect of the Eucharist. However, we do present the Eucharist as sacrifice in a manner suited to their age and level of understanding.

FOR THE TEACHER:

A thought before beginning

Memory is the temple wherein the past is gathered.
'Great is the power of memory, exceedingly great, O my God, a spreading limitless room within me.
Who can touch its depth!
Yet it is a faculty of soul and belongs to my nature.'

St Augustine

What am I trying to do?

To help children to remember and to begin to become conscious of the power of personal and collective memory.

Why?

So that they will begin to be aware that, as Christians, we need to remember the Life, Death and Resurrection of Jesus, and to understand the Eucharist as the most important time when we respond to the words of Jesus 'Do this in memory of me'.

> *We continue to teach the children the responses at Mass. This week we suggest that you focus on the acclamation after the consecration:*
>
> Let us proclaim the mystery of faith.
> Christ has died, Christ is risen, Christ will come again.
>
> Lamb of God, you take away the sins of the world, have mercy on us.
> Lamb of God, you take away the sins of the world, have mercy on us.
> Lamb of God, you take away the sins of the world, grant us peace.
>
> *These prayers are particularly relevant to those children preparing for First Communion.*

Overview of the Week

Song: *I Remember* Activity: *Remembering* Chatting about the picture Story: *Jenny and the Computer* Chatting about the story Prayertime	Continue song Chatting about their memory-object! Prayertime Activity: *Our Memories*	Continue song Activity: *Remembering the Story* Story: *A Special Meal* Chatting about the story Remember and Say Prayertime	Continue song Recall story: *A Special Meal* Poem: *Remember* Prayertime Art: *Wall Frieze: We Remember the Passover*	Worksheet Prayertime

Day One

SONG

I Remember

ACTIVITY

Remembering

Place a variety of pictures from old magazines and newspapers on a table or in a central position on the floor. Gather the children around the pictures and ask them to look carefully at them and to choose a picture that reminds them of something/some place/ someone. Ask them to bring the picture back to their desk with them.

CHATTING

...about the picture

Look at the picture you have chosen. Who would like to describe their picture for us? What/who is in your picture? Why did you choose this one and not another? What does your picture remind you of? Is it a happy time or a sad time? Would your picture remind someone else in the class of the same thing? Why/Why not? Do you think it is a good thing to remember? Why? What would happen if we didn't remember? Are there things that we sometimes forget? Tell us about a time when you forgot something? Sometimes we think we have forgotten something and suddenly someone says something or we see something and then we remember. Tell us about a time when this happened to you. Have you ever heard anybody say 'wait a minute, I'll remember it, it will come back to me'? What do you think they mean by that? Are there things we would like to forget? Why?

STORY

Jenny and the Computer

Note: *For children with little or no experience of computers, the sentences written in italics may be omitted.*

Jenny sat down to have her first ever 'go' on a computer. She just played around with it, pressing keys and clicking the mouse here and there. Computers are fun, Jenny decided.

She saw the word 'Save'. She clicked it to see what would happen. Nothing happened. She clicked again. Suddenly writing appeared on the screen. 'Help Help!' it said, 'Cannot Save. No Memory. Help!' Jenny read the words aloud. She wasn't sure what they meant but she clicked 'OK' in answer to it. Next thing, strange whirring and clicking noises came from the computer, the screen went completely blank and the printer took a fit of coughing and started spitting out blank pages!

Jenny was so startled that she hurriedly began pressing keys here, there and everywhere to make it stop. *She pressed 'Escape' – nothing. She tried 'Exit'; 'Delete'; the arrow keys. Still nothing.* She was about to ask her mammy for help when a black hole appeared, growing bigger and bigger, spinning deeper and deeper into the screen. Jenny pressed more buttons. *She pressed 'End' – No good. She pressed 'Enter'. She tried 'Shift',* but the black hole would not go away. Then, quite by accident, she pressed a key with the word 'Home' written on it. That seemed to do the trick because a picture gradually appeared in the middle of the hole. Jenny saw a woman in a white coat surrounded by computers, each one with a blank look on its face.

'Who are you?' Jenny whispered.

'I don't know,' the woman replied. 'I can't remember my name, I've lost my memory. You can help me search for it since you seem to have stumbled into my home.'

'Is this where you live?' Jenny asked.

'I seem to be in a bit of a black hole just at the moment,' the woman said, 'but I suppose this is in-or-around where I live.'

'Why are you in a hole?' Jenny asked.

'Why do you ask so many questions?' returned the woman. 'I'm in a hole because I've lost my memory. Without it I can't remember how to give my computers a memory,' she sighed.

'I didn't know computers have a memory,' said Jenny. 'What do computers need a memory for?'

'To store lots of information, facts and figures, like tables and spellings and documents and things,' said the woman. 'A computer is no use without a memory.'

'I have a memory,' said Jenny. 'I will tell you some things that I remember. I remember my holidays last year; I remember my birthday; I remember when we had a new baby in our family; I remember when we first got you and we plugged you in and I remember that every time I pushed….'

'But…' said the woman. She was about to explain that a person's memory is different to a computer's memory, but in an instant she found herself enthralled, listening to and sharing in Jenny's memory. Memories about her last birthday, her family's Christmas, the time her grandad died and how she cried… indeed, tears began to trickle down the woman's own face as she listened to Jenny.

With each tear, her own memories began to trickle back into her. Before long she joined in with Jenny. 'I remember when my granny died,' she said. 'I missed her telling me stories. My granny had wonderful stories.'

As they shared their happy memories and their sad memories, everything clicked back into place for the computer woman, and for her computers too. 'You have restored my memory,' she said to Jenny. 'Thank you so much.'

'Not at all,' said Jenny. 'I have enjoyed sharing memories with you. It has been fun. Do your computers enjoy sharing memories?' she asked.

'Jenny, tea-time,' her mother called.

'Aw… what a pity,' said Jenny, and she switched off the computer.

CHATTING

…about the story

Jenny was wondering if computers enjoyed sharing their memory. What do you think? Do you think a computer memory is similar to a human memory? In what way? Can you remember facts and figures like tables and spellings? Let's see… *(invite the children to spell a few simple words or recite any facts/tables they may have learned.)* Can you remember the address where your home is? Can you remember what your name is? The names of your family? The people in your class? Do you think computers are good at remembering these things? Do you think your memory is different from a computer memory? In what way? Do you think a computer can remember who it is/what its name is? Do you think a computer can remember sad things/happy things? Can you remember any sad or happy things? Let's share some of our sad and happy and funny and frightening memories. A computer's memory stores facts and information; a person's memory can do more than this. What do you think 'more' is?

Let's see if there are some things everyone in the class remembers, some things that have happened to us all at school, or happened to our school… *(spend some time recalling significant, memorable events in the life of the class).*

PRAYERTIME

Sign of the Cross.

Children place their memory picture in front of them on the desk.

Teacher *(as the candle is lit)*
Let us proclaim the mystery of faith.

All *(with gestures, repeating after teacher)*
Christ has died. *(arms crossed on chest, head bowed)*
Christ is risen. *(arms stretched out by the side of the body, palms facing upwards, head facing straight ahead)*
Christ will come again. *(arms raised high above the head)*

Teacher
We are now going to thank God for the memories that have come back to us today.

Look at your picture.
Now close your eyes and think of what it is this picture reminds you of.
Go into your inside world. Think about your memory and stay with it for a little while.
We thank God for the people we remembered today.
We thank God for the times we remembered today.
We thank God for the gift of remembering.

Open your eyes.
Let's thank God as we say:

All
Glory be to the Father…

Sign of the Cross.

Note: For Day Two, ask the children to bring to class something which captures or symbolises a

303

memory that they have. It might be a photo of someone who has died or is away from home. It might be a shell/stone from a summer holiday, etc. It can be any object associated with their memory.

Day Two

Continue song: *I Remember*

CHATTING

...about their memory-object!

Ask the children to place their object on the desk in front of them. Ask the children to work in pairs. One listens without interrupting while the other talks. Ask each of them to describe what it is she/he has brought in. Then, if they want to and feel comfortable about it, ask them to tell each other what memory the object captures.

Did you describe your object? Was that hard or easy to do? Why? Was it difficult to find something at home that reminded you of a particular memory? When you went home yesterday, did you talk to anyone about what you had to get? Did they help you to remember? What did they say? Do you think that you have a good memory? Do you ever collect things? Do people collect things so that they can remember something else? Tell us about someone you know who is like that.

Some of our memories are personal, they are special to us alone. Some memories belong to more than just one person, like our class memories. Our family has a memory too. It might be the family memory of someone's death, or someone's birth, or someone's wedding, or of a time when a member of the family was ill. Can you remember something which is special to your whole family? Would you like to tell us about it? Or would you prefer to draw a picture of it? You can choose because sometimes we have memories which we are happy to share and other times we prefer not to.

PRAYERTIME

For this prayertime, place a table in a central position. Decorate the table with a cloth and place a candle in the centre. The children will be asked to come forward and to place the object associated with their memory on the table and, if they wish, to make a simple statement like: 'I remember the summer holidays' or 'I remember my granny...'

Sign of the Cross.

Teacher *(as the candle is lit)*
Let us proclaim the mystery of faith.

All *(with gestures, repeating after teacher)*
Christ has died. *(arms crossed on chest, head bowed)*
Christ is risen. *(arms stretched out by the side of the body, palms facing upwards, head facing straight ahead)*
Christ will come again. *(arms raised high above the head)*

Teacher
Let's offer our memories to God.
We light our candle. We know that God is with us. God cares for each one of us.
Today we ask God to bless us as we remember.

We pray together:

All
We praise you, we bless you, we thank you.

Perhaps the teacher herself/himself could begin the process by placing an object on the table and making a simple statement. 'I remember _____.'

Invite the children to come forward and to place their memory-object on the table, and make a simple statement 'I remember _____' if they wish. After each group/row of children, pray the following response:

All
We praise, we bless you, we thank you.

Teacher
We ask you, God, to bless all our memories.
Keep us in your loving care now and always.
Amen.

Sign of the Cross.

ACTIVITY

Our Memories

Note: This activity follows from the prayertime. Now that the children have named their individual memory, the writing about it for the book 'Our Memories', honours its place within the collective memory of the class.

Give each child a sheet of paper on which they write about whatever they brought into school in relation to their memory. These pages can later be tied together to make a book entitled *Our Memories*.

Put the title: *'I remember'* at the top of their sheet.
Invite the children to decorate the page with pictures appropriate to their memory.
Ask the children to sign the end of the page.

Day Three

Continue song: *I Remember*

ACTIVITY

Remembering the Story

One child begins: 'I went to the park and I brought a football.'
The second child repeats this and adds something else: 'I went to the park and I brought a football… and a book to read.'
And so on, each child remembering what was said before and adding to it.

STORY

A Special Meal

It was the tenth day of the first month of the year. Levi's father was very busy. He was preparing lamb for a meal the family was going to have, later. 'Why does it have to be a one-year-old lamb? Why can't it be just any lamb at all?' Levi asked his father.

'Levi, I want you to go to the well. I need water to make bread,' his mother called just then. 'This is not bread-making day; you made bread yesterday,' said Levi, as she handed him the bucket. 'Why are you making bread today?' 'Go quickly, Levi,' she said, 'I am in a hurry. There is bread to be made, a feast to be prepared and still much packing-up to be done before nightfall'.

Later that night Levi's sister Judith awoke him from his sleep. 'Get up, get up!' she whispered as she shook him gently. 'You must get dressed.' 'Why do I have to get dressed? It is night time,' Levi asked his sister Judith as he tied his sandals. 'Why is this night different from all other nights?' 'Hurry,' she said, but she did not answer his question. She put a hat on his head and led him into the room where the rest of the family was gathered.

'Why are our neighbours here and why are they standing around the table? What is going on here?' he asked his mother. 'Hush Levi,' his mother whispered, as his father took some unleavened bread from the basket on the table in front of him. 'What kind of bread is this? Why is it flat? Why are we not eating our usual bread?' Levi asked his sister.

'Baruh atah adonai eloheinu,' his father said, as he blessed the bread and shared it out around the table. Levi pulled out a chair and went to sit down at the table. No one else sat down. 'Why don't you sit down if you are going to share our meal?' he asked Daniel, his neighbour. 'Not tonight, Levi,' Daniel said smiling. 'Why is this night different from all other nights?' Levi asked, for the second time. But everyone fell silent as Levi's father blessed the special lamb.

'*Baruh atah adonai eloheinu,*' his father said. Then he shared the lamb among all those who stood around the table. Levi watched. He had so many questions he wanted to ask, like, why were they all eating so quickly and so quietly? Why were they all dressed as if they were going on a journey and holding their walking sticks or staffs in their hands as they ate? Why all this special food, special bread and special lamb? And why had his family packed up all their belongings? Levi stopped eating. He cleared his throat and spoke in a loud determined voice. 'Why is this night different from all other nights?' he asked.

His father spoke. 'Tonight is a special night for our family and for our people. People will remember the story of this night. Our story will be told over and over again. Tonight, we do not sit down to eat, because we must be ready and waiting. God made a special promise to us that one night he would lead us out of this land where we are slaves to a special land where we will be free. Tonight is a special night; that is why we eat special food. You are right, Levi, tonight is different from all other nights.'

When we share our memories we make a connection with someone who belongs to the past or with something that happened in the past. It keeps that person or that event alive. When we come together to celebrate the Mass, the Risen Jesus is present to us in a very special way. At Mass we all share the memory of Jesus' life, the stories he told, the people he lived with and the things he did. We also share the memory of his Death and his Resurrection. Jesus wanted us to share these memories. At Mass we hear his words. He says, 'Do this in memory of me.' When we remember and share the Risen Jesus we know that he is alive, among us all. Jesus is present especially in Holy Communion. At the end of the Mass, as we leave, we know that these living memories help us all to live as Jesus wants us to.

Remember and Say

At Mass we remember how Jesus lived and died.
We remember people we knew.
They are all brought to life in our memory,
And like Jesus they'll live again too.

CHATTING

...about the story

Have you ever heard this story before? Can you remember where or when? How do you think Levi feels about all the things that make this night different? Have you ever been in a situation where everything felt different – perhaps there was a special meal in your home for some special occasion or other? We don't always have special meals in our own home – can you remember any special meals you have been to? Does the meal in the story remind you of any other meal? The Passover, the Last Supper and the Mass are special meals.

PRAYERTIME

Sign of the Cross.

Teacher (*as the candle is lit*)
Let us proclaim the mystery of faith.

All
Christ has died. Christ is risen. Christ will come again.

Teacher
The Mass helps us to remember Jesus and what he did and said.
Most of all, Jesus shows us how much God loves us and cares for us.
Today let us remember Jesus as we say:

Teacher *(with gestures, children repeating)*
Christ has died. *(arms crossed on chest, head bowed)*
Christ is risen. *(arms stretched out by the side of the body, palms facing upwards, head facing straight ahead)*
Christ will come again. *(arms raised high above the head)*

We remember how Jesus loved those who lived with him.

All *(with actions)*
Christ has died. Christ is risen. Christ will come again.

Teacher
We remember how he shared food with others.

All *(with actions)*
Christ has died. Christ is risen. Christ will come again.

Teacher
We remember that he loved children.

All *(with actions)*
Christ has died. Christ is risen. Christ will come again.

Teacher
We remember how Jesus died on the cross.

All *(with actions)*
Christ has died. Christ is risen. Christ will come again.

Teacher
We remember Jesus' love for us.

All *(with actions)*
Christ has died. Christ is risen. Christ will come again.

Teacher
We remember Jesus' great love for his Father.

All *(with actions)*
Christ has died. Christ is risen. Christ will come again.

Teacher
We remember that the Risen Jesus is with us when we come together at Mass.

All *(with actions)*
Christ has died. Christ is risen. Christ will come again.

Sign of the Cross.

Day Four

Continue song: *I Remember*

Recall story: *A Special Meal*

POEM

Remember

Remember when we came to school
And sat upon a tiny stool
And all the other kids were tall
And we were very, very small.
Remember!

Remember how we learned to play,
To read and write, to draw and pray,
And all the things we learned to do
And how we grew and grew and grew.
Remember!

Remember how we learned to love,
How not to kick or push or shove.
God helped us grow so big and strong
To help the little ones along.
Remember!
Christy Kenneally

PRAYERTIME

Sign of the Cross.

Teacher *(as the candle is lit)*
Let us proclaim the mystery of faith.

All *(with gestures)*
Christ has died. Christ is risen. Christ will come again.

Teacher
Close your eyes.
Place your hands gently on your lap.
Place your feet on the floor.

Go into your inside world where it is dark and quiet and safe and peaceful.
In your inside world you can imagine anything you like.

Think of a memory you have that is very special to you. Maybe it is a memory of your birthday last year, or when someone came to visit, or when a little baby sister or brother was born, or last Christmas when you opened your presents, or last Easter when you got an Easter egg. With your special inside voice tell God about your memory. Tell God why it is special to you. Thank God for this very special memory.

Open your eyes.
Stretch.

Let us proclaim the mystery of faith.

All
Christ has died. Christ is risen. Christ will come again.

Sign of the Cross.

A R T

Wall Frieze: We Remember the Passover

Ask the children to draw their own picture of the Passover meal.
Display the children's pictures around the caption 'We Remember the Passover'.

W O R K S H E E T

If you wish to use the worksheet or workbook page which accompanies this lesson, this is an appropriate time to do so.

P R A Y E R T I M E

Sign of the Cross.

All
Song: *I Remember*

Teacher
We light our candle. We remember that God is always with us.
Jesus ate the Last Supper with his friends before he died.
Today let us remember the people we love who have died.
We ask God to bless all who have died.
We pray together:

All
Eternal rest grant to them, O Lord.

Teacher
Think of someone you know who has died or someone you have heard people talk about who has died.
Let's ask God to grant rest to all the people we have in our minds.

We pray together:

All
Eternal rest grant to them, O Lord.

Teacher
May they rest in peace.
Amen.

Sign of the Cross.

I Remember

Geraldine Doggett

1. I re-mem-ber, I re-mem-ber
   peo-ple, pla-ces, hap-py times,—
   po-ems, songs and nur-s'ry rhymes.— These
   me-mo-ries I bring to-day.— Accept my gifts— oh Lord, I pray.—
   Lord, I pray.—

2. I remember, I remember
   All the stories people read
   About what Jesus did and said.
   These stories I bring today.
   Accept my gifts, oh Lord I pray, Lord I pray.

3. I remember, I remember
   Jesus sharing one last time
   With His friends the bread and wine.
   This bread and wine I bring today.
   Accept my gifts, oh Lord I pray, Lord I pray.

Lesson 5: A Time To Share Life

Love one another as I have loved you.
(John 15:12)

The cup of blessing that we bless, is it not a
sharing in the blood of Christ?
The bread that we break,
is it not a sharing in the body of Christ?
Because there is one bread,
we who are many are one body,
for we all partake of the one bread.
(1 Corinthians 10:16-17)

The Last Supper which Jesus shared with his
apostles on the night before he died
brought together the many ways in which he
had shared himself and his life and his love
with them. It was also the springboard from
which he sent them forth to continue to share
their life and their love with one another and
with others. He left them to do this with the
assurance that he would be with them.

As followers of Jesus today, we are challenged
to continue to live in our world in a way that
mirrors his exhortation to all his followers:
'love one another as I have loved you'. Shared
living is characterised by a spirit wherein
people share their stories, their memories and
their food. In the Eucharist, as followers of
Jesus, we come together and celebrate the way
in which we have shared our life and our love
with others in memory of Jesus. By taking part
in the Eucharistic meal we share Jesus' body,
which is his life, and go forth with a renewed
sense of our identity and our mission as his
followers in our world today.

FOR THE TEACHER:

A thought before beginning

May Christ dwell
in our hearts
through faith,
so that rooted
and grounded in Love
we may contemplate
the breadth and length,
the height and depth
of Christ's love
which surpasses
all knowledge.
Jean Beyer
(Based on Ephesians 3:17-18)

What am I trying to do?

To help the children to reflect on the ways in
which they share life with others, and to explore
how Jesus shared himself and his life with others.

Why?

So that they will understand the Eucharist as a
context wherein Jesus shares his life with us and
come to a deeper awareness of how they can
share their lives with others in memory of him.

Overview of the Week

	Continue song Story: *Jesus Visits* *Three Special Friends*		Continue song Revise poem	
Song: *Do this in* *Memory of Jesus*	Chatting about the story	Continue song Recall story	Worksheet Chatting about the	
Chatting about life	Did You Know?	Chatting about life	picture	
Art: *What Keeps the* *Life in Us?*	Remember and Say Activity: *Jesus-Heart*	Poem: *Shared Living* Did You Know?	Art: *Weaving our* *Lives*	Continue art
Prayertime	Prayertime	Prayertime	Prayertime	Prayertime

We continue to teach the responses for Mass. This week, focus on the Kyrie and the Sanctus:

Lord have mercy.
Lord have mercy.
Christ have mercy.
Christ have mercy.
Lord have mercy.
Lord have mercy.

Holy, holy, holy Lord,
God of power and might.
Heaven and earth are full of your glory.
Hosanna in the highest.
Blessed is he who comes in the name of the Lord.
Hosanna in the highest.

These prayers are particularly relevant to those children preparing for First Communion.

Day One

SONG

Do this in Memory of Jesus

CHATTING

…about life

Each one of us is alive. We each have a life. That life is in our bodies. Let's talk about that life. Have you ever been asked the question, 'How are you?' What does someone want to know when they ask that question? Turn to the person beside you. One of you ask the other, 'How are you?'

What answer did you get? Are there any other answers you could have got? When someone asks 'How are you?' they are usually asking about the life in your body, about how you are feeling. You say, 'I'm well' or 'I have a cold' or 'I was sick for a day or two but I'm better now', etc. We need to look after the life in our bodies. How can we do that? How does food help 'to keep the life in us'? What else do we need 'to keep the life in us' apart from food? *(Water, rest, health, etc.)*

At Mass we remember and we celebrate Jesus' Life, Death and Resurrection. Jesus gave himself to his followers in bread and wine at the Last Supper. At Mass we receive the Bread of Life which is Jesus and then go out to live like Jesus.

ART

Collage: What Keeps the Life in Us?

For each group you will need:
• Old magazines
• Scissors
• Adhesive

Ask the children to cut out pictures from magazines of all the things that we need 'to keep the life in us' – food, water, exercise, clothes, etc. Divide the children into several groups, giving a particular aspect to each group, for example, 'What keeps the life in us?,' 'Food that keeps us alive', 'Clothes that keep us warm', etc.

PRAYERTIME

Sign of the Cross.

Teacher *(as the candle is lit)*
For the air we share as we breathe together,
For the food we share as we eat together,
For the love we share as we live together,
We praise you, O God, and we bless you.

For food that nourishes our bodies.

All
We praise you, O God, and we bless you.

Teacher
For water that keeps us alive.

All
We praise you, O God, and we bless you.

Teacher
For rest that we take when we are feeling tired.

All
We praise you, O God, and we bless you.

Teacher
For our health to enjoy our life.

All
We praise you, O God, and we bless you.

Teacher
Thank you, God, for the life that flows through our bodies.
Thank you, God, for all living things.
All life comes from you.

All
Glory be to the Father…

Sign of the Cross.

Continue song: *Do this in Memory of Jesus*

STORY

Jesus Visits Three Special Friends
(Adapted from Luke 10:38-41)

Jesus had many friends. Among them he had twelve very close friends who walked with him all the time. He called them his apostles. He ate with them and talked with them. He listened to their stories, just as they listened to his. Sometimes, though, Jesus liked to be by himself. Sometimes he would leave his friends for a little while and go off on his own.

One day, Jesus and his apostles were walking towards the city. Jesus remembered that his good friends Martha, Mary and Lazarus lived just a little way off, in Bethany. He decided to call in on his way and pay them a visit since he had not seen them for a while. He told the apostles he was going off by himself, but he would meet up with them again in a day or two.

Martha and Mary and their brother Lazarus were delighted to see Jesus. They ran to greet him.
'You just called at the right time,' Martha said, 'tomorrow is the Sabbath and so we are having a special meal tonight.'
'Why don't you join us!' said Lazarus and Mary at once.
'I would love to,' Jesus replied, and all four of them walked back to the house together.

When the meal was ready, the table laid, and the wine poured, Jesus and his friends sat down to eat. 'Tell us everything that has happened since we saw you last, Jesus,' said Lazarus, passing the bread around. Jesus told them all about his travels; he told them that many people came to listen to him speaking; he told them about the little boy with the basket of loaves and fishes. 'Only for him,'

Jesus said, 'I don't know what we'd have done! But what about you, my friends,' he said, passing the wine around, 'how have things been going for you?'

'Oh, nothing very exciting ever happens around here,' said Mary laughing. 'One day is very much like another.'

'That's why we are so happy to see you,' agreed Lazarus. 'You tell such interesting stories.'

'Tell us a story now, Jesus,' Martha pleaded, 'it won't be long until you are gone, but at least we'll have your stories to remember you by until you come again.'

'Yes do, Jesus, tell us a story,' said Mary.

'If only everyone loved my stories as much as you do, my dear friends,' laughed Jesus, 'life would be so different!' Then he sat back and told them a story about a man going out to sow seeds and about all the adventures that happened to the different seeds he sowed.

And that was just the beginning. Because, one story led to another. 'Do you remember the time…' Lazarus began, and then he told a story about something Jesus had said or done; then Martha said, 'That reminds me of another time, do you remember…', and then she was off with yet another story. Then it was Mary's turn. And the stories and the memories and the meal went on late into the evening.

After a day or two, Jesus rejoined his apostles. They were glad to see him.

'Well, how are Mary and Martha and Lazarus?' asked John, the youngest apostle.

'They are very well,' Jesus replied, 'I had a wonderful time with them. We shared a meal and a story or two and we shared lots of memories. In fact,' said Jesus, pausing to think for a moment, 'we shared more than these – we shared our living, we shared our lives.'

'It sounds to me,' said Thomas, who had caught up with Jesus and John, '…that to share these things is to share something. I'm not sure what to call it, but it is something very deep.'

'I'd call it love,' said John.

'So would I,' said Jesus, and they walked on.

CHATTING

…about the story

Do you think Jesus and his three friends had a good time together? What makes you think so? Tell us about a meal you have shared like this, where stories were told and people remembered times they had spent together? Perhaps it was a wedding or a birthday or a family occasion. Or perhaps someone just arrived out of the blue. Tell us about it. Can you remember any stories that were told then? Can you remember what sort of meal you had? What memory/memories have you of the person/people involved? How do you think Mary and Martha and Lazarus felt when Jesus moved on? Do you think he ever called back to them again? Why?

Jesus said that they had shared more than a meal and stories and memories; he said they had shared each other's lives. What do you think he might have meant by that? Do others share your life at home? At school? What about your friends? Who are they? How do they share your living from day to day? What do you think about what John said – that this deep sharing of memories and meals and stories is also a way of sharing love? Do you share your love with others? Who do you share your love with?

DID YOU KNOW?

Jesus shared his life with us because he loves us.

Remember and Say

At Mass we take part together
In shared story, shared memory, shared meal.
In doing so, we share our lives,
In the presence of Jesus made real.

ACTIVITY

Jesus-Heart

Give each child a sheet of paper.
Ask them to draw a big heart. Make sure that
they leave room on the page so that they can
write a phrase around the edge of the heart.
Write the phrase 'Jesus said "Love one another
as I have loved you" ' on the blackboard.
Ask the children to write the phrase around
the heart.
Ask the children to draw Jesus in the centre of
the heart, sharing his stories, his memories,
his food and his life with his friends.

PRAYERTIME

Sign of the Cross.

Teacher *(as the candle is lit)*
For the air we share as we breathe together,
For the food we share as we eat together,
For the love we share as we live together,
We praise you, O God, and we bless you.

Jesus reminds us of God's love for us.
Jesus shared many stories with his friends. He
chatted and laughed with them.
He loved his friends. He shared everything
with them. He shared his life with them.
We can share Jesus' life too.
Today let's thank God for Jesus and for the life
he shares for and with us. We pray:

All
We praise you, we bless you, we thank you.

Teacher
Jesus shares food with his friends.

All
We praise you, we bless you, we thank you.

Teacher
Jesus shares stories with his friends.

All
We praise you, we bless you, we thank you.

Teacher
Jesus shares his life with his friends.

All
We praise you, we bless you, we thank you.

Teacher
Jesus shares his life for us.

All
We praise you, we bless you, we thank you.

Teacher
At Mass we remember how Jesus shares his life
for each and every one of us.
We thank God for Jesus as we say:

All
Our Father...

Sign of the Cross.

Day Three

Continue song: *Do this in Memory of Jesus*

Recall story: *Jesus Visits Three Special Friends*

CHATTING

...about life

Each one of us is alive. We have a life. We have
life in our bodies. We live through our bodies.
Our living can be about more than what
happens inside each one's own individual
body. Have you ever heard the question,
'How's life?' Where/When have you heard it?
Do you think there might be a difference

between the question we talked about yesterday – 'How are you?', and the question we are asking today – 'How's life?' What do you think is meant when someone says 'How's life?' What does a person want to know when they ask that question? Turn to the person beside you. One of you ask the other, 'How's life?'

What answer did you get? Can you think of any other questions which are similar to 'How's life?' Questions like 'How is it going?' or 'How are things?' or 'How are you getting on?' If you were asked, 'How is it going?' or 'How are things?' or 'How are you getting along?', what would you reply? When someone asks 'How's life?' or a similar question, they are asking about the things that are happening in your life as you live it every day; how you are getting along with others at home, at school, at play, etc., and if you are happy or sad or worried or excited about what's happening in your life as you live it from day to day.

DID YOU KNOW?

Living is about what happens among us as well as inside each one of us. Living is about the sharing of days and times and places and happenings and tasks and feelings between all of us. Jesus shared his life with others. He shared his life with those around him. He shares it with us too.

At Mass, through the stories we tell, the memories we recall, and the food we eat, we remember and celebrate the way Jesus shared his Life, Death and Resurrection. We are glad and say 'Thank you'. We try to share our lives with others too.

POEM

Shared Living

The man and woman, long ago,
Sat listening to the cold wind blow.
They huddled close to share the joy
Asleep in straw, their baby boy.

I share my home with two or three,
A little group, called family.
We share our birthdays, books and toys,
We share our dreams, our tears, our joys.

We share a classroom every day,
We learn to read and draw and pray.
Like bees, to happy humming hives,
We come each day to share our lives.
Christy Kenneally

PRAYERTIME

Sign of the Cross.

Teacher *(as the candle is lit)*
For the air we share as we breathe together,
For the food we share as we eat together,
For the love we share as we live together,
We praise you, O God, and we bless you.

Teacher *(children repeating)*
Sharing our stories, our memories, our life.
Talking and laughing and listening too.
This is what Jesus asks of us all
And it's something that our class can do.

All
Glory be to the Father…

Sign of the Cross.

Day Four

Continue song: *Do this in Memory of Jesus*

Revise poem: *Shared Living*

WORKSHEET

If you wish to use the worksheet or workbook page which accompanies this lesson, this is an appropriate time to do so.

CHATTING

...about the picture on pages 42 and 43

Who are the people in this picture? Is this how you eat at home? How is this meal different? Would you like to try eating like this? Look at the faces. How are these people getting on together? Imagine you are there too. What can you hear them saying to each other? What would you say to them?

ART

Weaving Our Lives

Note: In this activity each child is asked to represent her/his life in word and picture. As a sign that we share our lives with others and that all our lives are connected, strips which the children have made will be woven together as one.

For each child you will need:
• A strip of paper/card 2 x 15 ins (5 x 38 cms)
• Crayons/markers.

On the strip of paper/card ask each child to draw a series of small pictures that tell the class about themselves and their life. Children could also write words if they wish. At some point along the strip the children could write their name.

PRAYERTIME

Sign of the Cross.

Teacher *(as the candle is lit)*
For the air we share as we breathe together,
For the food we share as we eat together,
For the love we share as we live together,
We praise you, O God, and we bless you.

God is with us in a special way in the life of Jesus.
Today we ask God to bless us as we share our lives with one another each day at school.

All
God bless us and keep us, we pray.

Teacher
When we learn together, we share our lives.

All
God bless us and keep us, we pray.

Teacher
When we chat about our memories, we share our lives.

All
God bless us and keep us, we pray.

Teacher
When we tell stories to each other, we share our lives.

All
God bless us and keep us, we pray.

Teacher
When we love one another, we share our lives.

All
God bless us and keep us, we pray.

Teacher
God our Creator, be with us each and every day.

All
Sharing our stories, our memories, our life,
Talking and laughing and listening too.
That is what Jesus asks of us all
And it's something that our class can do.
Amen.

Sign of the Cross.

Day Five

Continue art: *Weaving Our Lives (if not already completed)*

PRAYERTIME

Note: In preparation for this prayertime clear a space on a wall in the classroom. The children will be asked to come forward and place their strip on the wall. For this the children will need some form of adhesive.

Sign of the Cross.

Teacher *(as the candle is lit)*
For the air we share as we breathe together,
For the food we share as we eat together,
For the love we share as we live together,
We praise you, O God, and we bless you.

Today we want to thank God for the life in our classroom that we share together.
We are going to watch as we see how the lives of everyone in this class are linked together.

All
Sharing our stories, our memories, our life,
Talking and laughing and listening too.

That is what Jesus asks of us all
And it's something that our class can do.
Amen.

Invite the children to come forward and to place their strip on the wall. The strips of paper/card can quite literally be woven and intertwined with one another.

All *(as each child returns to the desk)*
Thank you, God, for the life we share.

Teacher
Let's take time to look at all the different strips.
Look at all the different things we share with one another.
Look at all our different lives.
Look at how they are all connected with one another.

Close your eyes.
Think of all the different things you now know about the people in this class. With our inside voice thank God for all the chatting and listening, the laughing and working that has happened in the class. Thank God for the lives we share together.

Open your eyes.

All
Shared Living
The man and woman, long ago,
Sat listening to the cold wind blow.
They huddled close to share the joy
Asleep in straw, their baby boy.

I share my home with two or three,
A little group, called family.
We share our birthdays, books and toys,
We share our dreams, our tears, our joys.

We share a classroom every day,
We learn to read and draw and pray.
Like bees, to happy humming hives,
We come each day to share our lives.

Sign of the Cross.

Do This in Memory of Jesus

Cyril Murphy

Capo 2: Play D

Descant*

Sing! Sing! to Je - sus.

Refrain

Sing praise— and thanks to— Je - sus.

Lift! Lift! to Je - sus.

Lift up— your hearts to Je - sus.

Walk tall in the love of Je - sus.

Walk tall in the love of— Je - sus.

Do this in me-mory of,

Do this in me-mory of Him, of Him.

318

Do this in me-mory of Je - sus.

Do this in me-mory of Je - sus.

1. Take bread and wine, blessed and bro - ken,

live in your life the words He has spo - ken.

2. Trust in His love, walk in His ways,

share with the world His peace,— His praise.

* The descant is optional and, if used, should only be sung on choruses 2 & 3. It is included for use when children from older classes are singing with first class /P3 children, eg, at first communion celebration mass.

319

Lesson 6: Holy Spirit Help Us

If we live by the Spirit,
let us also be guided by the Spirit.
(Galatians 5:25)

The Holy Spirit will teach you everything and
remind you of all that I have said to you.
(John 14:26)

The Holy Spirit is the Spirit of God, the
third person of the Blessed Trinity. The
Spirit of God moved over the waters at the
dawn of creation. Whenever we see new life
we are in the presence of God's Spirit. Already
the children have become aware in an indirect
way of the presence of God's Spirit moving at
the heart of all life. The Spirit of God is active
in the world of nature and can be seen in the
changing of the seasons and in the beauty of
the world. Most clearly, we see God's Spirit in
action in the life of Jesus, in his efforts to
make God present and active in the world.

Jesus promised to send the Holy Spirit to his
followers to help them after his death. The
Holy Spirit came to the apostles at Pentecost
and comes to us in Baptism. Jesus promised
his followers that the Holy Spirit would help
them to remember all that he had taught
them and would help them to live as he had
asked them to.

The Spirit of Jesus can be seen at the heart of
human life. It is the spirit of love, joy, peace,
patience, kindness, goodness, truthfulness,
gentleness, trustfulness and self-control. When
we see these qualities in action in people's
lives, we see the Spirit of Jesus in action.

FOR THE TEACHER:

A thought before beginning

Come Holy Spirit
Word of God in mind and fire
Come my heart inspire.

Come Holy Spirit
God in the evening breeze
Come my soul refresh.

Come Holy Spirit
Breath of God in us dwelling
Come in me abide.
Rev Peter Coppen

What am I trying to do?

To introduce the children to the story of
Pentecost.

Why?

So that they will begin to be aware of the gift of
the Holy Spirit in their lives and be able to
respond to the promptings of the Spirit to live
and to love as Jesus asks us to.

Overview of the Week

Song: *Come Holy Spirit*	Continue song			
Did You Know?	Story: *The Story of Pentecost*		Continue song	Revise poem
Prayer to the Holy Spirit	Chatting after the story	Continue song	Recall story	Worksheet
Chatting about Jesus	Mime	Poem: *Help us Holy Spirit*	Revise poem	Activity: *Holy Spirit, Spirit of God*
Prayertime	Prayertime	Prayertime	Art: *The Spirit of God is in us*	Prayertime
			Prayertime	Now We Know

SONG

Come Holy Spirit

DID YOU KNOW?

Jesus promised his followers that he would send the Holy Spirit to help them to remember him and to live and to love as he had asked them to. The Holy Spirit came to us in Baptism. The Holy Spirit helps us to live and to love as Jesus asks us to.

Begin to teach the Prayer to the Holy Spirit:

Prayer to the Holy Spirit

Spirit of God in the heavens.
(Reach away up high)

Spirit of God in the seas.
(Make rippling movement with hands)

Spirit of God in the mountain-tops.
(Raise hands overhead – fingers meet to form a point)

Spirit of God in me.
(Hand gestures towards self)

Spirit of God in the sunlight.
(Hands bringing sunbeams towards the earth)

Spirit of God in the air.
(Spread fingers and move arms through space)

Spirit of God all around me.
(Extend arms wide and turn around)

Spirit of God everywhere.
(Extend hands to side, palms up, and raise them slowly)

Holy Spirit, Spirit of God, help me.
(Hands joined)

CHATTING

...about Jesus

What kind of things did Jesus do? Do you think he was a nice person to know and to be with or not? Why? Do you think the children liked to be with him? Why? Do you think the people on the hillside liked to be with him? Why? Do you think the woman at the well liked to be with him? Why? What sort of person do you think Jesus asks you to be? Is it easy or difficult to be that sort of person? Can you think of a time when you were that kind of person? A time at home? A time at school? A time with your friends? Can you think of a time when you were not?

PRAYERTIME

Sign of the Cross

Teacher *(as the candle is lit)*
We pray that as this candle burns, God's Spirit, the Holy Spirit, will light our lives with love, with kindness, with gentleness, with peace.

All
Glory be to the Father,
And to the Son,
And to the Holy Spirit.
As it was in the beginning,
Is now and ever shall be,
World without end. Amen.

Teacher
Holy Spirit, help us to be kind.

All
Holy Spirit, Spirit of God, help us.

Teacher
Holy Spirit, help us to be gentle.

All
Holy Spirit, Spirit of God, help us.

Teacher
Holy Spirit, help us to be at peace.

All
Holy Spirit, Spirit of God, help us.

Teacher
Holy Spirit, help us to love.

All
Holy Spirit, Spirit of God, help us.

Glory be to the Father...

Sign of the Cross.

Day Two

Continue song: *Come Holy Spirit*

STORY

The Story of Pentecost

The friends of Jesus were sad and lonely without him. They huddled together in a room all by themselves. Their faces were sad, their heads hung low, they sighed. They missed their friend. No one seemed to know what to do without him. Then suddenly as they huddled close together, they heard the sound of a breeze. It grew stronger and stronger until, in no time at all, a powerful wind filled the whole room. A bright light, like flames of fire, shone all around them. 'What's this? What is happening? What is going on?' they called out, jumping to their feet and raising their hands in alarm. At first they were afraid, but the wind kept blowing and the fiery light kept shining.

Then one of the friends suddenly remembered what Jesus had said: 'I will ask the Father and he will send you the Holy Spirit to be with you forever.' He too jumped to his feet, he was no longer afraid, his face had lost its sad look, he held his head high and he shouted in a loud voice above the noise of the wind, 'The Holy Spirit has come to us. The Holy Spirit Jesus promised is here with us now!'

'Of course, of course. It is the Holy Spirit,' the others shouted joyfully. Their faces lit up; they lifted up their hearts; they stood tall and straight; they danced for joy! They danced out of the room and out into the streets. Now they were no longer sad and lonely. Now they knew exactly what to do. They danced and sang in the streets; they told everyone about their friend Jesus; they told them about the Holy Spirit who had come into their lives this very day and filled their hearts with joy and gladness and courage. People looked and listened in amazement. 'You can be friends and followers of Jesus too,' they were told. The people wanted to know how they could become friends and followers of Jesus.

'You must be baptised, you must receive the Holy Spirit to give you joy and courage and wisdom. The Holy Spirit will help you to live as Jesus did.'

That day many many people were baptised. All those who received the Holy Spirit began to live in a new way. They shared whatever money and goods they had with each other; they prayed together; they stayed in each other's homes and they were always ready to help anyone who was in need of any kind.

But there was one very special thing they did. They came together on the Lord's day to pray. They would tell stories about Jesus and they would take bread, break it, bless it and share it out, just as Jesus had done at the Last Supper. The Holy Spirit was with them as they remembered Jesus in this way. The Holy Spirit stayed with them always, just as Jesus had promised.

CHATTING

...after the story

Can you remember a time in your life when you missed someone who had gone away? Why did you miss them? What kinds of things did you miss – things they'd do, say, just for being the way they were, etc? Who do you think would miss you if you went away? What are the special things about you that others would miss? Jesus' friends missed him. What special things about their friend do you think they missed most? How do you think the Holy Spirit helped the friends of Jesus?

Mime

Let's imagine we are all Jesus' friends huddled together in the room. How would we be sitting? What kind of look would be on our faces? How would we sigh? Let's think about Jesus. Let's tell each other what we miss about him.

Now we begin to hear a sound. At first it's very soft and low – let's make the soft, low whisper of a breeze. It gets stronger and louder. We huddle tighter together. We are afraid. The wind gets louder and louder. Let's try to imagine the strong, fiery light all around. Can you see it? Listen to the wind. See the light. Let's ask the questions the friends asked. What is it? What's happening? What's going on?

Let's think about Jesus our friend. Can you remember who he promised to send to help us? It's the Holy Spirit! Let's all shout and proclaim together – 'It's the Holy Spirit!' Now we are not afraid. Our faces change. How do they change? Our hearts and our spirits are lifted – we jump up, we dance and sing and clap all around the classroom, 'Hurray for the Holy Spirit!'

Chatting continued...

Now that we have received the Holy Spirit, how should we try to live? The people in the story began to live in a new way. What kinds of things did they do? What can we do to live like Jesus?

PRAYERTIME

Sign of the Cross.

Teacher (*as the candle is lit*)
Glory be to the Father,
And to the Son,
And to the Holy Spirit.
As it was in the beginning,
Is now and ever shall be,
World without end. Amen.

Let us praise God's Spirit alive in us and in the world.

We pray together: (*children, if necessary, repeating words after the teacher*)

Spirit of God in the heavens.
(*Reach away up high*)

Spirit of God in the seas.
(*Make rippling movement with hands*)

Spirit of God in the mountain-tops.
(*Raise hands overhead – fingers meet to form a point*)

Spirit of God in me.
(*Hand gestures towards self*)

Spirit of God in the sunlight.
(*Hands bringing sunbeams towards the earth*)

Spirit of God in the air.
(*Spread fingers and move arms through space*)

Spirit of God all around me.
(*Extend arms wide and turn around*)

Spirit of God everywhere.
(*Extend hands to side, palms up, and raise them slowly*)

Holy Spirit, Spirit of God, help me.
(*Hands joined*)

All
Glory be to the Father...

Sign of the Cross.

Day Three

Continue song: *Come Holy Spirit*

POEM

Help us Holy Spirit

Have you ever wondered,
Would you like to know
What meeting Jesus would be like
Two thousand years ago?

If you had been a poor man
Back in those ancient days
And you met Jesus on the road,
What do you think he'd say?

If you said, 'Sir, I'm hungry',
What do you think he'd do?
He'd take out any food he had
And share it all with you.

He'd share all that he had with you,
I feel quite sure he would,
For Jesus cared for everyone
And helped them when he could.

Now help us Holy Spirit
To try in our own way
To care and share as Jesus did
Back in those ancient days.
            Finbar O'Connor

PRAYERTIME

Sign of the Cross.

Teacher *(as the candle is lit)*
Glory be to the Father,
And to the Son,
And to the Holy Spirit.
As it was in the beginning,

Is now and ever shall be,
World without end. Amen.

Let us praise God's Spirit alive in us and in the world.

We pray together: *(children, if necessary, repeating words after the teacher)*

Spirit of God in the heavens.
(Reach away up high)

Spirit of God in the seas.
(Make rippling movement with hands)

Spirit of God in the mountain-tops.
(Raise hands overhead – fingers meet to form a point)

Spirit of God in me.
(Hand gestures towards self)

Spirit of God in the sunlight.
(Hands bringing sunbeams towards the earth)

Spirit of God in the air.
(Spread fingers and move arms through space)

Spirit of God all around me.
(Extend arms wide and turn around)

Spirit of God everywhere.
(Extend hands to side, palms up, and raise them slowly)

Holy Spirit, Spirit of God, help me.
(Hands joined)

All
Glory be to the Father...

Sign of the Cross.

Continue song: *Come Holy Spirit*

Recall story: *The Story of Pentecost*

Continue poem: *Help us Holy Spirit*

ART

The Spirit of God is in us

Ask each child to draw a big sunflower. On the circle in the centre of the sunflower ask them to write the following words:

The
Spirit of God
is in us

Then on the petals ask them to write their own name and the names of their family/relations and friends – as many as are needed to complete the flower.

or

Give each child a piece of paper cut in the shape of a petal. On the circle which will form the centre of the flower write the words:

The
Spirit of God
is in us

Ask the children to colour their petal yellow and to write their name on their petal. Then place the petals around the centre of the flower.

PRAYERTIME

Sign of the Cross.

Teacher *(as the candle is lit)*
Holy Spirit, I want to do what is right. Help me.
Holy Spirit, I want to live like Jesus. Guide me.
Holy Spirit, I want to pray like Jesus. Teach me.

Close your eyes.

Go into your inside world, where it's dark and quiet and peaceful, deep inside you where God's Spirit lives in your heart – the Holy Spirit which Jesus said he would send to his followers.
The Holy Spirit helps you to be gentle. Think of a time when you were gentle – with someone at home, with someone in school, with your friends. *(Pause)*

The Holy Spirit helps you to be loving. Think of a time when you were loving – at home, at school, when you were playing with your friends.
With your inside voice gently say, 'Holy Spirit, I want to do what is right. Help me.' *(Pause)*

The Holy Spirit helps you to be patient. Think of a time when you were patient, when you had to wait for something to happen, when someone was smaller and slower than you. *(Pause)*

The Holy Spirit helps us to be kind. Think of a time when you were kind to someone who was feeling sad or someone who was sick or someone who needed help with something.
With your inside voice gently say, 'Holy Spirit, I want to live like Jesus. Guide me.' *(Pause)*

The Holy Spirit has been helping you to live and to love like Jesus did. With your inside voice ask the Holy Spirit to help you always.
With your inside voice gently say, 'Holy Spirit, I want to pray like Jesus. Teach me.' *(Pause)*

Open your eyes.
We pray together:

All
Holy Spirit, Spirit of God, help me always.

Sign of the Cross.

Day Five

Revise poem: *Help us Holy Spirit*

WORKSHEET

If you wish to use the worksheet or workbook page which accompanies this lesson, this is an appropriate time to do so.

ACTIVITY

Holy Spirit, Spirit of God

For each child you will need:
- paper (a bright colour if possible)
- markers/crayons

Today we are going to ask the Holy Spirit to help us to be kind and gentle and loving with those who live at home. Think of someone in particular in your home. Think of something you can do for that person. Think of when you will do it. Imagine how the person will feel then.

Distribute the paper. On one side ask the children to write the name of or to draw a picture of the person at home whom they have thought about. Then ask them to write what they will do for that person.
On the other side ask them to write the prayer:
Holy Spirit, Spirit of God, help me.
Holy Spirit, Spirit of God, guide me.
Holy Spirit, Spirit of God, teach me.

PRAYERTIME

Sign of the Cross.

Song: *Come Holy Spirit*

Teacher *(as the candle is lit)*
Holy Spirit, Spirit of God, help us.

Let us praise God's Spirit alive in us and in the world.

All *(children, if necessary, repeating words after the teacher)*
Spirit of God in the heavens.
(Reach away up high)

Spirit of God in the seas.
(Make rippling movements with hands)

Spirit of God in the mountain-tops.
(Raise hands overhead – fingers meet to form a point)

Spirit of God in me.
(Hand gestures towards self)

Spirit of God in the sunlight.
(Hands bringing sunbeams towards the earth)

Spirit of God in the air.
(Spread fingers and move arms through space)

Spirit of God all around me.
(Extend arms wide and turn around)

Spirit of God everywhere.
(Extend hands to side, palms up, and raise them slowly)

Holy Spirit, Spirit of God, help me.
(Hands joined)

Poem: *Help us Holy Spirit*

Sign of the Cross.

NOW WE KNOW

Q. How does the Holy Spirit help us?

A. The Holy Spirit helps us to live like Jesus.

Come, Holy Spirit

Seán Creamer

Response:

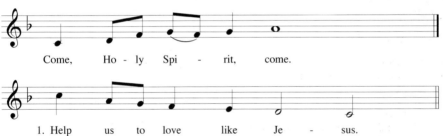

Come, Ho - ly Spi - rit, come.

1. Help us to love like Je - sus.

2. Help us to pray like Jesus.

3. Help us to be patient.

4. Help us to forgive others.

Lesson 7: Treasures From Long Ago

...if the root is holy,
then the branches also are holy.
(Romans 11:16)

O ur ancestors were a deeply spiritual people who experienced the powerful presence of the divine in the natural world. They possessed a strong sense of the sacredness of places, especially woods, rivers and springs. They lived close to nature, close to the elements and close to God. They valued culture too and placed great emphasis on the literary and poetic skills of their druids and priests. Their legacy of Christianity is with us to this day in the store of prayers, poems and artefacts which reflect the protective presence of God. We see this in a beautiful way in the following prayer from St Patrick's Breastplate, where the Trinity is being evoked.

> I bind unto myself today
> The strong name of the Trinity
> By invocation of the same
> The Three in One and One in Three.

Children love to hear legends and stories from long ago. In this lesson we tell the story of the Children of Lir, a story from our rich mythology and one that bridges the gap between the pre-Christian and Christian worlds.

To enable the children to enter more deeply into Celtic spirituality, the prayertimes focus in a particular way on the deep Celtic sense of connectedness between God's presence and all of life.

What am I trying to do?

To develop in the children an appreciation of the richness and depth of the Celtic culture.
To heighten their awareness of the sacredness of all living things and to tap into the protective presence of God in their lives.

Why?

So that they will have a Celtic sense of the sacredness of all things and be more aware of God's presence in life.

FOR THE TEACHER:

A thought before beginning

Beannacht

On the day when
            the weight deadens
            on your shoulders
and you stumble,
may the clay dance
to balance you.

And when your eyes
freeze behind
the grey window
and the ghost of loss
gets in to you,
may a flock of colours,
indigo, red, green
and azure blue
come to awaken in you
a meadow of delight.

When the canvas frays
in the curach of thought
and a stain of ocean
blackens beneath you,
may there come across the waters
a path of yellow moonlight
to bring you safely home.

May the nourishment of the earth be yours,
may the clarity of light be yours,
may the fluency of the ocean be yours,
may the protection of the ancestors be yours.

And so may a slow
wind work these words
of love around you,
an invisible cloak
to mind your life.
            J. O'Donohue

Overview of the Week

Song: *Round and Round/Christ Be Beside Me*		Continue song Did You Know? Chatting about music, song and dance		Worksheet
Story: *The Children of Lir*	Continue song Recall story	Activity: *Let's Listen and Move* or *Listen and Paint*	Continue song Activity: *Celtic Designs*	Chatting about the Celtic Cross
Chatting about the story	Remember and Say Art: *The Swans*			Art: *Celtic Cross*
Prayertime	Prayertime	Prayertime	Prayertime	Prayertime

Day One

SONG

Round and Round/Christ Be Beside Me

STORY

The Children of Lir

Once upon a time there were four children: Finola and her three brothers, Aedh and the twins Fiachra and Conn. Their mother had died and they lived with their father Lir. Soon Lir took a new wife, called Aoife. For a time everything went well. But over the years Aoife became resentful because she believed that Lir loved his children more than he loved her. As the children grew up Aoife wished she could get rid of them.

One day she took them to Lake Derravaragh to swim. While they were enjoying themselves in the water, Aoife cast a terrible spell on them. She turned the four beautiful children into four swans. The children were very upset. They pleaded with her to return them to their own shape. Aoife would not agree. She told them they would remain as swans for nine hundred years. They must spend three hundred years on this lake, another three hundred on the sea of Moyle between Ireland and Scotland, and another three hundred years in Innis Glorra in the Western Ocean. She gave them two small consolations: they would be able to speak with human voices and they would sing the sweetest songs in the world. Then she went away and left them.

When she returned to Lir she told him that his children had fallen into the lake and drowned. Lir did not believe her. He made her tell him the truth. When he heard what had really happened he turned her forever from his sight.

Lir went to the shores of the lake to see his children. They swam to him and begged him to change them back into their proper form. But, sadly, Lir did not have the power to do as they asked.

Everyone was very sad when they heard the story. They made a rule that no one should harm a swan from that day on.

The children spent three hundred years on the lake. They huddled together to keep themselves warm during the long winters. During the long summers they told each other stories and recalled memories of the happy times before Aoife came into their lives.

Near the end of the nine hundred years a man called Patrick came to Ireland. He spoke to the people about a loving God and his son Jesus. He told them how this loving God wanted them to love each other and to be just and

329

peaceful and kind to others. Many of the people followed the teaching of Patrick.

One day when the nine hundred years were coming to an end, Patrick came to the lake and saw the swans. He heard their sweet singing. He began to talk to them and they told him their story. Patrick was very sad. He wanted to help them. He told them that God – Father, Son and Holy Spirit – loved them and wanted to help them. He blessed them with Holy Water and immediately they changed back into their human form. But instead of four children, an old old woman and three very old men stood in front of Patrick.

Patrick baptised each of them. When they died, Patrick buried them together.

(Based on a version in
Mythology of the Celtic People)

CHATTING

...about the story

Note: *If there is a book of Celtic stories in the school/ class library, this would be a good week in which to read/tell some of them.*

This is a very old story. Do you know any old stories? Can you think of any other old Irish stories? Could you tell us another old Irish story? Story-tellers were always very important in Ireland. In Ireland a story-teller has a special name – '*seanchaí*'. Have you ever listened to a *seanchaí* telling a story? Do you know anyone who is good at telling stories? Do you think some people might be better at telling stories than others? What do you think is the difference between a good story-teller and a not-so-good story-teller?

Can you remember any of the names in the story? Did you notice anything about those names? Have we any of those names in the class/at home/know anyone who has one of those names? Can you think who the Patrick in the story might be? Stories about St Patrick are very old too. Could anyone tell us a story about St Patrick?

PRAYERTIME

Note: *In line with the Celtic focus of this lesson you might like to teach the children 'The Journey Prayer' through Irish. Children may repeat the prayer after the teacher until they become familiar with it.*

Sign of the Cross/Comhartha na Croise

Teacher *(as the candle is lit)*
Arise with me in the morning,
Travel with me through each day,
Welcome me on my arrival.
God, be with me all the way.

Dia na mBóithre
Éirigh liom ar maidin,
Siúil romham's mo dhiadh,
Cuir fáilte romham, tráthnóna,
Bí liom i ndeireadh an lae.

God is with us right here and now.
God is loving us now.
God is caring for us now.
God is blessing us now.
We light our candle.

Close your eyes.
Go into your inside world where it is quiet and peaceful. In your inside world feel God's care for you. Feel God's love for you. Feel God's love all around you. You can rest in the warmth of God's love. You are in God's love. With your special inside voice say 'Thank you, God, for caring for me'. Maybe there is something else you would like to tell God.

Let us ask God to be with us as we pray:

All
Arise with me in the morning,
Travel with me through each day,
Welcome me on my arrival.
God, be with me all the way.

Dia na mBóithre
Éirigh liom ar maidin,
Siúil romham's mo dhiadh,
Cuir fáilte romham, tráthnóna,
Bí liom i ndeireadh an lae.

Sign of the Cross/Comhartha na Croise

Day Two

Continue song: *Round and Round* or *Christ Be Beside Me*

Recall story: *The Children of Lir*

Remember and Say

Deep peace of the running wave to you.
Deep peace of the flowing air to you.
Deep peace of the quiet earth to you.
Deep peace of the shining stars to you.
Deep peace of the Son of Peace to you.

ART

The Swans

Ask the children to draw the swans. Using the figure '2' as an outline, ask the children to draw the head and body. Make feathers from torn tissue paper. Beginning at the swan's tail, carefully stick the end of each 'feather' down so that they overlap. For best effect, do not screw up the tissue paper but paste it flat. The children could draw a river or lake as the background.

PRAYERTIME

Sign of the Cross/Comhartha na Croise.

Teacher
We look up at the sky and we know that God is with us.
We breathe in the air and we know that God is with us.
We watch the stars at night and we know that God is with us.
Whenever we see goodness, we see a sign of

God's presence with us.
We light our candle.

Let us offer each other God's blessing. We know that God is present as we turn to one another with a blessing. Our blessing will be:

Teacher
Deep peace of the running wave to you.
Deep peace of the flowing air to you.
Deep peace of the quiet earth to you.
Deep peace of the shining stars to you.
Deep peace of the Son of Peace to you.

Let us now offer the blessing to each other.

***Note:** The teacher begins by blessing the class, and the children repeat the gestures and bless one another.*

Teacher
Deep peace of the running wave to you. *(open-hand gesture towards the class)*

All
Deep peace of the running wave to you. *(children repeat the hand gesture, turning to the child next to him/her)*

Teacher
Deep peace of the flowing air to you. *(open-hand gesture to the class)*

All
Deep peace of the flowing air to you. *(children repeat open-hand gesture to each other)*

Teacher
Deep peace of the quiet earth to you. *(open-hand gesture to class)*

All
Deep peace of the quiet earth to you. *(children repeat open-hand gesture to each other)*

Teacher
Deep peace of the shining stars to you. *(open-hand gesture to class)*

All
Deep peace of the shining stars to you. *(children repeat open-hand gesture to each other)*

Teacher
Deep peace of the Son of Peace to you. *(open-hand gesture to class)*

All
Deep peace of the Son of Peace to you. *(children repeat open-hand gesture to each other)*

Teacher

May the blessing of God be with us and may God keep us safe.

Sign of the Cross/Comhartha na Croise.

Day Three

Continue song: *Round and Round* or *Christ Be Beside Me*

Note: Play some Irish music or lilting music from the cassette tape.

DID YOU KNOW?

Long ago people gathered in neighbours' houses to sing, to tell stories and to play music. Sometimes they would have a few dances as well. If they didn't have anyone to play music for the dancing, they would sing the tune themselves as they danced. This was called 'lilting'. People had fun singing, dancing and playing music together. In Ireland, songs and singing have always been important. Some Irish songs are very old, telling very old stories. People used to sing to them without any music. This kind of singing is called 'traditional singing'. People do the same kind of thing today, at the *Fleadh Ceoil* or the *Seisiún*.

CHATTING

...about music, song and dance

Note: Any teacher who has a talent for any or all of the following may like to enrich the lesson by offering the children a 'live informal performance'.

Today, all around us, we can hear many different kinds of music. Let's see if we can name some of them.

Which kind of music do you like? Do you think you could tell a piece of Irish music apart from all the other kinds? How? What seems to be different about Irish music? In Ireland we have some musical instruments which are very old. Do you know the names of any musical instruments that are associated with Irish music? (Tin Whistle, Harp, Fiddle, Button Accordion, Uillean Pipes, Bodhrán, Wooden Flute, etc.) Does anybody have/play/know someone who plays one of these instruments? Let's listen to the sound that some instruments make and then see if we can name them (Flute, Fiddle, Bouzouki).

Most of us are very good at lilting. Let's lilt an Irish dance tune. Sometimes people did a dance on their own. Sometimes they danced in groups. Does anyone here do Irish dancing? Let's lilt again and dance together at the same time. Sometimes people sang songs without any music. Let's listen to an example of traditional singing.

ACTIVITY

Note: Listening and responding spontaneously to Irish music is the focus of this activity. The children respond to the music either through movement or art. Choose whatever alternative is most suitable to your situation. A large space, such as a hall, will be needed if the movement option is chosen.

Let's listen and move

Play a piece of Irish music. Ask the children to close their eyes. Ask them to listen carefully to the music, hearing it deep inside themselves. When they are ready, encourage them to move freely to the rhythm of the music. The dance movements should not be restricted to formal Irish dancing steps – encourage the children to create their own movements in line with how they experience and hear the music.

CHATTING

...after the movement

What was it like to close your eyes and listen to the music deep inside you? How did you decide to move to the music? Did you make up your own movements? Would anyone like to show us some of the different movements that they used?

Let's listen and paint

Note: Provide the children with a range of paints and large sheets of paper (old wallpaper would do).

Play a piece of Irish music. Ask the children to close their eyes. Ask them to listen carefully to the music, hearing it deep inside themselves. What colours and shapes do they think of as they listen to the music. When they are ready, encourage them to represent the music through colour and shape.

CHATTING

...after the painting

Ask the children to tell each other, in pairs, about what they have painted. Maybe a few children could be encouraged to show their painting to the class.

PRAYERTIME

Note: This prayer-round begins with the teacher giving a blessing to a child by laying her/his hands on the child's shoulder. The rest of the class, with

the teacher, say 'Deep peace of the running wave to you (name the child)'. This child then turns to the child next to her/him, lays her/his hands on the child's shoulder, while the rest of the class with the teacher say the second line of the prayer. The prayer-round continues in this way until each child has received and given a blessing.

This prayer-round works best if the children are gathered in a large circle. However, it will also work within the normal arrangement of the classroom.

Sign of the Cross/Comhartha na Croise

Teacher
We look at the sky at night and we know that God is with us.
We walk on the green grass and we know that God is with us.
We feel the rain on our faces and we know that God is with us.
We light our candle.
Let us offer each other God's blessing, knowing that God is always with us.

Our blessing will be:

Teacher *(children repeating)*
Deep peace of the running wave to you.
Deep peace of the flowing air to you.
Deep peace of the quiet earth to you.
Deep peace of the shining stars to you.
Deep peace of the Son of Peace to you.

Let us now offer a blessing to each other.

Class with teacher *(as teacher lays hands on child Number 1's shoulder)*
Deep peace of the running wave to you *(name)*.

Class with teacher *(as child Number 1 turns and lays hands on the shoulder of the child next to him/her)*
Deep peace of the flowing air to you *(name)*.

Class with teacher *(as child Number 2 turns and lays hands on the shoulder of the child next to her/him)*
Deep peace of the quiet earth to you *(name)*.

Class with teacher *(as child Number 3 turns and lays hands on the shoulder of the child next to her/him)*
Deep peace of the shining stars to you *(name)*.

Class with teacher *(as child Number 4 turns*

and lays hands on the shoulder of the child next to him/her)
Deep peace of the Son of Peace to you *(name).*

Class with teacher *(as child Number 5 turns and lays hands on the shoulder of the child next to her/him)*
Deep peace of the running wave to you *(name).*

(Continue the prayer-round until each child has received and given an individual blessing.)

Teacher
Let us put our hands on the shoulder of the person next to us:
May the blessing of God be with us and may God keep us safe.

Sign of the Cross/Comhartha na Croise

Day Four

Continue song: *Round and Round* or *Christ Be Beside Me*

 ACTIVITY

Celtic Designs

Choose one of the following activities:
- Ask the children to experiment with some simple circular Celtic designs. Use bright coloured markers to decorate.
- Make Celtic designs using Plasticine/Play-dough. Ask the children to roll out small pieces of Plasticine/Play-dough in snake-like shapes. Using the Plasticine/Play-dough experiment with various circular designs, ask the children to draw the design they have just made.
- Using a flattened piece of Plasticine/Play-dough as a base, ask the children to build a Celtic design.

- Taking their initials of their name, get the children to make a Celtic design around them. Decorate the initials using bright coloured markers.
- Ask the children to make a bookmark using some simple Celtic patterns.

 PRAYERTIME

Sign of the Cross/Comhartha na Croise.

Teacher
When we see the sky it reminds us of God.
When we look at the sea it reminds us of God.
When we hear the birds sing it reminds us of God.
We bless the deep peace of the world created by God.
We light our candle.

Teacher *(children repeating)*
Time and time and time again.
Praise God, praise God.

Teacher
Let us today offer our own blessings of deep peace by putting our own words to the prayer.
Close your eyes.
Now think of all the things that remind you of God.
Let us add them to our prayer.

Invite the children to substitute their own words:
Deep peace of the _____ to you.

Individual children can change the words while the class and teacher repeat the blessing after it has been said.

All
Deep peace of the running wave to you.
Deep peace of the flowing air to you.
Deep peace of the quiet earth to you.
Deep peace of the shining stars to you.
Deep peace of the Son of Peace to you.

Sign of the Cross/Comhartha na Croise.

Day Five

WORKSHEET

If you wish to use the worksheet or workbook page which accompanies this lesson, this is an appropriate time to do so.

CHATTING

...about the Celtic Cross
Today we are going to make a special cross. It's called a Celtic cross. What shape is a cross? Where would you find a cross? Does anyone have a chain with a cross on it? A Celtic Cross has a very special shape. Let's look at the shape of a Celtic Cross. *Draw an outline of a Celtic Cross on the blackboard.* What's the difference between the Celtic Cross and an ordinary cross? Some Celtic Crosses have pictures on them that tell stories from the Bible. Today we are going to make our own special Celtic Cross and we are going to write a special blessing on it.

ART

Celtic Cross

To make a Celtic Cross
- Begin by drawing a circle in the upper middle of a page.

- Draw two 'arms' on either side of the circle.
- From the base of the circle, draw a long rectangle for the shaft of the cross.
- From the top of the circle draw a short rectangle.
- Draw two semi-circles at each of the four corners of the cross.
- Ask the children to write one of the following inside each of the semi-circles: Deep, Peace, of, God.

Encourage the children to bring their Celtic Cross home and to give the blessing to someone they know.

PRAYERTIME

Sign of the Cross/Comhartha na Croise.

All
Song: *Christ Be Beside Me*

Teacher
As we light our candle we know that God is with us. God is with us night and day. Let us ask God to bless us and keep us always as we pray: May God bless us and keep us, we pray.

Teacher
Each morning as we get up.

All
May God bless us and keep us, we pray.

Teacher
Each day as we work in school.

All
May God bless us and keep us, we pray.

Teacher
Each evening as we play with our friends.

All
May God bless us and keep us, we pray.

Teacher
Each night as we lie in bed.

All
May God bless us and keep us, we pray.

Teacher
May God bless all those we love and keep them safe today and every day.

Close your eyes and think of someone you want to pray for.
With your inside voice ask God to be with that person every day.
Ask God to take care of her/him.

Teacher
We ask God's blessing on us all as we pray together.

All
Deep peace of the running wave to you.
Deep peace of the flowing air to you.
Deep peace of the quiet earth to you.
Deep peace of the shining stars to you.
Deep peace of the Son of Peace to you.
Amen.

Sign of the Cross/Comhartha na Croise.

Round and Round

Fran Hegarty

1. Sum - mer fades to au - tumn gold,
leaves fall to___ the ground.
Days are get - ting short - er as the
sea - sons turn a - round.
Au - tumn days get cold - er, soon the
win - ter winds___ will blow.
In be - tween comes Hal - low - e'en___ when the
chan - ges start to show.

Oh like the night—— time——
al - ways turns to day,
the tides they come and go—— but the
o - cean's here to stay.
The sea - sons change and yet—— it
all re - mains the same—— go - ing round and
round.

2. Winter snows melt away and buds are on the trees,
   Days are getting longer as the buds turn into leaves,
   Spring is here and sunshine soon will drive away the rain,
   When the summer's over, it will all go round again.

Coda:

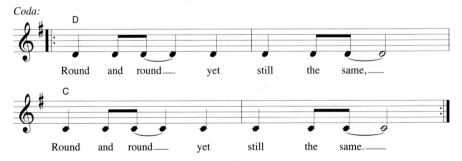

Round and round—— yet still the same,——
Round and round—— yet still the same.——

Christ Be Beside Me

Traditional

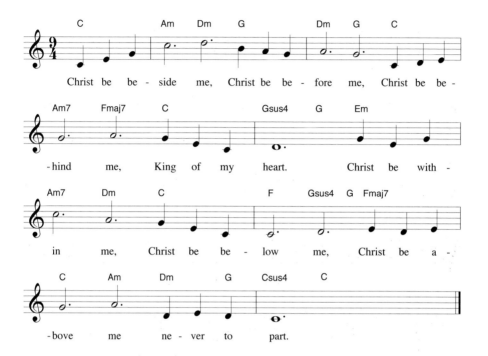

Christ be be - side me, Christ be be - fore me, Christ be be -
hind me, King of my heart. Christ be with -
in me, Christ be be - low me, Christ be a -
bove me ne - ver to part.

2. Christ on my right hand,
Christ on my left hand,
Christ all around me,
Shield in the strife.
Christ in my sleeping,
Christ in my sitting,
Christ in my rising,
Light of my life.

3. Christ be in all hearts,
Thinking about me,
Christ be on all tongues,
Telling of me.
Christ be the vision,
In eyes that see me,
In ears that hear me
Christ ever be.

O, give thanks to the Lord, for he is good;
for his steadfast love endures for ever.
(Psalm 107:1)

The school year is drawing to a close. The
year's work is done and the long summer
days beckon us forth. At this stage the
children have journeyed through the days,
weeks and months together. They have been
together through the exciting and the not-so-
exciting times. The year has provided them
with countless opportunities to explore what
it feels like to belong and to understand the
significance of belonging with others. By now
the children have reflected on their experience
of working together, playing together, telling
stories and sharing their lives with one
another. Hopefully they have learned what it
means to belong.

We began the year by focusing on the fact that
the children were moving into a new class.
They were moving out of a familiar situation
and moving into one which was strange and
unfamiliar. Then they were beginning the
process of belonging. Now they have done the
full circle and, in a process that is mirrored
time and again in the cycles of the seasons and
in the pattern of human life, the children are
ready to move on.

In this lesson, then, we celebrate the year, and
lead the children into a celebratory week of
story, game, fun and praise of God.

FOR THE TEACHER:

A thought before beginning

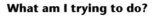

We shall not cease from
    exploration
And the end of all our exploring
Will be to arrive where we
    started
And to know the place for the first time.
    T. S. Eliot

What am I trying to do?

To provide a context for the children to reflect on
and appreciate their experience of belonging as a
class during the past year.

Why?

So that a context may be set within which they
can understand the concept of belonging to the
Christian community called Church.

Overview of the Week

Song: *Alive-O*				
Chatting about the year		Continue song		
		We Prepare		
Activity: *Favourite Times*	Continue song	Art: *Congratulations Cards*	Continue song, preparation	
Prayertime	Worksheet			
	Prayertime	Prayertime	Prayertime	Celebratory Ritual

Day One

SONG

Alive-O

CHATTING

...about the year

We are coming to the end of the year. Soon we will be on our summer holidays. How do you feel? What sort of things are you looking forward to? Tell us about some of the things you will do during the summer.

Can anyone remember what it was like when we started the year? How did you feel then? Let's look at our Enrolment Book. Let's look at some of the pictures of ourselves! Who remembers that day? Have we changed since then, I wonder? How? What about our Class Code? Do you think we have lived according to it? Could we have done better? How? Why? Would you change anything in it today? What?

Close your eyes and picture the year gone by. Now picture the best time during the year and tell us about it.

ACTIVITY

Favourite Times

Ask the children to draw a picture of a favourite time during the school year.

Cut out these pictures and make a collage of the class's favourite times. A possible caption could be 'Favourite Times'.

or

Make a bar-chart of the class's favourite time during the year.

PRAYERTIME

Sign of the Cross.

Teacher *(as the candle is lit)*
God of yesterday.
God of today.
God of tomorrow.

During the year we learned how to belong to this class. Sometimes it was easy, other times it was hard. During the year we spent a lot of time together. It was good to have others to share stories and fun, and maybe even tears, with. Let us praise God for bringing us safely through the year.

All
We praise you and bless you, O God.

Teacher
The school year has come to an end.

All
We praise you and bless you, O God.

Teacher
It was fun to be together.

All
We praise you and bless you, O God.

Teacher
It was good to belong to this class.

All
We praise you and bless you, O God.

Teacher
We thank God for all the time we have spent together.
Let us close our eyes and think of our favourite time.
Imagine yourself in that time. Imagine what it was like.

With your inside voice thank God for that time.

All *(sing)*
Time and time and time again.
Praise God, praise God.

Sign of the Cross.

Day Two

Continue song: *Alive-O*

WORKSHEET

Certificate of Belonging

Ask the children to decorate their Certificate of Belonging.
Encourage them to fill it in and to sign it.

PRAYERTIME

Sign of the Cross.

Teacher *(as the candle is lit)*
God of yesterday.
God of today.
God of tomorrow.

Today we thank God for all who helped us through the year.
We ask God to bless them and care for them.

For those at home.

All
God bless them and keep them, we pray.

Teacher
For our friends.

All
God bless them and keep them, we pray.

Teacher
For our principal _____ *(name).*

All
God bless him/her and keep him/her, we pray.

Teacher
For our vice-principal _____ *(name)* and all the teachers.

All
God bless them and keep them, we pray.

Teacher
For our school caretaker _____ *(name).*

All
God bless him/her and keep him/her, we pray.

Teacher
For our lollipop person _____ *(name).*

All
God bless him/her and keep him/her, we pray.

Teacher
For all those who have died.

All
God bless them and keep them, we pray.

Glory be to the Father…

Sign of the Cross.

Day Three

Continue song: *Alive-O*

Note: Over the next two days, involve the children in preparing for a celebratory presentation that will take place on Day Five.

We Prepare

Ask the children to recall:
* their favourite stories/poems
* their favourite songs
* their favourite games

Select one of each for the prayertime ritual on Day Five.

ART

Congratulations Cards

You will need:
- A sheet of paper for each child
- Markers/paints
- Scissors

Put the names of all of the children in a box. Ask each child to pull out a name. Ask them to make a congratulations card for that person. Discuss the design and shape of the card. Maybe it could include bits of poems/songs from the children's textbook or pictures of various stories, characters, etc.

On the inside of the card write a message, e.g. 'I'm Glad You Belong', 'Best Wishes', 'Thanks for a Great Year', 'It was Fun to Belong in the Class with You', 'We had Fun Together', 'We Are Alive-O'.

PRAYERTIME

Sign of the Cross.

Teacher *(as the candle is lit)*
God of yesterday.
God of today.
God of tomorrow.

God has been with us right through the year.
God is with us now.
God is with us as we congratulate each other at the end of our school year.
We sing:

All
Alive-O 3

Teacher
It is fun to celebrate. It is good to celebrate with one another.

God is with us when we celebrate together.
We ask God to bless each one of us as we come to the last week of the year.

All
Bless us, O God, we pray.

Teacher
Let us now give our congratulations to each other as we say 'well done!'

Invite each child to move around the class and give their congratulations card to their chosen person. (Perhaps they could shake hands.) Children then return to their own seat, hold hands and sing:

All *(sing)*
Time and time and time again.
Praise God, praise God.

or

Alive-O

Sign of the Cross.

Day Four

Continue song: *Alive-O*

Continue preparation

PRAYERTIME

Sign of the Cross.

Teacher *(as the candle is lit)*
God of yesterday.
God of today.
God of tomorrow.

Today we give praise to God for all the people we belong to. We pray:

All
We praise you and bless you.

Teacher
We belong to our families.

All
We praise you and bless you.

Teacher
We belong to our school.

All
We praise you and bless you.

Teacher
We belong to the Church.

All
We praise you and bless you.

Teacher
We belong to the parish of _____.

All
We praise you and bless you.

Teacher
We belong to God the Father, the Son and the Holy Spirit.

All
We praise you and bless you.

Teacher
Let us hold hands as we pray together in the words Jesus taught us and as we are led by the Holy Spirit.

All
Our Father...

Sign of the Cross.

Day Five

P R A Y E R T I M E

Celebratory Ritual

In preparation for the ritual arrange the room so that the children can sit in a circle. You might like to decorate the room with balloons and with the children's artwork. Place the Enrolment Book in the centre of the circle. Place the candle beside it.

Sign of the Cross.

All
Sing: *Together Again/Alive-O*

Teacher
Today is a special day. Today is our last day in this class. We have been together all year long. Maybe we are excited to know that the summer holidays are here. Maybe we feel sad because some of us will be saying goodbye to each other for a while. But it is now time to move on.

Let us light our candle.

Let us ask God to be with us as we move on.

All
God be with us on our way.

Teacher
As we say goodbye to this class.

All
God be with us on our way.

Teacher
As we say goodbye to each other.

All
God be with us on our way.

Teacher
As we begin our summer holidays.

All
God be with us on our way.

Teacher
We have had a good year together.
Let us thank God now for all that we have learned.

For songs to sing. Let us sing a favourite song now.

All
Song of children's choice
Thank you, God, for the songs to sing.

Teacher
For stories/poems to tell. Let us tell a story/poem now.

All
Story/poem of children's choice
Thank you, God, for the stories/poems to tell.

Teacher
For games to play. Let us play a game now.

All
Game of children's choice
Thank you, God, for the games to play.

Teacher
Thank you, God, for everything that we learned this year.
Thank you for the gift of each other.
Let us hold hands and say our poem.

All
Poem: *Where I Belong (Christy Kenneally)* *(Term 1, Lesson 5)*

Teacher presents the Certificate of Belonging to each child as the rest of the class applauds.

Teacher
May God bless us and keep us safe.

All
Amen.

Teacher
May God bless our families and friends.

All
Amen.

Teacher
May God bless each and everyone as we make the Sign of the Cross.

All
In the name of the Father,
And of the Son,
And of the Holy Spirit.
Amen.

Song: *Alive-O*

Sign of the Cross.

Alive-O!

Words: Clare Maloney
Music: Fran Hegarty

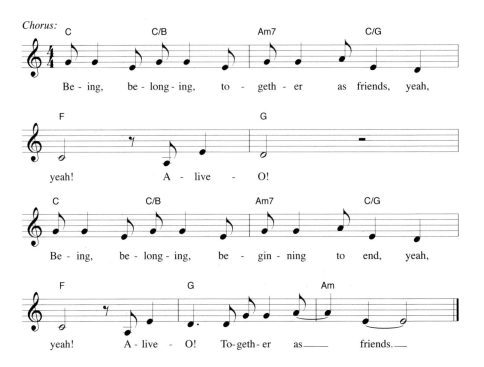

Chorus:

Be - ing, be - long - ing, to - geth - er as friends, yeah,

yeah! A - live - O!

Be - ing, be - long - ing, be - gin - ning to end, yeah,

yeah! A - live - O! To-geth- er as___ friends.___

1. Say Be! Say We! Say You! Say Me!
   Say Yes, Yes, YES! Because we are ALIVE-O!
   Say Sow! Say Grow! Ready, Steady, say GO!
   Say Hey! Praise God! Because we are ALIVE-O!

2. Say Do! Say Don't! Say Will! Say Won't!
   Be all you can be, because we are ALIVE-O!
   Say Try! Say True! Say Good through and through!
   Say Hey! Praise God! Because we are ALIVE-O!

Nativity Play

The Moment We've Been Waiting For

CHARACTERS
>   Mary
>   Joseph
>   Melchior
>   Balthasaar
>   Caspar
>   Naomi – a young shepherdess
>   Benjamin – a young shepherd
>   Isaac – a solo singer
>   A group of shepherds
>   Centurion
>   Simeon
>   Anna
>   A group of soldiers
>   A choir of angels
>   A group of innkeepers
>   A child carrying a star

For all the songs in this play, a choir, assembled nearby or on stage, may assist the singing. They should stand when they sing, and sit and watch when not singing.

ACTIVITY

During the singing of the opening song, the three wise men make their way through the audience and onto the stage. Melchior carries a 'telescope' (perhaps a tin-foil tube). Caspar carries a rolled-up map and various instruments such as a large blackboard-size protractor, a set-square etc. Balthasaar carries a compass (a home-made one, large enough to be clearly visible). As the song continues, they peer at the sky; study the map; examine the compass and swap instruments. They adopt many different poses and gestures for the duration of the song (such as scratching the head, as if puzzled; each king, in turn, pointing towards a different direction while the other two shake their heads in disagreement; sitting down and waiting, drumming fingers impatiently, and so on). They may also join in the singing.

ACT 1, SCENE 1

SONG

The three wise men sing this song, assisted by the choir.

Following A Star

Verse 1
Why are we waiting here, why?
Why are we waiting here, why?
Waiting for the joy and hope the baby brings
To us and to the world.

Chorus
We are the wise men,
Caspar, Melchior and Balthasaar.
We are the wise men,
Following a star.

Verse 2
Why are we watching here, why?
Why are we watching here, why?
Watching for a new star in the sky above
To guide us on our way.

Verse 3
Why are we wondering here, why?
Why are we wondering here, why?
Wondering if the road we're on will ever end,
If the new King will be there.

Melchior (*pointing in the direction of the ceiling at the back of the room/hall*)
Look at all those stars!

Balthasaar and Caspar (*each with one hand 'shading' their eyes as they very obviously peer at the audience*)
Never mind all those stars,
look at all these stars!

Melchior
They're not stars, not real stars…

Balthasaar
How do you know they're not real stars... they might be able to sing and dance and...

Caspar
This play could do with some good singers and actors. Let's ask them and see.

Melchior
Don't be silly! I mean they're not the kind of stars in the story.

Balthasaar and Caspar
What story?

Melchior
This story...

SONG

The kings, assisted by the choir, sing these words to the tune of 'Once Upon A Time'.

Verse 1
Gather round, and a story you will hear.
It's a story that's retold every year
About a baby, a manger and a star
And wise men from afar.
You can hear it in once upon a time.

Verse 2
Gather round and a story you will hear.
It's a story that's retold every year
About a mother, some shepherds, angels too.
Sing glory Allelu.
You can hear it in once upon a time.

All three stare silently for a moment.

Melchior
There is a new star in the sky tonight? I wonder why!

Balthasaar
That's what I'm wondering too.

Caspar
I wonder if it's a sign – a star-sign?

All three stare silently for another moment.

Balthasaar and Caspar
Why are we watching?

Melchior
Because we are waiting.

Balthasaar and Caspar
Why are we waiting? *(They begin to sing together, 'Why are we waiting, why are we waiting' etc.)*

Melchior *(impatiently)*
Because we are wise. All wise people watch and wait.

Balthasaar
I wonder why!

Caspar
Me too. *(Turning to Melchior)* Why do all wise people watch and wait, Melchior?

Melchior *(crossly)*
You two are only half-wise, otherwise you would know why. Wise people watch and wait because they don't want to miss anything. *(Melchior becomes excited.)* Watch out! The star is moving! *(He rushes around, gathering up the equipment, before heading off in the direction of the star.)*

Balthasaar *(in a laid-back voice)*
I see that.

Caspar *(equally laid back)*
I wonder why it's moving!

Balthasaar *(making no moves to follow the star)*
If something is moving, you can follow it.

Caspar *(making no moves either)*
True. You cannot follow a thing that does not move.

Balthasaar
You are a very wise man, Caspar.

Melchior *(rushes back on stage, agitated)*
Come along, come along, we must follow the star, hurry!

Balthasaar
Hurry, Caspar.

Caspar
Hurry Balthasaar.

The three hurry off stage.

SCENE 2

Centurion accompanied by soldiers and carrying a roll-book enters the stage. He/she addresses the audience directly.

Centurion
You there *(pointing at someone who may or may not have been planted there)* in the front row – where are you from?
(The person answers and, as they do so, the centurion pretends to write the details in the book.)
You must go to Bethlehem. Caesar's orders.
(The centurion repeats this process twice more.)

Melchior enters the stage and says with agitation:

Melchior
It'll take till Christmas to count all these at the rate you're going.

Centurion
Everyone must be counted. Caesar's orders.

He points as if to call out another person, but Melchior interrupts him.

Melchior
But we must move on, the story must be told tonight.

Centurion *(repeating)*
Everyone must be counted. Caesar's orders.

Melchior
I'll tell you what I'll do. *(He whispers in the centurion's ear and then turns, addressing the audience directly.)* Do you want to hear the rest of the story? Are you sure? Well then, you must all promise this centurion that as soon as this story is told tonight, you will all go to Bethlehem to sign Caesar's book. Do you promise? Louder…

Centurion *(to audience)*
Repeat after me – We promise.

Audience repeats: We promise.

To go to Bethlehem.

Audience repeats: To go to Bethlehem.

To be counted.

Audience repeats: To be counted.

Very well then. *(He leaves the stage, but just before he exits he turns to Melchior one last time and points a warning finger.)*

Remember – you promised!

Melchior
Now, let's get on with the story. *(He exits)*

SCENE 3

A long queue of people wind across the stage like a snake. Those at the front of the queue are the main speaking characters, Mary, Joseph, Naomi, Benjamin, Simeon and Anna.

They sing the following to the tune of 'The Passover Song'.

SONG

Chorus
Watching and waiting and waiting and watching.
Watching, waiting, wondering too.
Watching and waiting and waiting and watching
For a Saviour – a Saviour who *(last chorus 'A Saviour true')*.

Verse 1
Will lead us, to the freedom of God's kingdom,
Will tell us the story of God's love,
Will share the bread and wine of life with humankind,
And send us the Spirit from above.

Verse 2
Will teach us to call God 'Our Father',
Will heal the sick and comfort those who cry,
Will right the wrongs to those who've been ill-treated,
Bring new life to all those who've died.

Two soldiers enter the stage.

Soldier 1
That's enough of that noise.

Soldier 2
We could arrest you for singing such rebel songs. Be quiet and stand to attention for our centurion.

The centurion enters the stage, still carrying the

large roll-book from earlier. He pretends to do a rough head count. As he is doing so, the cross young woman says:

Naomi

Some day, we will have a true leader, someone to put these Roman soldiers in their place. *(The others in the queue nod and mumble assent.)* A leader from among our own people who will show everyone how to treat people fairly and justly.

Benjamin

We have been waiting for a leader like that for a long, long time. How much longer do we have to wait?

Simeon

My name is Simeon. I have spent my whole life watching and waiting for him. God will send us a leader, I am sure of it.

Anna

My name is Anna. I too have spent a lifetime watching and waiting for the one whom God promised to send. I have prayed. I know it will not be long now.

Naomi

Well, whenever he comes, it will not be a moment too soon.

Benjamin

Speaking of sooner – the sooner we get back to our flocks on the hillside, the better. They will be scattered far and wide by now. It'll take all night to gather them together.

Centurion

That's enough talking! Be quiet! *(Turning to his soldiers)* Who are all these people and where are they from? *(pointing to the queue on stage)*

Soldier 1

These are David's people and they have come from Nazareth.

Centurion

And who are all these? *(pointing to the audience)*

Soldier 2

These are all *(mentioning the name of the school)* and they come from *(mentioning the name of the locality)*.

Centurion *(repeating the names just mentioned)*

Never heard of them! Take the whole lot of them to the Scriptorium to sign up.

Handing the book to soldier 1, he says (obviously referring to the audience)

They don't look too intelligent.

(Turning from the soldier he addresses the audience)

Can you lot all write your own name? Well… speak up.

Allow a moment for an audience response. Shaking his head as he leaves the stage, the centurion says in a loud voice:

Definitely a rather 'stupid' lot! *(He turns to soldier 2)*

Now, we need to sort out our accommodation for the night. Are there any innkeepers in the queue?

Soldier 1

Anyone who has an inn, step forward.

A group of innkeepers step forward. They can be as numerous or as few as you wish. They sing to the tune of 'My Body Clock'.

SONG

Verse 1

Today is just the busiest we've been for quite some time,

With crowds of people queuing up and waiting just to sign.

They come from near, they come from far, all looking for a place.

We've never been so busy; we just cannot keep pace.

Chorus

I haven't got a room, no room for anyone.

I haven't got a room; no room, no room.

Verse 2 (The soldiers)

We are Caesar's soldiers, we're the rulers of this land

And what we soldiers want – we get! So, take heed! Understand!

Turn your guests out of their rooms; make way for Caesar's men

Or it'll be the worse for you, your families and your friends!

350

Chorus
We soldiers want a room; all rooms, every room.
We soldiers want a room; all rooms, all rooms.

Verse 3 (Joseph stepping forward with Mary)
We two have travelled far this day and Mary is with child.
We need a room where we can stay; the night is wet and wild.
The moment we've been waiting for is very soon to come.
Shepherds, kings and angels wait the birth of Mary's son.

Chorus (Mary and Joseph, while innkeepers and soldiers shake their heads)
Please let us have a room; one room, any room.
Please let us have a room; one room, one room.

Verse 4 (Melchior entering, and trying to hurry things along)
Not a room of any kind, or so the story goes,
Except for one kind woman, who's had children and she knows
That every newborn baby and its mother need a bed.
'I've a stable in the hills, you can go there,' she said.
'You can go there,' she said, 'go there and make a bed.
You can go there,' she said, 'go there, go there.' *(Melchior points off stage.)*

Melchior
That's that sorted out. Now, take all these people away to sign the book.

He ushers the soldiers, the centurion and the queue off stage and then he leaves himself. Mary and Joseph straggle along at the back of the queue.

Joseph
Sit down Mary. Take a moment to rest yourself. You must be tired out.

Mary *(sits down, Joseph sits beside her)*
Yes Joseph, let's take a moment to rest.

Mary and Joseph sing 'Mary, Our Mother'.

SONG

Mary, Our Mother

Chorus
Mary, our mother, the Lord is with you.
Guide us, protect us in all that we do.

Verse 1
Angel Gabriel said to you,
'You will be mother of Jesus.'

Verse 2
With Elizabeth you rejoiced,
'I will be mother of Jesus.'

Verse 3
In a manger in Bethlehem
You became mother of Jesus.

Mary
We have had many precious moments, Joseph, but right at this moment, we need to move on and find the stable where we can stay. I have a feeling this baby will be here soon.

SONG

Mary and Joseph walk a few 'laps' of the stage. As they do so, the choir sing two verses of 'Carol Of The Journey'.

SCENE 4

A group of shepherds sit around in a semi-circle. Naomi and Benjamin are standing, one on either side of the semi-circle, recounting their experience of earlier on in the day.

Naomi
Some day a leader will come from among our own people, who will put an end to the

soldiers' rule. Then we will never again have to sign our names in Caesar's book.

Benjamin
I have never seen such a long queue. It took ages to sign.

Third Shepherd
We have gathered all your sheep, as well as our own, for the night, so there is nothing for you to do. You look worn out. Sit down and take a rest. Isaac was just about to sing *The Lost Sheep* song for us.

They sit down. Isaac stands up and sings. The others join in the chorus.

SONG

The Lost Sheep

Verse 1
The poor little sheep, he started to weep
All lost and alone in the wood.
He didn't cry 'Mummy', he didn't cry 'Mum',
He just started bleating as loud as he could:
'Baa, baa, baa, I've lost my Ma-ma, maa, maa,
Baa, baa, baa, I've lost my Ma-ma.'

Verse 2
Back home in the shed, the mother sheep said,
'My baby is not by my side.'
She didn't cry 'Sonny', she didn't cry 'Son',
She just started bleating and here's what she cried:
'Maa, maa, maa, I've lost my baba, baa, baa.
Maa, maa, maa, I've lost my baba.'

Verse 3
The shepherd came in and said with a grin,
'See mother I've brought home your boy!'
He didn't cry 'Mummy'; she didn't cry 'Son',
They just started bleating aloud in their joy:
'Maa, maa, maa, I've found my baba, baa, baa.'
'Baa, baa, baa, I've found my mama!'

During the last chorus a choir of angels enter the stage and join in the singing. If there are a lot of angels to be 'got on stage', they could begin to enter during the last verse, singing along with

Isaac. The shepherds are so 'shocked' that their mouths drop open, they stare and forget to finish the song.

Melchior *(rushing on stage)*
Wait, wait! This is wrong. This is not part of the story. The angels are supposed to sing Glo-o-o-o-o-o ria in excelsis deo, not maa, maa, maa and baa, baa, baa!

Angel 1
Who are you?

Melchior
I'm Melchior, one of the three wise men.

Angel 2
Then it's you who are wrong – in the wrong place at the wrong time.

Angel 3
The wise men don't come into the story until the end.

Melchior
Yes I know, but for now I'm just supervising, to see that the story is told properly.

Angel 1
Well for now we're just joining in the song because it's a good song.

Angel 2
We sing the same Gloria song every year, it's nice to have a change.

Melchior
Very well, but can you get on with the proper story now please, otherwise, we may run out of time and we wise men might not get to see the baby at all! *(He exits)*

SONG

Angels sing the shepherds' verse of 'Carol of The Journey', followed by Gloria in Excelsis Deo. As they finish, Naomi becomes very excited.

Naomi
This is it! This is it! *(she shouts to the other shepherds).* This is the sign we have been

waiting and watching for, wondering who would be our leader!

Benjamin
She's right. All the watching and waiting and wondering is finally over! We must go and see this new baby who will be our Saviour!

The Other Shepherds (together)
But what about our sheep, our lambs? We can't just run off and leave them, they might wander away and get lost…

Angel 1
Don't worry about your sheep; we will look after them for you.

Melchior (hurrying on stage again)
Go on, go on, go on will you, or the story will never get to the end and we'll be wandering about from East to West for another year!

He ushers the shepherds off stage.

Angel 3 (to the other angels)
Do any of you know anything about minding sheep?

Angels shake their heads, shrug their shoulders and generally murmer 'No'.

Angel 2
I know, let's sing to them.

Angel 1
I say, I say, I say, what kind of songs do sheep like?

Angels (together)
We don't know; what kind of songs do sheep like?

Angel 1
Why lullabaa-aas of course!

All the angels exit the stage singing choruses of The Lost Sheep *song as they go.*

ACT 2, SCENE 1

Mary, carrying the baby, and Joseph, carrying a little lamb, enter stage and place the baby in a manger and the lamb beside it. They look at it for a moment, smiling.

Mary
This is the moment we've been waiting for, Joseph. It seems such a long time ago since the day the angel came and told me the good news… Do you remember, Joseph?

Joseph
Indeed I do. (*Leaving Mary's side and coming forward to address the audience.*)
The moment the angel appeared
Mary grew worried, and yet…

Mary (coming forward to join him)
The moment I first heard the news
Is a moment I'll never forget.

Joseph
The moment she left on her journey
Mary grew worried, and yet…

Mary
The moment Elizabeth hugged me
Is a moment I'll never forget.

Joseph
The moment I mentioned 'Bethlehem'
Mary grew worried, and yet…

Mary (looking at Joseph)
The moment you said 'I'll be with you'
Is a moment I'll never forget.

Joseph
The moment the keeper said 'No room'
We both grew worried, and yet…

Mary
The moment yon little lamb bleated
Is a moment I'll never forget.

Joseph (picking up the baby)
The moment the baby first cried
We both grew worried, and yet…

Mary
The moment our baby first smiled
We thought, this is the best moment yet!

All cast except the wise men and soldiers assemble on stage, grouped around the manger. All together, they say the poem.

POEM

The Crib Community

Amidst all the tinsel and glitter
And fuss and bother and din,
To our house every Christmas
A whole community moves in.

Several men, one woman, one baby,
Where on earth will they fit?
Sheep, lambs, a cow and a donkey,
With a manger and straw – and that's it!

After settling their babe in the manger
They arrange themselves out before him,
Then spend Christmas Days, feasting their gaze;
It's obvious they simply adore him!

Amidst all the hustle and hassle
There's something so graceful about them,
Although they don't say or do anything
It wouldn't be Christmas without them!

SONG

Led by a child carrying a star, Caspar and Balthasaar enter. They present their gifts as the choir sings the kings' verse of 'Carol Of The Journey'.

Naomi
Only two wise men! Shouldn't there be three?

Caspar and Balthasaar
There were three of us. We've watched and waited like the story says, now we are wondering…

Benjamin
Wondering … what are you wondering about at this late stage? The story is almost over, the baby is born.

Caspar and Balthasaar
We're wondering where Melchior has got to.

A great marching of feet is heard. Melchior, protesting loudly and being roughly escorted by soldiers, enters from the back of the hall/ performance area and makes his way on stage.

Melchior
You cannot arrest me. I am an Eastern king. You have no authority over me.

Centurion
You may be an Eastern king, but here in this country, Rome rules. OK! You are under arrest. You made a bargain and you did not keep it.

Naomi *(stepping forward)*
The moment has finally come: the beginning of the end of Roman rule in our country.

She takes the baby in her arms and shows it to the centurion.

This baby, born tonight in this stable, is our king. He will lead us to freedom from Rome's rule. You will see.

Centurion *(laughing mockingly)*
Hah! This is a king! A baby born in a stable … Show me his army, show me his might and his power! Hah! Go back to your sheep, girl, for sheep will be all this baby will ever lead.

Soldiers all laugh.

Anna *(Taking the baby from Naomi)*
You are right, soldier. This baby will grow up to be a shepherd, but he will be a good shepherd like King David, his ancestor.

Simeon *(stepping forward)*
Yes, you are right soldier, he will never have a powerful army like Caesar's. For he will always be on the side of those who have no power, no might.

Mary
You are only partly right, Naomi, for yes, this baby will be a great leader. But his kingdom will not be a particular place – it will be anywhere and everywhere that people live together in the spirit of Christmas, in the spirit of peace on earth and goodwill to all.

SONG

Angel choir sings their chorus of 'Carol of the Journey'.

When they finish, Melchior, who is still being held by the soldiers, attempts to go and give his gift to the baby. He struggles to break free.

Centurion
Where do you think you're going?

Melchior
Let me go, I must give my gift to the baby.

Centurion
If you were really a wise man, you would keep your gift for Caesar, to try and make up for breaking your bargain.

Melchior
It's not my fault that all those other people didn't turn up to sign your book. They promised me they would. It is they and not I who have broken the promise.

Caspar and Balthasaar
But they have turned up! Look, there they are *(pointing to the audience)*. They are just waiting for the story to be over. Then they will sign the book. *(Turning to address the audience)* Won't you?… won't you?…

Melchior *(still 'under arrest', speaks to the audience)*
I'll tell you what, if you agree to sign the book, then clap your hands now.

(Caspar, Balthasaar and the others on stage begin to clap their hands. Hopefully, the audience will join in.) Thank goodness for that! *(The soldiers let go of him and he presents his gift.)* At last, the story is all told *(with a great flourish)*. THIS is the moment we have all been waiting for!

Total cast shout
Hurray for Baby Jesus; Hurray for Christmas; Hurray, Hurray, Hurray!

Finale

SONG

Everyone sings

This Is The Moment

Verse 1
Mary and Joseph tried to find a place to stay in Bethlehem,
But they were turned away at every door.
They settled in a stable where baby Jesus was born.
'This is the moment we've been waiting for.'

Chorus
As the star rose in the sky on that first Christmas night,
Mary held him in her arms and held him oh so tight.
The moment had arrived and he gave a little smile to the world,
A smile to the world.

Verse 2
The sound of angels filled the sky,
The shepherds heard each word they sang:
'Go see the baby and wait no more.'
Three wise men in the morning light,
Found the star, it was so bright.
'This is the moment we've been waiting for.'

Mass of Peace

Seoirse Bodley

Kyrie

Gospel Acclamation

'I am the good shepherd,' says the Lord. 'I know my own sheep and my own know me.'

Sanctus

Ho - ly, ho - ly, ho - ly Lord;

God of pow'r and— might.

Hea - ven and— earth are— full of your glo - ry. Ho -

san - na in the high - est. Bless - ed is— he who—

comes in the name of the Lord. Ho - san - na in the high - est.

Consecration Acclamation

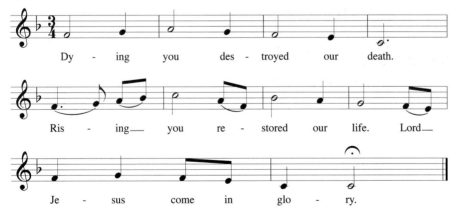

Dy - ing you des - troyed our death.

Ris - ing— you re - stored our life. Lord—

Je - sus come in glo - ry.

Great Amen

A - men.— A - men. A - men. A - men.

Agnus Dei

Lamb of God, you take a-way the sins of the world: have mer - cy on us.

Lamb of God, you take a-way the sins of the world: grant us— peace.

Celebration of First Holy Communion

Entrance Hymn
Happy in the Presence

Introduction
We have gathered here today with our families, our relations, and our friends. It is a good day. It is a good day for our parish/Christian community. It is a very special day for the girls and boys who are gathered around the table of the Lord to receive their First Communion. It is their day!

Priest invites each parent/guardian on behalf of the Christian community formally to welcome their son/daughter to this special cermony, by taking her/his hand and saying '_____ (name of child) you are very welcome to this very special celebration.'

So, girls and boys, as we gather today let us close our eyes and remember our time together as we prepared for this day:

We remember the year we have spent together. *Pause*

We remember all that we have learned. *Pause*

We remember the stories we have heard about Jesus. *Pause*

We give God thanks for the gift of life in ourselves and the gift of life that we share with others.

We give God thanks for all those who love us and who help us to grow and to learn.

We give thanks especially for Jesus who showed us how much God loves us and all people.

Opening Prayer
God our Creator, you love us like a loving father loves his children. You care for us like a loving mother cares for her children. Help us always to know that you are with us and to remember your love for us. We ask this through Jesus Christ our Lord. Amen.

Liturgy of the Word

First Reading *(Adapted from 1 John 3:1, 11, 23)*
See how much God loves us. God calls us his children. God takes care of us, so we must take care of one another. God loves us, and we must love one another. We must love one another as Jesus showed us.

The word of the Lord.

All
Thanks be to God.

Responsorial Psalm *(Psalm 99:1-5)*
1. Let everyone be happy,
    Let everyone be glad,
    Let everyone be full of joy
    and sing to the Lord.

Response: (Sing) Time and time and time again

2. We know the Lord is God
    who gives us life and breath,
    for we are God's own family
    and we belong to God.

Response: (Sing) Time and time and time again

or

We thank you, God, We Do

Gospel Acclamation
Sing: Alleluia (Easter)

Gospel Reading
We are the Greatest (Term 2: Lesson 3)

You might like to ask the children to sit around the sanctuary to hear the Gospel. Alternatively you might like to move down to the centre of the sanctuary or to the top of the aisle so that the children can be involved in the reading of the story.

Priest
The Gospel of the Lord.

All
Praise to you Lord Jesus Christ.

Song
We are the Greatest

Homily

Prayer of the Faithful
Priest
God, our Father, we come today to thank you for all your gifts. Help us to be generous and, like Jesus, to share our lives with others.

Reader
God, you care for us like a loving mother, you love us like a loving father. We thank you for all those who care for us at home.
We pray to the Lord.

All
Lord, hear our prayer.

Reader
You look after all people everywhere. God of love and compassion, we thank you for being with us all during this school year. We ask you to bless and to keep safe all those with whom we have learned and grown this year.
We pray to the Lord.

All
Lord, hear our prayer.

Reader
God our Creator, all time belongs to you. We thank you for all the days, the weeks and the months we have spent together in our class this year. We know that you were with us yesterday. We know that you are with us today. We ask you to be with us tomorrow.
We pray to the Lord.

All
Lord, hear our prayer.

Reader
As we look around us we see the beauty of the world that we live in. We thank you, God, for the changing seasons. We thank you especially for summer, the season we have now.
We pray to the Lord.

All
Lord, hear our prayer.

Reader
We thank you, God, our Creator, for the times when we have shared food with others. We ask you to bless all those who prepare our food for us every day.
We pray to the Lord.

All
Lord, hear our prayer.

Reader
God, we ask you to bless in a special way all our families and friends as the long summer holidays draw near.
We pray to the Lord.

All
Lord, hear our prayer.

Liturgy of the Eucharist

Preparation of the Gifts
(Sing): I Remember

1. We bring a clock:
   We share our time with others.

2. We bring our class code/crest:
   We share our work together as a class.

3. We bring bread:
   It is good to have others to share our food with.

4. We bring our favourite story book:
   It is good to have others to share our stories with.

5. We bring our candle:
   It reminds us that God is always with us.

6. We bring a bible:
   The Bible tells us God's story.

7. We bring our art work:
   We share our talents with one another.

8. We bring our enrolment book:
   We all belong to this class _____. We remember that together we belong to God's family.

9. We bring our name badges:
   We know that Jesus loves children. We know that we are the greatest!

10. We bring our banner:
    We share our good news with others.

Prayer over the Gifts
God our Father, we bring you our gifts, signs of the times we share with others. Jesus saw the goodness in children. You know the goodness that is deep inside each one of us here today. Help us always to grow in our love for you. We make our prayer through Jesus, your Son, who lives and reigns with you in the unity of the Holy Spirit, one God forever and ever. Amen.

Eucharistic Prayer for Masses with Children I

Sanctus
Holy, holy, holy Lord...

Proclamation of Faith
Christ has died
Christ has risen
Christ will come again.

Communion Rite

Our Father *(with actions)*

You might like to invite a few children to come forward to the sanctuary of the church and to show the rest of the congregation how to do the actions. Everyone (including the priest) is encouraged to pray the Our Father through word and gesture.

Sign of Peace
As all present offer each other a sign of peace they say the following prayer:
Deep peace of the running wave to you.
Deep peace of the flowing air to you.
Deep peace of the quiet earth to you.
Deep peace of the shining stars to you.
Deep peace of the Son of Peace to you.

Communion Hymns
Eat this Bread

Céad Míle Fáilte

Communion Prayers
Prayer before Communion
Lord Jesus, come to me.
Lord Jesus, give me your love.
Lord Jesus, come to me and give me yourself.

Lord Jesus, friend of children, come to me.
Lord Jesus, you are my Lord and my God.
Praise to you, Lord Jesus Christ.

Prayer after Communion
Lord Jesus, I love and adore you.
You're a special friend to me.
Welcome, Lord Jesus, O welcome.
Thank you for coming to me.

Thank you, Lord Jesus, O thank you
For giving yourself to me.
Make me strong to show your love
Wherever I may be.

Be near me, Lord Jesus, I ask you to stay
Close by me forever and love me, I pray.
Bless all of us children in your loving care
And bring us to heaven to live with you there.

I'm ready now, Lord Jesus.
To show how much I care.
I'm ready now to give your love
At home and everywhere. Amen.

Communion Reflection
God, our Creator,
We thank you for giving us your time;
time to run,
time to walk,
time to start,
time to stop,
time to drink,
time to eat,
time to wake,
time to sleep,
time to laugh,
time to cry,
time for hello,
time for goodbye,
time to work,
time to play,
time to watch,
time to pray.
Thank you, God,
for your time every day.
Amen.

or

Reflection for Parents/Guardians
(Term 2: Lesson 3)

Communion Litany
Priest
For Jesus the Light of the World.

All
We thank you, Lord our God.

Priest
For our parents and grandparents and families who love us.

All
We thank you, Lord our God.

Priest
For our friends who care for us.

All
We thank you, Lord our God.

Priest

For our school and our teachers who show us how to learn and grow.

All

We thank you, Lord our God.

Priest

For our church and our priests who are with us in a special way today.

All

We thank you, Lord our God.

Priest

For songs and stories and games to enjoy with others.

All

We thank you, Lord our God.

Concluding Rite

Final Blessing
Priest

God our Father, each day we see signs of your love and goodness all around us. Bless these children who today have shared in the Bread of Life. We make this prayer through Jesus Christ, your Son, who lives and reigns with you in the unity of the Holy Spirit, one God for ever and ever.

All

Amen.

Priest invites each parent/guardian to turn towards their daughter/son and to make the sign of the cross on her/his forehead, saying 'May God bless you _____ in the name of the Father and of the Son and of the Holy Spirit. Amen.'

The children then give their parents/guardians a hug as the congregation applauds.

Priest

May almighty God bless you, the Father, the Son and the Holy Spirit.

All

Amen.

Priest

Go in peace, to love and serve God and to share your joy and gladness with those you meet.

All

Thanks be to God.

Recessional Hymn
Do this in Memory of Jesus

Index of Songs by Title

Index of Stories by Title

Reflections for Parents